T0214536

Lecture Notes in Computer Science 11402

Commenced Publication in 1973
Founding and Former Series Editors:
Gerhard Goos, Juris Hartmanis, and Jan van Leeuwen

More information about this series at http://www.springer.com/series/7410

Brent ByungHoon Kang ·
JinSoo Jang (Eds.)

Information Security Applications

19th International Conference, WISA 2018
Jeju Island, Korea, August 23–25, 2018
Revised Selected Papers

 Springer

Editors
Brent ByungHoon Kang ⓘD
Korea Advanced Institute of Science
and Technology
Daejeon, Korea (Republic of)

JinSoo Jang ⓘD
Korea Advanced Institute of Science
and Technology
Daejeon, Korea (Republic of)

ISSN 0302-9743   ISSN 1611-3349   (electronic)
Lecture Notes in Computer Science
ISBN 978-3-030-17981-6   ISBN 978-3-030-17982-3   (eBook)
https://doi.org/10.1007/978-3-030-17982-3

LNCS Sublibrary: SL4 – Security and Cryptology

This Springer imprint is published by the registered company Springer Nature Switzerland AG
The registered company address is: Gewerbestrasse 11, 6330 Cham, Switzerland

Preface

The 19th World International Conference on Information Security and Application (WISA 2018) was held at Jeju Island, Korea, during August 23–25, 2018. The conference was supported by three research institutes: KISA (Korea Internet and Security Agency), ETRI (Electronics and Telecommunications Research Institute), and NSR (National Security Research Institute). The primary focus of WISA 2018 was on systems and network security including all other technical and practical aspects of security applications. This year, in particular, we sought to invite security researchers working on the embedded, unmanned, or autonomous systems and cyber-physical systems in general.

The program chair, Brent Byunghoon Kang of KAIST, prepared the programs with invaluable help from the highly regarded Program Committee members listed herein, many of whom have served in top security conferences such as IEEE S&P, ACM CCS, Usenix Security, NDSS. The conference received 53 submissions, covering all areas of information security, and finally selected 11 outstanding full papers and an additional 11 short papers out of 44 submissions that were carefully reviewed by the Program Committee. The excellent arrangements for the conference venue were led by the WISA 2018 general chair, Professor Manpyo Hong, and organizing chair, Okyeon Yi.

We were specially honored by the two keynote talks by Professor Dongyan Xu, Purdue University, on "A Cyber-Physical Approach to Robotic Vehicle Security," and by Professor Ahmad-Reza Sadeghi, TU Darmstadt, on "Trusted Execution Environments (TEE) and Autonomous Drone Systems." Also, we were delighted to have a special invited talk from Professor Mark M. Tehranipoor, on "Security Along SoC Design Lifecycle: Current Practices and Challenges Ahead."

Many people contributed to the success of WISA 2018. We would like to express our deepest appreciation to each of the WISA Program Committee and Organizing members as well as the paper contributors. Thanks to their invaluable support and sincere dedication, WISA 2018 was possible. We hope the following selected papers from WISA 2018 will contribute to the cyber-security solutions in autonomous vehicles, unmanned drones, and cyber-physical systems in general.

August 2018   Brent ByungHoon Kang

Organization

General Chair

Manpyo Hong   Ajou University, South Korea

Program Committee Chair

Brent ByungHoon Kang   KAIST, South Korea

Program Committee

Jason Hong	Carnegie Mellon University, USA
Lujo Bauer	Carnegie Mellon University, USA
Seong-je Cho	Dankook University, South Korea
Dooho Choi	ETRI, South Korea
Sangho Lee	Georgia Institute of Technology, USA
Eul Gyu Im	Hanyang University, South Korea
David Hyunchul Shim	KAIST (Aerospace Engineering), South Korea
Han-Lim Choi	KAIST (Aerospace Engineering), South Korea
Jinwhan Kim	KAIST (Mechanical Engineering), South Korea
Sang Kil Cha	KAIST, South Korea
Seungwon Shin	KAIST, South Korea
Marcus Peinado	Microsoft Research
Hyung Chan Kim	NSR, South Korea
Min Suk Kang	National University of Singapore, Singapore
Junghwan Rhee	NEC Laboratories America
Long Lu	Northeastern University
Yeongjin Jang	Oregon State University, USA
Gang Tan	Penn State, USA
Jong Kim	POSTECH, South Korea
Byoungyoung Lee	Purdue University, USA
Howon Kim	Pusan National University, South Korea
Ulrich Rührmair	Ruhr University Bochum, Germany
Ji Sun Shin	Sejong University, South Korea
Hyoungshick Kim	Sungkyunkwan University, South Korea
Yinqian Zhang	The Ohio State University, USA
Michael Franz	University of California, Irvine, USA
Aziz Mohaisen	University of Central Florida, USA

Kyu Hyung Lee   University of Georgia, USA
Ilsun You   Soonchunhyang University, South Korea

The 19th World International Conference on Information Security Applications
August 23–25, 2018, Lotte City Hotel, Jeju Island, Korea
http://www.wisa.or.kr

Contents

Systems Security

Analysis and Visualization of Threats

Applied Crypto

Short Papers

Security Analysis of Mobile Web Browser Hardware Accessibility: Study with Ambient Light Sensors

Sanghak Lee[1,2], Sangwoo Ji[1], and Jong Kim[1(✉)]

[1] Department of Computer Science and Engineering, Pohang University of Science and Technology (POSTECH), Pohang, South Korea
{uzbu89,sangwooji,jkim}@postech.ac.kr
[2] Defense Industry Technology Center (DITC), Pohang, South Korea

Abstract. Mobile web browsers are evolved to support the functionalities presented by HTML5. With the hardware accessibility of HTML5, it is now possible to access sensor hardware of a mobile device through a web page regardless of the need for a mobile application. In this paper, we analyze the security impact of accessing sensor hardware of a mobile device from mobile web page. First, we present the test results of hardware accessibility from mobile web browsers. Second, to raise awareness of the seriousness of hardware accessibility, we introduce a new POC attack LightTracker which infers the victim's location using light sensor. We also show the effectiveness of the attack in real world.

1 Introduction

HTML5 is a fifth hypertext markup language standard which have introduced many new features to keep pace with advances in computer performance and increased access to websites. HTML5 has aimed to reduce the necessity for plug-ins (e.g., Flash, Silverlight). Browsers that support HTML5 can play multimedia such as video and audio, utilize offline storage of web resource, and graphic work using canvas API without the assistance of external programs.

However, as the functionalities of HTML5 have increased, there have been a number of attack paths exploiting vulnerabilities of the functionalities. Numerous privacy attack methods have been reported using HTML5 features, for example browser fingerprinting through canvas API [10], and side-channel attack through Application Cache [24].

One new feature of HTML5 is hardware accessibility of web browsers. This feature has big security implication for mobile devices which have various types of sensor. On Android system, in order to access the hardware of a mobile device, it needs a capability called *permission*. Most of popular browsers require over eight *permissions* related to hardware access. In this environment, if the hardware access permission is given to a web browser and it does not have a fine access control mechanism for hardware, an attacker can create a malicious web server

© Springer Nature Switzerland AG 2019
B. B. Kang and J. Jang (Eds.): WISA 2018, LNCS 11402, pp. 3–15, 2019.
https://doi.org/10.1007/978-3-030-17982-3_1

and control the hardware of the connected user device without any restriction and get the hardware data.

In this paper, we investigate the security impact of hardware accessibility through mobile web browsers. First, to identify reality of hardware access problem and aware their risk, we investigate the security and privacy aspects and the current status of hardware access in various environments. We show accessible hardware components from various mobile web browsers and their access test results. Through this investigation, we show that most of popular browsers have no access restriction to motion sensor and ambient light sensor. Second, to show the seriousness of this hardware accessibility, we show the POC attack Light-Tracker using ambient light sensor. Most attack methods through mobile device hardware are concentrated only to using motion sensor. The risk of leaking light data is underestimated despite of the possibility of leaking privacy. To show the hardware access problem, we introduce LightTracker which infers the victim's location through ambient light sensor data. We show the evaluation results of LightTrack's effectiveness in real environments.

This paper is organized as follows. In Sect. 2, we show the hardware accessibility status in mobile environments. Section 3 introduces the POC attack LightTracker using web browser in mobile device. Section 4 shows the evaluation results of LightTracker. Finally, in Sect. 5, we conclude the work and discuss the future works.

2 Hardware Accessibility in Mobile Environments

In this section, we investigate the security & privacy aspects of hardware access and the current state of hardware access in various environments, i.e., combinations of mobile phone and web browsers.

2.1 Security and Privacy Consideration of Hardware Components

Web applications tend to have more accessibility to hardware of mobile devices. According to World Wide Web Consortium (W3C), mobile web applications can access the hardware data such as battery status [25], GPS [26], vibration [27], ambient light sensor [28], multimedia (camera, microphone) [29], and motion sensor [30].

W3C specification provides security & privacy consideration on hardware access within mobile browsers. Including these consideration, we investigate all concerns for each hardware component.

Battery Status. Battery status API shows current remaining power, charging status, and (dis)charging time of the hosting device. With tracking the change of the remaining power, it could leak the user's privacy [20]. To prevent such kind of threats, W3C suggests that web browsers should (1) not expose high precision data of battery, (2) enforce the user permission requirements, (3) inform the user of the API use, and (4) obfuscate the exposed value of the battery.

GPS. Web applications can access GPS data through Geolocation API. This API is used to retrieve the geographic location of a hosting device. This API directly exposes the user's location, so location data should be controlled with the user's perception, i.e., the browsers should acquire permission through a user interface, and this permission should be a revocable one.

Vibration. Vibrator is an actuator. Vibration functionality does not generate data to be used to leak privacy data. However, vibration stimuli can be used as an agitation source for privacy attack. For example, accelerators or gyroscopes may be subject to tiny imperfections during their manufacturing process [5]. Vibration API can help discovering those imperfections by introducing vibration patterns. Also, any unique imperfection can be used to fingerprint mobile devices. Moreover, continuous method calls for vibration could exhaust the battery power of the device which harms the availability or leads to privacy leaks [13].

Generic Sensor. Generic sensors consist of accelerometer, gyroscope, magnetometer, and ambient light sensor. When these sensors are in combination with other functionality, or used over time, user's privacy can be in risk by a simple attack such as user identification with fingerprinting. Numerous researchers propose various privacy attack methods using motion sensor data [4,32].

Multimedia. Allowing the access of multimedia data in mobile devices is directly related to the user's privacy. Leaking multimedia data itself can harm the confidentiality of the device [6], moreover other non-multimedia data can also be used to leak the user's private data, for example, embedding the user's location in the metadata of EXIF file.

2.2 Current Status of Hardware Access

Test Browser Selection. We test the hardware accessibility of mobile web browsers to identify how the real browsers handle security consideration described in 2.1. From the market share report of NETMARKETSHARE [19], we select representative mobile browsers such as Chrome, UC Browsers, Samsung Internet, and Firefox for hardware accessibility tests (Table 1). We exclude Safari browser because it is only for iOS, so we cannot compare this browser with

Table 1. Mobile browsers: numbers of downloads and tested version

Browser	Tested version	# of downloads
Chrome	58.0.3029.83	1,000,000,000+
UC Browser	11.3.2.960	100,000,000+
Samsung Internet	5.4.00-75	100,000,000+
Firefox	53.0.2	100,000,000+

other browsers in Android. Also, we select Firefox because of its high HTML5 acceptance score [8]. Note that all tested browsers require most of hardware access permissions such as *camera, microphone, GPS, network connection state,* and *vibration*. Therefore if browsers have no self-control mechanism while accessing the hardware, then web applications are able to access the hardware of the mobile device without any restrictions.

Hardware Access Test. We test the data accessibility of eight hardware components (i.e., camera, microphone, GPS, network connection state, vibration, motion, light, and battery status) of three different mobile devices, Galaxy Note3, Galaxy S5, and Nexus 5. For privacy-sensitive hardware components such as camera, microphone, and GPS, all tested browsers require user's permission to access the hardware component's data. However, other hardware components' data such as network connection state, vibration, motion sensor, ambient light sensor, and battery status could be accessed without permission, except the vibration by the Firefox browser. Also, we observe that each browser shows different access control policy to hardware. As we mentioned in Sect. 2.1, seemingly privacy-insensitive hardware in mobile devices can be used to leak the user's privacy.

Also, we survey whether each tested browser has setting options for the hardware access. The result shows that only the Chrome browser has the setting options for camera, microphone, and GPS (Fig. 1(a)). This option only covers the default access policy, whether asking first before allowing sites to use hardware component or completely blocking the access to the hardware component (Fig. 1(b)) (Table 2).

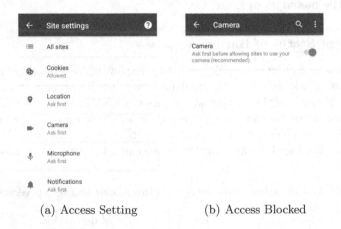

(a) Access Setting   (b) Access Blocked

Fig. 1. Setting options for the hardware access in Chrome

Table 2. Hardware access tests in mobile browsers (O: Required permission, X: Zero-permission, -: Not supported)

Device	Browser	Hardware							
		Camera	Mic	GPS	Network	Vibration	Motion	Light	Battery
Galaxy Note3	Chrome	-	-	-	X	X	X	-	-
	UC	O	O	O	-	X	X	-	-
	SI	O	O	O	X	X	X	-	-
	Firefox	O	O	O	X	O	X	X	-
Galaxy S5	Chrome	-	-	-	X	X	X	-	-
	UC	-	O	O	-	X	X	-	X
	SI	O	O	O	X	X	X	-	-
	Firefox	O	O	O	X	O	X	X	-
Nexus 5	Chrome	O	O	O	X	X	X	-	-
	UC	O	O	O	-	X	X	-	X
	SI	-	-	-	X	X	X	-	-
	Firefox	O	O	O	X	O	X	X	-

Table 3. Reported attack using hardware or its data in mobile devices (Accel: Accelerometer, Gyro: Gyroscope, Orient: Orientation, Magnet: Magnet)

Attack	Work	Access	Hardware
Inferring input	PIN Skimmer [22]	in-app	Camera, Microphone
	PIN Skimming [23]	in-app	Light sensor
	Keylogging by Mic [16]	in-app	Microphone
	ACCessory [21]	in-app	Accel
	Tapprints [14]	in-app	Accel, Gyro
	Accel side channel [1]	in-app	Accel
	Motion side channel [3]	in-app	Accel, Gyro
	TapLogger [31]	in-app	Accel, Orient
	TouchLogger [2]	in-app	Orient
	TouchSignatures [11]	in-browser	Accel, Gyro, Orient
Tracking	Route identification [17]	in-app	Accel, Gyro, Magnet
	ACComplice [7]	in-app	Accel
	Activity recognition [9]	in-app	Accel
	Peril tracking [18]	in-app	Accel, Gyro, Magnet
	Sensor fingerprinting [4]	in-browser	Accel, Gyro

2.3 Threat Models in Hardware Access

To better understand the security and privacy issues on hardware access in mobile devices, we performed a survey of attacks using sensor data through both browsers and applications. We classified the attacks into two classes, *Inferring input*, and *Tracking*, then we compare the access route and used hardware components of each attack (Table 3).

Inferring Input. Inferring input attacks consist of identifying the user's touch input to infer password/PINs using sensors such as camera, microphone, light, accelerometer, gyroscope, and magnetometer. Except PIN Skimmer [22], PIN Skimming [23], and Keylogging [16], most of the reported inferring input attacks exploit motion sensor data from accelerometer especially. The attacks exploit the characteristic; when the user types or touches a screen on his/her device, these actions induce the device orientation or motion traces which might be distinguishable from those of other actions.

Tracking. Tracking attacks include inferring the victim's route (or activity) and fingerprinting victim's device. Most of reported tracking attacks exploit motion sensor data as same as inferring input attacks. These kinds of attacks use the data whose variation is usually bigger than those of inferring input attacks. This feature is well fit for attacks through browsers; because browsers have a reduced sampling rate of sensors which is about 3–5 times slower than the original sampling rate [11,12], it is relatively hard to distinguish the small variation of data at browsers.

Through the investigation, we have observed that most of the reported attacks consider only motion sensors among zero-permission hardware components. Only PIN Skimming [23] uses the light data from ambient light sensors in mobile devices. The risk of leaking light data is underestimated despite of the possibility of side channel attack exploiting light data. Also, most attacks are conducted through applications, not browsers. However, attacks through browsers can expose a victim easier than attacks through applications, because browser-based attacks need no installation, but just need to allure the victim to the attacker's web pages.

3 POC: LightTracker

In this section, to raise the awareness of the risk of the ambient light sensor data, we introduce LightTracker, which infers the victim's location through ambient light sensor data. LightTracker is deployed on the attacker's server. When a victim visits the attacker's web pages, LightTracker collects the light data of the victim's mobile device. Next, LightTracker compares the collected data and predefined light map data to infer the victim's position.

3.1 Attack Procedure

We explain overall attack procedures of LightTracker (Fig. 2). It assumes that a victim visits the attacker's web pages. The attacker's web server includes JavaScript which makes the client's device leak the sensor data.

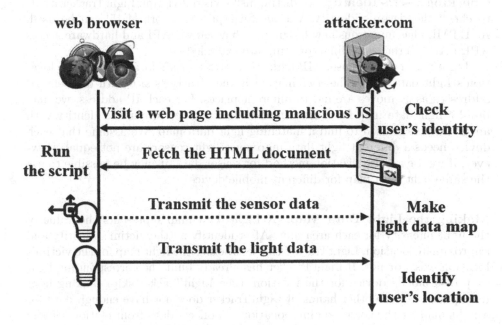

Fig. 2. Overall attack procedure of LightTracker

❶ A victim visits the web pages (attacker.com) which include a malicious JavaScript. Then the attacker checks the victim's identity, and examines whether this access is the victim's first visit or not. If this is the first visit, the attacker fingerprints the client browser. Note that we assume the user's IP address (subnet) represents the user's location.

❷ The client web browser starts to download the HTML document and runs the script.

❸ By running the script, the client browser transmits the sensor data to the attacker's server. To create light map, LightTracker manages the motion sensor data with light data. Note that this process is not mandatory if the server already has a light map for the victim; in this case, LightTracker requires no privilege to access motion sensor data.

❹ The client browser transmits the light data to the server. Then LightTracker checks the data with the map to identify the victim's location.

3.2   Attack Details

In this subsection, we explain details of the attack; checking user's identity, making light data map, and identifying user's location.

Checking User's Identity. To distinguish a visited victim, LightTracker needs to check the victim's identity. Various fingerprinting work [4,15] can be used. As HTML5 has numerous new features such as canvas API and hardware access API, attack surfaces for fingerprinting are extended.

LightTraker collects user's IP address to match user's location with the location's light data map. The user may visit the attacker's site with different IP addresses as he moves around to different places. For each IP address, we may build a light data map for a user's mobile device. Therefore user's identity with an IP address is used to find a matching light data map. We assume that each device needs a different light data map since light sensors are not equal. However, if we use a normalization method for sensor data, it may be possible to use the same light data map for different mobile devices.

Making the Light Data Map. A Light data map represents the value of the light intensity for each area unit. After identifying the victim's identity and approximate location, LightTracker checks whether the light map for the victim's location exists or not. If LightTracker has already built the corresponding light map of a mobile device for the location, then LightTracker skips making light map phase. On the other hands, if LightTracker does not have enough data for a light map for the corresponding location, it collects data from motion sensors (accelerometer, gyroscope, and magnetometer) to infer the victim's movements. By inferring this movement, LightTracker is able to make the naive geographic map [17]. At the same time, to make a light data map, LightTracker also gathers the ambient light sensor data and combines the data with each area unit of the geographic map. Note that collecting motion data is not mandatory. A light map data for a specific place can be generated if that place are physically accessible to the attacker. He or she can create more accurate light map and matches the map with the IP address of that place. In this way, LightTracker obtains more accurate light map than the map derived from the motion sensor data.

Identifying the User's Location. With the light data map, LightTracker can infer the current victim's location with transmitted light data from the victim's device. LightTracker compares the transmitted data with the value of unit areas in the light data map, and finds the exact location which has the most similar light value.

4   LightTracker Evaluation

We implemented a prototype of LightTracker and tested its effectiveness.

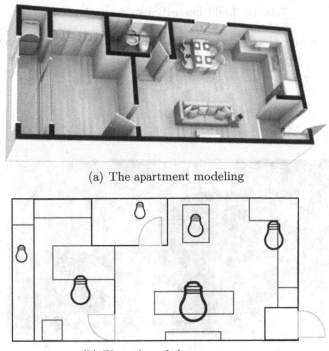

(a) The apartment modeling

(b) Floorplan of the apartment

Fig. 3. Modeling and floorplan of test environments used for testing LightTracker. Each bulb icon denotes a light source, and its size represents the light power of the source.

4.1   Test Environments

We tested the effectiveness of LightTracker in a typical apartment covering a $10 \times 6\,\mathrm{m}^2$ area and consisting of a living room connected to the bedroom and the toilet (Fig. 3(a)). We made a light map manually for an accurate location inferring. We used Samsung Galaxy Note3 as a test device and a Firefox browser to acquire ambient light data. We divided the apartment into $1 \times 1\,\mathrm{m}^2$ area units, and measured the ambient light data for each area.

4.2   Making Light Data Map

We measured the ambient light sensor data for each unit area 10 times, and recorded the mean value. With this data, we made a light map to test the effectiveness of LightTracker. The light intensity value is directly related to the distance from light sources. In Fig. 4, we visualized the light map in log scale, and it shows that we can infer the victim's location with the light intensity value.

Table 4. Light intensity data for each area

Light (lux)	8–16	16–32	32–64	64–128	128–256	256–512	512–1024	Total
Area (m²)	8.915	11.33	9.545	10.68	6.39	2.53	0.61	50
Percent (%)	17.83	22.66	19.09	21.36	12.78	5.06	1.22	100

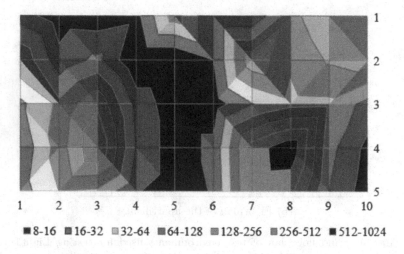

■8-16 ■16-32 ▫32-64 ■64-128 ■128-256 ■256-512 ■512-1024

Fig. 4. The light map visualization in log scale

4.3   Effectiveness Evaluation

With the light map, LightTracker significantly reduces candidates of victim's location (Table 4). In most case, the candidates are decreased to roughly 20% of total areas, through the light intensity value of that area. Especially, as the light intensity value is bigger, LightTracker infers a more accurate position. For example, among $50 \, \text{m}^2$ area, there exists only $1.22 \, \text{m}^2$ area whose light intensity value is over 512 lux. Also, as the number of divided areas in location data map increases, LightTracker can specify the victim's location more accurately. Moreover, as LightTracker can be combined with motion-based user tracking system orthogonally, it is possible to highly enhance the accuracy of user tracking.

5   Conclusion

In this paper, we investigated the security and privacy consideration of hardware access through mobile web browsers. Despite of the W3C specification and numerous in-app attacks, most popular browsers (e.g., Google Chrome, UC Browser, Samsung Internet, and Mozilla Firefox) do not have access control mechanism for motion sensor, vibration, battery status, and ambient light sensor. Although many researchers have shown attacks with motion sensor, ambient light sensor is underestimated despite of the possibility that it can be a medium of side-channel attacks. To raise the awareness of the risk of ambient light sensor, we have introduced a POC attack, LightTracker, which infers the victim's location. With the light data map, LightTracker can specify the victim's position accurately when the light intensity value is bigger.

Acknowledgement. This work was supported by the National Research Foundation of Korea (NRF) grant funded by the Korea government (MSIP) (No. 2017R1A2B4010914).

References

1. Aviv, A.J., Sapp, B., Blaze, M., Smith, J.M.: Practicality of accelerometer side channels on smartphones. In: Proceedings of the 28th Annual Computer Security Applications Conference, pp. 41–50. ACM (2012)
2. Cai, L., Chen, H.: TouchLogger: inferring keystrokes on touch screen from smartphone motion. HotSec **11**, 9 (2011)
3. Cai, L., Chen, H.: On the practicality of motion based keystroke inference attack. In: Katzenbeisser, S., Weippl, E., Camp, L.J., Volkamer, M., Reiter, M., Zhang, X. (eds.) Trust 2012. LNCS, vol. 7344, pp. 273–290. Springer, Heidelberg (2012). https://doi.org/10.1007/978-3-642-30921-2_16
4. Das, A., Borisov, N., Caesar, M.: Tracking mobile web users through motion sensors: attacks and defenses. In: Proceedings of the 23rd Annual Network and Distributed System Security Symposium (NDSS) (2016)
5. Dey, S., Roy, N., Xu, W., Choudhury, R.R., Nelakuditi, S.: AccelPrint: imperfections of accelerometers make smartphones trackable. In: NDSS (2014)
6. Diao, W., Liu, X., Zhou, Z., Zhang, K.: Your voice assistant is mine: how to abuse speakers to steal information and control your phone. In: Proceedings of the 4th ACM Workshop on Security and Privacy in Smartphones & Mobile Devices, pp. 63–74. ACM (2014)
7. Han, J., Owusu, E., Nguyen, L.T., Perrig, A., Zhang, J.: ACComplice: location inference using accelerometers on smartphones. In: 2012 Fourth International Conference on Communication Systems and Networks (COMSNETS), pp. 1–9. IEEE (2012)
8. HTML5TEST: how well does your browser support HTML5? (2017). https://html5test.com/results/mobile.html
9. Kwapisz, J.R., Weiss, G.M., Moore, S.A.: Activity recognition using cell phone accelerometers. ACM SigKDD Explor. Newsl. **12**(2), 74–82 (2011)
10. Laperdrix, P., Rudametkin, W., Baudry, B.: Beauty and the beast: diverting modern web browsers to build unique browser fingerprints. In: 2016 IEEE Symposium on Security and Privacy (SP), pp. 878–894. IEEE (2016)

11. Mehrnezhad, M., Toreini, E., Shahandashti, S.F., Hao, F.: TouchSignatures: identification of user touch actions and PINs based on mobile sensor data via JavaScript. J. Inf. Secur. Appl. **26**, 23–38 (2016)
12. Michalevsky, Y., Boneh, D., Nakibly, G.: Gyrophone: recognizing speech from gyroscope signals. In: USENIX Security, pp. 1053–1067 (2014)
13. Michalevsky, Y., Schulman, A., Veerapandian, G.A., Boneh, D., Nakibly, G.: PowerSpy: location tracking using mobile device power analysis. In: USENIX Security, pp. 785–800 (2015)
14. Miluzzo, E., Varshavsky, A., Balakrishnan, S., Choudhury, R.R.: TapPrints: your finger taps have fingerprints. In: Proceedings of the 10th International Conference on Mobile Systems, Applications, and Services, pp. 323–336. ACM (2012)
15. Mowery, K., Shacham, H.: Pixel perfect: fingerprinting canvas in HTML5. In: Proceedings of W2SP, pp. 1–12 (2012)
16. Narain, S., Sanatinia, A., Noubir, G.: Single-stroke language-agnostic keylogging using stereo-microphones and domain specific machine learning. In: Proceedings of the 2014 ACM Conference on Security and Privacy in Wireless & Mobile Networks, pp. 201–212. ACM (2014)
17. Narain, S., Vo-Huu, T.D., Block, K., Noubir, G.: Inferring user routes and locations using zero-permission mobile sensors. In: 2016 IEEE Symposium on Security and Privacy (SP), pp. 397–413. IEEE (2016)
18. Narain, S., Vo-Huu, T.D., Block, K., Noubir, G.: The perils of user tracking using zero-permission mobile apps. IEEE Secur. Priv. **15**(2), 32–41 (2017)
19. NETMARKETSHARE: Mobile/tablet top browser share trend (2017). https://www.netmarketshare.com/browser-market-share.aspx?qprid=1&qpcustomb=1
20. Olejnik, Ł., Acar, G., Castelluccia, C., Diaz, C.: The leaking battery. In: Garcia-Alfaro, J., Navarro-Arribas, G., Aldini, A., Martinelli, F., Suri, N. (eds.) DPM/QASA -2015. LNCS, vol. 9481, pp. 254–263. Springer, Cham (2016). https://doi.org/10.1007/978-3-319-29883-2_18
21. Owusu, E., Han, J., Das, S., Perrig, A., Zhang, J.: Accessory: password inference using accelerometers on smartphones. In: Proceedings of the Twelfth Workshop on Mobile Computing Systems & Applications, p. 9. ACM (2012)
22. Simon, L., Anderson, R.: PIN skimmer: inferring PINs through the camera and microphone. In: Proceedings of the Third ACM Workshop on Security and Privacy in Smartphones & Mobile Devices, pp. 67–78. ACM (2013)
23. Spreitzer, R.: PIN skimming: exploiting the ambient-light sensor in mobile devices. In: Proceedings of the 4th ACM Workshop on Security and Privacy in Smartphones & Mobile Devices, pp. 51–62. ACM (2014)
24. Van Goethem, T., Joosen, W., Nikiforakis, N.: The clock is still ticking: timing attacks in the modern web. In: Proceedings of the 22nd ACM SIGSAC Conference on Computer and Communications Security, pp. 1382–1393. ACM (2015)
25. World Wide Web Consortium: Battery status API (2016). https://www.w3.org/TR/battery-status/
26. World Wide Web Consortium: Geolocation API specification, 2nd (edn.) (2016). https://www.w3.org/TR/geolocation-API/
27. World Wide Web Consortium: Vibration API, 2nd (edn.) (2016). https://www.w3.org/TR/vibration/
28. World Wide Web Consortium: Ambient light sensor (2017). https://www.w3.org/TR/ambient-light/
29. World Wide Web Consortium: HTML media capture (2017). https://www.w3.org/TR/html-media-capture/

30. World Wide Web Consortium: Motion sensors explainer (2017). https://www.w3.org/TR/motion-sensors/
31. Xu, Z., Bai, K., Zhu, S.: TapLogger: inferring user inputs on smartphone touchscreens using on-board motion sensors. In: Proceedings of the Fifth ACM conference on Security and Privacy in Wireless and Mobile Networks, pp. 113–124. ACM (2012)
32. Yue, C.: Sensor-based mobile web fingerprinting and cross-site input inference attacks. In: 2016 IEEE Security and Privacy Workshops (SPW), pp. 241–244. IEEE (2016)

HapticPoints: The Extended PassPoints Graphical Password

Trust Ratchasan and Rungrat Wiangsripanawan[✉]

Department of Computer Science, Faculty of Science,
King Mongkut's Institute of Technology Ladkrabang, Bangkok, Thailand
{58605087,rungrat.wi}@kmitl.ac.th

Abstract. The most common issue of alphanumeric passwords is users normally create weak passwords for the reason that strong passwords are difficult to recognise and memorise. Graphical password authentication system is one of the approaches to address the issues of alphanumeric passwords memorability. Wiedenbeck et al. propose PassPoints in which a password is a sequence of any 5 to 8 user-selected click points on a system-assigned image. Nevertheless, PassPoints still faces the problem of predictable click points and shoulder surfing attack. In this paper, we propose an alternative graphical password system on smartphones called HapticPoints. By adding haptic feedback to PassPoints as additional decoy click points, the aforementioned problems can be prevented without needing users to do any additional memory task. We also conduct a user study to evaluate and compare the usability of HapticPoints and PassPoints.

Keywords: User authentication · Passwords · Graphical passwords · Usable security · Shoulder surfing attack · PassPoints

1 Introduction

Alphanumeric passwords are the most common approach for authentication but users normally create weak passwords for the reason that strong passwords are difficult to recognise and memorise [1,2].

Graphical passwords have been proposed to solve the memorability problem based on the studies which indicated that humans are better at recognising and recalling images than alphanumeric passwords [2,3]. Although some graphical passwords provide a high password space and are secure against password guessing attacks, they are difficult to use. This results in low login's success rate or longer login time [4], there is a trade-off between usability and cryptographic strength.

The previous studies [1,2] show that recognition-based graphical password systems require less human memory task than recall-based graphical password systems. In cued-recall graphical password systems, an external cue is provided to help users recall some information. Tulving and Pearlstone explained that

© Springer Nature Switzerland AG 2019
B. B. Kang and J. Jang (Eds.): WISA 2018, LNCS 11402, pp. 16–28, 2019.
https://doi.org/10.1007/978-3-030-17982-3_2

items in human memory might be available but not accessible for retrieval and showed that previously inaccessible information in a pure recall situation can be retrieved with the aid of a retrieval cue [3].

According to Biddle et al. [5], PassPoints is the cued-recall graphical password systems that has received high interest and is worth for extensive study. Originally, PassPoints extended Blonder's [6] idea by eliminating the predefined boundaries and allowing arbitrary images to be used. As a result, a user can click on any place on an image (as opposed to some pre-defined areas) to create a password. A tolerance around each chosen pixel is calculated. In order to be authenticated, the user must click within the tolerance of the chosen pixels.

The primary security problem of PassPoints is hotspots which happen when users tend to select similar click points as part of their passwords. Attackers who are able to gather knowledge of hotspots can use automated image processing techniques to build dictionary attack allowing them to more successfully guess PassPoints passwords [7,8]. Another concern of PassPoints is a shoulder-surfing attack. When a user clicks at his/her password click points, nearby attackers can observe what points user is clicking.

In this paper, we propose an alternative graphical password system on smartphones called HapticPoints. By adding haptic feedback to PassPoints as additional decoy click point, users can avoid hotspots and shoulder surfing attacks without having to remember any additional information. We also conduct a user study to evaluate and compare the usability of HapticPoints and PassPoints.

2   Graphical Password Systems

Graphical password systems are imaged-based authentication systems that works by allowing users to select images or points of the image as their passwords. They are an alternative way of solving the problem of using alphanumeric passwords [1,2]. Graphical passwords are easier to remember than text passwords for most people [4,9]. A study by Biddle et al. [5] classifies and compares stereotype of graphical passwords into Recall-based System, Recognition-based System and Cued-recallSystem.

Recall-based graphical password systems known as the drawmetric systems, these systems allow users to create passwords from drawing lines or points on empty spaces or a grid. This type of graphical password is the most difficult to memorize since users must remember all lines without any memorisation aid. Examples of recall-based graphical password systems are Draw-a-Secret (DAS) [10], BDAS [11], YAGP [12] and PassGo [13].

Recognition-based graphical password systems known as cognometric systems or searchmetric systems, this system require users to select a set of images to create a password, then user must recognize their images among decoys to log in. The images used are mostly people's faces, pictures, artwork, and biographies. Examples of recognition-based graphical password systems are Use Your Illusion (UYI) [14] and Deja vu [15].

Cued-recall graphical password systems also known as locimetric, these systems require user choose positions or points of an image during password creation and authentication, subjects are given hints (cues) at the time of recall. The cues are supposed to enable the subject to recall his/her memorised items. Examples of cued-recall graphical password systems are PassPoints [16] and Inkblot Authentication [17].

3   PassPoints

PassPoints is a cued-recall graphical password systems which proposed by Wiedenbec et al. [16] A password is a sequence of 5 users' selected click points (pixels) on a system-assigned image. The user selects points by clicking on them using a mouse. During login, re-entry of the click-points must be in the correct order, and accurate within a system-specified tolerance. The image acts as a memory cue to the location of the original chosen click-points as shown in Fig. 1.

The underlying images of PassPoints for creating a password are not restricted to any types of images. All types of images such as drawings, Perspective photos, Human face images can be used; users can even install their own images. Natural images help users remember complex passwords better [2,3]. This suggests that in a human context, the (conditional) entropy of a password will depend on the underlying image, and leads to the question: Given an image, how can we predict the (conditional) entropy of a click point in that image, within the context of PassPoint passwords.

Dirik et al. [7] analysed the password security of underlying images by computing the entropy of a click point by adding saliency points to the images, Next they compared the predictions produced by their model with data consisting of approximately 100 actual passwords selected by users. In these (very small) images their model was able to predict 70–80% of the user click positions. The results show that their model can be used to evaluate the suitability of an underlying image for the PassPoints system.

4   Threat Model

Biddle et al. [5] elaborates standard threats to password-based authentication systems and how they relate to graphical passwords. Based on their study, threats and attacks model faced in PassPoints. Attacks are classified as shoulder surfing attacks, brute force attacks, dictionary attacks and hotspots.

4.1   Shoulder Surfing Attack

Shoulder-surfing attack is a direct attack focused on the visual aspect of graphical passwords. When users are logging in or inputting passwords, attackers may directly observe or use external recording devices such as high resolution cameras and surveillance equipment to collect users' credentials.

Fig. 1. User interface of PassPoints.

Several existing graphical password systems tried to prevent shoulder surfing attacks adding more features or steps; however, these give significant usability drawbacks [18], especially in the time and effort required to log in which makes them less suitable for daily-usage authentication.

4.2 Brute Force Attack

Brute force attack is a trial and error method used to obtain information such as a user password by imitating the clicking on a password image. In a brute force attack, automated software is used to generate a large number of consecutive guesses as to the value of the desired data. An attack of this nature can be time and resource consuming. Success is usually based on computing power and the number of combinations tries rather than an ingenious algorithm.

The advantage to do offline brute force attacks is that with enough time and computing power, all passwords will be found. However, a full search of large password spaces is limited in practice by the time or processing power available. To minimise the threat of exhaustive attacks, the theoretical password space should be too large to search.

4.3 Dictionary Attack

The original idea involved guessing passwords from a relatively short pre-compiled list (dictionary) of high probability candidate passwords, based on assumptions about user behaviour. Massive dictionaries and powerful data structures have created a continuum from small dictionaries to prioritised brute force attacks with smart dictionary attacks combining time-memory trade-offs of brute force attacks with higher success probabilities of prioritised dictionaries, in some cases algorithmically generated [19].

Many users uses weak passwords which make it easier for attackers to guess using the graphical dictionary attack [20].

Previous studies [7,8] show that users' choices are predictable in most cued-recall based systems, so attackers can make use of this property. Attackers first collect images used by authentication systems, then processes and analyses the images to obtain the hotspots and patterns.

4.4   Hotspots

Hotspots [21] are remarkable points or areas of a password image with higher probability of being chosen by users as password click points. The attacks below target PassPoints itself, as opposed to evolved systems like PCCP [22]. Hotspots can be used as an important information in dictionary attack.

Success in exploiting hotspots with automated image processing tools has been reported (see Fig. 2) [7]. The most efficient hotspot attacks to date [8] harvest from different users a small sample of passwords for target images, using the component click-points to build "human-seeded" attack dictionaries. Another attack uses probability by using Markov model for its first order attack, and uses independent probability model for their second order attack assuming that click-points are independent of their predecessors.

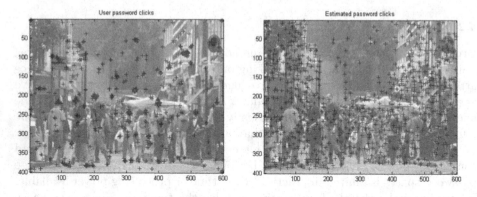

Fig. 2. Dirik et al. exploited hotspots with automated image processing

5   HapticPoints

We propose a graphical password authentication system on smartphones which extended from PassPoints called "HapticPoints". The aim of the work is to prevent Passpoints' aforementioned attacks - shoulder surfing, bruteforce, dictionary and hotspots attacks - without sacrificing usability and is practical to use. HapticPoints enhances PassPoints by randomly generating haptic feedback after a user clicks on a password click point to notify users that he/she needs to create additional decoy click points. The reason behind adding haptic feedback is when the haptic feedback vibrates, it is hard to observe by eyes or eavesdrop by ears. Thus, it is difficult for attackers to distinguish the actual click points from the decoy click points. We generate the numbers of decoy click points (p) by:

$$decoyPoints = ciel(actualPoints/2)$$

In HapticPoints graphical password authentication system, there are two usage phases: the registration phase and the login phase.

5.1 Registration Phase

Alshehri and Crawford [23] shows that their model can be used before users select the first click point without requiring any additional effort to guide suitable image selection for graphical passwords. By using their measurement for image selection that is based on overall image saliency and contents (see Fig. 2), they found that the more salient regions on an image, the higher the entropy of click points, and thus the higher the theoretical and practical password space.

Fig. 3. An example of saliency map

In the registration phase, users are allowed to choose their own images to create passwords then the image saliency is shown by using Deep Gaze [24] algorithm to inform the suitability of the image to prevent dictionary attacks. The following is the complete procedure:

1. User selects his/her password image from the phone, the password image can be any types of images.
2. The selected password image will be analysed and showed overall image saliency (see Fig. 3). At this step, The user will be informed that the more salient regions on the image, the stronger password that it could be.
3. If the user confirms to use the current image as his/her password, Create a password by clicking on the password image in the range from 4 to 6 points in sequence similarly to the original PassPoints.
4. User Confirms the password by re-entering it correctly. If the user incorrectly confirms his/her password could retry the confirmation or return to Step 3 or Step 1.

5.2 Login Phase

In login phase, users use passwords created during the registration phase to log into HapticPoints (see Fig. 4). The following is the complete procedure:

1. User starts clicking the first password click point of a password image.
2. If the haptic feedback vibrates, The user needs to create a decoy click point by clicking any area in the password image and If the haptic feedback does not vibrate, The user needs to click on the actual click point of the current password sequence.
3. User continues Step 1 and Step 2 until he/she finishes inputting password.
4. If users notices an error during login, he/she could cancel their login attempt and restart again in Step 1.

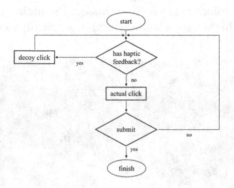

Fig. 4. HapticPoints login flow

6   Usability Evaluation

A prototype on android operating system as an application was developed and also 20 participants were recruited to involve in the experiment. These participants were 8 females and 12 males age between 24 to 32 from two different companies.

The experiment started with a tutorial phase, in which participants had to enter a PassPoints password followed by HapticPoints password on the smartphone. The application continued to challenge the participants as soon as both passwords had been entered successfully. Then, each participant had to create their own passwords.

We assessed usability with a combination of quantitative and qualitative metrics. A scheme's efficiency is measured by number of attempts required for successful login and the entry time required for a login, effectiveness is assessed with the recall success rate. The usability questionnaire provides qualitative data on user satisfaction based on participant ratings on Lewis' Post-Study System Usability Questionnaire (PSSUQ) to participants [25].

6.1 Login Attempts

Table 1 displays the number of attempts required for successful authentication of original PassPoints and HapticPoints. HapticPoints was taken slightly more attempts than PassPoints (PassPoints = 1.645 tries, HapticPoints = 1.709 tries and P = 0.759). A T-test analysis for PassPoints and HapticPoints password revealed no significant difference.

Table 1. Login attempts result (tries)

Scheme	Mean	S.d.	Min	Max	t-test
Original PassPoints	1.645	0.797	1	4	t = 0.308
HapticPoints	1.709	0.824	1	4	p = 0.759

6.2 Login Time

Table 2 displays the average login time required in a successful authentication of PassPoints and HapticPoints. Login time also gives no significant difference between PassPoints and HapticPoints from a T-test analysis (PassPoints = 8.421 s, HapticPoints = 10.278 s, P = 0.0782).

Table 2. Login time result (seconds)

Scheme	Mean	S.d.	Min	Max	t-test
Original PassPoints	8.421	3.838	3.35	15.52	t = 1.793
HapticPoints	10.278	4.178	4.01	17.37	p = 0.0782

6.3 Recall Success Rate

In PassPoints scheme, the recall success rate depends on forgetting the password length or clicking points outside the tolerance region. The experiment compared recall success rate between PassPoints and Haptic Points. The time range of the experiment was separated into two groups which are one hour and one week.

Table 3 compares the recall success rate for one hour test and one week test. From The T-test result shows that the recall success rate of both HapticPoints is similar to PassPoints.

Table 3. Recall success rate result (seconds)

	Scheme	Mean	S.d.	Min	Max	t-test
One hour test	PassPoints	95.97	9.347	75	100	t = 0.912
	HapticPoints	93.548	11.12	75	100	p = 0.365
One week test	PassPoints	67.741	29.006	0	100	t = 0.2002
	HapticPoints	66.129	33.259	0	100	p = 0.842

6.4 Usability Questionnaire (PSSUQ)

The user usability experiment was conducted by using the Lewis' Post-Study System Usability Questionnaire (PSSUQ) [20] which contains 19 usability questionnaire items perceived usefulness of the scheme in completing the given tasks (SysUse), perceived quality of displayed information (InfoQual), perceived quality of interface elements (InterQual), and perceived quality of overall satisfaction with the scheme (Overall). It uses Likert scale from "1" to "7". "1" means strongly disagree and "7" means strongly agree. Figure 5 shows the results for each scheme. A T-test found no significant differences between PassPoints and HapticPoints for any of the scores (t = 0.4412, P = 0.634).

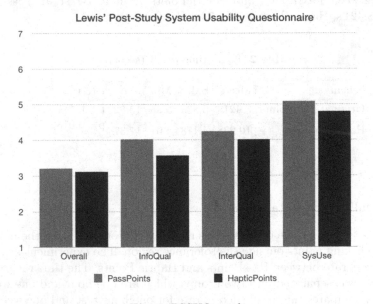

Fig. 5. PSSUQ result.

7   Security Evaluation

7.1   Brute Force Attack

We calculate the entropy of haptic points password to quantify the security of haptic points against brute force attacks. Entropy means the quantity of information inside the password space, i.e., all possible passwords, in bits.

We implement a prototype to a smartphone which has 5 in. display size, and the number of total tolerance squares is 60 (6 in horizontal and 10 in vertical). Table 4 shows and compares the calculated password entropy between the original PassPoints and HapticPoints. We can find that the password strength of HapticPoints 4 click points password is similar to PassPoints 6 click points password which also is equivalent to six-character text password consisting of numbers, lowercase, and uppercase characters. From the result, it shows that our proposed scheme is more secure than PassPoints in practice against brute force attacks.

Table 4. The entropy in bits of the original PassPoints compared with HapticPoints.

	Number of click point(s)		
	4	5	6
Original PassPoints Entropy	23 bits	29 bits	35 bits
HapticPoints Entropy	35 bits	47 bits	53 bits

7.2   Shoulder Surfing Attack

We followed the common approach of having participants act as shoulder surfers [26–29]. Participants acted as shoulder surfers and the experimenter acted the victim. This setup has the advantage that the experimenter could train password entry in advance, to ensure consistent entry speed and body posture for all participants. Thus, we evaluated a casual observer's ability to recognise a password entered by a trained user, compared to evaluating an expert shoulder surfer with a beginner user in the reverse setup. The average age of the participants was 29 years old. The youngest participant was 23 years old and the oldest was 44 years old.

The shoulder surfing experiment was conducted after the usability experiment. The right-handed experimenter sat at a table holding a smartphone as if entering a pass- word and the participant could position herself left, right, or behind the experimenter. We also limited the number of login attempts for shoulder surfers to 4 times.

The shoulder surfing result of PassPoints is 12 out of 20 (60%) shoulder surfers could crack the password but the result of HapticPoints is 1 out of 20 (5%) shoulder.

7.3 Dictionary Attack and Hotspots

In general graphical password systems are vulnerable to the threat of dictionary attacks. Attackers can collect the image of PassPoints and perform an automated image processing [8] to obtain hotspots and patterns. However we enhanced an ability to avoid dictionary attacks by adding image saliency [17,18]. A more complex image can provide more possible click points that users actually select, thus potentially encouraging the user to create a less guessable password, or at least one that is more computationally intensive and time consuming for an attacker. This also has the effect of spreading potential user password click points, and thus potential hotspots, over an image, which may make dictionary attacks that need to consider all hotspots less feasible.

8 Limitation

We can only increase the cost of shoulder surfing attack. If the attacker is able to observe multiple login sessions then clicking points may be revealed based on the intersection and correlation among the observations. HapticPoints is not fully resistant to shoulder surfing attack, but still stronger than PassPoints because if PassPoints passwords are being screen recorded or observed, attackers could possibly crack passwords in only one time.

9 Conclusion

We proposed HapticPoints, a PassPoints based graphical-password authentication system, which randomly adding haptic feedback to create decoy click points in a sequence of 4–6 click-points that user selects in the password image.

We also enhanced an ability to prevent dictionary attacks, hotspots in particular, by adding image saliency at the registration phase to inform the suitability of the user's password image selection. To prove that our scheme does work and practical to use, we implemented a prototype as an android application of HapticPoints and the original PassPoints to compare a number of failed login attempts, login time and recall success rate. In addition, we conducted a usability study of both schemes. The security analysis shows that HapticPoints provides stronger password strength and be able to prevent all attacks mentioned in the threat model better than PassPoints. To illustrate, HapticPoints provides 47 bits entropy (with 5 click points) against brute force attacks which is higher than PassPoints (29 bits). The experimental results shows that the PassPoints gave slightly better usability according to the T-test result but these differentiates are insignificant.

References

1. Li, J., Jiang, Y., Fan, R.: Recognition of biological signal mixed based on wavelet analysis. In: Jiang, Y., et al. (eds.) Proceedings of UK-China Sports Engineering Workshop, pp. 1–8. World Academic Union, Liverpool (2007)
2. Dewri, R., Chakraborti, N.: Simulating recrystallization through cellular automata and genetic algorithms. Model. Simul. Mater. Sci. Eng. 13(3), 173–183 (2005)
3. Gray, A.: Modern Differential Geometry. CRE Press (1998)
4. Florencio, D., Herley, C.: A large-scale study of web password habits. In: Proceedings of the International Conference on World Wide Web (WWW 2007), pp. 657–666 (2007)
5. Biddle, R., Chiasson, S., van Oorschot, P.: Graphical passwords: learning from the first twelve years. Carleton University - School of Computer Science, Technical report TR-11-01, 4 January 2011
6. Blonder, G.E.: Graphical passwords. United States Patent 5559961 (1996)
7. Dirik, A., Memon, N., Birget, J.: Modeling user choice in the passpoints graphical password scheme. In: Proceedings of the 3rd Symposium on Usable Privacy and Security, pp. 20–28. ACM (2007)
8. Thorpe, J., van Oorschot, P.: Human-seeded attacks and exploiting hot-spots in graphical passwords. In: Proceedings of 16th USENIX Security Symposium on USENIX Security Symposium, pp. 8:1–8:16. USENIX Association (2007)
9. Enso, B.: How Consumers Remember Passwords. Forrester Research Report, 2 June 2004
10. Jermyn, I., Mayer, A., Monrose, F., Reiter, M.K., Rubin, A.D.: The design and analysis of graphical passwords. In: Proceedings of USENIX Security Symposium (1999)
11. Dunph, P., Yan, J.: Do background images improve "Draw a Secret" graphical passwords? In: Proceedings of 14th ACM Conference on Computer and Communications Security, Virginia, USA, 28–31 October 2007, pp. 36–47. ACM Press, New York (2007)
12. Gao, H.C., Guo, X.W., Chen, X.P., Wang, L.M., Liu, X.Y.: YAGP: yet another graphical password strategy. In: Proceedings of 24th Annual Computer Security Applications Conference (ACSAC 2008), California, USA, 8–12 August 2008, pp. 121–129 (2008)
13. Tao, H.: Pass-Go, a new graphical password scheme. Master Thesis, University of Ottawa Canada, June 2006
14. Hayashi, E., Dhamija, R., Christin, N., Perrig, A.: Use your illusion: secure authentication usable anywhere. In: Proceedings of SOUPS 2008. ACM (2008)
15. Dhamija, R., Perrig, A.: Deja Vu: a user study using images for authentication. In: Proceedings of 9th USENIX Security Symposium (2000)
16. Wiedenbeck, S., Waters, J., Birget, J., Brodskiy, A., Memon, N.: PassPoints: design and longitudinal evaluation of a graphical password system. Int. J. Hum.-Comput. Stud. 63, 102–127 (2005)
17. Stubblefield, A., Simon, D.R.: Inkblot authentication. Microsoft Technical report MSR-TR-2004-85 (2004)
18. Wiedenbeck, S., Waters, J., Sobrado, L., Birget, J.: Design and evaluation of a shoulder-surfing resistant graphical password scheme. In: International Working Conference on Advanced Visual Interfaces (AVI), May 2006
19. Narayanan, A., Shmatikov, V.: Fast dictionary attacks on passwords using time-space tradeoff. In: ACM Conference on Computer and Communications Security (CCS), November 2005

20. Chiasson, S., et al.: Multiple Password Interference in Text Passwords and Click-Based Graphical Passwords. ACM (2009)
21. Gołofit, K.: Click passwords under investigation. In: Biskup, J., López, J. (eds.) ESORICS 2007. LNCS, vol. 4734, pp. 343–358. Springer, Heidelberg (2007). https://doi.org/10.1007/978-3-540-74835-9_23
22. Chiasson, S., Forget, A., Biddle, R., van Oorschot, P.: Influencing users towards better passwords: persuasive cued click-points. In: Human Computer Interaction (HCI), The British Computer Society, September 2008
23. Alshehri, M,N., Crawford, H.: Using image saliency and regions of interest to encourage stronger graphical passwords. In: ACSAC 2016, Los Angeles, CA, USA, December 2016
24. Kummerer, M., Theis, L., Bethge, M.: Deep Gaze I: boosting saliency prediction with feature maps trained on ImageNet. arXiv preprint arXiv:1411.1045 (2014)
25. Lewis, J.R.: IBM computer usability satisfaction questionnaires: psychometric evaluation and instructions for use. Int. J. Hum.-Comput. Interact. **7**, 57–78 (1995)
26. Nicholson, J.: Design of a multi-touch shoulder surfing resilient graphical password. Dissertation, Newcastle University (2009)
27. Tari, F., Ozok, A.A., Holden, S.: A comparison of perceived and real shoulder-surfing risks between alphanumeric and graphical passwords. In: SOUPS 2006. ACM (2006)
28. Kim, D., Dunphy, P., Briggs, P., Hook, J., Nicholson J., Olivier, P.: Multi-touch authentication on tabletops. In: CHI 2010. ACM (2010)
29. Zakaria, N.H., Griffiths, D., Brostoff, S., Yan, J.: Shoulder surfing defence for recall-based graphical passwords. In: SOUPS 2011. ACM (2011)

ADSaS: Comprehensive Real-Time Anomaly Detection System

Sooyeon Lee[✉] and Huy Kang Kim[✉]

Graduate School of Information Security, Korea University, Seoul, South Korea
{tndus95a,cenda}@korea.ac.kr

Abstract. Since with massive data growth, the need for autonomous and generic anomaly detection system is increased. However, developing one stand-alone generic anomaly detection system that is accurate and fast is still a challenge. In this paper, we propose conventional time-series analysis approaches, the Seasonal Autoregressive Integrated Moving Average (SARIMA) model and Seasonal Trend decomposition using Loess (STL), to detect complex and various anomalies. Usually, SARIMA and STL are used only for stationary and periodic time-series, but by combining, we show they can detect anomalies with high accuracy for data that is even noisy and non-periodic. We compared the algorithm to Long Short Term Memory (LSTM), a deep-learning-based algorithm used for anomaly detection system. We used a total of seven real-world datasets and four artificial datasets with different time-series properties to verify the performance of the proposed algorithm.

Keywords: Anomaly detection · SARIMA · STL · Real-time · Data stream

1 Introduction

Extremely vast data leads to severe challenges to a security administrator who should catch all the anomalies in real-time. Anomaly detection cannot be regarded as a human-work anymore. To automate the anomaly detection process, machine-learning-based and statistics-based anomaly detection have been researched within diverse research areas including network intrusion detection, fraud detection, medical diagnoses, sensor events and others. Despite the variety of such studies in recent years, most anomaly detection systems find anomalies in limited conditions. This is because not only a variety of attacks but also multiple sensors in a single device generate a different type of time-series. In the case of IoT devices, which are embedded with multiple sensors, it is inefficient to use independent anomaly detection algorithms to each different sensor. Anomaly detection systems that are resistant to various datasets should detect anomalies autonomously irrespectively of the time-series properties.

Also, the anomaly detection system should occupy as little memory as possible. Most of deep learning based anomaly detection systems are generally unsuitable for an environment such as IoT devices because of the limited memory and

© Springer Nature Switzerland AG 2019
B. B. Kang and J. Jang (Eds.): WISA 2018, LNCS 11402, pp. 29–41, 2019.
https://doi.org/10.1007/978-3-030-17982-3_3

light capacity. As most anomalies cause a critical problem to the medical system such as ventricular assist system, anomaly detection system must get less latency. Although there are many types of researches based on deep learning recently, deep learning approaches are not suitable to process data in real-time that changes frequently or has large data since it takes a lot of time to build a model compared to other algorithms.

The critical conditions of anomaly detection system for IoT devices or cloud network intrusion detection are as follows. First is accuracy, second is speed, third is the small size of the model and the last is domain universality [2,19]. We propose ADSaS, anomaly detection system using SARIMA and STL, to meet the four conditions. SARIMA is conventional time-series forecast method, and STL is a versatile and robust method for time-series decomposition. Aforementioned methods are commonly used for stationary and periodic time-series data [7]. In our experiments, however, integrating two methods shows better performance not only for periodic data but also for non-periodic data. Moreover, the size of the model and speed are optimized by undersampling and interpolation. For accuracy, we defined an anomaly window for evaluation and then judged how well ADSaS finds anomalies in various datasets.

The contributions of our system are as follows:

- Regardless of time-series properties, ADSaS detects anomalies with high precision and recall. We verify this by using the time-series from a variety of sources. With the development of Cyber-Physical Systems (CPS) or IoT devices, anomaly detection systems must detect anomaly autonomously and generically for applications.
- ADSaS detects various types of anomaly. (i.e., peak, dip, concept drift, contextual anomalies, and collective anomalies).
- ADSaS detects anomalies with short latency. We use two conventional time-series analysis methods and advance performance by undersampling. By undersampling time-series, time-series model is built much faster. Though undersampling causes loss of data, STL recovers that loss by decomposing prediction errors.
- ADSaS proceeds anomaly detection in real-time for every data stream.

2   Related Works

In particular, there have been studies such as automotive IDS [8], SCADA, control network [18] to detect anomalies for mission-critical and safety-critical systems. It is important to develop anomaly detection algorithm robustly for the efficiency of intrusion detection in a modern network environment such as cloud computing [9]. Anomaly detection in time-series is roughly divided to clustering-based approach [11,12] and forecast-based approach. Most of the forecast-based approaches perform anomaly detection based on the error with the predicted value.

Several machine learning techniques were introduced so far for anomaly detection system. LSTM network has been demonstrated to be particularly useful for anomaly detection in time-series [13]. Jonathan *et al.* [6] also presented a novel anomaly detection system to detect cyber attacks in CPS by using unsupervised learning approach, Recurrent Neural Network (RNN). Sucheta *et al.* [3] applied RNN and LSTM to detect anomalies in ECG signals. They used only a single data source, so did not show the generality of algorithms.

Some studies used diverse dataset sources to evaluate anomaly detection algorithm. Numenta used Hierarchical Temporal Memory (HTM) algorithm to detect anomaly detection capable for stream time-series [2]. HTM is a neural network, and every neuron in HTM remember and predict the value by communicating with each other. Since it is composed of a higher order than other neural networks, it may not be suitable for anomaly detection systems which require high speed. Yahoo suggested EGADS [10], plug-in-out anomaly detection framework, and they indicated that it is essential to use time-series features for anomaly detection. EGADS offers AR, MA, and ARIMA. Several studies [17] used ARIMA models to forecast time-series, but they did not process errors for a non-periodic dataset. SARIMA was also frequently used for time series prediction, but it was not applied to anomaly detection system [16].

3 Backgrounds

3.1 Time-Series Analysis

Power Spectral Density. Power spectral density is a simple but powerful method to find the frequency of the data [15]. Power spectral density of the signal (time-series data) describes the distribution of power which refers to frequency. Power spectral density graph shows clear peaks when the signal has evident frequencies.

Dickey-Fuller Test. Dickey-Fuller Test tests the null hypothesis that a unit root is present in an autoregressive model [5]. The unit root test is carried out under the null hypothesis test value $\gamma = 0$ against the alternative hypothesis of $\gamma < 0$. The unit root test is an analytical method for determining stationarity of the time-series. In ADSaS, when the p-value of the test is bigger than 0.0005, we reject the hypothesis and refer the time-series as non-stationary data.

STL. STL is an algorithm developed to decompose a time-series into three components namely: the trend, seasonality, and residuals (remainder) [4]. A trend shows a persistent increasing or decreasing direction in data, seasonality shows seasonal factors over a fixed period, and residuals mean noise of the time-series. For time-series analysis, residuals mainly considered as errors. In this paper, we use residuals of time-series to extract errors that are related to anomalies.

3.2   Time-Series Forecast Model

Autoregressive (AR) Model. AR model is used when a value from a time-series is regressed on previous values from the same time-series. When time-series data has white noise α_t, autoregressive parameter ϕ, an $AR(p)$ model Z_t at time t is defined as:

$$Z_t = \phi_1 Z_{t-1} + \phi_2 Z_{t-2} + \cdots + \phi_p Z_{t-p} + \alpha_t \tag{1}$$

Moving Average (MA) Model. MA model uses complicated stochastic structure to model time-series [14]. When time-series has white noise α_t, parameters of the model θ, a $MA(q)$ model Z_t at time t is defined as:

$$Z_t = \alpha_t - \theta_1 \alpha_{t-1} - \cdots - \theta_q \alpha_{t-q} \tag{2}$$

ARIMA. ARIMA model generalizes an ARMA model (AR+MA) by replacing the difference among previous values. An ARMA model is applicable only for stationary time-series, ARIMA is applicable for non-stationary time-series. $ARMA(p, q)$ model is given by:

$$Z_t - \phi_1 Z_{t-1} - \cdots - \phi_p Z_{t-p} = \alpha_t + \theta_1 \alpha_{t-1} + \cdots - \theta_q \alpha_{t-q} \tag{3}$$

$$\left(1 - \sum_{i=1}^{p} \phi_i L^i\right) Z_t = \left(1 + \sum_{i=1}^{q} \theta_i L^i\right) \alpha_t \tag{4}$$

In here, L is the lag operator of Z. $ARIMA(p, d, q)$ model has parameters p (the order of AR model), q (the order of MA model) and also d (the degree of differencing). When two out of the three parameters are zeros, the model is referred to as AR or MA or I. (i.e., ARIMA(1,0,0) is AR(1)) $ARIMA(p, d, q)$ model is defined as:

$$\left(1 - \sum_{i=1}^{p} \phi_i L^i\right) (1 - L)^d Z_t = \left(1 + \sum_{i=1}^{q} \alpha_i L^i\right) \alpha_t \tag{5}$$

SARIMA. SARIMA is a much more efficient model to express time-series with seasonality than ARIMA model. It has an additional parameter seasonal order called s. SARIMA is defined as $SARIMA(p, d, q)(P, D, Q)_s$. The parameters p, d, q are for non-seasonal part of the time-series, and P, D, Q are for seasonal part of the model. In other words, SARIMA creates models with both seasonal and non-seasonal data. For $s = 12$, SARIMA builds a time-series model with seasonality per 12 data points.

4   Methodology

ADSaS. ADSaS consists of three modules, dataset analysis module, forecasting module and error processing module. Let the vector x_t is the value of a system at time t. Real-time anomaly detection system should classify whether the value is an anomaly or not without using any data after the time t. First of all, by analyzing the proper size of the train set, dataset analysis module finds the frequency and stationarity of the given dataset. Then, forecasting module forecasts $x_{t+1}, x_{t+2}, x_{t+3}, \ldots$ by using train set (The size of forecast can be changed). When data stream x_{t+1} comes, error processing module calculates the residuals of the error and the cumulative probability of the residuals. If the cumulative probability is less or bigger then the threshold, ADSaS classifies the value as an anomaly and alert. For more accurate forecast model, only the normal value is fed back to the train set.

Data Analysis Module. STL and SARIMA, mainly used algorithms, work based on the properties of the time-series data. To get the properties, we use *Dickey-Fuller test* for stationarity and *power density spectra* for frequency. When data does not have stationarity, we use one day for default frequency.

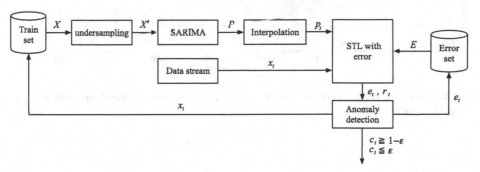

Fig. 1. The figure shows how the forecasting module and error processing module works.

Forecasting Module. SARIMA model has a s parameter that represents the seasonality frequency. If a time-series has regular change per one second and repeats every day, s should be at least 86400 to define time-series model. However, large s causes a huge amount of time, which is problematic for practical anomaly detection systems. The ADSaS uses undersampling and interpolation to shorten building time. Figure 1 is details about how the prediction and error processing works. First, we undersample the train set X to $X'(|X| \gg |X'|)$.

If the dataset is recorded at the five-minute interval, we adjust it at the one-hour interval by averaging them. Then, SARIMA model for train set is built to describe and forecast time-series. The interval of the model is one-hour, so we interpolate forecasts at the initial interval (in this case, five-minute) by using *cubic spline interpolation*. Where the predicted value is p_t and real value is x_t, absolute prediction error e_t is defined as $p_t - x_t$.

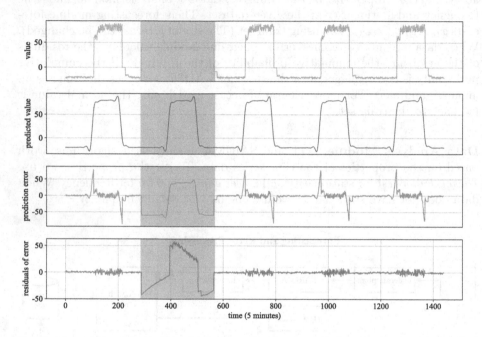

Fig. 2. Observed value, predicted value, prediction error, and residuals of error for the given time series data.

Error Processing Module. In the error processing module, prediction errors are decomposed by STL and the residuals are calculated. Although undersampling and interpolation arise a serious problem of missing actual data points, regularity of the errors due to lost data points diminishes the residuals. We model the residuals distribution as a rolling normal distribution, though the distribution of prediction errors is not technically a normal distribution. Where the sample mean μ, and variance σ^2 are given, the cumulative distribution function is calculated as follows:

$$F(x) = \int_{-\infty}^{x} \frac{e^{-\frac{(x-\mu)^2}{2\sigma^2}}}{\sigma\sqrt{2\pi}} \, dx \qquad (6)$$

We threshold $F(r_t)$ based on a user-defined parameter ε to alert anomalies[1]. If $F(r_t)$ is smaller than ε or greater than $1 - \varepsilon$, it is determined as anomaly.

Figure 2 is an example of error residuals[2] The error increment is occurred in the normal data (first jump) due to the undersampling and interpolation. However, it is judged to be a regular error by STL, so decomposed to trend or seasonality, no residuals. As the anomaly occurs, the residuals decreases/increases sharply. This causes the dramatic difference in residuals between regular errors and unexpected errors, so anomalies are detected by ADSaS easily.

5   Experimental Evaluation

5.1   Dataset

There are 11 datasets we used in the experiment, eight datasets from Numenta Anomaly Benchmark (NAB) [1] and three datasets from the P corporation, Korea's leading third-party online payment solution. NAB is a benchmark for evaluating anomaly detection algorithms, and it is comprised of over 50 labeled artificial and real-world datasets. Also, the real-world datasets from P are user login statistics, tracks the browser, service provider and login result status. The anomalies are labeled when the real attack attempts are held. All the anomalies were confirmed by P corporation.

All datasets except four datasets (NAB artificial jump datasets) are real-world datasets, which cover various fields, including CPU utilization, machine temperature, and user login statistics. The examples of datasets are shown in Fig. 3. Each dataset has different time series characteristics and anomaly types. For instance, dataset (b) has concept drift anomaly that it should not be detected as anomaly after the drift point. Dataset (c) disk write anomaly has lots of noises. NYC taxi dataset shows various anomalies (peak, dip and partial decrease).

5.2   Evaluation Metrics

We use precision, recall and F_1-score to evaluate the algorithm. When the actual anomaly is classified as an anomaly, it is true positive. False positive is when the normal data is classified to be an anomaly. False negative is when the anomaly is classified as normal, and true negative is when the normal data is classified as normal. Depending on the area, false positive may be more important than false negative to check performance or vice versa. We use F_1-score to evaluate both precision($\frac{TP}{TP+FP}$), which is an indicator of whether the anomalies detected by the algorithm is trusty and recall($\frac{TP}{TP+FN}$), which is an indicator of how many anomalies are detected by the algorithm. The metric of F_1-score is $2 \times \frac{Precision \times Recall}{Precision + Recall}$.

---

[1] We used $\varepsilon = 0.0005$ for experiments.
[2] Anomalies are colored with red.

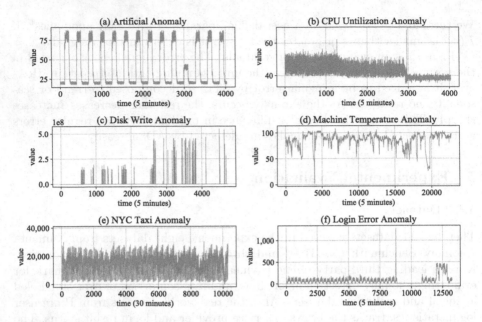

Fig. 3. The examples of the datasets.

Anomaly Window. We also define *anomaly window* to evaluate the performance of the algorithm. An anomaly may occur only at a certain point (peak, dip), but it may occur over a long period. It is not false positive to detect anomaly at the point immediately before or after the occurrence of an anomaly. It is essential to set the appropriate anomaly windows covering anomalies. Numenta defines their own anomaly windows for NAB dataset, but it is too large to distinguish whether the classification is right or wrong. We use small enough window size to prevent inept detection considered as true positive or true negative. In the case of anomalies occurring over a long period, it can be judged as a section composed of several anomaly windows. If the anomaly window is successfully detected in section, it is considered to be true positive after the detection.

6   Results

Table 1 shows the comparisons of precision, recall and F_1-score for algorithms from different kinds of sources. It shows that ADSaS yields the best overall datasets except one, NAB CPU. For NAB CPU, the algorithm that uses only LSTM shows the best result. LSTM algorithm, however, is a deep learning based algorithm that takes a lot of time to learn. In addition, for data such as NAB Jumps and P Login, which has periodicity and stationary, LSTM shows lowest F_1-score than other algorithms. Even LSTM with STL, F_1-score is slightly increased in periodic time-series, but it is decreased by about half in case of non-periodic data (NAB CPU).

Table 1. Comparison of results between algorithms.

Dataset	Total window	Anomaly window	Metrics	STL only	SARIMA only	LSTM only	LSTM with STL	ADSaS
NAB jumps	335	11–25	Precision	0.920	0.518	0.324	0.278	1.000
			Recall	0.910	0.727	0.500	0.750	1.000
			F_1-score	0.903	0.583	0.370	0.392	**1.000**
NAB CPU	335	4	Precision	0.800	0.143	0.833	0.308	1.000
			Recall	1.000	0.250	1.000	1.000	0.250
			F_1-score	0.889	0.182	**0.909**	0.471	0.400
NAB disk	394	1	Precision	0.025	0.026	0.049	0.018	1.000
			Recall	1.000	1.000	0.222	1.000	1.000
			F_1-score	0.049	0.051	0.049	0.018	**1.000**
NAB temperature	315	9	Precision	0.250	0.000	0.049	0.059	1.000
			Recall	0.222	0.000	0.222	0.625	0.500
			F_1-score	0.235	0.000	0.080	0.108	**0.667**
NAB taxi	214	9	Precision	0.533	0.000	0.176	0.161	1.000
			Recall	0.889	0.000	0.333	1.000	1.000
			F_1-score	0.667	0.000	0.231	0.277	**1.000**
P login	1,102	245	Precision	0.970	1.000	0.962	0.968	1.000
			Recall	0.922	0.307	0.307	1.000	1.000
			F_1-score	0.945	0.470	0.466	0.984	**1.000**
P browser	1,102	131	Precision	0.947	1.000	1.000	0.942	1.000
			Recall	0.954	0.588	0.924	0.992	1.000
			F_1-score	0.951	0.740	0.960	0.967	**1.000**
P provider	1,102	141	Precision	0.914	1.000	0.917	0.849	1.000
			Recall	0.979	0.057	0.936	1.000	0.993
			F_1-score	0.945	0.107	0.926	0.919	**0.996**

We note that in most datasets, an algorithm that uses only STL has the next highest F_1-score after ADSaS. In particular, as opposed to LSTM, it performed well for NAB Jumps and P Login which are periodic time-series. However, STL does not forecast anything, so it is impossible to automatically correct anomalies to normal values, which is possible in other algorithms. SARIMA only algorithm does not perform well in anomaly detection because its forecast accuracy is compromised by the undersampling and interpolation processes. For NAB disks, which is the noisiest dataset, all but ADSaS has very low F_1-score less than 0.05. This suggests that SARIMA, STL, and LSTM cannot handle noise alone, but combining SARIMA and STL shows remarkable performance at handling noise.

We also analyze the reasons why ADSaS performed poorly on NAB CPU dataset. ADSaS found only one of the four anomaly windows, which is the last anomaly window, the actual concept drift. ADSaS is unable to determine the first anomaly whether or not it is an anomaly because it is used as train set. This is a fatal disadvantage of ADSaS. Both SARIMA and STL require a data set of a certain size to be used as a train set to forecast or decompose time-series. ADSaS uses both algorithms, so the amount of data sets initially used for training is greater than others. However, since there are large enough datasets for anomaly detection in real business, this is not a big problem to ADSaS. In addition, ADSaS shows near-perfect accuracy for most datasets.

Figure 4 shows examples of the residuals and errors from each algorithm in NAB taxi dataset. The anomaly is determined by the cumulative distribution function of these data. There are five anomaly sections (including peak, dip, partial decrease), and a total number of anomaly windows is nine. First, ADSaS and STL have some similar forms but STL shows some bumps between the fourth and fifth anomaly sections which cause false positives. SARIMA generates a lot of errors regularly due to its uncertainty of forecasting. LSTM shows the lowest prediction error compared to other algorithms, but the prediction error is increased only at the point where peaks exist. For dip and partial decrease, where the value is suddenly reduced, the prediction error is low because LSTM quickly adjusts to the value.

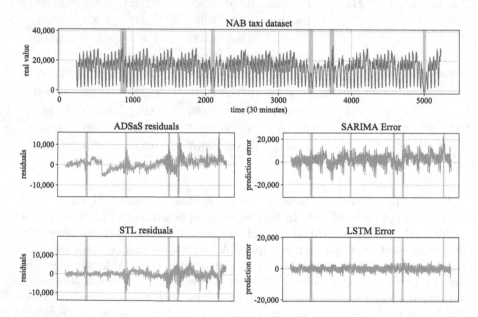

Fig. 4. Residuals or error of each algorithm for NAB taxi dataset. Anomaly windows are colored with red. (Color figure online)

Table 2. The latency of classification for each stream and model-build.

Algorithm	Model build (s)	Classify (s)
STL	0.000	0.189
SARIMA	3.776	0.000
LSTM	1982.410	0.001
ADSaS	3.992	0.187

Table 2 is a comparison of latency between algorithms. STL does not need to build a model, so only time-decomposition process increases latency. Unlike other algorithms, the time decomposition of STL is directly linked to anomaly detection and cannot proceed with batch. For SARIMA, the forecast size can be adjusted to help speed up the forecasting. In this experiment, SARIMA model predicts the daily data in advance. Therefore, anomaly classification using SARIMA is very fast because all it has to do is calculate the actual stream data difference. Although we used the LSTM model with 12 neurons, two hidden layer and *relu* activation function in this experiment, which is comparatively not a heavy model, LSTM took the 1982 seconds to build the model. As the number of neurons and hidden layers increases, building or updating LSTM's model takes an extraordinary amount of time.

7   Conclusions

By combining STL and SARIMA, we have presented algorithms to detect various anomalies in datasets from various sources. In addition, comparing with LSTM shows that conventional time-series analysis has better performance and accuracy than the deep-learning algorithm. In this paper, we have discussed the forecasting model SARIMA does not give accurate predictions, but STL is able to resolve incomplete predictions by decomposing the prediction errors. It supports the fact that the STL algorithm will be more useful in anomaly detection than other approaches in error processing, such as likelihood. We also showed that the conventional time-series techniques are applicable to noisy and non-stationary datasets (NAB Disk). We applied our algorithm to real online payment system data and showed that ADSaS can be applied directly to the real industry. ADSaS succeeded in detecting anomaly right at the time of the attack. In this experiment, only the SARIMA model is used as the time-series prediction algorithm, but other time-series models including GARCH model, that expresses white noises, can be used as a predictor module. Furthermore, we need to update our algorithms to detect anomaly using multivariate datasets because we conducted the experiments on datasets with only single variable.

Acknowledgements. This work was supported under the framework of international cooperation program managed by National Research Foundation of Korea (No. 2017K1A3A1A17 092614).

References

1. The numenta anomaly benchmark. https://github.com/numenta/NAB
2. Ahmad, S., Lavin, A., Purdy, S., Agha, Z.: Unsupervised real-time anomaly detection for streaming data. Neurocomputing **262**, 134–147 (2017)
3. Chauhan, S., Vig, L.: Anomaly detection in ECG time signals via deep long short-term memory networks. In: IEEE International Conference on Data Science and Advanced Analytics (DSAA), pp. 1–7. IEEE (2015)
4. Cleveland, R.B., Cleveland, W.S., Terpenning, I.: STL: a seasonal-trend decomposition procedure based on loess. J. Off. Stat. **6**(1), 3 (1990)
5. Dickey, D.A., Fuller, W.A.: Distribution of the estimators for autoregressive time series with a unit root. J. Am. Stat. Assoc. **74**(366a), 427–431 (1979)
6. Goh, J., Adepu, S., Tan, M., Lee, Z.S.: Anomaly detection in cyber physical systems using recurrent neural networks. In: IEEE 18th International Symposium on High Assurance Systems Engineering (HASE), pp. 140–145. IEEE (2017)
7. Hamilton, J.: Time Series Analysis. Princeton University Press, Princeton (1994)
8. Han, M.L., Lee, J., Kang, A.R., Kang, S., Park, J.K., Kim, H.K.: A statistical-based anomaly detection method for connected cars in internet of things environment. In: Hsu, C.-H., Xia, F., Liu, X., Wang, S. (eds.) IOV 2015. LNCS, vol. 9502, pp. 89–97. Springer, Cham (2015). https://doi.org/10.1007/978-3-319-27293-1_9
9. Kwon, H., Kim, T., Yu, S.J., Kim, H.K.: Self-similarity based lightweight intrusion detection method for cloud computing. In: Nguyen, N.T., Kim, C.-G., Janiak, A. (eds.) ACIIDS 2011. LNCS (LNAI), vol. 6592, pp. 353–362. Springer, Heidelberg (2011). https://doi.org/10.1007/978-3-642-20042-7_36
10. Laptev, N., Amizadeh, S., Flint, I.: Generic and scalable framework for automated time-series anomaly detection. In: Proceedings of the 21st ACM SIGKDD International Conference on Knowledge Discovery and Data Mining, pp. 1939–1947. ACM (2015)
11. Laxhammar, R., Falkman, G., Sviestins, E.: Anomaly detection in sea traffic-a comparison of the Gaussian mixture model and the kernel density estimator. In: 12th International Conference on Information Fusion, FUSION 2009, pp. 756–763. IEEE (2009)
12. Leung, K., Leckie, C.: Unsupervised anomaly detection in network intrusion detection using clusters. In: Proceedings of the Twenty-Eighth Australasian Conference on Computer Science, vol. 38, pp. 333–342. Australian Computer Society, Inc. (2005)
13. Malhotra, P., Vig, L., Shroff, G., Agarwal, P.: Long short term memory networks for anomaly detection in time series. In: Proceedings, p. 89. Presses universitaires de Louvain (2015)
14. Mills, T.C., Mills, T.C.: Time Series Techniques for Economists. Cambridge University Press, Cambridge (1991)
15. T.D.P. Studio: Cygnus research international. https://www.cygres.com/0cnPageE/Glosry/SpecE.html
16. Wang, Y., Wang, J., Zhao, G., Dong, Y.: Application of residual modification approach in seasonal ARIMA for electricity demand forecasting: a case study of china. Energy Policy **48**, 284–294 (2012)
17. Yaacob, A.H., Tan, I.K., Chien, S.F., Tan, H.K.: ARIMA based network anomaly detection. In: Second International Conference on Communication Software and Networks, ICCSN 2010, pp. 205–209. IEEE (2010)

18. Yu, S.J., Koh, P., Kwon, H., Kim, D.S., Kim, H.K.: Hurst parameter based anomaly detection for intrusion detection system. In: 2016 IEEE International Conference on Computer and Information Technology (CIT), pp. 234–240. IEEE (2016)

19. Zhang, Z.K., Cho, M.C.Y., Wang, C.W., Hsu, C.W., Chen, C.K., Shieh, S.: IoT security: ongoing challenges and research opportunities. In: IEEE 7th International Conference on Service-Oriented Computing and Applications (SOCA), pp. 230–234. IEEE (2014)

One-Pixel Adversarial Example that Is Safe for Friendly Deep Neural Networks

Hyun Kwon[1], Yongchul Kim[2], Hyunsoo Yoon[1], and Daeseon Choi[3(✉)]

[1] School of Computing, Korea Advanced Institute of Science and Technology,
Daejeon, South Korea
[2] Department of Electrical Engineering, Korea Military Academy, Seoul, South Korea
[3] Department of Medical Information,
Kongju National University, Gongju, South Korea
sunchoi@kongju.ac.kr

Abstract. Deep neural networks (DNNs) offer superior performance in machine learning tasks such as image recognition, speech recognition, pattern analysis, and intrusion detection. In this paper, we propose a one-pixel adversarial example that is safe for friendly deep neural networks. By modifying only one pixel, our proposed method generates a one-pixel-safe adversarial example that can be misclassified by an enemy classifier and correctly classified by a friendly classifier. To verify the performance of the proposed method, we used the CIFAR-10 dataset, ResNet model classifiers, and the Tensorflow library in our experiments. Results show that the proposed method modified only one pixel to achieve success rates of 13.5% and 26.0% in targeted and untargeted attacks, respectively. The success rate is slightly lower than that of the conventional one-pixel method, which has success rates of 15% and 33.5% in targeted and untargeted attacks, respectively; however, this method protects 100% of the friendly classifiers. In addition, if the proposed method modifies five pixels, this method can achieve success rates of 20.5% and 52.0% in targeted and untargeted attacks, respectively.

Keywords: Deep neural network (DNN) · Adversarial example · One-pixel attack · Differential evolution (DE)

1 Introduction

Deep neural networks (DNNs) [12] have been widely used for image recognition, speech recognition, pattern analysis, and intrusion detection. However, adversarial examples [15] are a serious threat to DNNs. An adversarial example is a distorted sample that adds a small amount of noise to the original sample; this can lead to misclassification of the DNN. Adversarial examples and their effects have been extensively studied.

In recent years, one-pixel adversarial attacks [14] have emerged as a threat to DNNs. Unlike conventional adversarial attacks, this method causes DNN misclassification by modifying a single pixel and is useful for applications such as

© Springer Nature Switzerland AG 2019
B. B. Kang and J. Jang (Eds.): WISA 2018, LNCS 11402, pp. 42–54, 2019.
https://doi.org/10.1007/978-3-030-17982-3_4

stickers. However, this method has not been considered for situations such as military scenarios, where enemy forces and friendly forces are mixed.

The adversarial example of friendly forces can be useful in situations such as military engagements. Because battlegrounds are shared by enemy forces and friendly forces, friend-safe adversarial examples [9] that can be misclassified by enemy classifiers and correctly classified by friendly classifiers could prove to be an invaluable tool. For example, it may be necessary to modify the road signs on a battlefield to deceive only the enemy's self-driven vehicles.

Thus, we propose an advanced one-pixel adversarial example that preserves the recognition of friendly classifiers. By modifying only one pixel, the proposed method can generate a one-pixel-safe adversarial example that can be misclassified by enemy classifiers and correctly classified by friendly classifiers. This paper makes the following contributions:

- First, we propose a one-pixel-safe adversarial example by modifying a single pixel in a DNN and systematically organize the frameworks of the proposed scheme.
- The proposed scheme has two configurations: targeted and untargeted attacks. The proposed method can generate the one-pixel-safe adversarial example in for both configurations.
- We used the CIFAR-10 dataset to validate the performance and analyze the success rates for targeted attack and untargeted attacks. In addition, we analyzed the performance of this method by modifying groups of three and five pixels.

The remainder of this paper is structured as follows: Sect. 2 reviews related works. Our proposed adversarial example attack is presented in Sect. 3. The experiments and evaluation are shown in Sect. 4, and a discussion of the proposed system is presented in Sect. 5. Finally, conclusions are given in Sect. 6.

2   Related Works

The study of adversarial examples was introduced by Szegedy et al. [15] in 2014. The main goal of using an adversarial example is to induce the DNN into making a mistake by adding a small amount of noise to the original image such that humans cannot tell the difference between the original and the distorted image.

The basic method for generating adversarial examples is described in Sect. 2.1. Adversarial examples can be categorized in three ways: recognition of an adversarial example, information on the target model information, and method for generation, as described in Sects. 2.2–2.4.

2.1   Adversarial Example Generation

The basic architecture that generates an adversarial example comprises two elements: a target model and a transformer. The transformer takes the original sample x and original class y as input data. Next, the transformer creates a transformed example $x^* = x + w$, with noise value w added to the original sample x as output; the transformed example x^* is given as input data to the target model. The target model then provides the transformer with the class probability results for the transformed example. Following this, the transformer updates the noise values w in the transformed example $x^* = x + w$ so that the other class probabilities are higher than the original class probabilities, while minimizing the distortion distances between x^* and x.

2.2 Categorization by Recognition of Adversarial Example

According to the class that the target model recognizes from the adversarial examples, we can divide these examples into two subcategories: targeted and untargeted. A targeted adversarial example is an adversarial example that causes the target model to recognize the adversarial image as a particular intended class. This can be expressed mathematically as follows:

Given a target model and original sample $x \in X$, the problem is an optimization problem that generates a targeted adversarial example x^*:

$$x^* : \operatorname*{argmin}_{x^*} L(x, x^*) \text{ s.t. } f(x^*) = y^*$$

where $L(\cdot)$ is the distance measure between the original sample x and the transformed example x^*, and y^* is the particular intended class. $f(\cdot)$ is an operation function that provides class results for the input values of the target model.

An untargeted adversarial example is an adversarial example that causes the target model to recognize the adversarial image as a class other than the original class. It can be expressed mathematically as follows:

Given a target model and original sample $x \in X$, the problem is an optimization problem that generates an untargeted adversarial example x^*:

$$x^* : \operatorname*{argmin}_{x^*} L(x, x^*) \text{ s.t. } f(x^*) \neq y$$

where $y \in Y$ is the original class.

Untargeted adversarial examples have the advantages of less distortion from the original image and shorter learning time when compared with targeted adversarial examples. However, targeted adversarial examples are more sophisticated attacks as they are misclassified as target classes chosen by the attacker.

2.3 Categorization by Information on Target Model

Depending on the amount of target information required, attacks that generate adversarial examples can also be divided into two types: white box attacks and black box attacks. However, black box attacks only require an input response; no additional information about the target is needed. In this paper, the proposed method is a white box attack that knows both the enemy and friendly classifiers.

2.4   Categorization by Method for Adversarial Example Generation

There are four typical attacks that generate adversarial examples. The first is the fast-gradient sign method (FGSM) [4], which can find x^* through L_∞:

$$x^* = x + \epsilon \cdot \text{sign}(\triangledown loss_{F,t}(x))$$

where F is an object function and t is a target class. In every FGSM iteration, the gradient is updated by ϵ from the original x, and x^* is found through optimization. This method is simple and demonstrates good performance.

The second attack is iterative FGSM (I-FGSM) [8], which is an updated version of the FGSM. Instead of changing the amount ϵ in each step, the smaller amount of α is updated and eventually clipped by the same ϵ:

$$x_i^* = x_{i-1}^* - \text{clip}_\epsilon(\alpha \cdot \text{sign}(\triangledown loss_{F,t}(x_{i-1}^*)))$$

The I-FGSM provides better performance than the FGSM.

The third type of attack is the Deepfool method [10], which is an untargeted attack and uses the L_2 distance measure. This method generates an adversarial example that is more efficient than the FGSM and as close as possible to the original image. To generate an adversarial example, this method constructs of a neural network and looks for x^* using linearization approximation. However, because the neural network is not completely linear, we must find the adversarial example through multiple iterations; i.e., it is a more complicated process than that of the FGSM.

The fourth attack method is the Carlini attack [2], which is the latest attack method and delivers better performance than the FGSM and I-FGSM. This method can achieve a 100% success rate, even against a distillation structure [11], which was recently introduced in the literature. The key principle of this method involves the use of a different objective function:

$$D(x, x^*) + c \cdot f(x^*)$$

Instead of using the conventional objective function $D(x, x^*)$, this method proposes a means to find an appropriate binary c value. In addition, it suggests a method to control the attack success rate even with some increased distortion by reflecting the confidence value as follows:

$$f(x^*) = \max(Z(x^*)_t - \max\{Z(x^*)_t : i \neq t\}, -k)$$

where $Z(\cdot)$ represents the pre-softmax classification result vector and t is a target class.

The four previously mentioned methods add a small amount of noise to the entire original sample, causing misclassification. In a recent study, Su et al. [14] proposed a one-pixel attack that causes misclassification by modifying a single pixel. In one-pixel attacks, differential evolution [3,13] is used as the optimizer. The advantage of one-pixel attacks is that they do not affect the rest of the pixels in the original sample. For example, a traffic sign could be attacked by modifying one pixel in the sign when it is deployed. In this paper, the proposed method is constructed by applying a similar one-pixel attack.

3 Proposed Method

To generate a one-pixel-safe adversarial example, we propose a network architecture that consists of a transformer, a friendly discriminator D_{friend}, and an enemy discriminator D_{enemy}, as shown in Fig. 1.

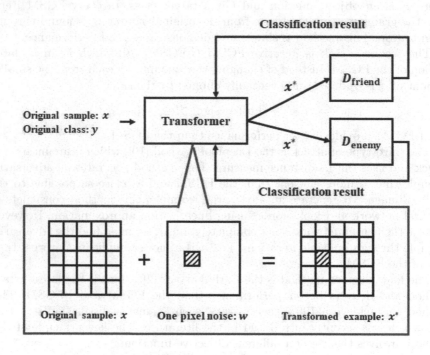

Fig. 1. Proposed architecture.

The transformer takes the original sample $x \in X$ and the original class $y \in Y$ as input and converts the original sample to the transformed example x^*. Furthermore, D_{friend} and D_{enemy} are pre-trained classifiers and are not changed during transformation. They take x^* as input and provide their classification result (i.e., confidence) to the transformer.

The goal of this architecture is to add one pixel of noise to the original sample so that the transformed example x^* is misclassified by D_{enemy} and correctly classified by D_{friend}. There are two configurations in which the transformed example x^* is incorrectly classified by D_{enemy}: the targeted adversarial and untargeted adversarial examples. In mathematical expressions, the operation functions of D_{enemy} and D_{friend} are denoted as $f^{enemy}(x)$ and $f^{friend}(x)$, respectively. Given the pre-trained D_{friend} and D_{enemy} and the original input $x \in X$, we have an optimization problem that generates the targeted adversarial example x^*:

$$x^* : \underset{x^*}{\operatorname{argmin}}\ L(x, x^*)\ \text{s.t.}\ f^{friend}(x^*) = y\ \text{and}\ f^{enemy}(x^*) = y^*,$$

where $L(\cdot)$ is the chosen measure of the distance between the original sample x and transformed example x^*, and $y^* \in Y$ is the target class chosen by the attacker. An untargeted adversarial example x^* is similarly generated:

$$x^* : \operatorname*{argmin}_{x^*} L(x, x^*) \text{ s.t. } f^{\text{friend}}(x^*) = y \text{ and } f^{\text{enemy}}(x^*) \neq y.$$

This procedure consists of pre-training D_{friend} and D_{enemy} and creating a transformation that generates a one-pixel-safe adversarial example, x^*. First, D_{friend} and D_{enemy} are trained to classify the original sample x.

$$f^{\text{friend}}(x) = y \in Y \text{ and } f^{\text{enemy}}(x) = y \in Y.$$

In our experiments, D_{friend} and D_{enemy} were trained to classify the original samples using CIFAR-10 with more than 92% accuracy. Second, the transformer accepts the original sample and original class as input and produces the transformed example x^*. For this study, we modified the transformer architecture given in [9,14], and defined x^* as

$$x^* = x + w,$$

where $x = (x_1, ..., x_n)$ is the original sample with n n-dimensional inputs and $w = (w_1, ..., w_n)$ is noise with n-dimension.

The classification results of x^* by D_{friend} and D_{enemy} are returned to the transformer. The transformer then calculates the total objection function, $f^T(x^*)$, and generates a one-pixel-safe adversarial example x^* by iteratively maximizing $f^T(x^*)$. $f^T(\cdot)$ is defined as

$$\operatorname*{maximize}_{x^*} f^T(x^*) = f_y^{\text{friend}}(x^*) + f_{y^*}^{\text{enemy}}(x^*) \text{ subject to } \|w\|_0 \leq d, \quad (1)$$

where $f_y^{\text{friend}}(x^*)$ and $f_{y^*}^{\text{enemy}}(x^*)$ are the objection functions of D_{friend} and D_{enemy}, and d is 1 as the one-pixel attack. In d dimension, all but one of the remaining pixels in the original sample are zero.

To satisfy the Eq. (1), the one-pixel attack uses differential evolution (DE) [3,13]. DE is a population-based optimization algorithm used to solve optimization problems for multiple models. During iteration, this method generates candidate solutions (children) based on the current solution (parent). By comparing the children with their parent, one of two solutions is selected; specifically, this method aims to find the solution with the highest fitness value. The DE equation [3,13,14] is as follows:

$$x_i(g + 1) = x_a(g) + F(x_b(g) + x_c(g)),$$

$$a \neq b \neq c,$$

where x_i is the element of the candidate solution; a, b, and c are arbitrary values; F is a scale parameter set; and g is the current generation index. When a candidate solution (child) is generated, the solution with the highest fitness values will survive by comparing the candidate solution (child) with the parent or current solution (parent). The above process is continued until the iteration is over. Using the DE method, our proposed method generates x^* by maximizing f^{T}.

To satisfy $f^{\mathrm{friend}}(x^*) = y$, $f_y^{\mathrm{friend}}(x^*)$ should be maximized as

$$\underset{x^*}{\mathrm{maximize}}\; f_y^{\mathrm{friend}}(x^*),$$

where y is the original class.

However, f^{enemy} presents two cases (targeted and untargeted adversarial examples).

To satisfy $f^{\mathrm{enemy}}(x^*) = y^*$, in targeted adversarial examples, $f_{y^*}^{\mathrm{enemy}}(x^*)$ should be maximized as

$$\underset{x^*}{\mathrm{maximize}}\; f_{y^*}^{\mathrm{enemy}}(x^*),$$

where y^* is the targeted class.

To satisfy $f^{\mathrm{enemy}}(x^*) \neq y$ in an untargeted adversarial example, $f_{y^*}^{\mathrm{enemy}}(x^*)$ should be maximized as

$$\underset{x^*}{\mathrm{maximize}}\; f_{y^*}^{\mathrm{enemy}}(x^*) \; = \underset{x^*}{\mathrm{maximize}}\; \{-f_y^{\mathrm{enemy}}(x^*)\},$$

where y is the original class. The procedure for generating a one-pixel-safe adversarial example is detailed in Algorithm 1.

Algorithm 1. one-pixel-safe adversarial example generation in a transformer.

Input: original sample x, one-pixel noise w, original class y, targeted class y^*, iterations r, dimension d.

Targeted adversarial example generation:
    $d \leftarrow 1$
    $x^* \leftarrow 0$
    for r step **do**
        $x^* \leftarrow x + w$
        Update w by $\underset{x^*}{\mathrm{maximizing}}\; f_y^{\mathrm{friend}}(x^*) + f_{y^*}^{\mathrm{enemy}}(x^*)$ subject to $\|w\|_0 \leq d$
    end for
    return x^*

Untargeted adversarial example generation:
    $d \leftarrow 1$
    $x^* \leftarrow 0$
    for r step **do**
        $x^* \leftarrow x + w$
        Update w by $\underset{x^*}{\mathrm{maximizing}}\; f_y^{\mathrm{friend}}(x^*) - f_y^{\mathrm{enemy}}(x^*)$ subject to $\|w\|_0 \leq d$
    end for
    return x^*

---

4   Experiment and Evaluation

Our experiments showed that the proposed scheme can generate a one-pixel-safe adversarial example that is incorrectly classified by enemy classifiers and correctly classified by friendly classifiers. We used the Tensorflow [1] library (a widely used open source library) for machine learning on a Xeon E5-2609 1.7-GHz server.

4.1 Experimental Method

In this experiment, we used the CIFAR-10 dataset [7] (planes, cars, birds, cats, deer, dogs, frogs, horses, boats, and trucks). The CIFAR-10 dataset consists of 50,000 training data and 10,000 test data. The experimental method consisted of (1) pre-training D_{friend} and D_{enemy} and (2) transforming the one-pixel-safe adversarial example.

First, during pre-training, D_{friend} and D_{enemy} were common Resnet networks [5]. Their configuration and training parameters are shown in Tables 2 and 3 of the appendix. 50,000 training data were used to train D_{friend} and D_{enemy}. During

Table 1. A one-pixel-safe adversarial example for each target class that was misclassified by D_{enemy} for each original sample: plane "0," cars "1," birds "2," cats "3," deer "4," dogs "5," frogs "6," horses "7," boats "8," and trucks "9."

testing, D_{friend} and D_{enemy} correctly classified the original samples with 92.15% and 92.31% accuracy, respectively.

Next, DE optimization was applied to generate the one-pixel-safe adversarial example [3,13]. The population size was 400, the scale parameter set was 0.5, the iteration was 100, and perturbation was 1. The initial population used the uniform distribution $U(1, 32)$ to generate the x–y coordinates, and the RGB values followed an average of 128 and a standard deviation of 127 for the Gaussian distribution. For a given number of iterations, the transformer updated the output x^* and provided it to D_{friend} and D_{enemy}, from which it receives feedback. At the end of the iterations, the transformation result x^* was evaluated in terms of the accuracy of D_{friend}, which was the attack success rate. In detail, the accuracy of D_{friend} is the coincidence rate between the original class and the output class of D_{friend}; the attack success rate is the rate at which D_{enemy} incorrectly classifies x^*. The attack success rate has two configurations: targeted and untargeted. The targeted attack success rate is the coincidence rate between the targeted class and the class output by D_{enemy}; the untargeted attack success rate is the rate of inconsistency between the original class and the output class of D_{enemy}.

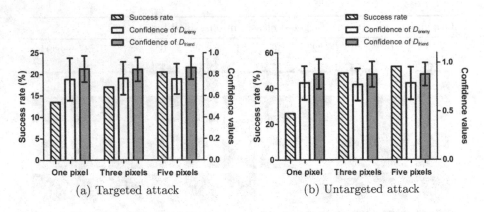

Fig. 2. The success rate and confidence of D_{enemy} and D_{friend} for 200 random adversarial examples generated by modifying one-, three-, and five-pixel attacks.

4.2 Experimental Results

The evaluation of one-pixel-safe adversarial examples is divided into targeted and untargeted adversarial examples. In addition, we analyzed the success rate and confidence by additionally modifying groups of three and five pixels.

Targeted Attack. Table 1 shows one-pixel-safe adversarial examples that were incorrectly classified as the targeted class by D_{enemy} and correctly classified as the original class by D_{friend} for each original sample. Furthermore, Table 1 shows that the one-pixel-safe adversarial example is similar to the original sample; specifically, there is a difference of only one pixel.

Figure 2(a) shows the success rate and confidence of D_{enemy} and D_{friend} for one-, three-, and five-pixel targeted attacks. In the one-pixel attack, the success rate was 13.5% where the target attack success rate and friend accuracy were 100%. The confidences of the one-pixel attack also showed that the values of 0.754 and 0.851 for D_{enemy} and D_{friend} were the highest fitness values. Thus, we know that it is more difficult to deceive the enemy classifier owing to the high confidence in the friend classifier. Figure 2(a) also shows that the success rate increased along with the number of changeable pixels. In the five-pixel attack, the success rate was 20.5%.

Untargeted Attack. Figure 2(b) shows the success rate and confidence of D_{enemy} and D_{friend} for one-, three-, and five-pixel untargeted attacks. In the one-pixel attack, the success rate was 26.0% when the untargeted attack success rate and the friend accuracy were 100%. Because untargeted attacks are easier to optimize than targeted attacks, the success rate of untargeted attacks was 12.5% higher. Similar to targeted attacks, Fig. 2(b) shows that the success rate increased along with the number of changeable pixels. In the five-pixel attack, the success rate was 52.0%.

5   Discussion

Attack Method Consideration. Our proposed method added one-pixel noise with strange colors to the original sample; however, human perception was maintained at 100%. In addition, one out of 3,072 pixels of CIFAR-10 is about 0.03% part, meaning one-pixel noise was very low.

We considered targeted or untargeted attacks depending on priority differences between the success rate and the goals of the target model misrecognition. If the success rate was more important, the attacker chose an untargeted attack. If an attacker wished to change the misclassification into a target class of their choice, they used a targeted attack.

The assumption of the proposed method was a white box attack that has identified the enemy and friendly classifiers. Since DE optimization searches for one pixel with the highest confidence value, the proposed method must know the classification results of D_{enemy} and D_{friend} to derive the input values.

Application. The one-pixel-safe adversarial example can be applied to practical applications (such as stickers). For example, once a traffic left sign has been deployed, a hybrid adversarial left sign can be generated by replacing one pixel that was generated in advance. Thus, a one-pixel-safe adversarial left sign can be misclassified as a right sign by an enemy vehicle and can be correctly classified as a left sign by a friendly vehicle.

Limitation. The proposed method has a lower success rate than the conventional one-pixel attack method. In the ResNet model [5], the conventional one-pixel attack achieved a higher success rate than the proposed method with 15.0% and 33.5% success rates for targeted and untargeted attacks, respectively. Since the proposed method has a higher recognition condition for a friendly classifier, it is difficult to confirm that a modification of one pixel satisfies a one-pixel-safe adversarial example. To increase the success rate of the proposed method, we must also increase the number of pixels that can be modified.

6   Conclusion

In this paper, we proposed a novel one-pixel-safe adversarial example by modifying a single pixel. The proposed method generated a one-pixel-safe adversarial example by adding one pixel of noise to the original sample, thereby causing misclassification for enemy classifiers and maintaining correct recognition for friendly classifiers. Experimental results on CIFAR-10 data confirmed that the proposed method showed a success rate of 13.5% and 26.0% for targeted and untargeted attacks, respectively. Although these rates are slightly lower than those of the conventional one-pixel method (15% and 33.5%), our proposed method protects 100% of friendly classifiers. When the proposed method was applied to five pixels, the success rates were 20.5% and 52.0% for targeted and untargeted attacks, respectively. This method can also be used in applications such as stickers.

In future work, we will expand the proposed method to new datasets, such as the ImageNet and Voice. In addition, future work will involve the implementation of new algorithms to improve upon the results achieved in these experiments. Finally, challenges related to countermeasures against our proposed method must be addressed.

Acknowledgement. This work was supported by National Research Foundation (NRF) of Korea grants funded by the Korean government (MSIT) (2016R1A4A1011761 and 2017R1A2B4006026) and an Institute for Information & Communications Technology Promotion (IITP) grant funded by the Korean government (MSIT) (No. 2016-0-00173).

Appendix

Table 2. D_{friend} and D_{enemy} model of 34-layer ResNet [5]

Layer type	Model shape
#1 layer Convolution+ReLU	[7, 7, 64]
Max pooling	[3, 3]
#2 layer Convolution+ReLU	[1, 1, 64]
#2 layer Convolution+ReLU	[3, 3, 64]
#2 layer Convolution+ReLU	[1, 1, 256]
#2 layer Repeat	3 times
#3 layer Convolution+ReLU	[3, 3, 128]
#3 layer Convolution+ReLU	[3, 3, 128]
#3 layer Repeat	4 times
#4 layer Convolution+ReLU	[3, 3, 256]
#4 layer Convolution+ReLU	[3, 3, 256]
#4 layer Repeat	6 times
#5 layer Convolution+ReLU	[3, 3, 512]
#5 layer Convolution+ReLU	[3, 3, 512]
#5 layer Repeat	3 times
Fully connected+ReLU	[1000]
Softmax	[10]

Table 3. D_{friend} and D_{enemy} model parameters.

Parameter	Values
Learning rate of SGD [6]	0.1
Momentum	0.9
Delay rate	1 (decay 0.0001)
Iteration	50,000
Batch size	128
Epochs	200

References

1. Abadi, M., et al.: TensorFlow: a system for large-scale machine learning. OSDI. **16**, 265–283 (2016)
2. Carlini, N., Wagner, D.: Towards evaluating the robustness of neural networks. In: 2017 IEEE Symposium on Security and Privacy (SP), pp. 39–57. IEEE (2017)
3. Das, S., Suganthan, P.N.: Differential evolution: a survey of the state-of-the-art. IEEE Trans. Evol. Comput. **15**(1), 4–31 (2011)
4. Goodfellow, I., Shlens, J., Szegedy, C.: Explaining and harnessing adversarial examples. In: International Conference on Learning Representations (2015)
5. He, K., Zhang, X., Ren, S., Sun, J.: Deep residual learning for image recognition. In: Proceedings of the IEEE Conference on Computer Vision and Pattern Recognition, pp. 770–778 (2016)
6. Ketkar, N.: Stochastic gradient descent. In: Ketkar, N. (ed.) Deep Learning with Python, pp. 111–130. Apress, Berkeley (2017). https://doi.org/10.1007/978-1-4842-2766-4_8
7. Krizhevsky, A., Nair, V., Hinton, G.: The CIFAR-10 dataset (2014). http://www.cs.toronto.edu/kriz/cifar.html
8. Kurakin, A., Goodfellow, I., Bengio, S.: Adversarial examples in the physical world. In: ICLR Workshop (2017)
9. Kwon, H., Kim, Y., Park, K.W., Yoon, H., Choi, D.: Friend-safe evasion attack: an adversarial example that is correctly recognized by a friendly classifier. Comput. Secur. **78**, 380–397 (2018)
10. Moosavi-Dezfooli, S.M., Fawzi, A., Frossard, P.: DeepFool: a simple and accurate method to fool deep neural networks. In: Proceedings of the IEEE Conference on Computer Vision and Pattern Recognition, pp. 2574–2582 (2016)
11. Papernot, N., McDaniel, P., Wu, X., Jha, S., Swami, A.: Distillation as a defense to adversarial perturbations against deep neural networks. In: 2016 IEEE Symposium on Security and Privacy (SP), pp. 582–597. IEEE (2016)
12. Schmidhuber, J.: Deep learning in neural networks: an overview. Neural Netw. **61**, 85–117 (2015)
13. Storn, R., Price, K.: Differential evolution-a simple and efficient heuristic for global optimization over continuous spaces. J. Glob. Optim. **11**(4), 341–359 (1997)
14. Su, J., Vargas, D.V., Kouichi, S.: One pixel attack for fooling deep neural networks. arXiv preprint arXiv:1710.08864 (2017)
15. Szegedy, C., et al.: Intriguing properties of neural networks. In: International Conference on Learning Representations (2014). http://arxiv.org/abs/1312.6199

Efficient Ate-Based Pairing
over the Attractive Classes of BN Curves

Yuki Nanjo[1][(✉)], Md. Al-Amin Khandaker[1], Masaaki Shirase[2],
Takuya Kusaka[1], and Yasuyuki Nogami[1]

[1] Graduate School of Natural Science and Technology,
Okayama University, Okayama, Japan
{yuki.nanjo,khandaker}@s.okayama-u.ac.jp
{kusaka-t,yasuyuki.nogami}@okayama-u.ac.jp
[2] Future University Hakodate, Hakodate, Hokkaido, Japan
shirase@fun.ac.jp

Abstract. This paper proposes two attractive classes of Barreto-Naehrig curve for ate-based pairing by imposing certain condition $\chi \equiv 7, 11 \pmod{12}$ on the integer χ that parameterizes the curve settings. The restriction results in an unparalleled way to determine a BN curve, its twisted curve coefficients, and obvious generator points. The proposed $\chi \equiv 11 \pmod{12}$ are found to be more efficient than $\chi \equiv 7 \pmod{12}$ together with pseudo 8-sparse multiplication in Miller's algorithm. The authors also provide comparative implementations for the proposal.

Keywords: Pairing · Tower of extension field ·
Barreto-Naehrig curve

1 Introduction

Pairing-Based Cryptography (PBC) provides several innovative protocols, e.g. ID-based encryption [6] and BLS short signatures [5] making it an inseparable tool of modern cryptography. The prerequisites for PBC are a pairing-friendly elliptic curve [9] and an efficient pairing algorithm. Over the years, several variants of Weil's pairing i.e. ate [7], χ-ate [15], optimal-ate [17] pairings have been evolved. However, to find a suitable pairing-friendly curve is a nontrivial task. In 2005 Barreto et al. [4] made a major breakthrough introducing parameterized pairing-friendly curve named as Barreto-Naehrig (BN) curve given as polynomial formulas of an integer. This work especially focuses on pairing in BN curve. A bilinear-pairing is an efficiently computable non-degenerate map $e : \mathbb{G}_1 \times \mathbb{G}_2 \to \mathbb{G}_3$. Typically, $\mathbb{G}_1$ and $\mathbb{G}_2$ are additive cyclic sub-groups of order r defined over a finite extension field $\mathbb{F}_{p^k}$ and $\mathbb{G}_3$ is a multiplicative cyclic subgroup of order r in $\mathbb{F}_{p^k}^*$. The embedding degree k ($k = 12$ for BN) is the smallest positive integer such that $r|(p^k - 1)$, where prime p and order r is given by polynomial formulas of integer χ.

© Springer Nature Switzerland AG 2019
B. B. Kang and J. Jang (Eds.): WISA 2018, LNCS 11402, pp. 55–67, 2019.
https://doi.org/10.1007/978-3-030-17982-3_5

When considering the pairing over BN curves, suitable parameter χ have to be found for which both p and r become an odd prime number. Then it comes to determining an elliptic curve $E : y^2 = x^3 + b$ to be a BN curve over the prime field $\mathbb{F}_p$. The probabilistic way to prove curve coefficient b is to choose a random b and check the group order until $\#E(\mathbb{F}_p) = r$. Moreover, a sextic twisted curve $E'(\mathbb{F}_{p^{12/d}})$ $(d = 6)$ also have to be determined, since the Miller's algorithm for pairing in BN curve is calculated over E'. However, E' could not be determined immediately since there exist two possible types of the twisted curve with $d = 6$. As noted above, these initial settings require time-consuming computation. In addition to this, when selecting the parameters, the following cautions are considered for an efficient implementation of pairing. The Parameters have an effect on efficient towering; another prerequisite of efficient finite field arithmetic; one of the pivotal factors of efficient pairing implementation. Also, the parameters with a small Hamming weight result in reducing calculation amount of the Miller's algorithm and final exponentiation. Moreover, the authors found that not all parameters end up efficient line evaluation of Miller's algorithm due to the type of twisted curve E'. However, the conditions of suitable parameters have not clearly given at this point. This paper overcomes the aforementioned challenges of efficient pairing in BN curve by restricting parameter as mentioned below.

Our Contribution: The major contribution of this paper can be summarized as (i) offering two attractive classes of BN curves by restricting integer χ as $\chi \equiv 7, 11 \pmod{12}$. (ii) The restriction also results in an efficient tower of extension field construction given in [1]. (iii) Instantaneously determining the coefficient b in BN curve and resulting obvious rational points overcomes the probabilistic approach. (iv) The twisted curve and its coefficients can also be determined easily from the condition on χ. (v) Proposed parameter satisfying $\chi \equiv 11 \pmod{12}$ enables more efficient implementation pairing. Moreover, the authors implemented several candidate curves and compared performances for the lower Hamming weight.

Previous Works: BN curve is one of the most widely studied pairing-friendly curves. The most relevant work similar to this is Costello et al.'s [8] proposal on restricting the parameter for BLS curve for embedding degree 24. They also mention the efficiency of the Miller's algorithm. This paper does not only describes more details applying pseudo 8-sparse multiplication but also focus on the small Hamming weight of the parameter.

Organization of this Paper: Section 2 overviews several necessary backgrounds. Sections 3 and 4 give the required details with theoretic proofs of the proposal. The implementation results are compared in Sect. 5 and Sect. 6 which draws the conclusion.

2   Fundamentals

This section shows that the details of the necessary fundamentals of pairing over BN curve to keep the reference and for easy explanation of rest of the paper.

BN Curves: Barreto-Naehrig curve [4] is a class of non super-singular (ordinary) pairing-friendly elliptic curves of embedding degree $k = 12$ defined as $E/\mathbb{F}_p$: $y^2 = x^3 + b$. Its characteristic p, order r and Frobenius trace t are given as follows:

$$\begin{cases} p = p(\chi) = 36\chi^4 + 36\chi^3 + 24\chi^2 + 6\chi + 1, \\ r = r(\chi) = 36\chi^4 + 36\chi^3 + 18\chi^2 + 6\chi + 1, \\ t = t(\chi) = 6\chi^2 + 1. \end{cases} \tag{1}$$

where χ is an integer. In what follows, the parameter χ is called *BN parameter* and the prime p is called *BN prime*. If $\#E(\mathbb{F}_p) = r$, E becomes a BN curve.

Tower of the Extension Field: Pairing requires arithmetic operations in embedded extension fields. It is important to consider the way to construct the extension field since it affects to the efficiency of the pairing. Therefore, this paper especially focuses on the construction of efficient tower of the extension field. Bailey et al. [2] proposed the optimal extension field by the towering irreducible binomials. In the context of the pairing over BN curve, where $k = 12$, one of the way to construct the efficient extension field proposed by Aranha et al. [1] as follows:

$$\begin{cases} \mathbb{F}_{p^2} = \mathbb{F}_p[\alpha]/(\alpha^2 - (-1)), \\ \mathbb{F}_{p^6} = \mathbb{F}_{p^2}[\beta]/(\beta^3 - (\alpha + 1)), \\ \mathbb{F}_{p^{12}} = \mathbb{F}_{p^6}[\gamma]/(\gamma^2 - \beta), \end{cases} \tag{2}$$

where p is a BN prime and α, β, γ are one of the roots of the modular polynomials of $\mathbb{F}_{p^2}, \mathbb{F}_{p^6}$ and $\mathbb{F}_{p^{12}}$. The set of the basis elements constructing $\mathbb{F}_{p^{12}}$ vector is denoted as $\{1, \alpha, \beta, \alpha\beta, \beta^2, \alpha\beta^2, \gamma, \alpha\gamma, \beta\gamma, \alpha\beta\gamma, \beta^2\gamma, \alpha\beta^2\gamma\}$.

Ate-Based Pairing: While BN curve is applied in different variants of pairings, e.g. ate [7], optimal-ate [17] and χ-ate [15] pairing; the groups $\mathbb{G}_1$, $\mathbb{G}_2$ and $\mathbb{G}_3$ for such ate-based pairings are defined as $\mathbb{G}_1 = E(\mathbb{F}_{p^{12}})[r] \cap \mathrm{Ker}(\phi - [1])$, $\mathbb{G}_2 = E(\mathbb{F}_{p^{12}})[r] \cap \mathrm{Ker}(\phi - [p])$, $\mathbb{G}_3 = \mathbb{F}_{p^{12}}^*/(\mathbb{F}_{p^{12}}^*)^r$. $E(\mathbb{F}_{p^{12}})[r]$ denotes rational points of order r and $[s]$ denotes s times scalar multiplication for a rational point. ϕ denotes the Frobenius mapping given as $\phi : (x, y) \mapsto (x^p, y^p)$. $\mathrm{Ker}(\cdot)$ is the kernel of $\cdot$, which means that $\mathrm{Ker}(\cdot)$ is a set whose elements are mapped to an initial point by $\cdot$. In what follows, we consider $P \in \mathbb{G}_1 \subseteq E(\mathbb{F}_p)$ and $Q \in \mathbb{G}_2 \subset E(\mathbb{F}_{p^{12}})$. Then, optimal-ate $e_\alpha(Q, P)$ and χ-ate $e_\zeta(Q, P)$ pairing are given as follows:

$$e_\alpha(Q, P) = \left\{ f_{6\chi+2, Q}(P) \cdot l_{[6\chi+2]Q, [p]Q}(P) \cdot l_{[6\chi+2+p]Q, [-p^2]Q}(P) \right\}^{\frac{p^{12}-1}{r}},$$

$$e_\zeta(Q, P) = \left\{ f_{\chi, Q}(P)^{(1+p^3)(1+p^{10})} \cdot l_{[\chi]Q, \phi^3([\chi]Q)}(P) \right.$$

$$\left. \cdot l_{[\chi]Q+\phi^3([\chi]Q), \phi^{10}([\chi]Q+\phi^3([\chi]Q))}(P) \right\}^{\frac{p^{12}-1}{r}}.$$

where the first term of e_α and e_ζ denotes the output of Miller's loop and the second and third terms are the line evaluations. An efficient way to calculate these line evaluation steps, called 7-sparse and pseudo 8-sparse multiplication are proposed in [12,14]. The details of the line evaluation are discussed in Sect. 4.

3   Attractive Classes of BN Curves

This section shows that the proposed classes of BN curves can result in efficient pairing implementations. Table 1 shows two classes of the BN curve parameter, categorized as *Class 1* and *Class 2*. The conditions $\chi \equiv 7$ (mod 12) and $\chi \equiv 11$ (mod 12) are satisfied by *Class 1* and *Class 2*, respectively. The advantages of choosing such parameters are following.

– The efficient towering of $\mathbb{F}_{p^{12}}$ given in Eq. (2) can be constructed (See Lemma 1 below).
– The coefficients of the curve $E/\mathbb{F}_p$ to be a BN curve can be determined uniquely. Once a BN parameter satisfying $\chi \equiv 7, 11$ (mod 12) is found, the BN curves are immediately given as $y^2 = x^3 + 2^{6l-1}$, $y^2 = x^3 + 2^{6l+1}$, where l is an integer (See Lemma 2 below). The curve $y^2 = x^3 + 2^{6l+1}$ can have an obvious generator point $(-2^{2l}, \pm 2^{3l})$. And also $y^2 = x^3 + 2^{6l-1}$ has $(-2^{2l}, \pm(-2)^{-1/2} \cdot 2^{3l})$, where -2 is a quadratic residue in $\mathbb{F}_p$ since -1 and 2 are quadratic non-residues in $\mathbb{F}_p$ (See Theorem 1).
– The correct twisted curves can also be determined uniquely. The parameter $\chi \equiv 7, 11$ (mod 12) results in twisted curve as $y^2 = x^3 + 2^{6l-1}(\alpha + 1)$, $y^2 = x^3 + 2^{6l+1}(\alpha + 1)^{-1}$ (See Lemma 3 below).

Table 1. Two attractive classes of the BN curve

Type	Condition of χ	Efficient towering	BN curve $E/\mathbb{F}_p$	Twisted curve $E'/\mathbb{F}_{p^2}$
Class 1	$\chi \equiv 7(\text{mod } 12)$	✓	$y^2 = x^3 + 2^{6l-1}$	$y^2 = x^3 + 2^{6l-1}(\alpha + 1)$
Class 2	$\chi \equiv 11(\text{mod } 12)$	✓	$y^2 = x^3 + 2^{6l+1}$	$y^2 = x^3 + 2^{6l+1}(\alpha+1)^{-1}$

3.1   Using Parameters Satisfying $\chi \equiv 7, 11$ (mod 12)

This subsection shows how the proposed condition of χ can result in efficient towering of $\mathbb{F}_{p^{12}}$ by using the theorem of quadratic and cubic residue in $\mathbb{F}_p$.

Theorem 1. *Let $(-)$ be the Legendre symbol and $(-)_3$ be a multiplicative function defined as follows:*

$$\left(\frac{\mu}{p}\right)_3 \begin{cases} = 1 & \text{if } \mu \text{ is a cubic residue in } \mathbb{F}_p, \\ \neq 1 & \text{if } \mu \text{ is a cubic non-residue in } \mathbb{F}_p. \end{cases}$$

If the characteristic p is a BN prime; quadratic and cubic residue properties for certain elements in $\mathbb{F}_p$ are given by the condition of BN parameter χ as follows:

$$(a) \quad \left(\frac{-1}{p}\right) = \begin{cases} 1 & if \ \chi \equiv 0 \ (\mathrm{mod} \ 2), \\ -1 & if \ \chi \equiv 1 \ (\mathrm{mod} \ 2). \end{cases} \tag{3a}$$

$$(b) \quad \left(\frac{2}{p}\right) = \begin{cases} 1 & if \ \chi \equiv 0, 1 \ (\mathrm{mod} \ 4), \\ -1 & if \ \chi \equiv 2, 3 \ (\mathrm{mod} \ 4). \end{cases} \tag{3b}$$

$$(c) \quad \left(\frac{2}{p}\right)_3 \begin{cases} = 1 & if \ \chi \equiv 0 \ (\mathrm{mod} \ 3), \\ \neq 1 & if \ \chi \equiv 1, 2 \ (\mathrm{mod} \ 3). \end{cases} \tag{3c}$$

Proof. For the details of the proof, please refer to [16, §5.1]. $\qquad\square$

Lemma 1. *If the characteristic p is a BN prime and χ satisfies $\chi \equiv 7, 11$ (mod 12), the efficient tower of the extension field given in Eq. (2) can be constructed.*

Proof. To construct $\mathbb{F}_p \xrightarrow{\alpha^2 - (-1)} \mathbb{F}_{p^2}$, $\alpha^2 - (-1)$ should be an irreducible polynomial over $\mathbb{F}_p$. Therefore, -1 has to be a quadratic non-residue in $\mathbb{F}_p$. Then, χ should be satisfying $\chi \equiv 1 \ (\mathrm{mod} \ 2)$ from Eq. (3a). In the similar way, when constructing $\mathbb{F}_{p^2} \xrightarrow{\beta^3 - (\alpha+1)} \mathbb{F}_{p^6} \xrightarrow{\gamma^2 - \beta} \mathbb{F}_{p^{12}}$, $(\alpha + 1)$ should be a quadratic and cubic non-residue in $\mathbb{F}_{p^2}$. This condition means that $2 \in \mathbb{F}_p$ has to be a quadratic and cubic non-residue as shown in the following equations.

$$(\alpha + 1)^{\frac{p^2 - 1}{2}} = ((\alpha + 1)^p (\alpha + 1))^{\frac{p-1}{2}} = 2^{\frac{p-1}{2}} = -1,$$

$$(\alpha + 1)^{\frac{p^2 - 1}{3}} = ((\alpha + 1)^p (\alpha + 1))^{\frac{p-1}{3}} = 2^{\frac{p-1}{3}} \neq 1.$$

According to Eqs. (3b) and (3c), if 2 is a quadratic and cubic non-residue in $\mathbb{F}_p$, χ should satisfy $\chi \equiv 1, 2 \ (\mathrm{mod} \ 3)$, $\chi \equiv 2, 3 \ (\mathrm{mod} \ 4)$. Therefore, the condition to construct efficient extension field is given by $\chi \equiv 1, 2 \ (\mathrm{mod} \ 3)$, $\chi \equiv 3 \ (\mathrm{mod} \ 4)$ which means $\chi \equiv 7, 11 \ (\mathrm{mod} \ 12)$. $\qquad\square$

From the proposed conditions, it is clear that it shrinks the probability of getting smaller Hamming weight (HW) of χ. Smaller Hamming weight (less than 6) is a catalyst for efficient Miller's algorithm and final exponentiation. Since, according to [3], for 128-bit security, the $\lfloor \log_2 \chi \rfloor = 114$ is expected. Therefore, an exhaustive search can result in smaller Hamming weight along with the proposed conditions.

3.2 Determining BN Curves and Twisted Curves

In this part, we show how uniquely the BN curves' and its twisted curves' coefficients can be determined in $E/\mathbb{F}_p$ and $E'/\mathbb{F}_{p^2}$, respectively. For the reference in our proof, we recall the theorem given by Shirase as follows:

Theorem 2. *Let p be a BN prime, and let $n_0 = n_0(\chi)$, $n_1 = n_1(\chi)$, $n_2 = n_2(\chi)$, $n_3 = n_3(\chi)$, $n_4 = n_4(\chi)$ and $n_5 = n_5(\chi)$ be polynomials defined as*

$$n_0(\chi) = 12\chi^2(3\chi^2 + 3\chi + 1), \qquad\qquad n_1(\chi) = 36\chi^4 + 36\chi^3 + 18\chi^2 + 1,$$
$$n_2(\chi) = 3(12\chi^4 + 12\chi^3 + 10\chi^2 + 2\chi + 1), \quad n_3(\chi) = 4(9\chi^4 + 9\chi^3 + 9\chi^2 + 3\chi + 1),$$
$$n_4(\chi) = 3(12\chi^4 + 12\chi^3 + 10\chi^2 + 4\chi + 1), \quad n_5(\chi) = 36\chi^4 + 36\chi^3 + 18\chi^2 + 6\chi + 1.$$

Then, the group orders of $E_2 : y^2 = x^3 + 2$ are determined as follows:

$$
\#E_2(\mathbb{F}_p) = \begin{cases}
n_0 & \text{if } \chi \equiv 0, 9 \ (\text{mod } 12), \\
n_1 & \text{if } \chi \equiv 7, 10 \ (\text{mod } 12), \\
n_2 & \text{if } \chi \equiv 5, 8 \ (\text{mod } 12), \\
n_3 & \text{if } \chi \equiv 3, 6 \ (\text{mod } 12), \\
n_4 & \text{if } \chi \equiv 1, 4 \ (\text{mod } 12), \\
n_5 & \text{if } \chi \equiv 2, 11 \ (\text{mod } 12).
\end{cases} \tag{4}
$$

Proof. Please refer to [16, §5.2]. □

Remark 1. The group orders n_0, n_1, n_2, n_3, n_4 and n_5 can be denoted as

$$n_0 = p + 1 - (3f + t)/2, \ n_1 = p + 1 - (3f - t)/2, \ n_2 = p + 1 - (-t),$$
$$n_3 = p + 1 - (-3f - t)/2, \ n_4 = p + 1 - (-3f + t)/2, \ n_5 = p + 1 - t,$$

where p is a BN prime, t is a Frobenius trace and $f = f(\chi) = 6\chi^2 + 4\chi + 1$ is an integer. From the definition [4], an elliptic curve which has the order $n_5 = r$ becomes BN curve.

Remark 2. The divisibility of the group order by 2 or 3 of the curve $E_b(\mathbb{F}_{p^k})$: $y^2 = x^3 + b$ depends on its coefficient. If the coefficient b is a cubic residue in $\mathbb{F}_{p^k}$, $\#E_b(\mathbb{F}_{p^k})$ is divisible by 2, since there exists an obvious rational point $(-b^{1/3}, 0)$ of order 2. Therefore, if p is a BN prime and b has a cubic residue property, $\#E_b(\mathbb{F}_p)$ can be determine as n_0 or n_3. Similarly, if the coefficient b is quadratic residue in $\mathbb{F}_p$, $\#E_b(\mathbb{F}_p)$ is divisible by 3 and determined as n_0, n_2 or n_4.

Lemma 2. *(i) The BN parameter χ satisfying $\chi \equiv 11$ (mod 12) results in the BN curve as $E_{2^{6l+1}}/\mathbb{F}_p : y^2 = x^3 + 2^{6l+1}$, where $l \in \mathbb{Z}$. (ii) If the parameter satisfies $\chi \equiv 7$ (mod 12), the curve $E_{2^{6l-1}}/\mathbb{F}_p : y^2 = x^3 + 2^{6l-1}$ always becomes BN curve.*

Proof. (i) If the BN parameter satisfies $\chi \equiv 11$ (mod 12), we first note that the group order $\#E_2(\mathbb{F}_p)$ is n_5 from Eq. (4) in Theorem 2. Then, let us consider a map from $E_{2^{6l+1}}$ to E_2 given as follows:

$$E_{2^{6l+1}} : y^2 = x^3 + 2^{6l+1} \rightarrow E_2 : y^2 = x^3 + 2, \ (x, y) \mapsto (2^{-2l}x, 2^{-3l}y).$$

It is easily found that the map is isomorphic in $\mathbb{F}_p$ since 2^{-2l} and 2^{-3l} are elements in $\mathbb{F}_p$. Therefore, we got the equation $\#E_{2^{6l+1}}(\mathbb{F}_p) = \#E_2(\mathbb{F}_p) = n_5$.

(ii) If the BN parameter satisfies $\chi \equiv 7 \pmod{12}$, the group order $\#E_2(\mathbb{F}_p)$ is n_1 from Eq. (4). Then, let us consider following twist mapping.

$$E_{2^{6l-1}} : y^2 = x^3 + 2^{6l-1} \to E_{2^{6l+1}} : y^2 = x^3 + 2^{6l+1}, \ (x, y) \mapsto (2^{\frac{2}{3}}x, 2y).$$

Since 2 is a cubic non-residue element in $\mathbb{F}_p$, the isomorphic mapping exists in $\mathbb{F}_{p^3}$ and we can say that $E_{2^{6l-1}}$ is a twisted curve of $E_{2^{6l+1}}$ with the twist degree 3. There exist two types of twist of degree 3. $E_{2^{6l-1}}$ has only two possible group orders given as $p + 1 - (3f_1 - t_1)/2$ or $p + 1 - (-3f_1 - t_1)/2$, where t_1 is the Frobenius trace of $E_{2^{6l+1}}(\mathbb{F}_p)$ and f_1 is computed by $4p = t_1^2 + 3f_1^2$ [13]. We can represent t_1, f_1 as $t_1 = t_1(\chi) = 6\chi^2 + 6\chi + 1$, $f_1 = f_1(\chi) = 6\chi^2 + 2\chi + 1$ since $\#E_{2^{6l+1}}(\mathbb{F}_p) = n_1$. Thus, the possible group order can be obtained as $n_5 = 36\chi^4 + 36\chi^3 + 18\chi^2 + 6\chi + 1$ and $n_3 = 4(9\chi^4 + 9\chi^3 + 9\chi^2 + 3\chi + 1)$. As discussed in Remark 2, when the group order of elliptic curves can be divisible by 2, coefficients of the curves should have cubic residue property. Here, $\#E_{2^{6l-1}}(\mathbb{F}_p)$ cannot have 2 as a factor since the curve coefficient 2^{6l-1} has cubic non-residue property. Finally we can find $\#E_{2^{6l-1}}(\mathbb{F}_p) = n_5$. According to Remark 1, the curves having the order n_5 become BN curve, $E_{2^{6l-1}}$ and $E_{2^{6l+1}}$ end up as BN curve for the respective conditions of χ. □

Next, we show the proof of the twisted curve $E'/\mathbb{F}_{p^2}$ can be determined as $y^2 = x^3 + 2^{6l-1}(\alpha + 1)$, $y^2 = x^3 + 2^{6l+1}(\alpha + 1)^{-1}$ for each parameters.

Lemma 3. *When $\mathbb{F}_{p^{12}}$ is constructed by Eq. (2), the correct sextic twist with E' can be obtained uniquely. If the parameter satisfies $\chi \equiv 7 \pmod{12}$, $E'_{2^{6l-1}}/\mathbb{F}_{p^2}$: $y^2 = x^3 + 2^{6l-1}(\alpha + 1)$ becomes twisted curve. When $\chi \equiv 11 \pmod{12}$, $E'_{2^{6l+1}}/\mathbb{F}_{p^2} : y^2 = x^3 + 2^{6l+1}(\alpha + 1)^{-1}$ becomes twisted curve.*

Proof. There exist two twists of E with the degree 6, E' has only two possible group orders given as $p^2 + 1 - (-3f_2 + t_2)/2$ or $p^2 + 1 - (3f_2 + t_2)/2$ [13], where t_2 is a Frobenius trace of E over $\mathbb{F}_{p^2}$ computed as $t_2 = t^2 - 2p$. f_2 is an integer calculated by $4p^2 = t_2^2 + 3f_2^2$. In the context of BN curve, t_2 and f_2 are given by $t_2 = t_2(\chi) = -36\chi^4 - 72\chi^3 - 36\chi^2 - 12\chi - 1$ and $f_2 = f_2(\chi) = (6\chi^2 + 1)(6\chi^2 + 4\chi + 1)$, respectively. Then, the possible group orders can be denoted as $4(324\chi^8 + 648\chi^7 + 756\chi^6 + 540\chi^5 + 288\chi^4 + 108\chi^3 + 30\chi^2 + 6\chi + 1)$ or $(36\chi^4 + 36\chi^3 + 18\chi^2 + 6\chi + 1)(36\chi^4 + 36\chi^3 + 30\chi^2 + 6\chi + 1)$. Thus, it is found that the twisted curve order becomes $\#E'(\mathbb{F}_{p^2}) = (36\chi^4 + 36\chi^3 + 18\chi^2 + 6\chi + 1)(36\chi^4 + 36\chi^3 + 30\chi^2 + 6\chi + 1)$ since E' has a unique order such that $r = r(\chi)|\#E'(\mathbb{F}_{p^2})$. It means that $E'(\mathbb{F}_{p^2})$ cannot divisible by 2. Therefore, the twisted curve E' coefficients should be a cubic non-residue in $\mathbb{F}_{p^2}$. Now in the case of the BN curve denoted as $y^2 = x^3 + 2^{6l+1}$, twisted curves can be denoted as $y^2 = x^3 + 2^{6l+1}(\alpha + 1)$ or $y^2 = x^3 + 2^{6l+1}(\alpha + 1)^{-1}$ since $(\alpha + 1)$ and $(\alpha + 1)^{-1}$ are quadratic and cubic non-residue in $\mathbb{F}_{p^2}$. Then, the cubic residue properties of each curve coefficients can be denoted as follows:

$$\left(2^{6l+1}(\alpha + 1)\right)^{\frac{p^2-1}{3}} = \left(\left(2^{6l+1}(\alpha + 1)\right)^{p+1}\right)^{\frac{p-1}{3}} = \left((2^{6l+1})^2 \cdot 2\right)^{\frac{p-1}{3}} = 1,$$

$$\left(2^{6l+1}(\alpha + 1)^{-1}\right)^{\frac{p^2-1}{3}} = \left(\left(2^{6l+1}(\alpha + 1)^{-1}\right)^{p+1}\right)^{\frac{p-1}{3}} = \left((2^{6l+1})^2 \cdot 2^{-1}\right)^{\frac{p-1}{3}} \neq 1.$$

Since the coefficient of E' needs to be a cubic non-residue in $\mathbb{F}_{p^2}$, the twisted curve is determined as $y^2 = x^3 + 2^{6l+1}(\alpha+1)^{-1}$. In the case of $y^2 = x^3 + 2^{6l-1}$, its twisted curves are also derived in the same way.   □

4   Implementation Pairing Using Attractive Classes

This section shows the overview of sparse multiplication techniques and describes the implementation difference between two classes.

4.1   Overview: Sparse Multiplication for Miller's Algorithm

It is well known that the line evaluation can be optimized by applying the 7-sparse multiplication [12]. Mori et al. [14] have shown a more efficient technique called the pseudo 8-sparse multiplication for BN curve in the affine coordinate.

Let $P(x_P, y_P)$ be a rational point in $\mathbb{G}_1$ and $Q(x_Q, y_Q)$ and $T(x_T, y_T)$ be rational points in $\mathbb{G}_2$. Let us consider the sextic twist given as

$$\psi_6 : E'(\mathbb{F}_{p^2}) \to E(\mathbb{F}_{p^{12}}), \quad (x_{Q'}, y_{Q'}) \mapsto (x_{Q'}z^{-1/3}, y_{Q'}z^{-1/2}),$$

where z is a quadratic and cubic non-residue in $\mathbb{F}_{p^2}$. Applying this mapping, Q and T can be considered as points $Q'(x_{Q'}, y_{Q'}) = (z^{1/3}x_Q, z^{1/2}y_Q)$ and $T''(x_{T'}, y_{T'}) = (z^{1/3}x_Q, z^{1/2}y_Q)$ on E'. Let the elliptic curve addition be $T' + Q' = R'(x_{R'}, y_{R'})$. Then, the line evaluation and elliptic curve addition (ECA) can be calculated as

$$A = \frac{1}{x_{Q'} - x_{T'}}, \quad B = y_{Q'} - y_{T'}, \quad C = AB, D = x_{T'} + x_{Q'}, \quad x_{R'} = C^2 - D$$

$$E = Cx_{T'} - y_{T'}, \quad y_{R'} = E - Cx_{R'},$$

$$l_{T',Q'}(P) = y_P - z^{-1/6}Cx_P + z^{-1/2}E. \tag{5}$$

Here, all the variables (A, B, C, D, E) are calculated as $\mathbb{F}_{p^2}$ elements. There exist 7 zero coefficients in Eq. (5) which lead to *7-sparse multiplication*.

The line evaluation can be more optimized by multiplying y_P^{-1} in both side of Eq. (5) as $y_P^{-1}l_{T',Q'}(P) = 1 - z^{-1/6}C(x_Py_P^{-1}) + z^{-1/2}Ey_P^{-1}$. One of the non-zero coefficient becomes 1 and it realizes more efficient multiplications. However, comparing with Eq. (5), it is found that they need a little more calculation for $x_Py_P^{-1}$ and y_P^{-1}. To minimize the computation overhead of $x_Py_P^{-1}$, let us consider the following isomorphic mapping.

$$\hat{E}(\mathbb{F}_p) : y^2 = x^3 + b\hat{z} \to E(\mathbb{F}_p) : y^2 = x^3 + b, \quad (x, y) \mapsto (\hat{z}^{-1/3}x, \hat{z}^{-1/2}y),$$

$$\hat{E}'(\mathbb{F}_{p^2}) : y^2 = x^3 + bz\hat{z} \to E'(\mathbb{F}_{p^2}) : y^2 = x^3 + bz, \quad (x, y) \mapsto (\hat{z}^{-1/3}x, \hat{z}^{-1/2}y),$$

where $\hat{z}$ is a quadratic and cubic residue in $\mathbb{F}_p$ defined as $\hat{z} = (x_Py_P^{-1})^6$. Then, a rational point $\hat{P} \in \hat{E}$ can be represented as $\hat{P}(x_{\hat{P}}, y_{\hat{P}}) = (x_P^3y_P^{-2}, x_P^3y_P^{-2})$. In the same way, $\hat{Q}', \hat{T}' \in \hat{E}'$ can be denoted as $\hat{Q}'(x_{\hat{Q}'}, y_{\hat{Q}'}) = (x_P^2y_P^{-2}x_{Q'}, x_P^3y_P^{-3}y_{Q'})$,

---

Algorithm 1. Pseudo 8-Sparse Multiplication for *Class 1*

Input: $a = (a_0 + a_1\beta + a_2\beta^2) + (a_3 + a_4\beta + a_5\beta^2)\gamma,\ b = 1 + b_4\beta\gamma + b_5\beta^2\gamma$
Output: $c = (c_0 + c_1\beta + c_2\beta^2) + (c_3 + c_4\beta + c_5\beta^2)\gamma$
where $a_i, b_j, c_i \in \mathbb{F}_{p^2}\ (i = 0, \cdots, 5, j = 4, 5)$

1	$t_0 \leftarrow a_0 b_4,\ t_1 \leftarrow a_1 b_5,\ t_2 \leftarrow a_0 + a_1,\ t_3 \leftarrow b_4 + b_5\ ;$	$(2\tilde{m}_2 + 2\tilde{a}_2)$
2	$t_2 \leftarrow t_2 t_3 - t_0 - t_1\ ;$	$(\tilde{m}_2 + 2\tilde{a}_2)$
3	$c_5 \leftarrow a_5 + t_2,\ c_4 \leftarrow a_4 + t_0 + a_2 b_5(\alpha + 1);$	$(\tilde{m}_2 + 3\tilde{a}_2 + \tilde{B}_2)$
4	$c_3 \leftarrow a_3 + (a_2 b_4 + t_1)(\alpha + 1);$	$(\tilde{m}_2 + 2\tilde{a}_2 + \tilde{B}_2)$
5	$t_0 \leftarrow a_3 b_4,\ t_1 \leftarrow a_4 b_5,\ t_2 \leftarrow a_3 + a_4,\ t_2 \leftarrow t_2 t_3 - t_0 - t_1;$	$(3\tilde{m}_2 + 3\tilde{a}_2)$
6	$c_0 \leftarrow a_0 + t_2(\alpha + 1),\ c_1 \leftarrow a_1 + (t_1 + a_5 b_4)(\alpha + 1);$	$(\tilde{m}_2 + 3\tilde{a}_2 + 2\tilde{B}_2)$
7	$c_2 \leftarrow a_2 + t_0 + a_5 b_5(\alpha + 1);$	$(\tilde{m}_2 + 2\tilde{a}_2 + \tilde{B}_2)$
	return $c;$	

$\hat{T}'(x_{\hat{T}'}, y_{\hat{T}'}) = (x_{\hat{P}}^2 y_{\hat{P}}^{-2} x_{T'}, x_{\hat{P}}^3 y_{\hat{P}}^{-3} y_{T'})$. Applying these rational points for line evaluation, $x_{\hat{P}} y_{\hat{P}}^{-1}$ becomes 1. Therefore, line evaluation can be optimized as

$$\hat{l}_{\hat{T}', \hat{Q}'}(\hat{P}) = y_{\hat{P}}^{-1} l_{\hat{T}', \hat{Q}'}(\hat{P}) = 1 - z^{-1/6}C + z^{-1/2}E y_{\hat{P}}^{-1}. \tag{6}$$

The remaining 7 zero and 1 one coefficients in Eq. (6) lead to an efficient multiplication called *pseudo 8-sparse multiplication*.

4.2 Line Evaluation for the Proposed Attractive Classes

Here, this paper describes the line evaluation for two classes of BN curves. In what follows, the cost of the multiplication, constant multiplication, squaring, addition/subtraction and inversion over $\mathbb{F}_{p^k}$ are represented as $\tilde{m}_k, \tilde{m}_{uk}, \tilde{s}_k, \tilde{a}_k$ and $\tilde{i}_k$, respectively. The costs of multiplication by $(\alpha + 1)$ and $(\alpha + 1)^{-1}$ are especially denoted as $\tilde{B}_2$ and $\tilde{B}_2^{-1}$.

Using Class 1: It is found that the sextic twist parameter z is $(\alpha + 1)$ since the twisted curve of *Class 1* is $E' : y^2 = x^3 + 2^{6l-1}(\alpha + 1)$ from Table 1. Therefore, the sextic twist mapping for *Class 1* is given as follows:

$$E'(\mathbb{F}_{p^2}) : y^2 = x^3 + 2^{6l-1}(\alpha + 1) \rightarrow E(\mathbb{F}_{p^{12}}) : y^2 = x^3 + 2^{6l-1},$$
$$(x, y) \mapsto ((\alpha + 1)^{-1/3}x, (\alpha + 1)^{-1/2}y) = ((\alpha + 1)^{-1}x\beta^2, (\alpha + 1)^{-1}y\beta\gamma).$$

Then, the line evaluation of the pseudo 8-sparse form can be obtained for the rational point $\hat{P} \in \hat{E}'(\mathbb{F}_p)$ and $\hat{Q}', \hat{T}' \in \hat{E}'(\mathbb{F}_{p^2})$ as follows:

$$\hat{l}_{\hat{T}', \hat{Q}'}(P) = 1 - (\alpha + 1)^{-1}C\beta^2\gamma + (\alpha + 1)^{-1}E y_{\hat{P}}^{-1}\beta\gamma. \tag{7}$$

Finally, the pseudo 8-sparse multiplication is calculated by Algorithm 1.

Using Class 2: The twist parameter z for E' from Table 1 is $(\alpha+1)^{-1}$. Therefore, the sextic twist mapping for *Class 2* is given as follows:

$$E'(\mathbb{F}_{p^2}) : y^2 = x^3 + 2^{6l+1}(\alpha+1)^{-1} \to E(\mathbb{F}_{p^{12}}) : y^2 = x^3 + 2^{6l+1},$$

$$(x,y) \mapsto ((\alpha+1)^{1/3}x, (\alpha+1)^{1/2}y) = (x\beta, y\beta\gamma).$$

Then, the line evaluation of the pseudo 8-sparse form can be obtained in affine coordinate for the rational point $\hat{P} \in \hat{E}'(\mathbb{F}_p)$ and $\hat{Q}', \hat{T}' \in \hat{E}'(\mathbb{F}_{p^2})$ as follows:

$$\hat{l}_{\hat{T}',\hat{Q}'}(P) = 1 - C\gamma + Ey_{\hat{P}}^{-1}\beta\gamma. \tag{8}$$

Therefore, Algorithm 2 shows the derived pseudo 8-sparse multiplication.

Algorithm 2. Pseudo 8-Sparse Multiplication for *Class 2*

Input: $a = (a_0 + a_1\beta + a_2\beta^2) + (a_3 + a_4\beta + a_5\beta^2)\gamma$, $b = 1 + b_3\gamma + b_4\beta\gamma$
Output: $c = (c_0 + c_1\beta + c_2\beta^2) + (c_3 + c_4\beta + c_5\beta^2)\gamma$
where $a_i, b_j, c_i \in \mathbb{F}_{p^2}$ $(i = 0, \cdots, 5, j = 4, 5)$

1	$t_0 \leftarrow a_0 b_3, \ t_1 \leftarrow a_1 b_4, \ t_2 \leftarrow a_0 + a_1, \ t_3 \leftarrow b_3 + b_4;$	$(2\tilde{m}_2 + 2\tilde{a}_2)$
2	$t_2 \leftarrow t_2 t_3 - t_0 - t_1;$	$(\tilde{m}_2 + 2\tilde{a}_2)$
3	$c_4 \leftarrow a_4 + t_2, \ c_3 \leftarrow a_3 + t_0 + a_2 b_4(\alpha+1);$	$(\tilde{m}_2 + 3\tilde{a}_2 + \tilde{B}_2)$
4	$c_5 \leftarrow a_5 + t_1 + a_2 b_3;$	$(\tilde{m}_2 + 2\tilde{a}_2)$
5	$t_0 \leftarrow a_3 b_3, \ t_1 \leftarrow a_4 b_4, \ t_2 \leftarrow a_3 + a_4, \ t_2 \leftarrow t_2 t_3 - t_0 - t_1;$	$(3\tilde{m}_2 + 3\tilde{a}_2)$
6	$c_2 \leftarrow a_2 + t_2, \ c_1 \leftarrow a_1 + t_0 + a_5 b_4(\alpha+1);$	$(\tilde{m}_2 + 3\tilde{a}_2 + \tilde{B}_2)$
7	$c_0 \leftarrow a_0 + (t_1 + a_5 b_3)(\alpha+1);$	$(\tilde{m}_2 + 2\tilde{a}_2 + \tilde{B}_2)$
	return $c;$	

Comparing Class 1 and Class 2: Table 2 shows the calculation costs of the sextic twist, computation of line evaluation/ECA, and pseudo 8-sparse multiplication for *Class 1* and *Class 2*. It is easily found that *Class 1* requires more $\tilde{B}_2$ and $\tilde{B}_2^{-1}$ computation, making it costlier than *Class 2*. This cost incurs due to the twist coefficient z. The details of the costs are given by $\tilde{B}_2 = 2\tilde{a}_1$ and $\tilde{B}_2^{-1} = 2\tilde{m}_{u1} +$

Table 2. Calculation cost of the sextic twist, line evaluation and ECA and pseudo 8-sparse multiplication for proposed classes

Type	Sextic twist	Line evaluation and ECA		Pseudo 8-sparse multiplication
		$\hat{T} \neq \hat{Q}$	$\hat{T} = \hat{Q}$	
Class 1	$2\tilde{B}_2^{-1}$	$3\tilde{m}_2 + \tilde{m}_{u2} + \tilde{s}_2$ $+6\tilde{a}_2 + \tilde{i}_2 + 2\tilde{B}_2^{-1}$	$3\tilde{m}_2 + \tilde{m}_{u2} + 2\tilde{s}_2$ $+ 7\tilde{a}_2 + \tilde{i}_2 + 2\tilde{B}_2^{-1}$	$10\tilde{m}_2 + 17\tilde{a}_2 + 5\tilde{B}_2$
Class 2	0	$3\tilde{m}_2 + \tilde{m}_{u2}$ $+ \tilde{s}_2 + 6\tilde{a}_2 + \tilde{i}_2$	$3\tilde{m}_2 + \tilde{m}_{u2}$ $+ 2\tilde{s}_2 + 7\tilde{a}_2 + \tilde{i}_2$	$10\tilde{m}_2 + 17\tilde{a}_2 + 3\tilde{B}_2$

$2\tilde{a}_1$. Although the costs are seemingly insignificant than other $\mathbb{F}_p$ operations, however, they appear repeatedly in line evaluation, ECA calculation and sparse multiplication in the Miller's algorithm for more than 114 times. Therefore, the authors suggest that using *Class 2* is a better choice for efficient pairing implementation.

5   Experimental Result

This section gives details of the experimental implementation. The source code can be found in Github[1]. The big integer arithmetic is implemented using the mpz_t data type of GMP [11] library. In what follows, multiplication, squaring, addition/subtraction/negation and inversion in $\mathbb{F}_p$ are denoted as M, S, A and I, respectively. This paper assumes that $M = 5A$, $S = 4.5A$ and $I = 30A$ for performance comparison (based on the average time of 1 million $\mathbb{F}_p$ operations). The pairings are implemented by using pseudo 8-sparse multiplication for the Miller's algorithm (see Sect. 4) and Fuentes-Castaneda et al.'s [10] final exponentiation algorithm. Table 3 shows the computational environment. The parameters of the proposed classes of the BN curve at the 128-bit security level are given in Table 4. Table 5 shows the operation count based on the counter in the implementation code. The result also shows the average execution time of 100 pairings.

Table 5 shows that Miller's algorithm using *Class 2* is more than 3.9% efficient than *Class 1*. It is also found that the performance of *Class 2* for the parameter of the Hamming weight 6 is close to the *Class 1* with the Hamming weight 4. According to Table 5, the efficiency precedence can be expressed as $(ii) > (i) \approx (iv) > (iii)$. Therefore, the authors conclude that *Class 2* is a better choice for efficient pairing implementation. The total cost in execution time is subject to the environment. However, the time cost is coherent with the operation count.

Table 3. Computational Environment

CPU	Memory	Compiler	OS	Language	Library
Intel(R) Core(TM) i7-7567U CPU @ 3.50 GHz	8 GB	GCC 4.2.1	macOS High Sierra 10.13.6	C	GMP ver 6.1.2 [11]

Table 4. Proposed classes of the parameter at the 128-bit security level (four types)

Type	χ	HW	BN curve	Twisted curve
(i) Class 1[a]	$2^{114} + 2^{101} - 2^{14} - 1$	4	$y^2 = x^3 + 32$	$y^2 = x^3 + 32(\alpha + 1)$
(ii) Class 2	$2^{114} + 2^{84} - 2^{53} - 1$	4	$y^2 = x^3 + 2$	$y^2 = x^3 + 2(\alpha + 1)^{-1}$
(iii) Class 1	$2^{114} + 2^{78} + 2^{51} - 2^{38} - 2^{36} - 1$	6	$y^2 = x^3 + 32$	$y^2 = x^3 + 32(\alpha + 1)$
(iv) Class 2	$2^{114} + 2^{94} + 2^{55} - 2^{53} - 2^3 - 1$	6	$y^2 = x^3 + 2$	$y^2 = x^3 + 2(\alpha + 1)^{-1}$

[a] Proposed by Barbulescu et al. [3].

---

[1] http://github.com/YukiNanjo/BN12_attractive.

Table 5. Operation count and execution time using proposed classes

Type	Pairing operations		Time [ms]	M	S	A	I
(i) Class 1	Miller's Alg.	Opt-ate	5.17	1696	9062	35770	125
		χ-ate	4.88	1658	8893	35241	120
	Final Exp.		4.79	1428	8131	43102	1
(ii) Class 2	Miller's Alg.	Opt-ate	4.88	1201	9061	34774	125
		χ-ate	4.75	1183	8892	34285	120
	Final Exp.		4.71	1428	8131	43102	1
(iii) Class 1	Miller's Alg.	Opt-ate	5.24	1728	9234	36298	129
		χ-ate	5.03	1674	8979	35505	122
	Final Exp.		4.94	1428	8455	44446	1
(iv) Class 2	Miller's Alg.	Opt-ate	5.04	1217	9233	35270	129
		χ-ate	4.82	1191	8978	34533	122
	Final Exp.		4.86	1428	8455	44446	1

6   Conclusion

This paper has proposed two attractive classes of BN curves for the efficient pairing implementation which result in not only constructing an efficient tower of the extension field but also instantaneously determining BN curve, its twisted curves and obvious generator points. Moreover, this paper clearly describes that the implementation difference of the Miller's algorithm between two classes applying pseudo 8-sparse multiplication. The authors conclude that Class 2 curve ($\chi \equiv 11 \pmod{12}$) is a better choice for efficient pairing. As a future work, the authors would like to examine the similar technique for other pairing-friendly curves.

Acknowledgement. This work was supported by the Strategic Information and Communications R&D Promotion Programme (SCOPE) of Ministry of Internal Affairs and Communications, Japan.

References

1. Aranha, D.F., Karabina, K., Longa, P., Gebotys, C.H., López, J.: Faster explicit formulas for computing pairings over ordinary curves. In: Paterson, K.G. (ed.) EUROCRYPT 2011. LNCS, vol. 6632, pp. 48–68. Springer, Heidelberg (2011). https://doi.org/10.1007/978-3-642-20465-4_5
2. Bailey, D.V., Paar, C.: Efficient arithmetic in finite field extensions with application in elliptic curve cryptography. J. Cryptol. **14**(3), 153–176 (2001)
3. Barbulescu, R., Duquesne, S.: Updating key size estimations for pairings. J. Cryptol. **2018**, 1–39 (2018). https://doi.org/10.1007/s00145-018-9280-5

4. Barreto, P.S.L.M., Naehrig, M.: Pairing-friendly elliptic curves of prime order. In: Preneel, B., Tavares, S. (eds.) SAC 2005. LNCS, vol. 3897, pp. 319–331. Springer, Heidelberg (2006). https://doi.org/10.1007/11693383_22
5. Boneh, D., Boyen, X.: Short signatures without random oracles. In: Cachin, C., Camenisch, J.L. (eds.) EUROCRYPT 2004. LNCS, vol. 3027, pp. 56–73. Springer, Heidelberg (2004). https://doi.org/10.1007/978-3-540-24676-3_4
6. Boneh, D., Lynn, B., Shacham, H.: Short signatures from the Weil pairing. In: Boyd, C. (ed.) ASIACRYPT 2001. LNCS, vol. 2248, pp. 514–532. Springer, Heidelberg (2001). https://doi.org/10.1007/3-540-45682-1_30
7. Cohen, H., et al.: Handbook of Elliptic and Hyperelliptic Curve Cryptography. CRC Press, Boca Raton (2005)
8. Costello, C., Lauter, K., Naehrig, M.: Attractive subfamilies of BLS curves for implementing high-security pairings. In: Bernstein, D.J., Chatterjee, S. (eds.) INDOCRYPT 2011. LNCS, vol. 7107, pp. 320–342. Springer, Heidelberg (2011). https://doi.org/10.1007/978-3-642-25578-6_23
9. Freeman, D., Scott, M., Teske, E.: A taxonomy of pairing-friendly elliptic curves. J. Cryptol. $23(2)$, 224–280 (2010)
10. Fuentes-Castañeda, L., Knapp, E., Rodríguez-Henríquez, F.: Faster hashing to $\mathbb{G}_2$. In: Miri, A., Vaudenay, S. (eds.) SAC 2011. LNCS, vol. 7118, pp. 412–430. Springer, Heidelberg (2012). https://doi.org/10.1007/978-3-642-28496-0_25
11. Granlund, T.: The GMP development team: GNU MP: the GNU multiple precision arithmetic library, 6.1. 0 edn. (2015)
12. Grewal, G., Azarderakhsh, R., Longa, P., Hu, S., Jao, D.: Efficient implementation of bilinear pairings on ARM processors. In: Knudsen, L.R., Wu, H. (eds.) SAC 2012. LNCS, vol. 7707, pp. 149–165. Springer, Heidelberg (2013). https://doi.org/10.1007/978-3-642-35999-6_11
13. Hess, F., Smart, N.P., Vercauteren, F.: The Eta pairing revisited. IEEE Trans. Inf. Theory $52(10)$, 4595–4602 (2006)
14. Mori, Y., Akagi, S., Nogami, Y., Shirase, M.: Pseudo 8-sparse multiplication for efficient ate-based pairing on Barreto-Naehrig curve. In: Cao, Z., Zhang, F. (eds.) Pairing 2013. LNCS, vol. 8365, pp. 186–198. Springer, Cham (2014). https://doi.org/10.1007/978-3-319-04873-4_11
15. Nogami, Y., Akane, M., Sakemi, Y., Katou, H., Morikawa, Y.: Integer variable chi-based ate pairing. Pairing 5209, 178–191 (2008)
16. Shirase, M.: Barreto-Naehrig curve with fixed coefficient - efficiently constructing pairing-friendly curves (2010)
17. Vercauteren, F.: Optimal pairings. IEEE Trans. Inf. Theory $56(1)$, 455–461 (2010)

A Study on the Vulnerability Assessment for Digital I&C System in Nuclear Power Plant

SungCheol Kim[1(✉)], IeckChae Euom[1(✉)], ChangHyun Ha[1(✉)],
JooHyoung Lee[1(✉)], and BongNam Noh[2(✉)]

[1] KEPCO KDN, Naju, Republic of Korea
kimsungcheol17@gmail.com, icelaken@gmail.com,
koreabomb89@gmail.com, metalicred@gmail.com
[2] Chonnam National University, Gwangju, Republic of Korea
bbong@jnu.ac.kr

Abstract. NPP (Nuclear Power Plant) Operators have approached the problem of cyber security by simply keep up with the never-ending stream of new vulnerability alerts from suppliers and groups like ICS-CERT. Keeping Cyber Security Compliance, NPP Owner must patch vulnerabilities according to their CVSS Score. In fact, NPP Owner often has to deal with hundreds of vulnerabilities, which is not a trivial task to carry out. Unfortunately, the CVSS Score has been shown to be poor indicator for actual exploitation in NPP. This paper analyzes Vulnerability Assessment Methodology about Critical digital asset in NPP. And then give an effective methodology. It approaches the cyber security regulations of NPP from a technical vulnerability point of view, where any given Critical Digital Asset can be assessed for vulnerabilities.

Keywords: Vulnerability assessment · CVSS · Nuclear Power Plant

1 Introduction

NPP (Nuclear Power Plant) Operators have approached the problem of cyber security by simply keep up with the never-ending stream of new vulnerability alerts from suppliers and groups like ICS-CERT. Keeping Cyber Security Compliance, NPP Owner must patch vulnerabilities according to their CVSS (Common Vulnerability Scoring System) Score. In fact, NPP Owner often has to deal with hundreds of vulnerabilities, which is not a trivial task to carry out. Unfortunately, the CVSS Score has been shown to be poor indicator for actual exploitation in NPP.

There are two big problems with CVSS in the NPP. First, it doesn't tell us much about the NPP impact of vulnerability. Second, the scores published in official advisories are often just plain wrong, more importantly. It is not considered by environment of NPP. CVSS is meant to provide an abbreviated summary of vulnerability. Chiefly it is a means to quickly convey how serious a vulnerability is by showing both how easy a vulnerability is to exploit, as well as what the impacts of exploitation are.

Faced with regulatory commitments, NPP Operators have approached the problem of cyber security by simply attempting to apply nation's committed catalog of cyber security requirements to every Critical Digital Asset under evaluation. When new

© Springer Nature Switzerland AG 2019
B. B. Kang and J. Jang (Eds.): WISA 2018, LNCS 11402, pp. 68–80, 2019.
https://doi.org/10.1007/978-3-030-17982-3_6

Vulnerabilities are discovered, the issue is documented in the CAP (Corrective Action Program). CAP Evaluations should consider the attack vectors associated with the vulnerabilities.

There are many ways to describe vulnerabilities depending on the organization, programmatic policies and procedures, supply chain, asset or characteristics. Vulnerabilities are weaknesses in information system, system procedures, controls, or implementations the can be exploited by a threat source. Predisposing conditions are properties of the organization, mission/business process, architecture, or information systems that contribute to the likelihood of a threat event [1].

Although software weakness and flaws are technical vulnerabilities, they are a result of the supply chain, and are mitigated using programmatic security methods such as monitoring security advisories, patch management, and anti-malware. Most of the sources describe these types of vulnerabilities and seek to identify specific weakness and flaws. These types of specific software and hardware vulnerabilities are discovered after components are deployed in the field. Every day, a number of specific hardware, firmware, or application software vulnerabilities are identified such as ICS-CERT Advisory. New vulnerabilities are either discovered or introduced every day, making it impossible to predict future specific vulnerabilities.

A more efficient and effective approach to vulnerability assessment methodology is required. It can be used to demonstrate effective vulnerability assessment for any CDA or functional group of CDAs selected for evaluation by facility operator.

2 Related Research

2.1 Definition of CVSS

CVSS is one of a vulnerability assessments method that developed under the United States' NIAC (National Infrastructure Assurance Council). This rating system is designed to provide open and universally standard severity ratings of software vulnerabilities. It allows security administrators to effectively respond by classifying the severity of the vulnerability and determining the priority of the emergency response.

2.2 CVSS V3.0

CVSS v1.0 and v2.0 is early version of the rating system. CVSS v2.0 is classified into Base Metric, Temporal Metric, and Environmental Metric. Base Metric, which has the greatest impact on vulnerability scores, is divided into Attack Vector, Access Complexity, Authentication, Confidentiality, Availability, and Integrity.

However, in the case of v2.0, there were limitations in conducting detailed evaluation on items such as Access Complexity and Authentication. So CVSS v3.0 complemented the existed v2.0 issues, and the improvements are as follows.

Privileges Required. Authentication issues was introduced to measure how many times an attacker would have to be authenticated to penetrate the target system, but NVD (National Vulnerability Database) announced that 90% or more was None, which proved ineffective. So in v3.0, the Authentication value is removed and the attacker's authority to attack is presented as a new value [2].

Scope. The concepts of confidentiality, integrity, availability were limited to the effects on the host operating system, and new criteria for the extent of the damage were suggested to allow evaluation of whether the extent of damage is limited or derivable.

User Interaction. CVSS added a new value about whether the users need to interact with each other for the success of the attack so attacker could suggest whether the user's intervention is needed or not [3].

CVSS v3.0 is divided into three Metrics that Base, Temporal and Environmental Metrics called B.T.E Metrics. Each Metrics' score consists of 0 to 10 points that indicate severity of vulnerability [4] (Table 1).

Table 1. Components of CVSS

- Attack Vector
- Attack Complexity
- Privileges Required
- User Interaction
- Scope
- C.I.A

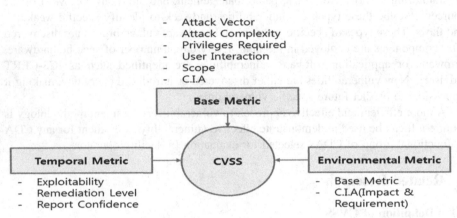

Base Metric. It is calculated by vulnerability's intrinsic characteristic that network connectivity, authentication, access complexity and possibility of impacting on C.I.A (confidentiality, integrity, availability). Base Metric is composed of two sets of metrics: the Exploitability metrics and the Impact metrics [3] (Table 2).

Table 2. Base Metric diagram

The Exploitability metrics reflect the characteristics of the thing that is vulnerable, which we refer to formally as the vulnerable component. Therefore, each of the exploitability metrics listed below should be scored relative to the vulnerable component, and reflect the properties of the vulnerability that lead to a successful attack [3] (Table 3).

Table 3. Exploitability metrics

Division	Metric value	Severity
Attack Vector	Network (Remotely Exploitable)	High
	Adjacent (Same Network)	Low-high
	Local (Not bound to network stack)	Medium
	Physical (Need physical access)	Low
Access Complexity	Low (Do not need any access conditions)	High
	High (Need several steps to access a target)	Low
Privileges Required	None (Unauthorized privileges)	High
	Low (Basic user capabilities)	Medium
	High (Administrative capabilities)	Low
User Interaction	None (Automatically exploitable)	High
	Required (Need specific actions)	Low
Scope of Damage	Unchanged (Limited to same authority)	Low
	Changed (Different authority)	High

Attack Vector value will be larger the more remote (logical, and physical) an attacker can be in order to exploit the vulnerable component.

Access Complexity describes the conditions beyond the attacker's control that must exist in order to exploit the vulnerability.

Privileges Required. It describes the level of privileges an attacker must possess before successfully exploiting the vulnerability.

User Interaction. It determines whether the vulnerability can be exploited solely at the w ill of the attacker, or whether a separate user must participate in some manner.

Scope of Damage. It is the scope that whether the damage is independent network or spread to wide network [5].

The Impact metrics refer to the properties of the impacted component. Whether a successfully exploited vulnerability affects one or more components, the impact metrics are scored according to the component that suffers the worst outcome that is most directly and predictably associated with a successful attack (Table 4).

Table 4. Impact metrics

Division	Metric value	Severity
Confidentiality	High (Total loss of data)	High
	Low (Some loss of data)	Low
	None (No loss of data)	None
Integrity	High (Modify all files)	High
	Low (Need some control for modification)	Low
	None (No files to modify)	None
Availability	High (Able to fully deny access to resources)	High
	Low (Able to deny some access to resources)	Low
	None (No impact)	None

Confidentiality. It measures the impact to the confidentiality of the information resources managed by a software component due to a successfully exploited vulnerability.

Integrity. It refers to the trustworthiness and veracity of information.

Availability. It refers to the loss of availability of the impacted component itself, such as a networked service.

Temporal Metric. This metrics measure the availability of attack code or exploit techniques, the level of vulnerability treatment and the reliability of the vulnerability. The level is calculated to reflect the availability of attack code and the value changes over time [3] (Table 5).

Table 5. Temporal metrics

Division	Metric value	Severity
Exploit Code Maturity	Not defined	N/A
	High	High
	Functional (Functional exploit code available)	Medium
	PoC (Some code available)	Medium-Low
	Unproven (No exploit code available)	Low
Remediation Level	Not defined	N/A
	Unavailable	High
	Workaround (Unofficial solution ex: create an own patch etc.)	Medium
	Temporary Fix (Official but temporary ex: hotfix, tool etc.)	Medium-Low
	Official Fix	Low
Report Confidence	Not defined	N/A
	Confirmed	Medium
	Reasonable	Medium-Low
	Unknown	Low

Exploit Code Maturity. It measures the likelihood of the vulnerability being attacked, and is typically based on the current state of exploit techniques and exploit code availability.

Remediation Level. It is the level of security controls that the less official and permanent a fix, the higher the vulnerability scored.

Report Confidence. The more vulnerability is validated by the vendor or other reputable sources, the higher the score.

Environmental Metric. Environmental Metric is calculated as the magnitude of the damage, the extent of the damage, and the security requirements as the vulnerability succeeds in the attack. This metrics enable the analyst to customize the CVSS score depending on the importance of the affected IT asset to a user's organization.

Therefore, this metrics need to be considered all the metrics as mentioned above [3].

2.3 US Nuclear Power Plant's Vulnerability Assessment

In general, IT systems and I&C systems have differences in requirements in the areas of communication, accessibility and operation, so it should be considered differently such as deriving vulnerability items. Likewise ICS-CERT a support group for the NCCIC (National Cyber Security and Communications Integration Center) analyzes and announces industry-specific vulnerabilities.

Secure and safe operation of critical NPPs is very important for the national security, human health and safety and economic vigor of the nations. The safe operation, security and reliability of this critical infrastructure are becoming a vital national concern. Management of security vulnerabilities is of great importance as cyber infringement accidents in national infrastructures could be large and cause social disruption. Safety is most significant issue in most of the NPP (Nuclear Power Plants system), they are aged and could not be changed easily.

Table 6. US NPP's Assessment method [5]

NPP I&C systems can be grouped into two categories: safety CDAs (Critical Digital Assets) and non-safety CDAs. Safety CDAs can be further graded as either safety-critical or important-to-safety. Safety systems require higher reliability, functionality, and availability than non-safety systems. For example, PLC which is grouped into safety CDA is a small-scale industrial computer designed to withstand the various environments of the infrastructure operation site. PLC uses control logic or control program to perform operations related to input/output devices and mounts RTOS such as vxworks (Table 6).

CVE-2017-0144 is vulnerability in Microsoft that allows local or remote users to write malicious scripts using Windows Fonts files. In a general IT system, the vulnerability can be solved with a simple patch, but it is not easy to apply to NPPs. Considering these characteristics, NEI (Nuclear Energy Institute) has announced a case for nuclear industry using CVSS and NVD.

ALNOTS (Alert Notifications System). It is automated system that managed by INPO (Institute of Nuclear Power Operations) that provide nuclear licensees a uniform and consistent means to ensure cyber security threat notifications and vulnerabilities are properly screened. Also, ensures licensees are notified of alerts and advisories that require further evaluation or action (Table 7).

Table 7. US NPP's Assessment Result example [5]

CDA Grouping	Microsoft Windows
Vulnerability Description	Microsoft Windows Graphics Component Flaws
Vulnerability Ref Number	CVE-2017-0144
Applicable in Attack Vectors	A Local or remote user can create content with specially crafted embedded fonts that will trigger a flaw
Security Controls	Data diode or air gap isolation for remote user Local user exploitation is addressed y CDAs being located in Vital area or room under continuous surveillance
Required to exploit the vulnerability	Physical CDA access
Defense-in-depth for corrective actions	No remedial or corrective actions required for CDAs behind a data diode or air-gapped isolated because exploitation of this vulnerability requires physical access

This case helped US nuclear licensees conduct effective vulnerability management. It also provided direction on how to manage the vulnerability of the sensitive nuclear control system [1].

3 The Proposed Methodology

3.1 Background

As shown in the case of the US, an effective evaluation system for the NPPs is also required in the domestic nuclear power field. NPPs are one of the main infrastructures of the country and causes serious damage when it is attacked. To prevent the damage caused by unauthorized change of malicious SW and unpredictable result of the change of logic control device (set-point, shut down, etc.), we analyze the vulnerability that is continuously announced, and evaluation system should be made considering these characteristics.

3.2 Assessment Methods

CVSS is a system for assessing the risk by scoring the evaluation items for security vulnerabilities. Unlike the US, it is not easy to introduce automated systems into the Korean nuclear control system. Also we do not have vulnerability database that able to integrate management. NVD is integrated database that under the responsibility of the Department of Homeland Security and NIST (National Institute of Standards and Technology) is running the NVD. NVD has a large number of vulnerability codes called CVE. So using NVD, we conducted four stages of vulnerability assessment [2] (Table 8).

Table 8. Vulnerability assessment workflow

Collect Information	Classify Vulnerability	Re-Evaluation	Mitigate Vulnerability
• Use NVD to monitor all vulnerabilities about NPPs CDA	• Classify CVSS(CVSS≥7.0) • Grouping CDA as vendor/model/product/version	• Consider network diagram, access management, supply chain etc.	• Technical support • Reduce vulnerabilities • Effective management

Collect information we have monitored vulnerability status that specific to CDA using NVD that records and manages 14,000 new vulnerabilities per year.

NVD includes well-known vulnerabilities and mitigation, and provides useful data regarding digital I&C cyber security. When collecting vulnerability from this database, a keyword would be used as 'controller', 'PLC', 'QNX', 'vxworks' etc. [6].

Classify vulnerability we selected vulnerabilities as an action target that classified as "Critical (CVSS $\geq$ 7.0)" from NVD. It showed us that approximately 8,400 vulnerabilities are specific to CDA.

Re-evaluation. Then, we identified hardware and software characteristic and collected applicable vulnerabilities. We analyzed the impact of vulnerability on CDA using KEPCO KDN's own impact analysis table. It is composed of communication interface, protocol, CDA locations, system connectivity and OS security management function etc. Using those, the CVSS score is recalculated considering the basic attributes of the CDA, the environment and the importance of the assets. And an action target that classified as "Critical (CVSS $\geq$ 7.0)" from NVD is about 110 vulnerabilities (Table 9).

Table 9. KEPCO KDN's impact analysis table (example)

Division	Metric Value	Example
CDA Attributes (type 1)	Communication Interface	RS-232C
	Communication Protocol	Modbus/TCP/IP
	CDA Location	VA (Vital Area)
	System connectivity	Independent Network
CDA Attributes (type2)	Account Management	Yes (Admin, user)
	Audit Function	No (Log etc.)
	Encryption Function	Yes (TCP, SSH etc.)
	Media connectivity	Yes (USB, CD etc.)
	Communication connectivity	No (Independent NW)
	Application Service	Yes (Markvie)
Applicability	CVE Information	CVE-2017-8487
	Applicable attack vector	Wireless connectivity
	Applied security control	No use remote service
	Exploit methods	Physical or remote
	corrective action for Defense-in-depth	Need Approvals

CDA Attributes (type 1) refers to CDA's network connectivity and configuration.

CDA Attributes (type 2) refers to CDA's hardware and software characteristic that could be handled by end-user.

Applicability refers to CVE information such as release date, summary of the code. Also, it finds out exploit methods that which function would be exploitable to assets such as remote service, physical access, supply chain, portable media, wired connectivity etc. (Table 10).

Table 10. Score arithmetic expression [3]

Division	Example
Formula	* Base Score = (.6 * Impact + .4 * Exploitability – 1.5) * f(Impact) * Impact = 10.41 * (1 – (1 – ConfImpact) * (1 – IntegImpact) * (1 – AvailImpact) * Exploitability = 20 * Access Complexity * Authentication * Access Vector * f(Impact) = 0 if Impact = 0; 1.176 otherwise
Weight	* Access Complexity = High: 0.35, Medium: 0.61, Low: 0.71 * Authentication = None: 0.704, Single: 0.56, Multiple: 0.45 * Access Vector = Local: 0.395, Adjacent: 0.646, Network: 1 * Confidentiality = None: 0, Partial: 0.275, Complete: 0.660 * Integrity = None: 0, Partial: 0.275, Complete: 0.660 * Availability = : None: 0, Partial: 0.275, Complete: 0.660

As mentioned on the *3.1 Background*, NPPs are one of the main infrastructures of the country and causes serious damage when it is attacked. Therefore NPPs' information should be handled very carefully, which means weight of confidentiality, integrity, and availability should be considered critical. So NPPs' C.I.A marks "Complete" as default.

Mitigate vulnerability. We have reported to vendor and CDA manager the results and gave them technical support. Through these works, licensees could make high attack barrier, prevent zero-day attacks, and enhance security consciousness.

3.3   Case.1 (PLC: Automatic Seismic Trip System)

This system monitors seismic sensor signals to protect the reactor when large-scale seismic waves occur, and automatically stops the reactor when the sensor signal reaches the set points. It contains several sub system and PLC has QNX operate system. QNX has vulnerability, code number CVE-2004-1390, that remote attackers could execute arbitrary code (Table 11).

Table 11. CDA Attack Vector

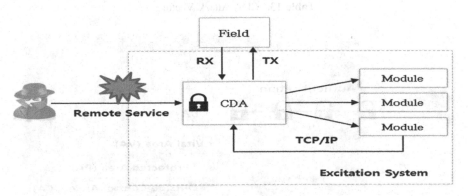

If attacker uses this vulnerability for exploit, remote access would be needed. This CDA does not use remote service. So Attack Vector has checked as Local. There is no account management function in PLC so that "Authentication" is N/A. N/A has same meaning as Multiple. Because Multiple checks means the highest level of security. Also any other CDA attributes can impact on vulnerability therefore CVE-2004-1390 could not be abused by attacker (Table 12).

Table 12. Re-Score summary

Code	Base-Score	Re-Score
CVE-2004-1390	10	6.9
Attack Vector	Network	Local
Access Complexity	Low	High
Authentication (UI/PR)	None	Multiple
C.I.A	Complete	Complete

- There is no connection point with other system, only TCP/IP is used internally
- Type 2 attributes are not supported: N/A
- Physical access control: port seal, cabinet locking devices etc.

3.4   Case.2 (Man-Machine Interface: Excitation System)

The exciter is a device that supplies DC power to the rotor of the generator, and the means of supplying the DC power to the main generator and forming the rotor into an electromagnet is called excitation. The exciter receives the alternating current from the excitation transformer, outputs the rectified current through the phase control, and supplies it to the generator excitation power source. In order to control the generator voltage automatically, the generator voltage and current signals are supplied to the input of the controller.

MMI (Man-machine Interface) is generally installed on MCR (Main Control Room) and excitation room. Also MMI is composed of remote and local PC based on Linux. MMI has vulnerability, code number CVE-2018-10124, that local users could cause DoS (Denial of Service) due to validation errors (Table 13).

Table 13. CDA Attack Vector

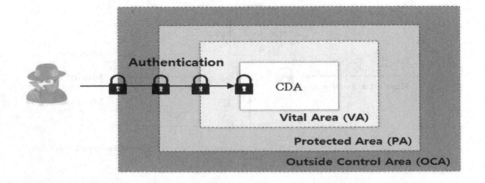

If attacker uses this vulnerability for exploit, physical access would be needed. But Excitation system has security controls that anyone who access should get approval in advance. And this system has physical control which is port seal and cabinet locking devices. Only authorized persons could access MMI. Any other CDA attributes can impact on vulnerability therefore CVE-2018-10124 could not be abused by attacker (Table 14).

Table 14. Re-Score summary

Code	Base-Score	Re-Score
CVE-2018-10124	6.9	5.9
Attack Vector	Local	Local
Access Complexity	Medium	High
Authentication (UI/PR)	None	Multiple
C.I.A	Complete	Complete

- There is no connection point with other system, only TCP/IP is used internally
- Type 2 attributes are supported and periodic management is conducted
- Physical access control: port seal, cabinet locking devices etc.

4 Conclusions

CVSS is meant to provide an abbreviated summary of vulnerability. It is means to quickly convey how serious a vulnerability is by showing both how easy a vulnerability is to exploit, as well as what the impacts of exploitation are.

There are problems with CVSS in the Nuclear Power Plant. It doesn't tell us much about the Nuclear Power Plant impact of vulnerability. More importantly, the scores, published in official advisories, are not reflecting CDA Attributes.

This paper proposes efficient methodology to assess CDA's vulnerability in NPP. Use of CDA Attributes and CDA's Exploitability greatly enhance the actual implementation of effort in assessment.

References

1. NIST Special Publication 800-82: Guide to Industrial Control Systems Security. Revision 2 (2015)
2. Ahn, J.: Research on software vulnerability scoring systems, p. 23 (2013)
3. Common Vulnerability Scoring System v3.0: Specification Document
4. Ahn, J.: Quantitative scoring system on the importance of software vulnerabilities, p. 4 (2015)
5. Shank, J.: Cyber Alert & Notification System Update (2016)
6. Skybox Security Vulnerability and Threat Trends Report (2018)
7. Jang, D.: A study on the IoT software and network vulnerability assessment system, pp. 4–6 (2017)

8. Song, J.G.: A cyber security risk assessment for the design of I&C systems in nuclear power plants, pp. 1–3 (2012)
9. Kostadinov, V.: Vulnerability assessment as a missing part of efficient regulatory emergency preparedness system for nuclear critical infrastructure (2011)
10. Holt, M.: Nuclear Power Plant Security and Vulnerabilities. Congressional Research Service, Washington, DC (2014)

IP Address Mutation Scheme Using Vector Projection for Tactical Wireless Networks

Jong-Kwan Lee[✉]

Cyber Warfare Research Center, Korea Military Academy, Seoul, Korea
jklee64@kma.ac.kr

Abstract. The static address configuration of networks and hosts allows attackers to have enough time to discover target networks and systems. On the other hands, the defenders always lack of time to respond because they can take action after attacker's explicit behaviors. To eliminate the attacker's asymmetric advantage of time, randomization of addresses have been suggested as Moving Target Defense (MTD) which is a promising technique to make the attacker's reconnaissance activities difficult by dynamically changing network properties. In this paper, I propose the address mutation scheme using vector projection for tactical wireless networks that are a leader node centric hierarchical structure. In the proposed scheme, the addresses in the same networks are mutated with a simple vector operation by fully distributed manner and the mutated addresses are shared to all the members in the internal networks. Unlike the conventional schemes, all addresses associated with network entities for data delivery are mutated. I evaluate the performance of the proposed scheme by numerical analysis and experimental simulations. The results show that the proposed scheme could effectively randomize the addresses in tactical wireless networks.

Keywords: Moving Target Defense · Address mutation ·
Tactical wireless networks

1 Introduction

1.1 Moving Target Defense (MTD)

In general, network configuration, security mechanisms, and system information are static in a traditional passive defense system. Thus, an attacker can gather information about the target system and have enough time to identify and analyze the vulnerability. On the other hand, the defender must be prepared for all possible attacks until the attack signatures are correctly identified, and the response time is not sufficient since the attack is explicitly identified and then a specific response is selected. Therefore, in cyber space, the attacker who is able to select the attack time and the target system is generally more advantageous than the defender [1–3]. This asymmetry between the attacker and the defender has forced the activity in cyberspace to be basically a game against the defender. MTD (Moving Target Defense) technology is an active defense concept that can transform such a cyber paradigm [4].

© Springer Nature Switzerland AG 2019
B. B. Kang and J. Jang (Eds.): WISA 2018, LNCS 11402, pp. 81–92, 2019.
https://doi.org/10.1007/978-3-030-17982-3_7

MTD technology minimizes information and vulnerability exposure of the target system by dynamically changing the main attributes of the objects to be protected, such as network, platform, software, and data, over time. Suppose an attacker has successfully collected information related to the target system at a particular point in time. However, at the time of the attack, the target system transitions to another state, which making the information collected by the attacker meaningless. MTD technology that changes network attributes increases the complexity of attacker's reconnaissance activities and ultimately blocks attacking activities. In order for the attacker's attack to be finally executed, the data collection and vulnerability analysis for the target system should be sufficiently preceded. Attackers will collect information about the target system in a variety of passive and active ways, such as eavesdropping data flowing in the middle of the network or passing specific data to the target system to analyze its response. Attackers are known to spend considerable time and effort in these reconnaissance activities. The MTD technology for mutating attributes does not block the attacker's reconnaissance activity, but makes it difficult to analyze the collected data and makes the use of the collected data meaningless.

1.2   Related Works

MTD techniques can be classified with the type of attributes to be mutated. In this paper, I consider MTD technique to mutate network attributes. Various techniques for varying network attributes have been proposed [5]. Similar to the NAT (Network Address Translation) concept, the techniques that dynamically convert the IP of each host between communicating hosts can effectively hide the actual IP of the host outside the network. On the other hand, DESIR (Decoy-enhanced seamless IP randomization) [6] constructs a virtual network by adding a number of decoy servers that use the same address range as the real servers, in order to reduce the attacker's network scan efficiency and cause analysis confusion. The changed IP address information of the real server is sent to a separate authentication server. Clients that want to access the real server request the IP address of the real server to the authentication server. That is, the IP address information of the authentication server cannot be changed. Therefore, if an attacker disables the authentication server, there is a risk that the use of the entire network may be restricted. Random Port and Address Hopping (RPAH) scheme [7] creates virtual IP address (*vIP*) and virtual port address (*vPort*) very dynamically using a random value generation function that uses the current time, host ID, and service ID as input values, assuming that all servers and clients share the secret key in advance and are synchronized with each other. The actual address information (*rIP*, *rPort*) is not changed and packets are transmitted using the virtual address. In order to request a new connection to a specific server, the RPAH scheme also obtains the changed address information of the server to access through the DNS server or the authentication server. That is, there is a vulnerability that cannot change the address information of the DNS server or the authentication server like the DESIR technique.

1.3 Tactical Wireless Networks

Tactical wireless networks are characterized by wireless transmission that radio waves can be transmitted to unintended unauthorized nodes. Therefore, the attacker's reconnaissance activity is relatively easy compared to a wired network. On the other hand, the tactical wireless network repeats network configuration and withdrawal depending on its mission and purpose. That is, it is an ad hoc network in which there is no network infrastructure because it is temporarily operated in a certain area for a certain period of time. In general, the communication nodes can share necessary information among the network members before deploying in the operation area. The network is generally layered structure and has a leader node to take account of the efficiency of military missions. However, since the limited radio resources are shared by the members, the network transmission capacity is limited. Therefore, we need MTD technology considering characteristics of tactical wireless network which is distinctly different from wired based commercial network.

In this paper, I propose an IP address mutation scheme that can change the IP address of all communication entities in the same network through common information that is calculated based on received data from the leader node. If the IP address of a particular node changes, the new IP address should be informed to the network members. The DESIR and the RPAH are schemes for individually transmitting the changed IP address information of the node to the necessary members through the third communication entity (DNS server, authentication server, etc.). Therefore, it is not possible to change the address of an entity that is capable of delivering a changed IP address. The existence of an object that cannot change IP address can be critical security vulnerability because it can cause a critical failure of the network operation by a cyber-attack. In the proposed scheme, the changed IP address information is not explicitly transmitted and is shared with the network members by calculating individually. Moreover, the changed IP address information is implicitly transmitted to the members belonging to other networks groups through a layered network structure. Therefore, a third party entity for notifying the changed IP address information is unnecessary. That is, there is an advantage that the IP address information of all communication entities can be changed unlike existing schemes.

This paper is composed as follows. The system model and the threat model are described in Sect. 2. We explain the specific IP mutation procedure of the proposed scheme in Sect. 3 and analyze the performance in Sect. 4. Finally, we conclude in Sect. 5.

2 System and Threat Model

The structure of the layered wireless tactical network considered in this paper is shown in Fig. 1. A network is composed of multiple layers, and each network uses different frequencies. There are many member nodes in each hierarchical network, one of which is a leader node. A leader node of a certain layer may be a member node of an upper layer. For example, Fig. 1, the node h is the leader node of the network A of the layer 1 and the member node of the network C of the layer 2.

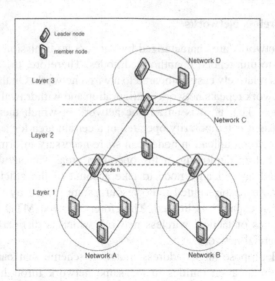

Fig. 1. Tactical wireless network structure

The leader node transmits the data of the upper layer to the lower layer and the data of the lower layer to the upper layer when necessary. To perform this role, the leader node has two IP addresses. The leader node transmits the basic data for the IP mutation to the network members. On the other hand, all nodes have a fixed IP address, *rIP*, which does not change, and a virtual IP address, *vIP*, which changes periodically. An attacker located within the wireless transmission range can obtain information about the frequency used in the network through frequency scanning. Therefore, it is possible to receive data that is transmitted by the legitimate nodes. However, the attacker does not know the IP address information used by the legitimate nodes and uses an arbitrary IP address to access the target system.

3 Address Mutation Scheme Using Projection Matrix

In this section, the projection matrix that is the rationale of the proposed scheme, the address mutation procedures, and data flow between the internal and external network members, are described. Table 1 shows the notation used in this paper.

3.1 Projection Matrix

The proposed scheme basically transforms the IP address by projecting the IP address vector used for each network into an arbitrary vector. When the number of network members is n, the vector $\bar{r}$ and vector $\bar{c}$ are expressed as follows

$$\bar{r} = [\text{rIP}_1, \text{rIP}_2, \cdots \text{rIP}_n] \tag{1}$$

$$\bar{c} = [cIP_1, cIP_2, \cdots cIP_n] \tag{2}$$

The projection matrix for projecting the vector $\bar{r}$ to a vector $\bar{c}$ is as follows

$$P = \frac{c \cdot c^T}{c^T \cdot c} \tag{3}$$

On the other hand, $\bar{t} = P \cdot \bar{r}$ is the result of projecting the vector $\bar{r}$ to a vector $\bar{c}$.

Table 1. Notation

rIP_i	Fixed IP address for i^{th} node
vIP_i	Mutation IP address for i^{th} node
cIP_i	i^{th} value in reference information vector transmitted by a leader node
uIP_i	i^{th} value in available IP address to be assigned
$\bar{r}, \bar{v}, \bar{c}$	Vectors with elements of rIP_i, vIP_i and cIP_i
U, V	Sets with elements of uIP_i and vIP_i

3.2 Address Mutation Procedure

The IP address is periodically mutated based on the reference information vector $\bar{c}$ that is transmitted by the leader node. The period in which the leader node transmits the reference information is a system parameter that can vary according to network threat and security requirements.

The leader node constructs a reference information vector $\bar{c}$ by selecting n values randomly within the available address range that do not overlap with each other, and transmits it to the member nodes. Member nodes generate vector $\bar{t}$ by projecting vector $\bar{r}$ to vector $\bar{c}$. By the way, it can be possible that an element of the vector $\bar{t}$ is not be an element of the set of available addresses, U. Therefore, it is necessary to map the element of the vector $\bar{t}$ to the element of the set U. In the proposed scheme, the elements of the vector $\bar{t}$ are compared with the elements of U, and the vector $\bar{q}$ is obtained by mapping the elements of U with the smallest value difference. Since the vector $\bar{q}$ is derived from the vector projected into the vector $\bar{c}$, the correlation between the vector $\bar{q}$ and the vector $\bar{c}$ is very high. Moreover, vector $\bar{c}$ is transmitted in wireless environments and is likely to be exposed to attackers. Therefore, if the correlation between two vectors is high, the possibility of estimating the vector $\bar{q}$ from the vector $\bar{c}$ is also high. In order to solve this vulnerability, the proposed scheme rearranges the element position of the vector $\bar{q}$ in a way that is defined beforehand among member nodes, and finally obtains the mutation address vector, $\bar{v}$. This can greatly reduce the correlation between the two vectors.

These processes are performed independently in each hierarchical network, and the leader node mutually shares the result of address change. Also, each node shares the mutated IP address of the member nodes receiving the same reference information vector. Algorithm 1 shows the IP address change procedure of the proposed scheme.

Algorithm 1 address mutation algorithm of the proposed scheme, which is conducted in a fully distributed manner by all network members.

$\bar{t} = P \cdot \bar{r}$

for i = 1 to n

$\qquad q_i = \underset{uIP_j \in U}{\operatorname{argmin}} (t_i - uIP_j)^2$

$\qquad q_i = \operatorname{argmin} (t_i - uIP_j)^2$

end for

$\bar{v} = rearrange(\bar{q})$

3.3 Data Transmission to Internal Network Members

As described in Sect. 3.2, nodes know the mutated address information of member nodes in the same network. When node *i* transmits data to node *j* in the same network, the source IP is set to *vIP$_i$* and the destination IP is set to *vIP$_j$*. That is, instead of using a fixed IP address for data transmission, only the mutated IP address is used. Moreover, the IP address used for data transmission is periodically mutated. Therefore the effect of the scanning attack can be reduced.

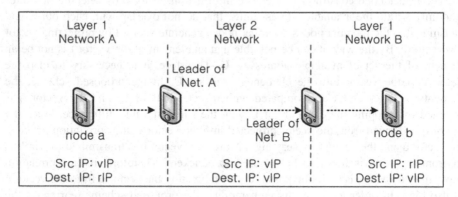

Fig. 2. Source and destination IP address in external communication

3.4 Data Transmission to External Network Members

Figure 2 shows the type of source and destination IP address when transmitting data to external network members in the proposed scheme. At the time of data transmission, the source IP is set to *vIP* and converted to *rIP* by the leader node of the destination. On the other hand, the destination IP is set to *rIP* and converted to the *vIP* by the leader node of the source network. *rIP* is used only for the network of the sender and receiver, and not for the intermediate network.

In order to transmit data to the external network, frequency conversion must be performed via the leader node because different frequencies are used for each network. The leader node discards the packet if the source address of the received data is not an element of the vector $\bar{v}$. Therefore, the attacker must acquire the *vIP* of the internal member first in order to scan the external member node. However, since the IP address information of the internal member is not only mutated but also the address of the external member node is periodically mutated, the effect of the scanning attack on the external member node is reduced. Table 2 show parameters and its values for performance analysis.

Table 2. Parameters and its value for performance analysis

T	Mutation period
S	Scanning attack trial rate
M	Address mutation rate
$n(U)$	Number of available addresses, 200
$n(V)$	Number of nodes in a network, 1–100
$R (= S \times T)$	Number of scanning attack during time T, 1–50

4 Performance Analysis

To analyze the performance of the proposed scheme, I define the address leakage probability, P_L which is the ratio the number of addresses assigned to a network member to the number of addresses leaked by the scanning attack within time T. For ease of analysis, it is assumed that $n(U)$ and $n(V)$ are the same, and P_L for the internal scanning attack and the external scanning attack are respectively examined.

I analyze the overhead caused by the proposed scheme and investigate the correlation between the reference information vector that is transmitted by the leader node and the mutation address vector that is calculated by each member. And I discuss the advantages of the proposed scheme.

4.1 Leakage Probability by Internal Scanning Attack

In the proposed scheme, the address is mutated every time T. It means that the mutation address is valid only for time T. The random variable X represents the number of addresses leaked by the scanning attack during time T. The mutation rate per unit time is $1/T$. If the scan rate per unit time is S, then the number of scanning attacks during time T, R, can be expressed as the product of S and T. Assuming that the attacker knows the information about the address range assigned to the specific network, the probability that the attacker obtains more than one address information during time T is as follows

$$P(X > 0) = 1 - \prod_{i=0}^{R-1} \left(1 - \frac{n(V)}{n(U) - i}\right), \quad n(U) \geq n, R. \tag{4}$$

If the attacker does not know the information about U (that is, there is no information about the address range), the probability of obtaining address information by the scanning attack sharply decreases. This is because the value of $n(U)$ becomes very large. On the other hand, the expected value of the random variable X is calculated as follows

$$E(X) = \sum_{i=1}^{n(V)} i \times P(X = i). \tag{5}$$

The attacker will not scan more than twice for the same IP address during time T. Therefore, scanning addresses is a sampling without replacement problem. In the viewpoint of a specific node, the probability of leakage by internal attack, $P_L^{(I)}$, is the value of $E(X)$ divided by $n(V)$ in Eq. (5).

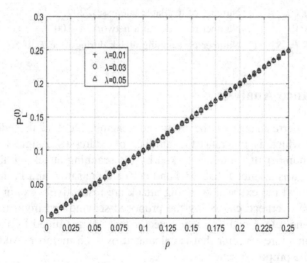

Fig. 3. Address leakage probability according to λ and ρ in internal scanning attack

Figure 3 represents $P_L^{(I)}$ with the variation of ρ and λ. ρ is the ratio of the number of available addresses ($n(U)$) to the number of scanning attacks (R) during time T, and λ is the ratio of the number of available addresses ($n(U)$) to the number of assigned addresses ($n(V)$). Intuitively, as R increases, the number of leaked addresses increases, and as $n(U)$ increases, the number of leaked addresses decreases because more addresses need to be scanned. Therefore, as shown in Fig. 3, $P_L^{(I)}$ increases as ρ increases. However, there is no influence by λ. It is a natural result because the number of assigned IP in a network is not related to the leakage probability in the viewpoint of a specific node.

4.2   Leakage Probability by External Scanning Attack

In order to attempt a scanning attack on the external network, the address information of the internal member node should be acquired first. Therefore, it is assumed that the attacker attempts to scan the external member node after the scanning attack on the internal network is successful. Figure 4 represents the probability of leakage by an external scanning attack, $P_L^{(E)}$, with the variation of ρ and λ.

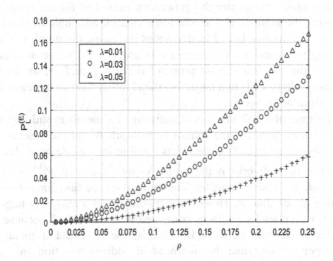

Fig. 4. Address leakage probability according to λ and ρ in external scanning attack

As shown in the Fig. 4, as ρ increases, $P_L^{(E)}$ increases because attacker makes more attack attempts. However, contrary to the internal scanning attack, the probability of leakage increases as λ increases. Large λ means that there are many addresses assigned to the network. Note that a specific IP address in the internal network is not required for the external scanning attack. Any assigned IP address can be used for the external scanning attack. Therefore, an attacker's internal scanning attack can be terminated earlier as the λ is larger, and more attempts can be made for an external scanning attack. For this reason, as shown in Fig. 4, $P_L^{(E)}$ increases as λ increases. On the other hand, Figs. 3 and 4 show that $P_L^{(E)}$ is always smaller than $P_L^{(I)}$ when ρ and λ are the same. This is a natural result because an external scanning attack is possible after an internal scanning attack succeeds.

The performance analysis results show that increasing $n(U)$ or shortening time T can mitigate the effect of an attacker's internal and external scanning attacks. Since the address information is mutated after time T, even if the address information is leaked, the leaked address information can be utilized only by the attacker for a maximum time T. That is, since the attacker must repeatedly attempt to scan at every time T, it is possible to effectively respond to the scanning attack by using the address mutation scheme.

4.3   Overhead Analysis

The proposed scheme incurs the overhead that the leader node periodically transmits the reference information vector. Therefore, the overhead depends on the size of the reference information vector, the generation period, and the number of leader nodes. The size of the reference information vector increases in proportion to the number of network members, but the number of transmissions does not increase because only the leader node transmits the reference information vector.

On the other hand, the shorter the generation period of the reference information vector is, the more the number of transmission increases, although the size of the vector does not change. As the number of leader nodes increases, the number of messages to be shared among the leader nodes increases. In order to exchange data, an additional overhead due to the communication protocol occurs. Therefore, an increase in the number of transmissions leads to a larger overhead rather than an increase in the size of the reference information vector.

Consider the case of m sub-networks consisting of n members and $2m$ sub-networks consisting of $n/2$ members. Let the former be network A and the latter be network B. The number of members in both networks is equal to $n \times m$. Assume that the address range available to the networks is the same. As we have seen, $P_L^{(E)}$ is smaller as the number of network members is smaller. Therefore, it can be said that network B is safer against scanning attack than A. However, network B has a relatively large number of transmissions between leader nodes as compared with network A because the number of leader nodes is large in network B. That is, the overhead is greatly increased. Therefore, the performance and the overhead of address mutation are in a trade-off relationship and should be appropriately selected in consideration of network size, security threat, and security demand level.

4.4   Similarity Analysis Between Vectors

The reference information vector $\bar{c}$ is transmitted periodically in wireless environment by the leader node. Therefore, if the reference information vector is not encrypted, it can be easily obtainable by an attacker. If an attacker can easily infer mutation address vector $\bar{v}$ from vector $\bar{c}$, it could be a serious security threat. The proposed scheme obtains the vector $\bar{t}$ by projecting the fixed address vector $\bar{r}$ to the reference information vector $\bar{c}$. Then, the vector $\bar{q}$ is obtained by mapping the elements of the vector $\bar{t}$ to the available addresses, the element positions of the vector $\bar{q}$ are rearranged, and finally the mutation address vector $\bar{v}$ is obtained.

The Pearson correlation coefficient was calculated to measure the similarity between these vectors. The Pearson correlation coefficient has a range of -1 to 1, 1 if the two vectors are the same, 0 if they are completely different, and -1 if they are the opposite. Table 3 shows the average of the absolute value of the correlation coefficient between $\bar{c}$ and $\bar{t}$, $\bar{v}$, $\bar{q}$.

Since the vector $\bar{t}$ is the result of projecting the vector $\bar{r}$ onto the vector $\bar{c}$, the correlation coefficient with the vector $\bar{c}$ is always 1. The correlation coefficient between vector $\bar{q}$ that is the result of mapping vector $\bar{t}$ to an available address, is somewhat lower than 1, but its influence is almost negligible, and the degree of lowering of the correlation coefficient depends on the distribution of available addresses. On the other hand, the correlation coefficient between vector $\bar{c}$ and vector $\bar{v}$, which rearranged the positions of the elements irregularly, was significantly lowered to 0.3 or less. That is, it is not easy to predict the vector $\bar{v}$ even if the attacker obtains the vector $\bar{c}$. Also, since a vector $\bar{c}$ is newly generated every time T, it is difficult for an attacker to obtain a meaningful vector $\bar{v}$.

Table 3. Average absolute Pearson correlation coefficients between vectors

Vectors	$\bar{c}, \bar{t}$	$\bar{c}, \bar{q}$	$\bar{c}, \bar{v}$
Correlation coefficient	1	0.998	0.2744

4.5   Advantage of the Proposed Scheme

The proposed scheme has two advantages over the existing scheme. First, the addresses of all communication entities required for data transmission are mutated. In the case of the existing research [5, 6, 8], the address of the DNS or the authentication server for processing the query of the communication opponent's mutated address information is not changed. Communication entities that perform this function become the weakest part of the address mutation network. If an attacker can exploit the vulnerability of this communication entity, the entire network operation is restricted. However, since the proposed scheme can easily share the mutation address information for internal member nodes and the mutation address information of the external member nodes is distributed and managed by the leader nodes, the problem of single point of failure can be mitigated.

Second, the address of the internal node is needed to scan the external member nodes. If the source address is not the address of the internal node, the leader node does not forward the data to the outside. In other words, the defense against scanning attacks is multi-stepped, and the success probability of a scanning attack is greatly reduced.

5   Conclusion

In this paper, I proposed an address mutation scheme using a projection matrix in a tactical wireless network, in which it has a hierarchical structure. A node can acquire mutated address information for all the network members at once including the leader node by projecting the address information vector to the reference information vector that is transmitted by the leader node. Unlike the existing scheme, address information of all communication entities directly involved in data transmission is mutated. Each node can effectively respond to an attacker's internal and external scanning attacks by using mutated address information. Even if the address information used by the attacker's scanning attack is leaked, the address information is periodically mutated, so that the leaked information becomes meaningful information for the attacker only for a certain period of time.

As a result of analyzing the leakage probability and overhead of the proposed scheme, it was confirmed that the larger the available address range and the smaller the address to be assigned, the better the performance. On the other hand, the overhead caused by the amount of reference information vector transmitted by the leader node, and the number of network members and leader nodes is the tradeoff relationship with the performance on the proposed scheme. Therefore, the network should be designed with the consideration these factors.

References

1. Beraud, P., Cruz, A., Hassell, S., Meadows, S.: Using cyber maneuver to improve network resiliency. In: 2011 - MILCOM 2011 Military Communications Conference, Baltimore, MD, pp. 1121–1126 (2011)
2. Carroll, T.E., Crouse, M., Fulp, E.W., Berenhaut, K.S.: Analysis of network address shuffling as a moving target defense. In: 2014 IEEE International Conference on Communications (ICC), Sydney, NSW, pp. 701–706 (2014)
3. Wang, S., Zhang, L., Tang, C.: A new dynamic address solution for moving target defense. In: 2016 IEEE Information Technology, Networking, Electronic and Automation Control Conference, Chongqing, pp. 1149–1152 (2016)
4. Tang, H., Sun, Q.T., Yang, X., Long, K.: A network coding and DES based dynamic encryption scheme for moving target defense. IEEE Access 6, 26059–26068 (2018)
5. Cai, G.-L., Wang, B.-S., Hu, W., Wang, T.-Z.: Moving target defense: state of the art and characteristics. Front. Inf. Technol. Electron. Eng. 17(3), 1122–1153 (2016)
6. Sun, J., Sun, K.: DESIR: Decoy-enhanced seamless IP randomization. In: IEEE INFOCOM 2016 - The 35th Annual IEEE International Conference on Computer Communications, San Francisco, CA, pp. 1–9 (2016)
7. Luo, Y.B., Wang, B.S., Wang, X.F., Hu, X.F., Cai, G.L., Sun, H.: RPAH: random port and address hopping for thwarting internal and external adversaries. In: 2015 IEEE Trustcom/BigDataSE/ISPA, Helsinki, pp. 263–270 (2015)
8. Wu, J.: Meaning and vision of mimic computing and mimic security defense. Telecommun. Sci. 30(7), 17 (2014)
9. Jafarian, J.H., Al-Shaer, E., Duan, Q.: An effective address mutation approach for disrupting reconnaissance attacks. IEEE Trans. Inf. Forensics Secur. 10(12), 2562–2577 (2015)

Parallel Implementations of CHAM

Hwajeong Seo[1], Kyuhwang An[1], Hyeokdong Kwon[1], Taehwan Park[2],
Zhi Hu[3], and Howon Kim[2(✉)]

[1] Hansung University, Seoul, Republic of Korea
hwajeong84@gmail.com, tigerk9212@gmail.com, hdgwon@naver.com
[2] Pusan National University, Busan, Republic of Korea
pth5804@gmail.com, howonkim@gmail.com
[3] Central South University, Changsha, China
huzhi_math@csu.edu.cn

Abstract. In this paper, we presented novel parallel implementations of CHAM-64/128 block cipher on modern ARM-NEON processors. In order to accelerate the performance of the implementation of CHAM-64/128 block cipher, the full specifications of ARM-NEON processors are utilized in terms of instruction set and multiple cores. First, the SIMD feature of ARM processor is fully utilized. The modern ARM processor provides 2×16-bit vectorized instruction. By using the instruction sets and full register files, total 4 CHAM-64/128 encryptions are performed at once in data parallel way. Second, the dedicated SIMD instruction sets, namely NEON engine, is fully exploited. The NEON engine supports 8×16-bit vectorized instruction over 128-bit Q registers. The 24 CHAM-64/128 encryptions are performed at once in data parallel way. Third, both ARM and NEON instruction sets are well re-ordered in interleaved way. This mixed approach hides the pipeline stalls between each instruction set. Fourth, the multiple cores are exploited to maximize the performance in thread level. Finally, we achieved the 4.2 cycles/byte for implementation of CHAM-64/128 on ARM-NEON processors. This result is competitive to the parallel implementation of LEA-128/128 and HIGHT-64/128 on same processor.

Keywords: CHAM · ARM-NEON processor · Parallel computation · Software implementation

1 Introduction

Modern processors support Single Instruction Multiple Data (SIMD) instruction sets, including SSE/AVX for INTEL and NEON for ARM, respectively. Since the SIMD instruction sets can issue multiple tasks in single instruction, traditional Single Instruction Single Data (SISD) based implementations can be accelerated by using SIMD instruction sets. Recently, many block cipher implementations, including LEA, HIGHT, SIMON, and SPECK, were re-programmed in SIMD instruction sets and achieved much higher performance than previous classical works [13,14,16]. Furthermore, the modern processors support multiple

© Springer Nature Switzerland AG 2019
B. B. Kang and J. Jang (Eds.): WISA 2018, LNCS 11402, pp. 93–104, 2019.
https://doi.org/10.1007/978-3-030-17982-3_8

cores/threads and each core/thread performs the task in parallel way. The most well-known multiple core framework is OpenMP and many works also evaluated the maximum performance of block cipher implementations by using OpenMP library, including LEA and HIGHT [15,21]. In this paper, we exploit a parallel computing power into the novel lightweight block cipher, CHAM, which was released at ICISC'17 by NSR [10]. The CHAM block cipher can be efficiently implemented in both platforms ranging from low-end embedded microprocessors to high-end personal computers. Contrary to previous implementations of CHAM block cipher, which mainly focused on serial computations on embedded processors, this paper introduces the feasibility of parallel implementation of CHAM on modern ARM-NEON processors. To improve the performance, we fully exploit the SIMD architectures with novel techniques. It is also worth to note that all the proposed methods are not limited to CHAM implementation but this can be applied to the other cryptography implementations with simple modifications.

The remainder of this paper is organized as follows. In Sect. 2, the basic specifications of CHAM block cipher and target ARM-NEON platform are described. In Sect. 3, the compact parallel implementations of CHAM block cipher on ARM-NEON platform are described. In Sect. 4, the performance of proposed methods in terms of execution timing is evaluated. Finally, Sect. 5 concludes the paper.

2 Related Works

2.1 CHAM Block Cipher

Lightweight cryptography is a fundamental technology to reduce the hardware chip size and accelerate the execution time for the Internet of Things (IoT) devices. Recently, a number of block ciphers have been designed for being lightweight features. The approaches are largely divided into two approaches, including Substitute Permutation Network (SPN) and Addition-Rotation-XOR (ARX). For the SPN architecture, PRESENT and GIFT block ciphers received the attention. The SPN block ciphers utilize the simple 4-bit S-BOX and permutation to achieve the high security as well [1,5]. For the ARX architecture, HIGHT, LEA, SPECK, SIMON, and CHAM block ciphers have been proposed. The ARX block cipher exploit the simple ARX operations [2,8–10].

In ICISC 2017, a family of lightweight block ciphers CHAM was announced by the Attached Institute of ETRI [10]. The family consists of three ciphers, including CHAM-64/128, CHAM-128/128, and CHAM-128/256. The CHAM block ciphers are of the generalized 4-branch Feistel structure based on ARX operations. The ARX operations ensure high performance on both software and hardware platforms and security against the timing attack. Particularly, the CHAM block cipher does not require updating a key state by using of $stateless-on-the-fly$ key schedule. With above nice features, the implementation of CHAM block ciphers achieved outstanding figures. In this paper, we targeted the most lightweight variant of CHAM, namely CHAM-64/128, for lightweight

Table 1. Instruction set summary for ARM

Mnemonics	Operands	Description	Cycles
ADD	Rd, Rr	Add without carry	1
EOR	Rd, Rr	Exclusive OR	1
ROL	Rd, Rr, #imm	Rotate left through carry	1
ROR	Rd, Rr, #imm	Rotate right through carry	1

Table 2. Instruction set summary for NEON

Mnemonics	Operands	Description	Cycles
VADD	Qd, Qn, Qm	Vector addition	1
VEOR	Qd, Qn, Qm	Vector exclusive-or	1
VSHL	Qd, Qm, #imm	Vector left shift	1
VSRI	Qd, Qm, #imm	Vector right shift with insert	2

implementations. However, this work is not limited to only CHAM-64/128, but the technique is also easily applied to other variants such as CHAM-128/128 and CHAM-128/256.

2.2   ARM-NEON Processor

Advanced RISC Machine (ARM) is an instruction set architecture (ISA) design by ARM for high-performance 32-bit embedded applications. Although ARM cores are usually larger and more complex than 8-bit AVR and 16-bit MSP processors, most ARM designs also have competitive features, in terms of low power consumptions, high-speed computations, and high code density. The ARM family has developed from the traditional ARM1 to advanced Cortex architectures in these days. They provide large number of pipeline stages and various caches, SIMD extensions and simple load/store architecture. Most instructions of the ARM are computed in a single cycle except memory access and some arithmetic instructions. In particular, the inline-barrel shifter instruction allows the shifted/rotated second operand without loss of clock cycles before the main operations. The load and store operations are performed in multiple data. Their 32-bit wise instructions mainly used for ARX architectures are described in Table 1.

NEON is a 128-bit SIMD architecture from the modern ARM Cortex-A series. One of the biggest difference between traditional ARM processors and new ARM-NEON processors is SIMD features. The NEON engine offers 128-bit wise registers and instructions. Each register is considered as a vector of elements of the same data type and this data type can be signed/unsigned 8-bit, 16-bit, 32-bit, or 64-bit. The detailed instructions for ARX operations are described in Table 2. This feature provides a more precise operation in various word sizes, which allows us to perform multiple data in single instruction, and the NEON engine can accelerate data processing by at least 3X that provided by ARMv5 and at least 2X that provided by ARMv6 SIMD instructions. This nice structure have accelerated the implementations by converting single instruction single data model to SIMD in previous works. In CHES 2012, NEON-based cryptography implementations including Salsa20, Poly1305, Curve25519, and Ed25519 were presented [4]. In order to enhance the performance, the authors provided novel bit-rotation, integration of multiplication, and reduction operations exploiting NEON instructions. In CT–RSA'13, ARM–NEON implementation of Grøstl shows that 40% performance enhancements than the previous fastest ARM implementation [7]. In HPEC 2013, a multiplicand reduction method for ARM-NEON was introduced for the NIST curves [6]. In CHES 2014, the Curve41417 implementation adopts 2-level Karatsuba multiplication in the redundant representation [3]. In ICISC 2014, Seo et al. introduced a novel 2-way Cascade Operand Scanning (COS) multiplication for RSA implementation [17,18]. In ICISC 2015, Seo et al. introduced a efficient modular multiplication and squaring operations for NIST P-521 curve [19]. Recently, Ring-LWE implementation is also accelerated by taking advantages of NEON instructions [11].

For the case of ARM implementations for ARX block ciphers, LEA block cipher implementations have been actively studied. First LEA implementation utilized the basic 32-bit ARM instruction set for high performance [8]. In [20], the parallel implementation of LEA was suggested, which utilized the SIMD instruction sets for high performance. In particular, the interdependency between each instruction set is optimized and multiple plaintexts and round keys are used in parallel way. In [15,21], the LEA block cipher is efficiently implemented in ARM and NEON instruction sets. Afterward, the compact ARM and NEON implementations are performed in interleaved way. This approach hides the latency of ARM computations into NEON computations and enhances the performance significantly. In [15], the auxiliary function is implemented with 4-bit wise LUT operation supported in NEON architecture (vtbl), which translates the auxiliary function into two 4-bit wise LUT operations. In [13,14], lightweight block ciphers, including SIMON and SPECK, are efficiently implemented over ARM-NEON processor. For the case of new lightweight CHAM block cipher, there are no ARM–NEON implementations. In this paper, we introduce a new implementation technique and new ARM–NEON results for CHAM block cipher.

3   Proposed Parallel Implementations of CHAM-64/128

In this section, we investigate the compact implementations of CHAM-64/128 on ARM–NEON processors. Particularly, we targeted the most lightweight variant of CHAM (i.e. CHAM-64/128) for lightweight implementations. However, this work is not limited to only CHAM-64/128, but the technique is also easily applied to other variants such as CHAM-128/128 and CHAM-128/256.

Table 3. 32-bit instructions over 32-bit ARM, where R1 and R0 represent destination and source registers

Addition	Exclusive-or	Right rotation by 31
ADD R1, R1, R0	EOR R1, R1, R0	ROR R1, #31

3.1 Parallel Implementation in ARM

CHAM-64/128 block cipher can be efficiently implemented on the 16-bit processor, because the platform provides 16-bit wise addition, bit-wise exclusive-or, and rotation operations, which are main 16-bit ARX operations for CHAM-64/128 block cipher. However, our target processor is 32-bit ARM processor and it is inefficient to implement the 16-bit wise operations in 32-bit ARM instructions described in Table 3, since the half of word is not utilized.

In order to optimize the 16-bit operations in 32-bit instruction sets, legacy ARM SIMD instruction set (UADD16 R1, R1, R0) is utilized. The instruction set divides the 32-bit registers into lower 16-bit and higher 16-bit and performs 2 16-bit addition in parallel way (like 2-way SIMD). Since the bit-wise exclusive-or does not generate the carry bits, the ARM instruction set is directly used without modification. The CHAM-64/128 block cipher requires 16-bit wise left rotation by 1-bit and 8-bit offsets. In order to establish the 2-way 16-bit wise rotation, the new rotation techniques are exploited. In Algorithm 1, the descriptions of left rotation by 1-bit for 2 16-bit variables are given. Unlike 32-bit wise rotation, ARM processor does not support 16-bit wise computations. For this reason, two mask variables (0x0101 and 0xFEFE) are set. Both mask variables are used to separate the 32-bit rotated input data into overflow bits and original bits. Afterward, both bits are integrated into one, which generates the rotated outputs. In Algorithm 2, the descriptions of left rotation by 8-bit for 2 16-bit variables are given. Similarly, one mask variable (0x0F0F) is used to handle the bits.

Algorithm 1. Left rotation by 1-bit for 2 16-bit variables

Input: input data (R1), mask values (0x0101: R2, 0xFEFE: R3), temporal
    variable (R4)
Output: output data (R0)
1: ROR R0, R1, #31
2: AND R4, R0, R2
3: AND R0, R0, R3
4: ADD R0, R0, R4, ROR#16

For the data load, only 32-bit wise access is available in 32-bit ARM processor. However, the word size of CHAM-64/128 is 16-bit and SIMD instruction requires 16-bit wise alignments. For this reason, all input data should be finely

Algorithm 2. Left rotation by 8-bit for 2 16-bit variables

Input: input data (R1), mask values (0x0F0F: R2), temporal variable (R3)
Output: output data (R0)
1: AND R3, R1, R2
2: ROR R1, R1, #8
3: AND R1, R1, R2
4: ADD R1, R1, R3, ROR#24

---

aligned before performing the parallel computations. The detailed descriptions are given in Algorithm 3. In Algorithm 3, 4 plaintexts are transposed in parallel way. In Step 1 and 3, lower 16-bit plaintexts are extracted[1]. In Step 2 and 4, the lower 16-bit part of other plaintexts are added to the extracted plaintext. In Step 5–10, the higher 16-bit plaintexts are extracted and combined. Similarly in Step 11–20, the remaining plaintexts are transposed. After the encryption, transposed data sets are re-ordered to the original format.

For the register level optimization, we assigned 8 registers for plaintext, 3 registers for mask variables, 2 register for temporal storage, and 1 register for memory pointer in encryption. The round keys are stored in the stack and the variables are directly accessed through the stack pointer. This is available since the round key size is very short for CHAM block ciphers.

3.2   Parallel Implementation in NEON

The basic 16-bit wise ARX operations of CHAM-64/128 block cipher are established with NEON instructions (See Table 4) and 24 encryptions are performed at once. This implementation assumes that all encryption shares same round key pair. For this reason, only one round key is loaded and duplicated from ARM register to the NEON registers, which reduces the number of memory access to load the round key pairs. Similar to the ARM SIMD approach, input data should be re-ordered to meet the SIMD friendly data format. The transpose operation is performed with 12 NEON transpose instruction sets. The detailed descriptions are given in Algorithm 4. In each 128-bit Q register, 2 64-bit plaintexts are stored. In order to align the data into 16-bit wise, two different transpose operations are required. First the operands are transposed by 16-bit wise. Afterward, the data is transposed again by 32-bit wise and this outputs the finely 16-bit aligned results. For the register level optimization, we assigned 12 registers for plaintext and 4 registers for temporal storage. This ensures 24 CHAM-64/128 encryptions at once.

3.3   Interleaved Implementation

ARM processor and NEON engine are independent processing units, which means that they can issue the computations independently. This parallel feature can be utilized to improve the performance by hiding the latency of ARM

---

[1] UXTH instruction only extracts lower 16-bit from 32-bit register.

Algorithm 3. Transpose operation for 4 plaintext in parallel way

---

Input: input data (R5--R12)
Output: output data (R2--R9)
 1: UXTH R2, R5
 2: ADD R2, R2, R7, LSL#16

 3: UXTH R3, R9
 4: ADD R3, R3, R11, LSL#16

 5: LSR R4, R5, #16
 6: ROR R7, R7, #16
 7: ADD R4, R4, R7, LSL#16

 8: LSR R5, R9, #16
 9: ROR R11, R11, #16
10: ADD R5, R5, R11, LSL#16

11: UXTH R7, R6
12: LSR R9, R6, #16
13: ADD R6, R7, R8, LSL#16

14: UXTH R7, R10
15: LSR R11, R10, #16
16: ADD R7, R7, R12, LSL#16

17: ROR R8, R8, #16
18: ADD R8, R9, R8, LSL#16

19: ROR R12, R12, #16
20: ADD R9, R11, R12, LSL#16

Table 4. 16-bit instructions over 128-bit ARM-NEON, where Q1 and Q0 represent destination and source registers

Addition	Exclusive-or	Right rotation by 9
VADD.I16 Q1, Q1, Q0	VEOR Q1, Q1, Q0	VSHL.I16 Q1, Q0, #9
		VSRI.16 Q1, Q0, #7

operations into that of NEON [15]. In sequential order, the processing time is exactly the sum of ARM and NEON execution timing while parallel order hides the ARM timing into NEON timing. The interleaved CHAM-64/128 encryption is performed as follows.

$$\text{Load} \rightarrow \text{Transpose} \rightarrow \text{Encryption} \rightarrow \text{Transpose} \rightarrow \text{Store}$$

Throughout the execution, Transpose and Encryption routines are performed in interleaved way. Only, LOAD and STORE routines are sequentially per-

---

Algorithm 4. Transpose operation for 24 plaintext in parallel way

---

Input: input data (Q0--Q11)
Output: output data (Q0--Q11)
 1: VTRN.16 Q0, Q1
 2: VTRN.16 Q2, Q3
 3: VTRN.16 Q4, Q5
 4: VTRN.16 Q6, Q7
 5: VTRN.16 Q8, Q9
 6: VTRN.16 Q10, Q11

 7: VTRN.32 Q0, Q2
 8: VTRN.32 Q1, Q3
 9: VTRN.32 Q4, Q6
10: VTRN.32 Q5, Q7
11: VTRN.32 Q8, Q10
12: VTRN.32 Q9, Q11

---

formed since it has inter-dependency between ARM and NEON instruction sets. In the interleaved CHAM implementation, 24 CHAM encryptions in NEON engine and 4 CHAM encryption are performed within optimized execution timing. This approach significantly reduces the computation timing for ARM processor and enhances the performance.

3.4   Multiple Thread Utilization

Recent ARM-NEON processors have multiple cores and each core can perform independent work loads in parallel way. In order to exploit the full specifications of multiple processing, SIMT programming library, namely OpenMP, is a good candidate. The target device has four physical cores, which can lead to theoretically 4 times of performance improvements. The basic implementations are parallelized using OpenMP library. The detailed program codes are

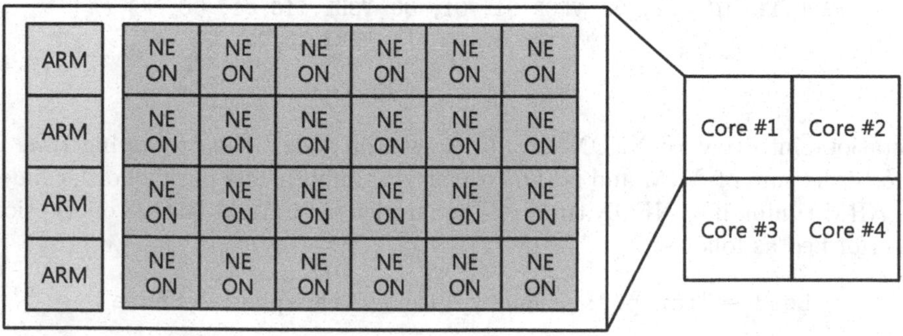

Fig. 1. Detailed architectures of parallel CHAM-64/128 encryptions in multiple cores

Table 5. Parallel implementation of CHAM-64/128 in OpenMP

```
#pragma omp parallel private(id) shared(PLAINTEXT)
    #pragma omp for
        for(id=0;id<TOTAL;id++)
            CHAM-64/128_Encryption(ROUNDKEY,PLAINTEXT[id]);
```

described in Table 5. The id variables are critical data and defined as `private`. The `PLAINTEXT` is defined as `shared` variables. The `PLAINTEXT` is indexed by id variables, which ensures that each thread accesses to different data. Since we assigned each encryption operation into single thread, the four different CHAM-64/128 encryption routines are performed in four different cores. As we can see in Fig. 1, 4 encryption (ARM) and 24 encryptions (NEON) in each core are performed, simultaneously. Total 112 (28×4) parallel encryptions are performed at once in 4 different cores.

4 Evaluation

To evaluate the performance of the CHAM-64/128 block cipher on the ARM–NEON processor, we used a Raspberry Pi 3 Model B (Cortex–A53 quad-core processor). For the ARM-NEON processor, we measured the execution time in both single-core and multiple-core cases. The performance is measured in system time function.

The comparison results are drawn in Table 6. The previous CHAM-64/128 implementation on ARM instruction sets achieved the 134 cycle/byte [10]. Since the work does not utilize the NEON instruction set and target processor is the low-end processor, the low performance is achieved. Unlike previous works, we utilized the ARM SIMD instruction sets and tested over high-end processors. The ARM SIMD based implementation utilizes four CHAM-64/128 encryptions at once and it enhances the performance by 65% for ARM platform. To the best of my knowledge, this is the first parallel implementation of CHAM-64/128 block cipher. For this reason, we only report our results in Table 6. The NEON requires 13.9 clock cycles per byte for CHAM-64/128 implementations. This is 3.26× faster than ARM SIMD based implementation. The both ARM and NEON implementations are finely integrated together, which hides the latency for ARM instruction sets. The results show 4.3% performance enhancements.

The performance is accelerated again by exploiting the full multiple cores in the platforms. Since the target platform is quad-core architecture, it improves the performance by increasing the number of threads. Interestingly, the performance decreases when the number of threads is larger than the number of cores, because many number of threads requires a number of context-switching procedures and this causes performance bottleneck (See Fig. 2). Finally, fully parallelized CHAM-64/128 implementations achieved the 4.2 cycle/byte with 4

Table 6. Comparison of CHAM-64/128 encryptions on ARM/NEON architectures, c/b: cycle/byte, a: one way communication over Cortex-M3 processor.

Method	Speed (c/b)	Instruction
Koo et al. [10]	134[a]	ARM
Proposed method ver 1	45.6	ARM
Proposed method ver 2	13.9	NEON
Proposed method ver 3	13.3	ARM–NEON

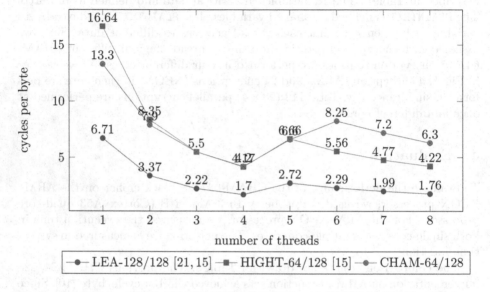

Fig. 2. Comparison of LEA-128/128, HIGHT-64/128, and CHAM-64/128 block ciphers results on ARM-NEON processors (Raspberry Pi 3) in terms of execution time (cycles per byte) depending on the number of threads

threads. This is not exactly four times faster than single core but this is the highest CHAM-64/128 performance reported ever. Compared with other lightweight block ciphers such as LEA-128/128 and HIGHT-64/128, the proposed CHAM-64/128 implementations show very competitive results.

5   Conclusion

In this paper, we presented new parallel implementation methods for CHAM-64/128 block cipher on representative SIMD platforms, namely ARM-NEON. We firstly optimized the both ARM and NEON implementations after then both methods are performed in interleaved way. The implementation results are further accelerated by taking advantages of multiple cores. Finally, we achieved performance enhancement up-to 13.3 cycle/byte with single core implementation, which is 90% faster than previous implementations on ARM processors.

By enabling the features of multiple cores, we achieved 4.2 cycle/byte which improved again the our single core results by 68.4%.

The proposed methods improved the CHAM-64/128 block cipher on ARM-NEON platforms. For this reason, there are many future works remained. First, we can directly improve the similar ARX block ciphers such as SPECK and SIMON. Recent works by [13,14] do not consider any techniques covered in this paper. For this reason, we expect high performance enhancements by using the proposed methods. Second, we only explore the ARM-NEON platform. However, INTEL and AMD processors also provide SIMD instructions such as AVX and SSE. Since the SIMD instructions are very similar to NEON instructions, this can be directly applied to the other SIMD instruction sets. Furthermore, these platforms support multiple cores and multiple threads. We can further explore the strong features of OpenMP on these platforms.

Acknowledgement. This work was partly supported by the National Research Foundation of Korea (NRF) grant funded by the Korea government (MSIT) (No. NRF-2017R1C1B5075742) and the MSIT (Ministry of Science and ICT), Korea, under the ITRC (Information Technology Research Center) support program (2014-1-00743) supervised by the IITP (Institute for Information & communications Technology Promotion). Zhi Hu was partially supported by the Natural Science Foundation of China (Grant No. 61602526).

References

1. Banik, S., Pandey, S.K., Peyrin, T., Sasaki, Y., Sim, S.M., Todo, Y.: GIFT: a small present. In: Fischer, W., Homma, N. (eds.) CHES 2017. LNCS, vol. 10529, pp. 321–345. Springer, Cham (2017). https://doi.org/10.1007/978-3-319-66787-4_16

2. Beaulieu, R., Treatman-Clark, S., Shors, D., Weeks, B., Smith, J., Wingers, L.: The SIMON and SPECK lightweight block ciphers. In: 2015 52nd ACM/EDAC/IEEE Design Automation Conference (DAC), pp. 1–6. IEEE (2015)

3. Bernstein, D.J., Chuengsatiansup, C., Lange, T., Schwabe, P.: Kummer strikes back: new DH speed records. In: Sarkar, P., Iwata, T. (eds.) ASIACRYPT 2014. LNCS, vol. 8873, pp. 317–337. Springer, Heidelberg (2014). https://doi.org/10.1007/978-3-662-45611-8_17

4. Bernstein, D.J., Schwabe, P.: NEON crypto. In: Prouff, E., Schaumont, P. (eds.) CHES 2012. LNCS, vol. 7428, pp. 320–339. Springer, Heidelberg (2012). https://doi.org/10.1007/978-3-642-33027-8_19

5. Bogdanov, A., et al.: PRESENT: an ultra-lightweight block cipher. In: Paillier, P., Verbauwhede, I. (eds.) CHES 2007. LNCS, vol. 4727, pp. 450–466. Springer, Heidelberg (2007). https://doi.org/10.1007/978-3-540-74735-2_31

6. Faz-Hernández, A., Longa, P., Sánchez, A.H.: Efficient and secure algorithms for GLV-based scalar multiplication and their implementation on GLV-GLS curves. In: Benaloh, J. (ed.) CT-RSA 2014. LNCS, vol. 8366, pp. 1–27. Springer, Cham (2014). https://doi.org/10.1007/978-3-319-04852-9_1

7. Holzer-Graf, S., et al.: Efficient vector implementations of AES-based designs: a case study and new implemenations for Grøstl. In: Dawson, E. (ed.) CT-RSA 2013. LNCS, vol. 7779, pp. 145–161. Springer, Heidelberg (2013). https://doi.org/10.1007/978-3-642-36095-4_10

8. Hong, D., Lee, J.-K., Kim, D.-C., Kwon, D., Ryu, K.H., Lee, D.-G.: LEA: a 128-bit block cipher for fast encryption on common processors. In: Kim, Y., Lee, H., Perrig, A. (eds.) WISA 2013. LNCS, vol. 8267, pp. 3–27. Springer, Cham (2014). https://doi.org/10.1007/978-3-319-05149-9_1

9. Hong, D., et al.: HIGHT: a new block cipher suitable for low-resource device. In: Goubin, L., Matsui, M. (eds.) CHES 2006. LNCS, vol. 4249, pp. 46–59. Springer, Heidelberg (2006). https://doi.org/10.1007/11894063_4

10. Koo, B., Roh, D., Kim, H., Jung, Y., Lee, D.-G., Kwon, D.: CHAM: a family of lightweight block ciphers for resource-constrained devices. In: International Conference on Information Security and Cryptology, ICISC 2017 (2017)

11. Liu, Z., Azarderakhsh, R., Kim, H., Seo, H.: Efficient software implementation of ring-LWE encryption on IoT processors. IEEE Trans. Comput. (2017)

12. Osvik, D.A., Bos, J.W., Stefan, D., Canright, D.: Fast software AES encryption. In: Hong, S., Iwata, T. (eds.) FSE 2010. LNCS, vol. 6147, pp. 75–93. Springer, Heidelberg (2010). https://doi.org/10.1007/978-3-642-13858-4_5

13. Park, T., Seo, H., Lee, G., Khandaker, M.A.-A., Nogami, Y., Kim, H.: Parallel implementations of SIMON and SPECK, revisited. In: Kang, B.B.H., Kim, T. (eds.) WISA 2017. LNCS, vol. 10763, pp. 283–294. Springer, Cham (2018). https://doi.org/10.1007/978-3-319-93563-8_24

14. Park, T., Seo, H., Kim, H.: Parallel implementations of SIMON and SPECK. In: 2016 International Conference on Platform Technology and Service (PlatCon), pp. 1–6. IEEE (2016)

15. Seo, H., Jeong, I., Lee, J., Kim, W.-H.: Compact implementations of ARX-based block ciphers on IoT processors. ACM Trans. Embed. Comput. Syst. (TECS) **17**(3), 60 (2018)

16. Seo, H., Kim, H.: Low-power encryption algorithm block cipher in JavaScript. J. Inform. Commun. Converg. Eng. **12**(4), 252–256 (2014)

17. Seo, H., Liu, Z., Großschädl, J., Choi, J., Kim, H.: Montgomery modular multiplication on ARM-NEON revisited. In: Lee, J., Kim, J. (eds.) ICISC 2014. LNCS, vol. 8949, pp. 328–342. Springer, Cham (2015). https://doi.org/10.1007/978-3-319-15943-0_20

18. Seo, H., Liu, Z., Großschädl, J., Kim, H.: Efficient arithmetic on ARM-NEON and its application for high-speed RSA implementation. Secur. Commun. Netw. **9**(18), 5401–5411 (2016)

19. Seo, H., et al.: Faster ECC over $\mathbb{F}_{2^{521}-1}$ (feat. NEON). In: Kwon, S., Yun, A. (eds.) ICISC 2015. LNCS, vol. 9558, pp. 169–181. Springer, Cham (2016). https://doi.org/10.1007/978-3-319-30840-1_11

20. Seo, H., et al.: Parallel implementations of LEA. In: Lee, H.-S., Han, D.-G. (eds.) ICISC 2013. LNCS, vol. 8565, pp. 256–274. Springer, Cham (2014). https://doi.org/10.1007/978-3-319-12160-4_16

21. Seo, H., et al.: Parallel implementations of LEA, revisited. In: Choi, D., Guilley, S. (eds.) WISA 2016. LNCS, vol. 10144, pp. 318–330. Springer, Cham (2017). https://doi.org/10.1007/978-3-319-56549-1_27

Logarithm Design on Encrypted Data
with Bitwise Operation

Joon Soo Yoo, Baek Kyung Song, and Ji Won Yoon[✉]

School of Information Security, Korea University, Seoul, South Korea
{sandiegojs,baekkyung777,jiwon_yoon}@korea.ac.kr

Abstract. Privacy-preserving big data analysis on cloud systems is becoming increasingly indispensable as the amount of information of the individuals is accumulated on our database system. As a way of maintaining security on cloud system, Homomorphic Encryption (HE) is considered to be theoretically eminent protecting against privacy leakage. However, insufficient number of operations on HE are developed, hindering many research developers to apply their knowledgeable techniques on this field. Therefore, we propose a novel approach in constructing logarithm function based on mathematical theorem of Taylor expansion with fundamental arithmetic operations and basic gate operations in usage. Moreover, we present a more accurate way of deriving answers for logarithm using square and shift method.

Keywords: Fully Homomorphic Encryption · Logarithm · TFHE · Cloud security

1 Introduction

There has been a significant increase in the demand defending one's privacy as the development of data mining techniques evolve rapidly in our current society. Needless to say, privacy issue has become one of the world's controversy that has to be overcome from any type of adversaries. In this response, many of the current researches such as differential privacy focuses on data mining while preserving privacy [1]. Although differential privacy has achieved remarkable results in respect to protecting original data against malicious data analyst, there still exist limitations in protecting against malignant server [2].

Homomorphic Encryption (HE) is one of the solutions that provide perfect security between the user and the server in the aid of profound mathematical background. This is due to the fact that HE performs operation with encrypted messages sent by the user and returns the outcome without obtaining any knowledge. However, with the perfect scheme that HE has, it struggles with time that takes to perform even basic operations such as addition, subtraction, multiplication and division. Fortunately, TFHE (Fast Fully Homomorphic Encryption over the Torus) library developed by Chillotti et al. has speed up operations in great amount by applying gate-by-gate bootstrapping technique, saving time in

© Springer Nature Switzerland AG 2019
B. B. Kang and J. Jang (Eds.): WISA 2018, LNCS 11402, pp. 105–116, 2019.
https://doi.org/10.1007/978-3-030-17982-3_9

experiments [3,4]. However, only a few operations such as AND, OR, NOT and etc have been designed, troubleshooting other developers' inflow in the research field.

Thus, our goal of this paper is to build logarithm operation using TFHE library to further contribute in building up HE library functions. We utilized Taylor expansion of three to five terms to approximate logarithm function and compared their speed and accuracy, respectively. Furthermore, we developed more accurate way of obtaining result of logarithm by using square and shift method, having inspired by the idea from [5]. In the end, we will compare their speed and accuracy to conclude optimal operation for logarithm among the two approaches that we have presented.

2   Background

In this section, we lay out brief explanation of HE and FHE. Next, we discuss about approximation of logarithm with Taylor series in terms of its mathematical basis in plaintext. Finally, the analysis of shift and square method is presented in the same manner.

2.1   Homomorphic Encryption

Homomorphic Encryption is an encryption scheme based on the property that decryption of operations on ciphertexts matches the result of the operations performed on the plaintexts. In other words, it can be written as $x \triangle y = \mathbb{D}[\mathbb{E}[x] \triangle \mathbb{E}[y]]$ where $\mathbb{E}[\cdot]$ and $\mathbb{D}[\cdot]$ denote encryption and decryption, respectively. Specifically, in the case of cloud computing system, one can query a task with his or her plaintexts to a server without revealing them. The server merely performs the task of the ciphertexts given and returns the outcome to the user without being informed of any clue.

Various HE scheme and libraries have been proposed, where the first Homomorphism was introduced by Rivest, Adleman, and Dertouzou in 1978 [6]. Since then, HE has contrived a way to deal with numerous limitations including noise accumulation on encryption stage, which had to restrict number of operations. The problem was solved by bootstrapping procedure proposed by Gentry suggesting FHE (Fully Homomorphic Encryption), which effectively removes noise each time encryption operation is performed [7].

TFHE Library. TFHE (Fast Fully Homomorphic Encryption over the Torus) library, developed by Chillotti et al. is one of the open source libraries based on FHE. The library allows to perform bootstrapping in less than a second, boosting speed to save lots of time for implementation. Basically, the library provides secret keys and cloud keys for private encryption and secure export to the server, respectively. With private keys, the message is safely encrypted and outsourced to the cloud using the public key. The cloud performs operation task that the user requested and returns the outcome without revealing any information of the data.

2.2 Taylor Series Expansion Approach

It is well-known that Taylor expansion can represent a function in a series as for approximation. In this sense, the logarithm can be expressed in a linear combination of polynomials. Therefore, the solution for logarithm can be derived approximately with the fundamental arithmetic operations.

In general, Taylor series of a real-valued function $f(x)$ that is differentiable at a real number $x = a$ can be expanded in a power series such that

$$\sum_{n=1}^{\infty} \frac{f^{(n)}(a)}{n!}(x-a)^n = f(a) + \frac{f'(a)}{1!}(x-a) + \frac{f''(a)}{2!}(x-a)^2 + \cdots \quad (1)$$

where $f^{(n)}$ is denoted by nth derivative of f and $n!$ is denoted by the factorial of n.

Therefore, since $\ln x$ is differentiable for all values of $x \in (0, \infty)$, it can be rewritten as a power series at $a = 1$ such that

$$\ln x = \sum_{n=1}^{\infty} (-1)^{n+1} \frac{(x-1)^n}{n}$$

$$= x - 1 - \frac{(x-1)^2}{2} + \frac{(x-1)^3}{3} - \cdots$$

where $x \in (0, 2)$. $log_a x$ can be derived by $\frac{log_e x}{log_e a}$ when the value of $\ln x$ is obtained.

2.3 Square and Shift Approach

Square and shift method is adopted as our proposition of the second approach. The method requires simple basic operations such as shift and addition which are fast in HE experiment environment.

First, let $x, y \in \mathbb{R}$, and the goal is to find y such that

$$y = log_a x \quad (2)$$

$log_a x$ can be obtained by $y = \frac{log_2 x}{log_2 a}$ since our initial step begins with solving $log_2 x$. Put

$$y_1 = log_2 x \quad (3)$$

Now, we normalize y_1 to interval $[0, 1)$ in order to apply our algorithm that requires division and multiplication. Representing y_1 in a binary form such that $\forall b_i$ of 0 or 1

$$y_1 = b_1 \times 2^{-1} + b_2 \times 2^{-2} + b_3 \times 2^{-3} + \cdots \quad (4)$$

To apply our algorithm, (4) can be represented in a parenthetical nested form such that

$$y_1 = 2^{-1}(b_1 + 2^{-1}(b_2 + 2^{-1}(b_3 + \cdots))) \quad (5)$$

By substituting (5) into $x = 2^{y_1}$, we obtain

$$x = 2^{2^{-1}(b_1 + 2^{-1}(b_2 + 2^{-1}(b_3 + \cdots)))} \tag{6}$$

From this point, we can recursively extract bits of log_2x by square and shift method.

In our first step of iteration, we square x to obtain first bit of y_1.

$$x^2 = 2^{b_1} \times 2^{2^{-1}(b_2 + 2^{-1}(b_3 + 2^{-1}(b_4 + \cdots)))} \tag{7}$$

Since b_1 is either 0 or 1, we can separate into two cases for the analysis of bits of y_1.

1. If $b_1 = 0$, then $x^2 = 2^{2^{-1}(b_2 + 2^{-1}(b_3 + 2^{-1}(b_4 + \cdots)))}$.
2. If $b_1 = 1$, then $x^2 = 2 \times 2^{2^{-1}(b_2 + 2^{-1}(b_3 + 2^{-1}(b_4 + \cdots)))}$.

Both of the equation share the common factor $2^{2^{-1}(b_2 + 2^{-1}(b_3 + \cdots))} \in [1, 2)$ which implies that x^2 is larger than or equal to 2 if and only if $b_1 = 1$, otherwise $b_1 = 0$.

In our next step, we analyze the value of x^2 and if x^2 is greater than or equal to 2, we divide x^2 by 2 with its mantissa set to 1. For other cases, leave x^2 as it is and set mantissa to 0. In this way, we are left with $x^2 = 2^{2^{-1}(b_2 + 2^{-1}(b_3 + 2^{-1}(b_4 + \cdots)))}$ at the end of the second step. The repetition follows and thus we are able to recursively apply the steps to extract the remaining bits of y_1.

3   Implementation Method

Representation of Array in TFHE Library. TFHE performs operations on a bit-by-bit basis in accordance with the other FHE cryptosystems. However, TFHE represents an array in the inverse direction thereby positioning msb (most significant bit) to the far right.

Notation of HE Operations. In this paper, we performed several HE operations to implement the approaches for designing logarithm. Table 1 elaborates notation of HE operations to prevent confusion with plaintext operations.

3.1   Implementation of Taylor Series Expansion

Taylor series is a power series that are calculated from the values of the derivatives of a function at a single point. The problem arises when we attempt to draw the first value of Eq. (1), $f(a)$. The term contains logarithm that is unobtainable except at a point $a = 1$, since $\ln 1 = 0$. Thus, we have only taken at the single point $a = 1$ for approximation.

In order to design logarithm with Taylor expansion in Homomorphic scheme, it is crucial to consider time complexity regarding gate and arithmetic operations. Since multiplication and division operation takes considerably longer time

Table 1. Notation of HE functions and symbols

Operation	HE function	Symbol
AND	$bootsAND$	⟁
NOT	$bootsNOT$	⊘
Addition	$HomAdd$	⊕
Subtraction	$HomSub$	⊖
Multiplication	$HomMult$	⊗
Division	$HomDiv$	✳

than the other operations, it is recommended to avoid the operations for designing an efficient algorithm. However, Taylor series contain power sums in which multiplication operations are frequently performed requiring great amount of time. Therefore the key point in the implementation of Taylor series are number of terms to be utilized to approximate logarithm that are directly related to speed and accuracy. In this sense, we have only taken three to five terms of the power series for the approximation of logarithm to balance between speed and accuracy. The time complexity and accuracy will be explained in the discussion section.

To proceed our algorithm, the first step is to create divisor arrays. It can be seen at the figure how we designed divisors in an array in the inverse order (Fig. 1).

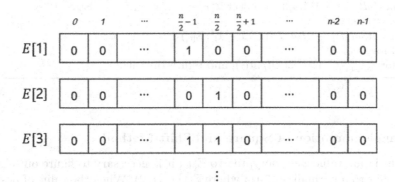

Fig. 1. Design of divisors

Then we need to build each terms of Taylor series. Specifically, Homomorphic property and its related operations are conducted as it can be seen in the following:

$$\mathbb{E}[x-1] = \mathbb{E}[x] \ominus \mathbb{E}[1]$$
$$\mathbb{E}[(x-1)^2] = \mathbb{E}[x-1] \otimes \mathbb{E}[x-1]$$
$$\mathbb{E}[(x-1)^3] = \mathbb{E}[(x-1)^2] \otimes \mathbb{E}[x-1]$$
$$\vdots$$
$$\mathbb{E}[(x-1)^{n-1}] = \mathbb{E}[(x-1)^{n-2}] \otimes \mathbb{E}[x-1]$$
$$\mathbb{E}[(x-1)^n] = \mathbb{E}[(x-1)^{n-1}] \otimes \mathbb{E}[x-1]$$

Next, each of the terms $\mathbb{E}[(x-1)^n]$ are divided using $HomDiv$ operation with its corresponding divisor $\mathbb{E}[n]$, respectively. Then, $\mathbb{E}[\ln x]$ can be obtained using Homomorphic addition and subtraction as follows.

$$\mathbb{E}[\ln x] = \mathbb{E}[x-1] \ominus \frac{\mathbb{E}[(x-1)^2]}{\mathbb{E}[2]} \oplus \frac{\mathbb{E}[(x-1)^3]}{\mathbb{E}[3]} \ominus \cdots \qquad (8)$$

The general case of Taylor series for HE is listed in the following algorithm.

Algorithm 1. Taylor series approximation of Logarithm

  – **Input** : n-bit real number x, number of terms used for approximation n
  – **Output** : $log_e x$

1: Create n divisors in array rows.
2: $HomSub$ $\mathbb{E}[x]$ by $\mathbb{E}[1]$ to obtain $\mathbb{E}[x-1]$.
3: $HomMult$ $\mathbb{E}[x-1]$ itself to collect $\mathbb{E}[x-1]$, $\mathbb{E}[x-1]^2$, $\cdots$, $\mathbb{E}[x-1]^n$
4: **for** $i = 1 : n$ **do**
5:     $\mathbb{E}[output(i)] \leftarrow HomDiv(\mathbb{E}[x-1]^i, \mathbb{E}[i])$
6: **end for**
7: Perform $\sum_{i=1}^{n}(-1)^{i+1}\mathbb{E}[output(i)]$ and return the value.

3.2 Implementation of Square and Shift Method

Since the input value x is encrypted to $\mathbb{E}[x]$, it is necessary to figure out digit of $\mathbb{E}[x]$ to shift to a normalized form where $\mathbb{E}[x] \in [1, 2)$. When the value of position of msb is obtained, we can shift $\mathbb{E}[x]$ into our desired form. Thus, our algorithm can be categorized into four main parts in the following:

1. Normalization of $\mathbb{E}[x]$ is performed.
2. Application of square and shift method is conducted to extract bits of $\mathbb{E}[y]$, where $y = log_2 x$.
3. Obtain integer part of normalized $\mathbb{E}[y]$.
4. Divide $\mathbb{E}[y]$ by $\mathbb{E}[log_2 a]$ to obtain $\mathbb{E}[log_a x]$.

Algorithm 2. Algorithm for normalization of $\mathbb{E}[x]$

- **Input** : n-bit real number x
- **Output** : Normalized $\mathbb{E}[x]$

1: Larger than or equal compare $\mathbb{E}[x]$ with $\mathbb{E}[2^{-\frac{length}{2}+1}]$, $\mathbb{E}[2^{-\frac{length}{2}+2}]$, $\cdots$ $\mathbb{E}[2^{-\frac{length}{2}-1}]$ and store their values in *output* array.
2: Add all the values of *output* elements and put it in *out_sum*.
3: Subtract *out_sum* by $\mathbb{E}[\frac{length}{2}]$ and save the value at *out_sum*.
4: Build Shift variables S and their corresponding shifted b to A.
5: Perform Equal comparison of S and *out_sum* and store it in EQ.
6: for all EQ and its corresponding A, execute $EQ \oslash A$ and store it in A.
7: Add all the values of A elements and save it in C.

Normalization. Algorithm 2 illustrates normalization of $\mathbb{E}[x]$ by shift operation. We perform Homomorphic larger than or equal comparison in the first stage, where the outcome of the function yields $\mathbb{E}[1]$ if $\mathbb{E}[x]$ is greater than or equal to $\mathbb{E}[2^{-\frac{length}{2}+1}]$, $\mathbb{E}[2^{-\frac{length}{2}+2}]$, $\cdots$ $\mathbb{E}[2^{\frac{length}{2}-1}]$ and otherwise $\mathbb{E}[0]$. By summation of all the outcomes and deduction of $\mathbb{E}(\frac{length}{2})$ yields $\mathbb{E}(out\_sum)$ which is the desired number of shift to the normalized $\mathbb{E}[x]$. It might be convenient to perform $\mathbb{E}[2^{out\_sum}] \otimes \mathbb{E}[x]$, however, regarding efficiency, it takes more time considering multiplication operation involved. Thus, we propose a more efficient way to shift $\mathbb{E}[x]$ by utilizing AND operation, which takes very short amount of time compared to the multiplication operation. Next, we define corresponding shift variable and its shifted outcome of $\mathbb{E}[x]$, A to iteratively perform equal comparison. The equal comparison operation of the shift variable and *out_sum* returns EQ, where EQ is $\mathbb{E}[1]$ if two comparer is the same and otherwise $\mathbb{E}[0]$. Then, bitwise operation of $EQ \oslash A$ and their summation gives the value of shifted outcome of $\mathbb{E}[x]$.

Square and Shift Method. In plaintext, we can determine whether x^2 is greater than or equal to 2, which then we can decide the direction of shift operation. Specifically $\frac{length}{2}$th bit of MC is decisive since $MC[\frac{length}{2}]$ is the extracted bit of y and also it determines whether x^2 is over than 2. However, it is not possible to use if condition to decide the shift direction of $\mathbb{E}[x^2]$ in ciphertext. Therefore, $MC[\frac{length}{2}] \oslash lb \oplus MC[\frac{length}{2}] \oslash MC$ is applied either to obtain left shift of x or to obtain x without the shift operation.

Integer part of $log_2 x$ is to simply copy *out_sum* array. This is due to the fact that the value of *out_sum* is equal to finding digit where the digit in binary representation of the outcome represents the integer part of $\log_2 x$. Lastly, it requires division to acquire $\log_a x$ which is the result of $\log_2 x$ divided by $\log_2 a$. This is because $log_a x = \frac{log_2 x}{log_2 a}$.

Algorithm 3. Algorithm for Logarithm using square and shift method

- **Input** : Normalized $\mathbb{E}[x]$ and base a
- **Output** : $\mathbb{E}[log_a x]$

1: **for** $i = 0 : \frac{length}{2} - 1$ **do**
2:     $MC \leftarrow C \otimes C$
3:     $final[i] \leftarrow MC[\frac{length}{2}]$ // extract bits of $log_2 x$
4:     $lb \leftarrow \text{LeftShift}(MC)$
5:     $x \oslash lb \leftarrow MC[\frac{length}{2}]$
6:     $nx \leftarrow bootsNOT(MC[\frac{length}{2}]) \oslash MC)$
7:     $C \leftarrow x \oplus nx$
8: **end for**
9: **for** $j = 0 : \frac{length}{2} - 2$ **do**
10:     $final[j + \frac{length}{2}] \leftarrow out\_sum[j]$ // integer part of $log_2 x$
11: **end for**
12: $result \leftarrow \text{HomDiv}(final, log_2 a)$

4   Experimentation Result

In this section, the method proposed in the previous section is verified through experiments. Experimental environment was implemented in i7-7700 3.60 GHz, 16.0 GB RAM, Ubuntu 16.04.3 LTS, and the actual implementation was on TFHE version 1.0. The section provides detailed results of the comparison of the two methods regarding their time complexity and accuracy.

We start from Taylor series method elucidating accuracy in respect to the number of terms. Secondly, accuracy of the square and shift method will be explained and finally the time complexity of the two methods will be analyzed.

4.1   Accuracy of Taylor Series Method

Our method approximated logarithm at a single point, $a = 1$, which produced a very close likeliness result in a small neighborhood of x, where $x \in (0.5, 1.5)$ with actual logarithm function that can be explicitly checked from Fig. 2(a).

In addition, the accuracy in a small boundary increases as more terms of Taylor series are added, which can be seen from the Fig. 2(b) with the proximate view of Fig. 2(a).

$$\ln x = x - 1 - \frac{(x-1)^2}{2} + \frac{(x-1)^3}{3} - \cdots + (-1)^{n+1}\frac{(x-1)^n}{n} + O(x^{n+1})$$

$$\therefore error = \ln x - \sum_{k=1}^{n}(-1)^{k+1}\frac{(x-1)^k}{k} = O(x^{n+1})$$

However, the distinction between the Taylor series and logarithm becomes more clear with $x \in (2, \infty)$, since the error, $O(x^{n+1})$ diverges as x goes to the infinity. In short, our approach of Taylor expansion can be applied in a small neighborhood of $a = 1$ with high accuracy.

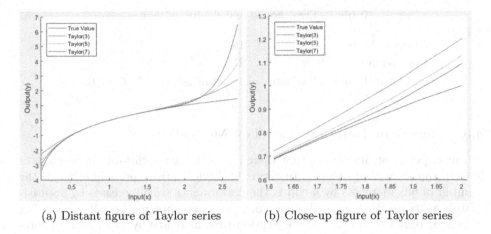

(a) Distant figure of Taylor series   (b) Close-up figure of Taylor series

Fig. 2. Comparison of Taylor series approximation and true value of logarithm

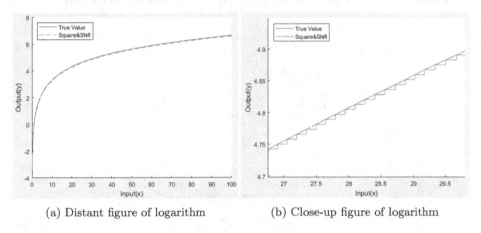

(a) Distant figure of logarithm   (b) Close-up figure of logarithm

Fig. 3. Comparison of square and shift approximation and true value of logarithm

4.2   Accuracy of Square and Shift Method

The approximation using square and shift method provides highly accurate solution for logarithm that can be noticeably viewed from Fig. 3(a). The mechanism extracts $\frac{length}{2} - 1$ bits of the correct answer for the logarithm.

Figure 3(b) illustrates the proximate view of Fig. 3(a) where $x \in (26.5, 30)$ with square and shift design in a cascade shape. The pattern is derived from the design of our algorithm that $\frac{length}{2}$th bit of mantissa are rounded off. Therefore, error bound of the mechanism is $\frac{length}{2}$. The following table summarizes error bound and significant figures of its corresponding bits (Table 2).

Table 2. Error bound and significant figures

Number of bits	8	16	32
Error bound	2^{-3}	2^{-7}	2^{-15}
Significant figures	1st of integer	2nd of mantissa	4th of mantissa

4.3   Time Complexity Between Two Methods

In our experiment, it appears that there exists linear relationship between data length and logarithm of time. In terms of Taylor series approximation, if the number of bits increases by n times, the performance time increases by approximately n^2 time. However, in the case of square and shift method, if the number of bits increases by n times, the execution time increases by roughly n^3. Therefore, the time difference of the two methods is $O(n^3)$. Figure 4 visualizes the comparison of the two mechanisms with respect to their execution time.

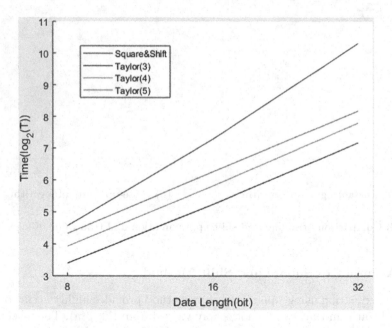

Fig. 4. Comparison of execution time

5   Conclusion

In this paper, we introduced two methods for constructing HE of logarithm and compared their performance time and accuracy through experiments. We conclude that the square and shift mechanism can be more generally utilized for Homomorphic logarithm. Even though Taylor series' execution has lighter computation than the square and shift method, its accuracy is low in the most cases except the neighborhood of $a = 1$.

In the case of Taylor series, high accuracy in the neighborhood of $a = 1$ is the motivation of adhering the same strategy that can be applied not only at a point $a = 1$, but all the intervals of x. In this way, we can obtain more accurate answers for $logx$. Specifically, the idea is to build Homomorphic operation of nth derivatives and find the value of $\ln a$ from the Eq. (1) in Sect. 2.

Square and shift method can be better designed with increased number of significant digits by rearranging number of bits of mantissa. This will facilitate enlargement of error bounds, thereby escalating accuracy.

6   Future Application

The future aspect of the design of logarithm is its high applicability to various fields of study because it is one of the fundamental operations. One way is to design exponential function with the similar algorithm that we have presented. The special case of Taylor expansion, namely Maclaurin series, applies to establishment of exponential function.

$$a^x = 1 + \frac{x \ln a}{1!} + \frac{(x \ln a)^2}{2!} + \frac{(x \ln a)^3}{3!} + \cdots \tag{9}$$

Likewise, it is necessary to define number of terms to determine accuracy and speed for approximation.

Moreover, in a a broader aspect, logarithm can be associated with data science and machine learning [8]. Particularly, logistic regression is one of the examples that logarithm can be used. In such case, we can apply the log operation to remove the exponents of the likelihood function to a linear combination [9,10]. With the proper design of exponential function and logarithm, logistic regression can be established so that users without any knowledge of HE can possibly request data analysis to the server in the future.

Acknowledgement. This research was supported by the MSIP (Ministry of Science, ICT & Future Planning), Korea, under the IITP (Institute for Information & communications Technology Promotion) support program (2017-0-00545).

References

1. Jain, P., Gyanchandani, M., Khare, N.: Differential privacy: its technological prescriptive using big data. J. Big Data 5(1), 15 (2018)
2. Dwork, C., Roth, A., et al.: The algorithmic foundations of differential privacy. Found. Trends® Theor. Comput. Sci. 9(3–4), 211–407 (2014)
3. Chillotti, I., Gama, N., Georgieva, M., Izabachène, M.: Faster fully homomorphic encryption: bootstrapping in less than 0.1 seconds. In: Cheon, J.H., Takagi, T. (eds.) ASIACRYPT 2016. LNCS, vol. 10031, pp. 3–33. Springer, Heidelberg (2016). https://doi.org/10.1007/978-3-662-53887-6_1

4. Chillotti, I., Gama, N., Georgieva, M., Izabachène, M.: Improving TFHE: faster packed homomorphic operations and efficient circuit bootstrapping. Cryptology ePrint Archive, Report 2017/430 (2017)
5. Turner, C.: A fast binary logarithm algorithm. In: Streamlining Digital Signal Processing: A Tricks of the Trade Guidebook, pp. 281–283, Wiley, Hoboken (2012)
6. Rivest, R., Adleman, L., Dertouzos, M.: On data banks and privacy homomorphisms. Found. Secure Comput. 4(11), 169–180 (1978)
7. Gentry, C.: Fully homomorphic encryption using ideal lattices. In: STOC, vol. 9 (2009)
8. Zaki, M.J., Meira, W., Meira, W.: Data Mining and Analysis: Fundamental Concepts and Algorithms. Cambridge University Press, Cambridge (2014)
9. Nasrabadi, N.: Pattern recognition and machine learning. J. Electron. Imaging 16, 049901 (2007)
10. Hogg, R., McKean, J., Craig, A.: Introduction to Mathematical Statistics, 2nd edn. Pearson Education, London (2005)

Network Deployments of Bitcoin Peers and Malicious Nodes Based on Darknet Sensor

Mitsuyoshi Imamura[1,2](✉) and Kazumasa Omote[1](✉)

[1] University of Tsukuba, Tennodai 1-1-1, Tsukuba 305-8573, Japan
ic140tg528@gmail.com, omote@risk.tsukuba.ac.jp
[2] Nomura Asset Management Ltd.,
1-11-1 Nihonbashi, Chuo-ku, Tokyo 103-8260, Japan

Abstract. Bitcoin depends on Peer-to-Peer (P2P) network in a major way and shares the connecting IP address list with the nearest peer. In addition, the blockchain which is the basic technology can be accessed by anyone, and the transaction stored in the block can be checked anytime. Recent research has reported that anonymity of such a bitcoin P2P network is low, regardless of whether peer uses the anonymizers like TOR to keep the anonymity. This fact shows the risk of the malicious users being able to use this public information without exception. However, when the malicious user is hiding behind the network and browsing public information, it is difficult to distinguish between a malicious user and a honest one, and it is a challenge to detect signs of hidden threats. In this research, we propose a data mining approach to analyze by combining two kinds of IP address distributions: Bitcoion peer and malicious node (not in the bitcoin network), in order to obtain characteristics of hidden users. As a result, we confirmed that the nodes, which matched the first 24 bits of the IP address in the bitcoin network peer, sent the packet to the darknet. The contribution of this paper is three-fold: (1) we employ a novel approach to analyze a bitcoin network using Darknet dataset, (2) we identify the malicious node in the same network as the honest peer, and (3) we clarify the network deployments of Bitcoin peers and malicious nodes.

Keywords: Darknet analysis · Bitcoin · Cybersecurity

1 Introduction

In recent years, Bitcoin is attracting attention as a rapidly expanding service on the network. Bitcoin is a system based on Peer-to-Peer (P2P) network and Blockchain which created by volunteers according to a whitepaper [22] released by anonymous authors "Satoshi Nakamoto". Since it is a system using innovative technologies such as blockchain, it has been widely researched as an interesting topic in the academic field [6].

© Springer Nature Switzerland AG 2019
B. B. Kang and J. Jang (Eds.): WISA 2018, LNCS 11402, pp. 117–128, 2019.
https://doi.org/10.1007/978-3-030-17982-3_10

In a survey [14] focused on anonymity of Bitcoin, researchers classify review papers into three different categories, which is Blockchain analysis, Traffic analysis, and Mixing. Blockchain analysis means analyzing transaction information recorded in a distributed managed ledger on a bitcoin network. Transaction analysis (network analysis) means analyzing a bitcoin network composed of P2P. The analyzed data includes the network traffic transmitted through the bitcoin P2P network and the IP address information of the peer. Mixing means a technique to shuffle the relationship between the senders address and the receiver address in order to increase anonymity of the system. Although network analysis is a challenging work, it is quite important by the paper [14]. In a relatively-recent research [21] using dataset such as the bitcoin P2P network traffic or blockchain transaction, clustering and characterization based on public information reduce anonymity and break the privacy of Bitcoin users. Therefore, it is important to detect signs of malicious users.

In order to collect signs of malicious users, there is a method of deploying a trap-based monitoring system that collects abnormal communication on the network. "The darknet sensor" is one of the basic monitoring system [4,9,23]. The darknet means the IP address space which can be routed and not assigned to the host. The darknet sensor is used for research to detect malicious users.

In this research, we focused on using the two different IP address distributions and analyzed the characteristics of threats latent on a port-basis using darknet sensor and bitcoin user's IP address. The contribution of this paper is three-fold: (1) we employ a novel approach to analyze a bitcoin network using Darknet dataset, (2) we identify the malicious node in the same network as the honest peer, and (3) we clarify the network deployments of Bitcoin peers and malicious nodes.

The remaining articles are organized as follows: Sect. 2 illustrates the background of the technology and the review of related literature, Sect. 3 reports the research method used and analysis results. Thereafter Sect. 4 discusses the results. Finally, the conclusion is described in Sect. 5.

2   Background and Related Work

This section provides an overview of bitcoin network and darknet, and then summarizes the latest research trends.

2.1   Bitcoin Network

In order to help understand our approach, we first explain the mechanism of the bitcoin network to link the analysis using darknet sensor dataset and the bitcoin network. Bitcoin maintains P2P networks around the world with two important mechanisms, "Peer Discovery" and "Connecting to Peers".

Those mechanisms are as follows:

Peer Discovery. In the initial peer connection, in order to discover active peers, the non-connecting peer (initiator) queries the domain lists which called hard-coded DNS seeds managed by Bitcoin community members. If there is no response within 60 s, it queries the domain lists using hard-coded IP address. When a peer restarts the service, it queries the peer that succeeded in the connection.

Connecting to Peers. After an initiator discovers the destination peer, it tries to establish the TCP connection to the destination using the network port number 8333. When the TCP connection is successful, a version message including the version number of the communication protocol, block information and current time is transmitted to the initiator. Because the peer at the connection destination responds with the verack message and the version message, it transmits a verack message and establishes the connection. When a connection is then established between peers, the initiator sends an addr message (peer information including its own IP address) and a getaddr message (a request for another peer's IP address list) to the peer at the connection destination. This allows the peer to find a new peer to connect, and it can inform other peers that the peer has newly joined the bitcoin network. A peer always maintains an outgoing connection with eight peers and can keep up to 125 connections with in-between connections from peers.

In the case of the no-action peer that has not sent a message for more than 30 min among connected peers, the peer sends a ping message and checks the activation status of the adjacent peer. When the peer activation status cannot be confirmed and 90 min have elapsed, the peer regards the connection as disconnected and removes it from the connection list.

Besides checking the activation status, the initiator also sent the addr message to the peer when receiving a getaddr message, or sending an addr message at 24-h intervals.

An important knowledge is that a peer communicates with only the peers which is described in its own IP address list. Therefore, it usually doesn't start communicating with peers that don't appear in the list. If there are peers that initiate communication, we can consider the possibility of a threatening peer.

Also, we know that one threat in the bitcoin network is a small group such as a botnet. This group poses different threats depending on the purpose.

Huang et al. [15] reports a comprehensive survey on mining bots used for mining applications. The mining bot exploits CPU resources without realizing it.

Heilman et al. [13] report the eclipse attack on bitcoin P2P network using bots that undermines bitcoin's core security guarantees, allowing attacks on the mining and consensus system, including N-confirmation double spending and adversarial forks in the blockchain.

In contrary to other researches which trying to earn profits directly with bots, several researches are considering a case of indirectly attacking by damaging the trust of the system. Neudecker et al. [20] reports a simulation model for analysis of attacks on the bitcoin P2P network. It discusses the concept of attacks and the motivation of attackers by simulation. According to this report, the attacker's peer can behaves in the attack phase to increase the probability of connecting with honest nodes. The target of such attacks is primarily personal information.

In [21], researchers assess whether combining blockchain and network information may facilitate the clustering process. According to this report, only a small share of clusters is conspicuously associated with a single IP address. Also, only a small number of IP addresses shows a conspicuous association with a single cluster.

Bojja et al. [5] reports the practical anonymity attacks on bitcoin network. According to this work, in the current network, there are enemies such as botnets that do spy activities linking users with transactions. This problem is not unique to Bitcoin: Many spinoff cryptocurrencies (known as altcoins) use similar technologies and thus suffer from the same lack of anonymity in their P2P networks. The Bitcoin community responds to these problems as appropriate.

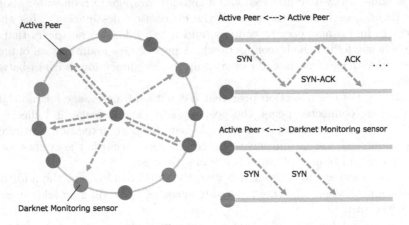

Fig. 1. Darknet sensor on network

2.2   Darknet

For the word "darknet" used in this research, we can mainly refer to two meanings. One is an unauthorized network formed by servers and programs used for trading illegal drugs and personal information. This includes technologies and services involved in illegal acts such as anonymous communication protocols such as TOR [8] or BitTorrent [7]. The other is the name of a packet addressed to a routable and unassigned IP address and is used to generate various cyber threat information such as scanning activity, distributed denial of service attack (DDoS attack) and, malware identification [10]. Since Bitcoin is sometimes used as a currency of illegal transactions, it is often related to the meaning of the former such as described in the previous research [19], however, in this research, it is referred to as the meaning of the last one.

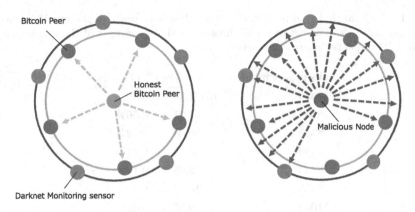

Fig. 2. Behavior of an honest Bitcoin peer (left) and a malicious node (right)

One of the effective way to monitor Internet activity is to employ passive monitoring using sensors or traps such as darknet [10,16]. A trap based monitoring system is deployed in the network to collect malicious activities. The darknet is one of them, and it is a network sensor acting in passive mode. Figure 1 shows the darknet sensor does not respond when a request packet is sent to IP addresses in the darknet.

Previous research [10] reports that the darknet has been used in the following researches: (1) probes or scanning activities due to worms, bots and other automated exploit tools; (2) DDoS attacks due to victims reply (backscatter) packets to spoofed IP addresses; (3) other activities such as misconfiguration and political events.

In a systematic summary of darknet research [10], the research subjects of the Darknet are categorized into three categories: (1) development and setup of the darknet (development), (2) measurement and analysis of the darknet data by the deployed sensor (packet analysis), (3) in tools and techniques for visualization and representation of packets (visualization). Our study is categorized in (2).

Also, various large-scale projects [2,24,25] are active in the darknet, and then the dataset used in this research is provided by the Network Incident analysis Center for Tactical Emergency Response (NICTER) project [16,17] which is one of them. Survey studies [10,12] report that the data set of NICTER project is used for anti-malware research, and the research results [4,9,23] is actively published. The current research [3] reports that this dataset attracts attention as a research targets such as big data and data mining.

3   Analysis and Results

In this section, we analyze by combining two kinds of IP address distributions: Bitcoion peer and non-Bitcoin malicious node, in order to obtain characteristics of hidden users.

Table 1. Our analyzed results from the network service ports of the top 10 ranked in the bitcoin network. The "# of peers" means the daily averages of the number of the peer and "% of peers" means the ratio.

Open port number	# of peers	% of peers
8333	10451.24	95.60%
8334	61.71	0.56%
8555	56.64	0.52%
8338	23.16	0.21%
28333	12.68	0.12%
8335	10.93	0.10%
11080	9.57	0.09%
8341	9.28	0.08%
9001	8.98	0.08%
18333	8.76	0.08%
8433	7.76	0.07%

3.1   Network Service Port Based Mapping

Figure 2 shows the service port based behavior of the bitcoin peer and non-Bitcoin malicious node using the darknet sensor. The inner circle shows a bitcoin network where the bitcoin peer exists and the external circle represents the other networks. The darknet sensors are hidden in the other networks. The honest Bitcoin peer is shown in the left figure, whose peer communicates only with the peers that exist in the bitcoin network, but doesn't communicate with other networks. On the other hand, the non-Bitcoin malicious node is shown in the right figure, when the malicious node tries to communicate regardless whether or not the Bitcoin peer exists. Therefore, there is a possibility for malicious node to communicate with a darknet sensor that was deployed as a trap on the other networks.

When conducting port-based analysis, we confirm that the default Bitcoin port (8333/tcp) is used as the service port in the bitcoin network. Table 1 shows the results of examining the ports used by the IPv4 address peers on the bitcoin network that can be accessed during the period from Mar. 1, 2018 to May. 31, 2018, using the data obtained from Bitnodes [1].

In this result, we find that more than 95% peers are using the default 8333/tcp port. The 8333/tcp port is not the well-known port numbers which are used in general applications. Therefore, it is reasonable to consider the 8333/tcp port as a Bitcoin port when conducting the port-based analysis. Then we confirm whether or not there is communication with the 8333/tcp port of the darknet sensor. We evaluate datasets collected at the darknet sensors hosted by NICTER [16] from Jan. 1, 2011 to May. 31, 2018. Figure 3 shows the total packet amount per day for the 8333/tcp port that reached the darknet sensor. In particular, we would like to pay attention to this result by Fig. 3. This figure means that packets

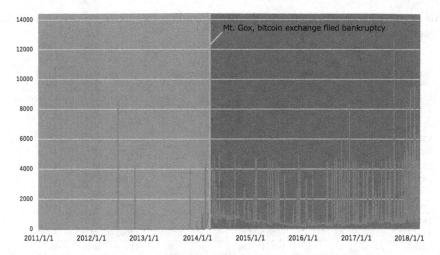

Fig. 3. The amount of daily total packets for 8333/tcp port, reached to the darknet (Color figure online)

which are never reached can be observed by darknet sensor from a certain point of time. The red vertical line refers to Feb. 24, 2014, which means that Mt.Gox (bitcoin exchange) went bankruptcy. From the figure, this day is a change point where a lot of packets becomes to reach to the darknet. We found that a certain packet started to reach the darknet, which is appeared as a spike.

3.2 Network Analysis of the Combining Two Kinds of IP Address Lists

A darknet sensor dataset has the IP address lists of senders which scans the Internet using 8333/tcp port. On the other hand, Bitcoin peer has the IP address lists of peer in the bitcoin network. Therefore, combining the above two kinds of IP address lists, we can acquire a new feature of the IP address in the bitcoin network. This approach is classified as a data mining method using two kinds IP address information.

Table 2 shows the relationship between the nodes sending the packet to the darknet and the peers on the bitcoin network in more detail. Bitcoin peers mean the number of the daily unique peer of accessible IPv4 addresses using 8333/tcp port on the "Bitcoin network" in Table 2 during the period from Mar. 1, 2018 to May. 31, 2018. "The Malicious nodes" means the number of the daily unique node sending packets to the darknet in the same period. "First 24 bit match (IPv4)" represents the number of peers that the peer matches the third octet of the IP address in the bitcoin network peer, in the same period. As a result, we confirm that the node, which matches the first 24 bits of IP address in the bitcoin network peer, send the packets to the darknet, and these peers are classified into two types. The outline of classification is shown in Fig. 4.

The first 24 bit of IP address (IPv4) in one non-Bitcoin malicious node is the same as the bitcoin peer and these two nodes have a sequential number, for the

Table 2. The relationship between the nodes sending the packet to the darknet and the peers on the bitcoin network

Day	Mar-18			Apr-18			May-18		
	Bitcoin peers	Malicious nodes	First 24 bit match (IPv4)	Bitcoin peers	Malicious nodes	First 24 bit match (IPv4)	Bitcoin peers	Malicious nodes	First 24 bit match (IPv4)
1	13830	24	6	12784	30	6	12099	85	6
2	14005	29	6	12684	30	6	12044	29	6
3	13742	27	6	12858	82	6	12096	27	5
4	13564	35	9	12805	25	6	12086	29	6
5	13704	21	6	12831	27	6	12024	33	6
6	13926	80	6	12881	28	6	11936	29	6
7	13352	24	6	12803	27	6	12189	27	6
8	12959	22	6	12744	49	6	11999	83	6
9	13900	26	6	12876	29	6	12075	26	6
10	14190	24	6	12940	84	6	12015	24	6
11	14151	25	6	12787	22	6	12092	30	6
12	14180	24	4	12714	26	6	11894	26	6
13	14493	88	4	12575	29	6	11900	46	8
14	14715	23	6	12168	29	6	11954	27	6
15	14855	63	6	12106	31	6	12102	78	6
16	12962	29	6	12146	28	6	11940	27	6
17	13464	242	6	12075	81	6	11843	34	6
18	14317	38	6	12163	29	6	11805	26	6
19	14347	246	6	12134	26	6	11675	30	6
20	14390	298	6	12112	29	6	11630	33	6
21	14100	152	5	12066	25	6	11723	34	6
22	14050	287	6	12089	28	6	11795	86	6
23	14138	285	6	12113	28	6	11695	31	6
24	14169	1346	7	12066	82	6	11626	33	6
25	13931	1322	11	12136	28	6	11349	32	6
26	14332	1576	7	12141	31	6	11301	30	6
27	14343	471	6	12151	25	6	11137	29	6
28	13809	33	6	12052	30	6	11606	24	6
29	14518	33	6	11936	25	6	11610	87	6
30	14028	173	6	11976	31	6	11590	30	6
31	13335	28	6				11528	34	6

whole period. In the another case, the first 24 bits of IP address (IPv4) is the same and they are on the network.

4 Discussion

In this section, we deeply discuss our results in the previous session. We focus on the change point which was observed in the darknet sensor described in Fig. 3, and the current existing peer IP address on the bitcoin network.

We consider that this changing point makes the malicious user motivated to search for bitcoin peers to attack. We consider that this changing point makes the malicious user motivated to search or attack for bitcoin peers. We consider that steady packets are for scanning purposes, and abnormally packets are for attack

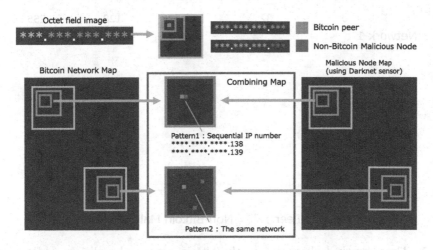

Fig. 4. IP address pattern of the Bitcoin peers sending the packets to the darknet

purposes. However it is difficult to classify them with this information alone. In the scanning purposes case, it may be possible for such searching to become a guide to find the new compromised point of the malicious user. For example, there are two types of wallets that the user uses, "Bitcoin core" and "Simplified payment verification (SPV)". Bitcoin core requires the high cost to store the big block. As compared to Bitcoin core, SPV wallets are gaining popularity due to less overhead or resources and then are reduced the bandwidth consumption. However, previous researches [11,18] report that SPV wallets are not safe against attack. In the attack purposes case, we can guess that it is an attack classified as an eclipse attack requiring reboots as reported in the previous research [13]. We think that a TCP SYN flooding is chosen as a means of restarting.

Then, we confirm the activity status of the current malicious peers. We observed that several nodes sent packets to the darknet. Especially, it is interesting that the node exists on the same network as the bitcoin peer. Figure 5 shows the network deployment map on the fourth octet of the node's IP address which matches to the first 24 bits on the bitcoin network, on May. 31, 2018. Note that we don't describe the concrete positions of the fourth octet because of anonymity of peers. From these results, we found the four patterns in the arrangement of peers. "Network 1" is the case that the existing bitcoin peer's IP address and malicious node's IP address have a sequential number. "Network 2" is the case that the IP address of the node and peer are the most distant at the subnet level. "Network 3" is the case that the IP addresses of the node and peer are allocated at the same subnet level. Finally "Network 4" is the case that the IP addresses of the node and peer are allocated at the nearest subnet level. In Network 1 and 3, there is a possibility that the nearest Bitcoin peer is related to a malicious node. Furthermore, in Network 1, 2, 3 and 4, there is a possibility that the node which is located inside the firewall managed by the organization is infected with malware and then tries to search a peer in the hot standby.

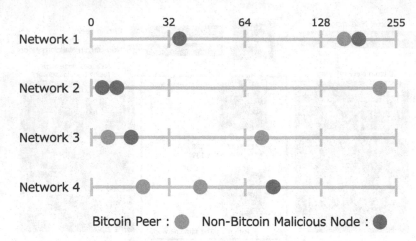

Fig. 5. The network deployments on the bitcoin peers and malicious nodes which matched the first 24 bits of the IP address on May. 31, 2018

5   Conclusion

In this research, we focused on the behavior of malicious node trying to connect excessively for information gathering and analyzed signs of threats latent on a port basis using Darknet observation information. As a result, we confirmed that the node which matched the first 24 bits of the IP address in the bitcoin network peer, sent the packets to the darknet, in which there were sequential IP number nodes.

The contribution of this paper is three-fold: First, in order to obtain the information which is not obtained only by the normal behaviour of bitcoin network, we proposed a new data mining approach to analyze bitcoin network using darknet which detects abnormal behaviour. Then, as a result of classification according to the location of IP addresses, malicious nodes were classified in the same network area as the bitcoin peer. Finally, we clarified the mapping characteristics in the network area of honest and malicious nodes.

As a future work: (1) In the darknet sensor, since only the scanning packets are confirmed, we would like to confirm more detailed information on communication by analyzing the traffic-based data after establishing the TCP connection; (2) Instead of researching the malicious node directly, we can analyze the characteristics of near-peers at the subnet level.

References

1. Bitnodes. https://bitnodes.earn.com/. Accessed 13 Mar 2018
2. Bailey, M., Cooke, E., Jahanian, F., Nazario, J., Watson, D., et al.: The internet motion sensor-a distributed blackhole monitoring system. In: NDSS (2005)

3. Ban, T., Eto, M., Guo, S., Inoue, D., Nakao, K., Huang, R.: A study on association rule mining of darknet big data. In: 2015 International Joint Conference on Neural Networks (IJCNN), pp. 1–7. IEEE (2015)
4. Ban, T., Zhu, L., Shimamura, J., Pang, S., Inoue, D., Nakao, K.: Detection of botnet activities through the lens of a large-scale darknet. In: Liu, D., Xie, S., Li, Y., Zhao, D., El-Alfy, E.-S.M. (eds.) ICONIP 2017. LNCS, vol. 10638, pp. 442–451. Springer, Cham (2017). https://doi.org/10.1007/978-3-319-70139-4_45
5. Bojja Venkatakrishnan, S., Fanti, G., Viswanath, P.: Dandelion: redesigning the bitcoin network for anonymity. Proc. ACM Meas. Anal. Comput. Syst. 1(1), 22 (2017)
6. Brandão, A., Mamede, H.S., Gonçalves, R.: Systematic review of the literature, research on blockchain technology as support to the trust model proposed applied to smart places. In: Rocha, Á., Adeli, H., Reis, L.P., Costanzo, S. (eds.) World-CIST'18 2018. AISC, vol. 745, pp. 1163–1174. Springer, Cham (2018). https://doi.org/10.1007/978-3-319-77703-0_113
7. Cohen, B.: Incentives build robustness in BitTorrent. In: Workshop on Economics of Peer-to-Peer Systems, vol. 6, pp. 68–72 (2003)
8. Dingledine, R., Mathewson, N., Syverson, P.: Tor: the second-generation onion router. Technical report, Naval Research Lab, Washington DC (2004)
9. Eto, M., Inoue, D., Song, J., Nakazato, J., Ohtaka, K., Nakao, K.: Nicter: a large-scale network incident analysis system: case studies for understanding threat landscape. In: Proceedings of the First Workshop on Building Analysis Datasets and Gathering Experience Returns for Security, pp. 37–45. ACM (2011)
10. Fachkha, C., Debbabi, M.: Darknet as a source of cyber intelligence: survey, taxonomy, and characterization. IEEE Commun. Surv. Tutor. 18(2), 1197–1227 (2016)
11. Gervais, A., Capkun, S., Karame, G.O., Gruber, D.: On the privacy provisions of bloom filters in lightweight bitcoin clients. In: Proceedings of the 30th Annual Computer Security Applications Conference, pp. 326–335. ACM (2014)
12. Hatada, M., Akiyama, M., Matsuki, T., Kasama, T.: Empowering anti-malware research in Japan by sharing the MWS datasets. J. Inf. Process. 23(5), 579–588 (2015)
13. Heilman, E., Kendler, A., Zohar, A., Goldberg, S.: Eclipse attacks on bitcoin's peer-to-peer network. In: USENIX Security Symposium, pp. 129–144 (2015)
14. Herrera-Joancomartí, J.: Research and challenges on bitcoin anonymity. In: Garcia-Alfaro, J., et al. (eds.) DPM/QASA/SETOP -2014. LNCS, vol. 8872, pp. 3–16. Springer, Cham (2015). https://doi.org/10.1007/978-3-319-17016-9_1
15. Huang, D.Y., et al.: Botcoin: monetizing stolen cycles. In: NDSS. Citeseer (2014)
16. Inoue, D., et al.: Nicter: an incident analysis system toward binding network monitoring with malware analysis. In: WOMBAT Workshop on Information Security Threats Data Collection and Sharing, WISTDCS 2008, pp. 58–66. IEEE (2008)
17. Inoue, D., et al.: An incident analysis system NICTER and its analysis engines based on data mining techniques. In: Köppen, M., Kasabov, N., Coghill, G. (eds.) ICONIP 2008. LNCS, vol. 5506, pp. 579–586. Springer, Heidelberg (2009). https://doi.org/10.1007/978-3-642-02490-0_71
18. Kaushal, P.K., Bagga, A., Sobti, R.: Evolution of bitcoin and security risk in bitcoin wallets. In: 2017 International Conference on Computer, Communications and Electronics (Comptelix), pp. 172–177. IEEE (2017)
19. Kethineni, S., Cao, Y., Dodge, C.: Use of bitcoin in darknet markets: examining facilitative factors on bitcoin-related crimes. Am. J. Crim. Justice 1–17 (2017)

20. Neudecker, T., Andelfinger, P., Hartenstein, H.: A simulation model for analysis of attacks on the bitcoin peer-to-peer network. In: 2015 IFIP/IEEE International Symposium on Integrated Network Management (IM), pp. 1327–1332. IEEE (2015)
21. Neudecker, T., Hartenstein, H.: Could network information facilitate address clustering in bitcoin? In: Brenner, M., et al. (eds.) FC 2017. LNCS, vol. 10323, pp. 155–169. Springer, Cham (2017). https://doi.org/10.1007/978-3-319-70278-0_9
22. Satoshi, N.: Bitcoin: a peer-to-peer electronic cash system (2008). http://www.bitcoin.org/bitcoin.pdf
23. Yamauchi, S., Kawakita, M., Takeuchi, J.: Botnet detection based on non-negative matrix factorization and the MDL principle. In: Huang, T., Zeng, Z., Li, C., Leung, C.S. (eds.) ICONIP 2012. LNCS, vol. 7667, pp. 400–409. Springer, Heidelberg (2012). https://doi.org/10.1007/978-3-642-34500-5_48
24. Zanero, S.: Observing the tidal waves of malware: experiences from the wombat project. In: 2010 Second Vaagdevi International Conference on Information Technology for Real World Problems (VCON), pp. 30–35. IEEE (2010)
25. Zseby, T., et al.: Workshop report: darkspace and unsolicited traffic analysis (DUST 2012). ACM SIGCOMM Comput. Commun. Rev. 42(5), 49–53 (2012)

Systems Security

VODKA: Virtualization Obfuscation Using Dynamic Key Approach

Jae-Yung Lee, Jae Hyuk Suk$^{(\boxtimes)}$, and Dong Hoon Lee$^{(\boxtimes)}$

Graduate School of Information Security, Korea University, Seoul, Korea
{2017572003,sjh2268,donghlee}@korea.ac.kr
http://protocol.korea.ac.kr

Abstract. The virtualization obfuscation technique is known to possess excellent security among software protection techniques. However, research has shown that virtualization obfuscation techniques can be analyzed by automated analysis tools because the deobfuscate virtualization obfuscation methodology is fixed. In this situation, additional protection techniques of the virtualization structure have been studied to supplement the protection strength of virtualization obfuscation. However, most of the proposed protection schemes require a special assumption or significantly increase the overhead of the program to be protected.

In this paper, we propose a delayed analysis method for a lightweight virtualization structure that does not require a strong assumption. Hence, we propose a new virtual code protection scheme combining an anti-analysis technique and dynamic key, and explain its mechanism. This causes correspondence ambiguity between the virtual code and the handler code, thus causing analysis delay. In addition, we show the result of debugging or dynamic instrumentation experiment when the additional anti-analysis technique is applied.

Keywords: Virtualization obfuscation · Dynamic key · Anti-analysis · Software protection

1 Introduction

1.1 Motivation

In modern society, Information technology is rapidly developing, and developers are producing software according to demand. Software produced/sold can only be used with a valid license key. However, in the man at the end (MATE) environment [1] as in Fig. 1a, the malicious user analyzes this software for his own benefit, as shown in Fig. 1b, obtains the internal algorithm and sensitive data, and uses it without payment. In addition, a malicious user can cause monetary damage to a developer by transforming an internal algorithm to create similar software and distribute. Therefore, it is necessary to study software protection techniques to cope with malicious users. Various kinds of software protection techniques have been studied [2–4]. Among them, software obfuscation is

© Springer Nature Switzerland AG 2019
B. B. Kang and J. Jang (Eds.): WISA 2018, LNCS 11402, pp. 131–145, 2019.
https://doi.org/10.1007/978-3-030-17982-3_11

(a) Man at the end   (b) Attacker tries to reverse program

Fig. 1. Target to protect environment (a) and attacker situation (b)

a technique that has been studied to delay the software analysis time. Software obfuscation techniques are used to protect the intellectual property of developers. Obfuscation divided into four categories [5,6], which are layout obfuscation, data obfuscation, control-flow obfuscation, and preventive obfuscation. A study is available that gathers the most information of obfuscated programs by performing dynamic analysis other than the virtualization obfuscation technique among control-flow obfuscation techniques. Although the virtualization obfuscation technique is known to possess a higher degree of protection compared to other obfuscation techniques, the technique is not always secure; many previous researchers have identified the limitations of virtualization obfuscation and presented the results of its deobfuscation [7–11].

This is because the analysis method is somewhat fixed when the virtualization structure is revealed statically, and many additional protection techniques of the virtualization structure have been studied as a countermeasure. However, the existing additional protection schemes for virtualization structure proposed in the past are most likely to require a strong assumption or significantly increase the performance overhead of a protected program. We will introduce these studies in Sect. 2.

In this paper, we propose a delayed analysis method for a lightweight virtualization structure that does not require a strong assumption. Hence, we propose a new virtual code protection scheme combining an anti-analysis technique and dynamic key, and explain its mechanism. The protection target herein is software containing important algorithms or important data (e.g. license key).

1.2   Contribution

- We herein present the existing anti-analysis techniques and conduct an experiment to prevent the analysis using various analysis tools. The experimental results are used as a basis for protecting the virtualization structure herein as well as a basis for the future design of new software protection schemes.
- The proposed virtualization obfuscation technique provides code integrity and the anti-analysis of protected software by applying code encryption that combines anti-analysis and dynamic key.
- As encryption and decryption are applied in units of basic blocks, the performance degradation is less than when encryption and decryption are applied in units of bytecodes.

– The anti-analysis technique used in the proposed virtualization obfuscation technique cannot easily enter the virtualization structure and the dynamic key additionally obscures the correspondence relationship between the virtual code and the handler code. This is because there's only one basic block that is revealed in decrypted form at a time; thus, the functionality analysis can be effectively delayed until an attacker acquires all basic blocks.

1.3 Paper Organization

The paper is organized as follows: Sect. 2 introduces the related work and summarizes the limitations of each study. Section 3 explains the background knowledge required to understand this paper, and Sect. 4 provides an overview of VODKA and its detailed description. In Sects. 5 and 6 respectively, we present a VODKA implementation and a security analysis of the proposed technique. Finally, Sect. 7 presents the conclusions.

2 Related Work

[2] proposed a virtualization obfuscation technique that divides the virtualization registers into two structures and adds a virtual code called a register rotation instruction (RRI) to complicate the analysis of the virtual registers. Here, RRI is a self-generated instruction that translates the position of a register allocated to a virtualization structure. In this example, the position of a virtual register stored in memory is transformed according to an argument value in the RRI. However, a limitation exists in which the correspondence between the virtual code and the handler code cannot be protected.

[3] presents various versions of virtualization structure for each level. As the level increases, the strength of the cryptographic primitives used becomes stronger; this also strengthens the security of the virtualization structure and allows the user to specify the virtualization level according to the software to be protected. However, even in the final version with the highest protection strength, the security of the static key is required to be secured. The limitation of [3] lies in establishing these strong assumptions.

[4] is a technique for creating various virtualization structures in software and selecting one at execution time. At each execution, the protection chooses a different virtualization structure to defend against a cumulative attack. A cumulative attack is an attack that finds information about protection techniques in relatively simple software with the same protection technique and simplifies the analysis of more complex software using this information. In [4], the performance degradation depends on the number of virtualization structures created in the applied software. This technique has a limitation in that no separate protection technique is applied to the selection algorithm of the virtualization structure.

3   Background

3.1   Virtualization Obfuscation

Virtualization obfuscation embeds a virtualization structure within the software and virtualizes the protected code, allowing the virtual code that cannot be executed on a typical CPU to execute.

In general obfuscation techniques, because packing or encrypted codes or data are restored to their original form, they can be restored through dynamic analysis. However, the virtualization obfuscation technique is advantageous in that it is resistant to dynamic analysis because the virtualized code is not restored to the original code. However, because the performance degradation may occur during the emulation of virtual code by inserting a virtualization structure, it is not often used with other additional protection techniques.

When applying the virtualization obfuscation technique, the following components are inserted into the software.

- Dispatcher
    - Dispatcher involves fetching/decoding an virtual code from memory and jumping to the corresponding handler code segment.
- Virtual Code
    - It is the code that modifies the original code to be protected to enable the decoding by the dispatcher. Even a simple instruction of a typical CPU will grow from tens to thousands of lines within the virtualization structure.
- Handler Code
    - The handler code defines the functionality of the virtual code.
- Virtual Register
    - The virtualization structure updates the data values similarly to a typical CPU. Hence, virtual registers exist within the virtualization structure, and the number of registers depends on the virtualization obfuscator.
- Virtual Stack
    - In stack-based virtualization structure, all data-passing operations through a virtual stack, whereas registers and memory never exchange data directly.

3.2   Dynamic Key and Static Key

Using the code-based dynamic key in our proposed method can prevent an attacker from bypassing by modifying the anti-analysis implementation code. Therefore, in this subsection, we explain the dynamic key and the static key in Table 1 before explaining the proposed technique.

In this study, we used dynamic keys for protection strength and it caused low overhead than other related works. This dynamic key can be generated by the following, among others: code-based key, time-based key, and flow-based key.

Because dynamic keys provide integrity by default, code-based keys provide code integrity [12] (tamper resistance), and time-based keys [13] provide time

Table 1. Comparing static and dynamic keys

Method	Advantages	Disadvantages	Key generation point
Dynamic key	- Static analysis can not obtain information about the key - It has the effect of verifying the integrity according to the components	Increases the program overhead to higher than that of static key	During program execution
Static key	Causes low performance degradation	An attacker can reverse the program to easily obtain the key	Always in the code section

integrity (anti-analysis). Finally, the flow-based key can provide additional flow integrity (control-flow integrity). However, because the time-based key can be misleading according to the software time measurement method and the flow-based key also can protect anti-analysis routine but compared to code-based key, it is more complicated to be implemented and causes more overhead as well. So, we propose a scheme using the code-based dynamic key.

3.3   Dynamic Binary Instrumentation (DBI)

Many limitations exist in software manual analysis. Hence, automated software analysis tools are required. This section describes the automatic software analyzer DBI and introduces the DBI's representative tool, i.e., Intel's Pintool.

DBI is a method of analyzing binary behaviors when executing software by inserting an instrumentation code in the software. In most cases, the instrumentation code will be entirely transparent to the software that it is injected to. This highlights one of the key differences between static binary analysis and dynamic binary analysis. Rather than considering what may occur, dynamic binary analysis has the benefit of operating on what actually occurs. DBI cannot analyze the overall code execution path of the software, but it compensates for these shortcomings by providing more detailed execution states [14].

A typical DBI tool is Intel's Pintool (PIN). PIN uses a large set of APIs called Pintool that can be used to write customized plugins for analysis. PIN's instrumentation engine allows Pintool to insert a customized plugin. The plugin can intercept the execution of a target program to insert user-defined code such as instruction counting, dynamic-link library (DLL) counting, memory writing and instruction collecting. Other debuggers or instruction tracing tools are available for behavioral analysis, but many reversers used Pintool because it can be customized according to the specific conditions, instead of a simple instruction or function (including DLL) tracking.

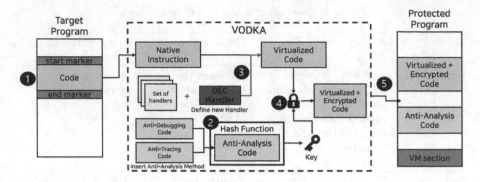

Fig. 2. Overview of our approach

4   Approach

The proposed method performs virtualization obfuscation as shown in Fig. 2.

1. The user inserts the markers into the code section for virtualization obfuscation to specify the region of obfuscation.
2. The hash value of the designed anti-analysis routine is calculated. Anti-
   analysis uses specific functions to determine the presence of debugging. Specific functions extract properties that appear when performing debugging.
3. The basic virtual code and the newly added DEC handler code are created.
   A description of the DEC handler will be provided later.
4. Encryption is performed using the virtual code from step 3 and the hash key
   calculated in step 2.
5. Finally, the raw virtual code and encrypted virtual code from step 4 are
   inserted into the program(In this paper, we assume that first basic block of
   total virtual code is revealed statically), and the designed anti-analysis code
   is inserted to end the VODKA operation.

The code block (dotted red box) of the last step is created as shown in Fig. 3.
The code encryption and decryption methods designed are as follows, and here
the **basic block** is a straight-line code sequence with no branches in except to
the entry and no branches out except at the exit [15]:

Encryption step:

1. Divide the virtual code of the virtualization obfuscation into n basic blocks.
2. Divide the hash value by the number of blocks divided.
3. The virtual code are encrypted with hash key by the XOR operation.

Decryption step: Because the decryption process step is more difficult and
more important than the encryption step, it is explained using two algorithms:
The first case (Algorithm 1) is the case when the executed virtual code block has
conditional jump instruction in the end that is not taken or has a call statement;

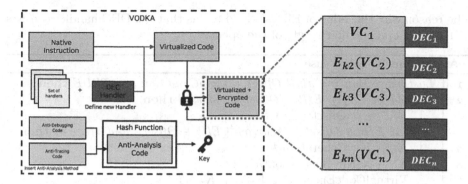

Fig. 3. Detailed VODKA code block structure (Color figure online)

the second case (Algorithm 2) is the case when the executed virtual code block has JCC in the end that is taken; the definitions of the variables in the algorithm are the same as those in Table 2.

Table 2. VODKA notations

Notation	Description
VC_i	i-th Virtual Code Block
K_i	i-th Key for Encryption/Decryption
$Flag[i]$	i-th Flag of Encryption/Decryption
EIP	Extended Instruction Pointer of Virtual Machine

Algorithm 1. Not taken Case

---

1 **if** *LastInstruction* == *CALL* ‖ *JumpCondition* == *FALSE* **then**
2   K_n = KeyGeneration(n);
3   K_{n-1} = KeyGeneration($n-1$);
4   VirtualCodeEncryption(VC_{n-1}, K_{n-1});
5   VirtualCodeDecryption(VC_n, K_n);
6      $Flag[n] = 0$;
7      $Flag[n-1] = 1$;   /* 0: Decryption, 1: Encryption */
8   EIP += 2;   /* DEC Handler size */
9   Goto *Dispatcher*;

The first algorithm is when the branch instruction in the executed block is CALL or does not taken the JCC instruction. In this case, first the encryption/decryption key is generated (KeyGeneration), the next block (VC_n) is decrypted (VirtualCodeDecryption) to execute the virtual code, and the currently executed block (VC_{n-1}) is encrypted to hide the virtual code of it. Finally, set the *Flag* value corresponding to the block and modify the *EIP* register value.

The reason why the value of EIP is added to 2 is that the DEC handler consists of 1 byte of op-code and 1 byte of the operand.

Algorithm 2. Taken case

1 **if** $LastInstruction == JMP\ Offset\ ||\ JumpCondition == TRUE$ **then**
2   **if** $Addr(n-1) \leq EIP + Offset < Addr(n)$ **then**
3 | $EIP + = Offset;$
4   **else if** $EIP + Offset \geq Addr(n)\ ||\ EIP + Offset < Addr(n-1)$ **then**
5      $K_k = \text{KeyGeneration}(k);$
6      $K_{n-1} = \text{KeyGeneration}(n-1);$
7      $\text{VirtualCodeEncryption}(VC_{n-1}, K_{n-1});$
8      $\text{VirtualCodeDecryption}(VC_k, K_k);$
9      $Flag[k] = 0;$
10     $Flag[n-1] = 1;$
11     $EIP + = Offset;$
12   Goto Dispatcher;

The second algorithm, contrary to the first algorithm, taken the JCC instruction in the executed block. In this case, two situations exist: the first is to jump into a block that has already been decrypted, and the second is to jump to another block which is encrypted. In the first case, one simply changes the EIP address to the desired address. However, in the second case, a key for decrypting the jump target block (VC_k) and a key for encrypting the block (VC_{n-1}) containing the jump instruction are generated at (KeyGeneration) function; subsequently, the encryption and decryption (VirtualCodeEncryption, VirtualCodeDecryption) function is performed. Finally, the $Flag$ value is set to correspond to the block and the EIP register value is modified.

5 Implementation

In this section, we demonstrate how VODKA encrypts and decrypts virtual code. Our implement environment OS is Windows 10, building language is C++.

5.1 Code Encryption

Figure 4 shows before and after applying VODKA to the program. Figure 4a shows the code with general virtualization obfuscation[1] applied, and Fig. 4b shows the encrypted virtual code with VODKA.

5.2 Code Decryption

We using Ollydbg observed the process of decrypting the encrypted virtual code. The result of decrypting is shown in Fig. 5. The red dotted block in Fig. 5a is

---

[1] https://github.com/nlog2n/x86obfuscator.

(a) Before applying VODKA   (b) After applying VODKA

Fig. 4. Before and After applying VODKA

the virtual code block encrypted by VODKA. The block is encrypted until it is executed. When executing the encrypted block, first the encrypted code block is decrypted using the key, and then the virtual code block is executed. The decrypted virtual code is shown in Fig. 5b. This whole process uses the newly defined DEC handler from VODKA.

```
Address  Hex dump                                                ASCII
0040611B 9F 86 9D 9D 94 4C 7D 87 91 27 E8 A0 CC 7A D4 15
0040612B A3 BF 5B 1B 19 0A 82 2C B7 59 68 10 B0 09 0F 03
0040613B BF 86 D0 05 8C 48 68 65 BC 2E EB A0 F9 7A D8 11
0040614B A3 63 69 3B 20 0B 82 60 CA 55 6E 15 71 FF F6 F7
0040615B 60 79 D5 81 7E 8E 66 6A 9A 2F 9C A8 DE 58 D0 46
0040616B BD 91 5E 5B 2B 1D 82 64 CF 59 6C 26 2A EB 14 18
0040617B 9E DD 90 BB 01 00 00 00 53 BB 00 20 40 00 8B 1B
0040618B FF D3 E9 05 00 00 00 AC 19 52 7A D5 60 9C E8 FA
0040619B 03 00 00 5F 5D 33 DB 03 DF B8 44 3F 00 00 03 D8
004061AB 89 2B 5A 33 ED 03 EF B8 58 3F 00 00 03 E8 89 55
004061BB 00 5D 33 D2 03 D7 BB 5C 3F 00 00 03 D3 89 2A 5A
```

(a) Before code decryption

```
Address  Hex dump                                                ASCII
0040611B 00 00 4D 1C 1C 00 00 E2 0B 08 02 00 09 20 04 00
0040612B 00 00 14 00 32 01 00 00 66 04 04 05 00 F9 05 0B
0040613B 20 00 00 84 04 04 15 00 26 01 01 00 3C 20 08 04
0040614B 00 DC 26 20 0B 00 00 4C 1B 08 02 00 C1 0F FC FF
0040615B FF FF 05 00 F6 C2 1B 0F 00 00 76 08 1B 02 00 53
0040616B 1E 2E 10 40 00 16 00 48 1F 04 00 33 9A 1B 1E 10
0040617B 00 5B 90 BB 01 00 00 00 53 BB 00 20 40 00 8B 1B
0040618B FF D3 E9 05 00 00 00 AC 19 52 7A D5 60 9C E8 FA
0040619B 03 00 00 5F 5D 33 DB 03 DF B8 44 3F 00 00 03 D8
004061AB 89 2B 5A 33 ED 03 EF B8 58 3F 00 00 03 E8 89 55
004061BB 00 5D 33 D2 03 D7 BB 5C 3F 00 00 03 D3 89 2A 5A
```

(b) After code decryption

Fig. 5. The code decrypt process observed by ollydbg (Color figure online)

6 Evaluation

6.1 Performance Analysis

In order to evaluate the additional performance overhead when applying VODKA, we show the result of measuring execution time after applying basic virtualization (BV) obfuscation, VMProtect [16] (VMP), Themida [17] (TMIN, with the fastest virtualization obfuscation option[Red-Tiger]) and VODKA to various programs. Results are shown in Table 3, Fig. 6a and b.

Table 3. Measuring program execution time

Target program	VO tool				
	Orig (ms & KB)	BV (ms & KB)	VMP (ms & KB)	TMIN (ms & KB)	**VODKA (ms & KB)**
HelloWorld	0.1800 (ms) 7 (KB)	0.2885 (60.28%↑) 17 (142.86%↑)	0.6394 (255.22%↑) 745 (10,543%↑)	0.2667 (48.17%↑) 2,318 (33,014%↑)	**0.2736 (52%↑) 17.7 (152%↑)**
CRC32	0.1870 (ms) 8 (KB)	0.3427 (83.26%↑) 20 (150%↑)	0.1981 (5.94%↑) 780 (9,650%↑)	0.3216 (71.98%↑) 2,346 (29,225%↑)	**0.4543 (142%↑) 24.8 (210%↑)**
AES	0.2099 (ms) 19 (KB)	0.4906 (133.73%↑) 31 (63.16%↑)	1.0107 (381.52%↑) 747 (3,832%↑)	0.6587 (213.82%↑) 2,403 (12,547%↑)	**0.6260 (198%↑) 38.4 (101%↑)**
Base64	0.2556 (ms) 9 (KB)	0.5833 (128.21%↑) 21 (133.33%↑)	1.3368 (423.00%↑) 724 (7,944%↑)	0.9016 (252.66%↑) 2,263 (25,044%↑)	**0.7663 (200%↑) 29.8 (231%↑)**
StringProcess	0.1992 (ms) 7 (KB)	0.3539 (77.66%↑) 20 (185.71%↑)	0.6861 (244.43%↑) 725 (10,257%↑)	0.7138 (258.33%↑) 2,363 (33,657%↑)	**0.5160 (159%↑) 30.1 (330%↑)**

VO: Virtualization Obfuscation, Orig: Original, BV: Basic Virtualization, VMP: VMProtect, TMIN: Themida

6.2 Anti-analysis

Before applying anti-analysis [18,19] to the virtualization obfuscation technique proposed herein, we implemented[2] various anti-analysis techniques and tested them with various analysis tools. Among the frequently used tools currently, Ollydbg [20], WinDbg [21], Pintool [22], and DynamoRIO [23] were selected as analytic tools. Ollydbg and WinDbg are debugging tools (can only execute on Window OS), and Pintool and DynamoRIO are DBI tools (can execute on Linux and Windows OS). The experimental results are shown in Table 4.

6.3 Security Analysis

In this section, we present the security analysis of the proposed VODKA herein. First, we explain how code tampering is prevented in the software with VODKA; subsequently, we explain what happens when code tampering occurs, and why it is safe for static analysis and dynamic analysis.

---

[2] https://github.com/jaeyung1001/Anti-Debugging.

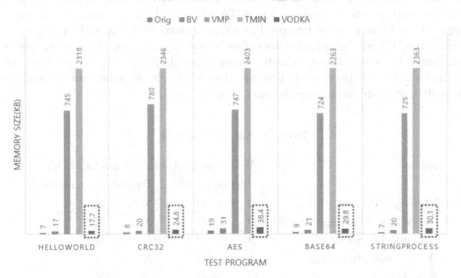

(a) Memory Overhead

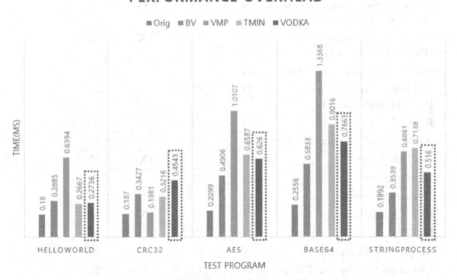

(b) Performance Overhead

Fig. 6. Overhead measuring

Tamper Resistance. In the proposed VODKA, the anti-analysis routine is embedded; therefore, the attacker can perform the analysis only by modifying the anti-analysis routine to analyze the protected program. However, VODKA generates a hash key based on the corresponding anti-analysis routine and proceeds to encryption/decryption. Figure 7a is result of execute original program. Figure 7b is a result of the executed program applied VODKA without any code tampering. When the attacker modified anti-analysis code, the correct key is not generated and cannot execute correctly as shown in Fig. 7c, because the virtual code is not decrypted correctly. Therefore, the attacker cannot analyze the software while modifying the anti-analysis code.

Table 4. Anti-analysis test

Method	Anti-analysis (Detect: O, Undetect: X)			
	Ollydbg	WinDbg	Pintool	sDynamoRIO
IsDebuggerPresent	O	O	X	X
CheckRemoteDebuggerPresent	O	O	X	X
OutputDebugString	O	O	X	O
OutputDebugStringBug	O	O	X	O
FindWindow	O	O	X	X
NtSetInformationThread Debugger Detaching	O	O	X	O
NtQueryInformationProcess (ProcessDebugFlags)	O	O	O	X
NtQueryInformationProcess (ProcessDebugPort)	O	O	X	X
Hardware BreakPoints (SEH)	O	O	X	O
Hardware BreakPoints (GetThreadContext)	O	O	X	X
RDTSC	O	O	O	X
NtQueryPerformanceCounters	O	X	O	X
GetTickCount	O	X	X	X
timeGetTime	O	O	X	X
GetSystemTime	O	X	X	X
INT 3 Exception	O	O	X	X
INT 2D	O	O	X	X
Single Step Detection	O	O	O	X
Unhandled Exception Filter	O	O	X	X
CloseHandle	X	O	X	X
Prefix Handling	O	O	O	X
Memory Breakpoints	O	X	O	X
ReadTEB	O	O	X	O
PEB NtGlobalFlag	O	O	X	X
PEB BeingDebugged	O	O	X	X
Self-Debugging	O	O	O	X

(a) Results of original program.

(b) Result execution of program applied with VODKA.

(c) When a program applied with VODKA has code modification.

Fig. 7. The execution result of programs

Static Analysis. VODKA is protected against static analysis. This is because the dynamic key is generated only when the software is executing as shown in Table 1. Therefore, the key is not exposed when analyzing statically. Hence, VODKA is safe for static analysis because the attacker cannot decrypt the encrypted virtual code with only static analysis. However, if an attacker statically finds key generation routine and calculate the decrypt key to decrypt the code, it can bypass our mechanism. It is our future work to supplement this.

Dynamic Analysis. Dynamic analysis is the most effective method to analyze software. Software using VODKA can obtain the decryption key of a block when a basic block is executed by dynamic analysis; however, it requires all revealed virtual code blocks ($VC_1, VC_2, ..., VC_n$) to determine the functionality of the program. However, VODKA requires at least n times memory dumps to analyze the functionality of the virtual code since there is no point in time when multiple blocks are decrypted at once. In addition to the difficulties of basic virtualization obfuscation analysis, VODKA is safe for dynamic analysis.

7   Conclusion

We herein proposed a delayed analysis method for a lightweight virtualization structure that does not require strong assumptions. We introduced VODKA, a new virtualization obfuscation technique combining an anti-analysis technique and dynamic key. Anti-analysis techniques are directly implemented and tested with various available analysis tools that is commonly used to provide a basis for the design of new software protection techniques in the future. For future work, we will focus on effective attacks against virtualization obfuscation and its additional protection techniques suggested at related works.

Acknowledgement. This work was supported as part of Military Crypto Research Center (UD170109ED) funded by Defense Acquisition Program Administration (DAPA) and Agency for Defense Development (ADD).

References

1. Banescu, S., Collberg, C., Pretschner, A.: Predicting the resilience of obfuscated code against symbolic execution attacks via machine learning. In: Proceedings of the 26th USENIX Security Symposium (2017)
2. Wang, H., Fang, D., Li, G., Yin, X., Zhang, B., Gu, Y.: NISLVMP: improved virtual machine-based software protection. In: 2013 9th International Conference on Computational Intelligence and Security (CIS), pp. 479–483. IEEE (2013)
3. Averbuch, A., Kiperberg, M., Zaidenberg, N.J.: Truly-protect: an efficient VM-based software protection. IEEE Syst. J. **7**(3), 455–466 (2013)
4. Kuang, K., Tang, Z., Gong, X., Fang, D., Chen, X., Wang, Z.: Enhance virtual-machine-based code obfuscation security through dynamic bytecode scheduling. Comput. Secur. **74**, 202–220 (2018)
5. Collberg, C., Thomborson, C., Low, D.: A taxonomy of obfuscating transformations. Technical report, Department of Computer Science, The University of Auckland, New Zealand (1997)
6. Banescu, S., Pretschner, A.: A tutorial on software obfuscation. In: Advances in Computers. Elsevier, Amsterdam (2018)
7. Rolles, R.: Unpacking virtualization obfuscators. In: 3rd USENIX Workshop on Offensive Technologies (WOOT) (2009)
8. Liang, M., Li, Z., Zeng, Q., Fang, Z.: Deobfuscation of virtualization-obfuscated code through symbolic execution and compilation optimization. In: Qing, S., Mitchell, C., Chen, L., Liu, D. (eds.) ICICS 2017. LNCS, vol. 10631, pp. 313–324. Springer, Cham (2018). https://doi.org/10.1007/978-3-319-89500-0_28
9. Coogan, K., Lu, G., Debray, S.: Deobfuscation of virtualization-obfuscated software: a semantics-based approach. In: Proceedings of the 18th ACM Conference on Computer and Communications Security, pp. 275–284. ACM (2011)
10. Yadegari, B., Johannesmeyer, B., Whitely, B., Debray, S.: A generic approach to automatic deobfuscation of executable code. In: 2015 IEEE Symposium on Security and Privacy (SP), pp. 674–691. IEEE (2015)
11. Guillot, Y., Gazet, A.: Automatic binary deobfuscation. J. Comput. Virol. **6**(3), 261–276 (2010)
12. Park, M.C., Koo, W.K., Suh, D.G., Kim, I.S., Lee, D.H.: TSTR: two-stage tamper response in tamper-resistant software. IET Softw. **10**(3), 81–88 (2016)
13. Lee, K.J., Kim, S.H., Lee, D.H.: Anti-debugging scheme with time-based key generation. J. Secur. Eng. **10**, 291–304 (2013)
14. Dynamic binary instrumentation. http://uninformed.org/index.cgi?v=7&a=1&p=3
15. Basic block. https://en.wikipedia.org/wiki/Basic_block
16. VMProtect. http://vmpsoft.com/
17. Themida. https://oreans.com/
18. LordNoteworthy: Public malware techniques used in the wild: virtual machine, emulation, debuggers, sandbox detection (2018). https://github.com/LordNoteworthy/al-khaser
19. Hong, S.H., Park, Y.S.: The design and implementation of pin plugin tool to bypass anti-debugging techniques, pp. 33–42, October 2016

20. OllyDbg. http://www.ollydbg.de/
21. WinDbg.   https://developer.microsoft.com/en-US/windows/downloads/windows-10-sdk
22. Pintool.   https://software.intel.com/en-us/articles/pin-a-dynamic-binary-instrumentation-tool
23. DynamoRIO. http://www.dynamorio.org/

Reliable Rowhammer Attack and Mitigation Based on Reverse Engineering Memory Address Mapping Algorithms

Saeyoung Oh and Jong Kim[(✉)]

Department of Computer Science and Engineering,
Pohang University of Science and Technology (POSTECH),
Pohang, Republic of Korea
{osy4997,jkim}@postech.ac.kr

Abstract. Rowhammer attacks intentionally induce bit flips to corrupt victim's data whose integrity must be guaranteed. To perform sophisticated rowhammer attacks, attackers need to repeatedly access the neighboring rows of target data. In DRAM, however, the physical addresses of neighboring rows are not always contiguous even if they are located before or after a target row. Hence, it is important to know the mapping algorithm which maps between physical addresses and physical row indexes not only for an attack but also for protection.

In this paper, we introduce a method to reverse engineer the exact mapping algorithm and demonstrate that the assumption in previous rowhammer work is faulty. In addition, we introduce a novel and efficient rowhammer method and improve existing mitigations that has a security hole caused by the faulty assumption. Finally, we evaluate the effectiveness of the proposed attack and show that the proposed mitigation almost perfectly defends against rowhammer attacks.

Keywords: Rowhammer bug · Reverse engineer ·
Memory address mapping

1 Introduction

In the last decades, DRAM has evolved dramatically. Researchers and manufacturers have devoted many efforts to increase the capacity of DRAM memory. As a consequence, the recent DRAM achieves high cell density, and thus, can hold large amounts of data. Despite the benefit, the development also brought side effects such as hardware faults which threaten data integrity.

A rowhammer attack is a representative attack abusing a disturbance error which is one of the high-density DRAM hardware faults. This attack corrupts target data by maximizing the effects of disturbance errors. In specific, the attacks

© Springer Nature Switzerland AG 2019
B. B. Kang and J. Jang (Eds.): WISA 2018, LNCS 11402, pp. 146–158, 2019.
https://doi.org/10.1007/978-3-030-17982-3_12

repeatedly access the neighboring rows of the target row that contains the target data. Although rowhammer attacks exploit a hardware fault, the attacks are performed at the software level without direct access to the hardware.

One of the requirements for rowhammer attacks is that attackers need to access the neighboring rows of the target row in the same bank. However, the mapping information between the user-level locations (e.g., virtual addresses or physical addresses) and physical locations on DRAM (e.g., row and bank information) is not available publicly. Therefore, it is not straightforward to access the upper and lower neighboring rows in the same bank.

To find the mapping, previous work has reverse engineered the mapping algorithm between physical addresses and physical DRAM bank indexes [10,14]. Using the mapping algorithm for banks, it is possible to track down bank indexes with physical addresses. However, no method has been proposed to find the exact mapping algorithm for rows, although a part of the mapping algorithm is already revealed [4]. To defend against the rowhammer attacks, a mitigation also has to understand the mapping algorithm since it has to locate the exact neighboring rows. However, due to the difficulty of knowing row-mapping information, previous work has used a naïve assumption that DRAM rows are arranged identically to the sequence of physical addresses [1,3]. If the assumption is faulty, these mitigations will not work as the intended way.

In this paper, we introduce a method to reverse engineer the mapping algorithm for rows. This method exploits the insight that rowhammer induces bit flips only on the neighboring rows. Based on this method, we demonstrate the invalidity of the commonly presumed assumption that physically contiguous rows have also contiguous physical addresses, and propose a novel and precise mapping algorithm-aware rowhammer attack. Also, we show that this invalid assumption causes a security hole in existing mitigation methods, and improve the existing mitigation by using our method to reverse engineer the mapping algorithm. Finally, we evaluate our attack and mitigation methods.

The contributions of our research are as follows:

- We introduce a method to reverse engineer the DRAM row organization and discover the mapping algorithm for rows. To the best of our knowledge, no such method has been used by the previous work to reverse engineer the organization of DRAM modules.
- We propose a novel and precise rowhammer attack with exact mapping algorithm.
- We explain a security hole of existing mitigations and improve one of the mitigations using our exact mapping algorithm.

2   Background

In this section, we introduce DRAM organization and a rowhammer bug. In addition, we explain the prior work to reverse engineer the DRAM mapping algorithm.

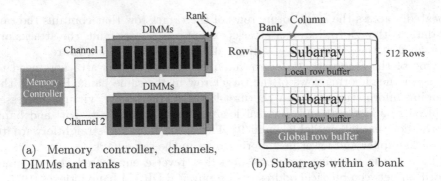

(a) Memory controller, channels, DIMMs and ranks

(b) Subarrays within a bank

Fig. 1. DRAM organization.

2.1 DRAM Organization

DRAMs are hierarchically organized (Fig. 1a). Channels connect a memory controller to Dual Inline Memory Modules (DIMMs). Modern DIMMs can have at most eight ranks which denote sets of DRAM chips. Each rank has multiple banks and banks contain numerous cells that store the voltage representing logical data. All cells are connected horizontally and vertically through wordlines and bitlines. The horizontally and vertically connected cells are respectively called rows and columns (Fig. 1b).

The 2D array of cells is subdivided into several subarrays [7]. Each subarray is composed of 512 rows and has regularity, which indicates that the subarray internal organizations are same as each other. All the cells in one subarray are connected to one local row buffer, and all local row buffers are connected to one global row buffer (Fig. 1b). All row buffers store and amplify the voltage of DRAM data to a recognizable level.

The data on the DRAM cells are volatile because the voltage representing the data is leaked over time, leading to data loss. Therefore, the voltage is maintained by refreshing cells periodically before the voltage drops below the threshold (the indicator to determine whether the data is 0 or 1).

2.2 Rowhammer

Since DRAM chips have been compressed remarkably to increase the capacity within limited space, many hardware faults have emerged [2,5,6]. One of the hardware faults is a disturbance error which hazards data integrity due to interferences of adjacent cells.

Rowhammer is a method to intentionally induce the disturbance error. Rowhammer is performed by repeatedly and rapidly accessing a DRAM row (called an aggressor row). This process accelerates the effect of the disturbance error, that corrupts the neighboring rows (called target rows or victim rows) of the aggressor row.

Double-sided rowhammer, an effective method to induce bit flips, was introduced in [12]. Double-sided rowhammer repeatedly accesses both upper and lower neighboring rows of a target row, while the single-sided rowhammer repeatedly accesses only a single neighboring row to induce bit flips on the target row. To corrupt target data by using double-sided rowhammer (or single-sided rowhammer) exquisitely, it is necessary to know the user-level address (i.e., virtual address) of upper and lower neighboring rows in the same bank. Previous work [11,13] has introduced the methods to know the virtual addresses that correspond to the physical addresses of potential neighboring rows. However, since these methods are performed with the unproven assumption that contiguous rows have contiguous physical addresses, the potential neighboring rows may not be actual neighboring rows. Therefore, to precisely corrupt the target row, attackers need to know the exact physical addresses corresponding to the neighboring rows in the same bank.

2.3 Mapping Algorithm

To access data on DRAM module, the memory controller locates the data on DRAM by referring to mapping algorithm. The mapping algorithm determines the location of data on DRAM and is composed of several physical address bits. Since it must map the physical address to the hierarchies of DRAM, the algorithm consists of sub-mapping algorithms for channels, modules, ranks, banks, and rows.

The mapping algorithm for banks is reverse engineered in previous work [10, 14]. By using a timing method which is related to row buffers, this work reveals that the mapping algorithm for banks is composed of XORed combinations of certain physical address bits. In contrast, the mapping algorithm for rows cannot be reverse engineered with the method which is used in the work. While it is possible to find which physical address bits compose the mapping algorithm for rows, it is impossible to identify how the composed bits of physical address determine the physical location of rows. This means that it is possible to distinguish whether the row of a certain physical address is different from the rowhammer target row in the same bank, but it is impossible to identify the exact upper and lower rows of the target row.

3   Reverse Engineering Mapping Algorithm

While the mapping algorithm for banks is reverse engineered, the mapping algorithm for rows cannot be reverse engineered using the timing method. Therefore, previous work [1,3,14] has naïve assumption that physical rows are arranged identically to physical addresses. According to the prior assumption, two rows are physically contiguous if the physical addresses of these rows are contiguous in the same bank.

Let r represent a row address composed of $\{b_0, b_1, \ldots, b_n\}$, b_i be the ith row bit, where n is the number of bits on a logical row address. The row index function on prior assumption is:

$$LRow(r) = \sum_{i=0}^{n} 2^i b_i, \tag{1}$$

where r is a row address. These bits of a row address can be extracted from a physical address by using the previous methods [10, 14]. We call this function (1) a logical row index function in this paper. Previous work has not demonstrated that the logical row index function is used in the real architecture.

The goal of this section is to find the real mapping algorithm. We can express the mapping algorithm as:

$$PRow(r) = \sum_{i=0}^{n} 2^i F_i(r) \tag{2}$$

We call this function (2) a physical row index function in this paper and the goal of this section is to find the $F_i(r)$ that is assumed to consist of physical address bits.

Before explaining our method in detail, we assume that 512 contiguous logical rows constitute one physical subarray and the mapping algorithm of one DRAM subarray also works for all DRAM subarrays. These assumptions seem reasonable due to the regularity of DRAM subarrays [5]. Therefore, we only focus on the lower 9 bits of a row address because each DRAM subarray consists of 512 ($=2^9$) rows.

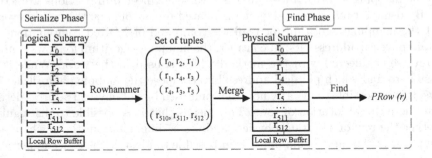

Fig. 2. Overall procedure of reverse engineering.

We reverse engineer the mapping algorithm in two steps. First, we arrange DRAM rows in sequential order by using rowhammer. We refer to this step as row serialization. Second, we manually find the mapping algorithm with the serialized rows, that is finding the function $F_i(r)$. The overall procedure of reverse engineering is shown in Fig. 2.

3.1   Row Serialization

In this subsection, we describe how to serialize rows of the single subarray in physical order to find the exact mapping algorithm. The key idea of row serialization is that *rowhammer induces bit flips only on the neighboring rows of an aggressor row*. We can identify the neighboring rows of aggressor rows by detecting the rows that have been corrupted by the rowhammer.

For convenience, we first define the following primitives:

- r_n is a row address which is composed of $\{b_0, b_1, b_2, ..., b_i\}$, where i is the number of bits on row address r_n.
- $sr_{n,m}$ is a row that is sandwiched between rows r_n and r_m.
- $Dhammer(r_n, r_m)$ returns the set of the rows that have been corrupted by double-sided rowhammer when r_n and r_m are aggressor rows.
- $Shammer(r)$ returns the set of the rows that have been corrupted by single-sided rowhammer when r is an aggressor row.

We perform double-sided rowhammer with all the combinations of two rows within a single DRAM subarray to find a row that is sandwiched between two rows. A single DRAM subarray consists of 512 rows, so the number of cases is at most $\binom{512}{2} = 130,816$. Thus, we argue that the time required to perform the rowhammer with two selected rows is feasible. We check which rows have been corrupted by double-sided rowhammer on the selected rows r_n and r_m. By this process, we can find the set of $Dhammer(r_n, r_m)$, which is related to $sr_{n,m}$. However, the set of $Dhammer(r_n, r_m)$ may contain rows that are adjacent to the other sides of the aggressor rows in addition to the sandwiched rows due to the effects of single-sided rowhammer. Therefore, we remove the effect of single-sided rowhammer by excluding the sets of $Shammer(r_n)$ and $Shammer(r_m)$ from $Dhammer(r_n, r_m)$ by performing additional single-sided rowhammer on r_m and r_n.

Ideally, $Dhammer(r_n, r_m) - Shammer(r_n) - Shammer(r_m)$ must have only one row $sr_{n,m}$ because only one sandwiched row can be between two aggressor rows. Therefore, except for two boundary rows (the 0th row and the 512th row) which are not affected by double-sided rowhammer, 510 tuples $(r_n, sr_{n,m}, r_m)$ can be obtained within a single DRAM subarray. This tuple indicates a sequence of physically contiguous rows. After obtaining the tuple, we can infer overall row arrangements due to the subarray regularity.

With the tuples, we can reconstruct a subarray by using the following rules:

- If two tuples, $(r_{n_1}, sr_{n_1,m_1}, r_{m_1})$ and $(r_{n_2}, sr_{n_2,m_2}, r_{m_2})$ exist such that $sr_{n_1,m_1} = r_{n_2}$ and $r_{m_1} = sr_{n_2,m_2}$, then the two tuples can be merged into $(r_{n_1}, r_{n_2}, r_{m_1}, r_{m_2})$.
- If two tuples, $(r_{n_3}, sr_{n_3,m_3}, r_{m_3})$ and $(r_{n_4}, sr_{n_4,m_4}, r_{m_4})$ exist such that $r_{m_3} = r_{n_4}$, then the two tuples can be merged into $(r_{n_3}, sr_{n_3,m_3}, r_{m_3}, sr_{n_4,m_4}, r_{m_4})$.

Using this method, we can ideally merge all of the tuples into one sequentially ordered tuple, that is, the physical sequence of 512 rows within a single DRAM subarray.

The success of row serialization depends on the number of corrupted rows after performing double-sided rowhammer. However, some rows might not be corrupted. To resolve this problem, we focus on the subarray regularity, which means that every subarray is organized identically. Due to this regularity, undiscovered tuples in one subarray can be obtained from another subarray.

3.2 Finding Mapping Algorithm

Next, we use the serialized rows to find the mapping algorithm of physical row indexes $PRow(r_n)$ (or $F_i(r)$). As we mentioned, the input of this function (2) is a row address and the output is a physical row index. We manually find the function $PRow(r)$ by exploiting the insight that the discovered tuple $(r_n, sr_{n,m}, r_m)$ implies $PRow(r_n) + 1 = PRow(sr_{n,m})$ and $PRow(r_m) - 1 = PRow(sr_{n,m})$, which means that the rows of the tuple are sequentially contiguous.

3.3 Row Address Mapping Schemes

We tested six DDR3 modules of three major DRAM manufacturers with this method to reverse engineer the mapping algorithm (Table 1). By using this method, we discovered two mapping algorithm schemes, which are address mirroring and row twisting. As a result, we demonstrate that the prior assumption is faulty.

Address Mirroring. The first scheme is observed only on one rank[1] of two-rank DRAM modules for all of the experimented manufacturers. The other rank is subject to either the logical row index function or row twisting. The physical row index function is (we mark the components which are different from the logical row index function in bold):

i	0	1	2	3	4	5	6	7	8
$F_i(r)$	b_0	b_1	b_2	$\mathbf{b_4}$	$\mathbf{b_3}$	$\mathbf{b_6}$	$\mathbf{b_5}$	$\mathbf{b_8}$	$\mathbf{b_7}$

JEDEC [4] documents this scheme, called address mirroring that is deployed to increase throughput by cross-wiring some wires on one rank. We can identify that our discovered physical row index is address mirroring because the index of address mirroring in the JEDEC standard is exactly identical with ours. The sameness implies that our method to reverse engineer is valid to find the exact physical address.

---

[1] In fact, it is impossible to distinguish the rank bits and bank bits from the existing reverse engineering method. However, since we can track the difference of mapping algorithm for each rank, we can infer which bit of the bank bits is a rank bit.

Row Twisting. The second scheme is observed only on DRAMs from A manufacturer, and we call the scheme row twisting. The physical row index function is (we mark the components which are different from the logical row index function in bold):

i	0	1	2	3	4	5	6	7	8
$F_i(r)$	b_0	$\mathbf{b_1} \oplus \mathbf{b_3}$	$\mathbf{b_2} \oplus \mathbf{b_3}$	b_3	b_4	b_5	b_6	b_7	b_8

According to our experimental result, the row twisting function is applied after address mirroring. For example, when a module is affected by both row twisting and address mirroring, the bit swap of b_3 and b_4 is first performed (due to address mirroring) and the swapped b_3 (originally b_4) is XORed with b_2 and b_1 later (due to row twisting). Therefore, we infer that row twisting is an internal mechanism of DRAM chip unlike address mirroring which is a mechanism at a circuit level. We also infer that row twisting is somehow related to twisted wordline schemes [8,9].

Table 1. Address mirroring and row twisting on DDR3 modules of three major manufacturers.

Tag	Manufacturer	Model	# of ranks	Mirroring	Twisting
A	SAMSUNG	M378B5273DH0-CK0	2	✓	✓
B		M378B5273DH0-CH9	2	✓	✓
C		M378B5173QH0-CK0	1		✓
D	HYNIX	HMT351U6CFR8C-PB	2	✓	
E		HMT351U6CFR8C-H9	2	✓	
F	MICRON	MT16JTF51264AZ-1G6M1*	2	✓	

*In this case, there are not enough bit flips to reverse engineer the mapping algorithm. However, since some bit flips are induced in rowhammer experiments with only address mirroring, we infer that this module is affected only by address mirroring.

4   Mapping Algorithm-Aware Rowhammer

If attackers know the exact mapping algorithm for rows, the attackers can perform more effective rowhammer attack by inducing more exploitable bit flips. In addition, attackers can exquisitely perform rowhammer attacks because the attackers can locate the exact upper/lower neighboring rows of the target row. We refer to this method as mapping algorithm-aware rowhammer.

We give an example of rows that are vulnerable to rowhammer attacks (Fig. 3). For simplicity, we assume that the DRAM module is affected by only address mirroring. When the faulty assumption is applied, the upper row is Row_b

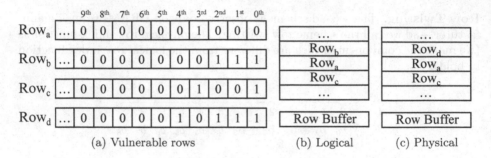

(a) Vulnerable rows   (b) Logical   (c) Physical

Fig. 3. Vulnerable rows on address mirroring. The upper row in logical index (b) and the upper row in physical index (c) is different about Row_a.

and the lower row is Row_c with respect to Row_a (Fig. 3b). However, the upper row of Row_a in address mirroring is actually Row_d, not Row_b (Fig. 3c). The logical row indexes of Row_a, Row_b, Row_c and Row_d are 8, 7, 9 and 23, but their physical row indexes are 16, 7, 17 and 15, respectively.

We evaluate the effectiveness of mapping algorithm-aware rowhammer. To evaluate the effectiveness, we measured the number of bit flips that were caused by double-sided rowhammer. We exploited three kinds of double-sided rowhammer:

(i) R1 is performed with the assumption that physically contiguous rows have contiguous physical addresses.

(ii) R2 is performed with the assumption that row indexes are affected only by address mirroring.

(iii) R3 is performed with the assumption that row indexes are affected by both address mirroring and row twisting.

We performed these three types of rowhammer on the memory space that is different from the subarray used in the experiment of Table 1. We tested on two modules: one was inferred to be affected only by address mirroring (module D); the other was inferred to be affected by both address mirroring and row twisting (module A) by our proposed method. We measured the number of bit flips on two processors, Sandy Bridge (i7-2600) and Haswell (i5-4460).

Although the prior assumption is faulty, R1 showed considerable bit flips (Fig. 4). The abnormal result is because some physical rows are sequential like logical rows, or single-sided rowhammer has shown an effect even if the attack uses double-sided rowhammer. However, module A shows the largest number of bit flips by R3 (25% more bit flips than R1 on average), and module D shows the largest number of bit flips by R2 (12% more bit flips than R1 on average). This experimental result shows that the proposed attack method, mapping algorithm-aware rowhammer, is more efficient than the conventional method regardless of processor types.

Also, this experimental result validates that our discovered mapping algorithm is correct.

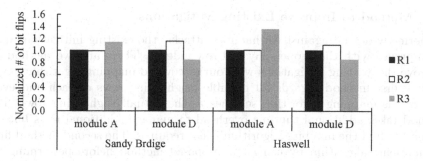

Fig. 4. Normalized number of bit flips. The number of bit flips for each case is normalized to R1.

5 Improved Mitigation

In this section, we explain existing mitigations and how the mitigations can be attacked by rowhammer attacks. Then, we improve Anvil, one of the existing mitigation methods, and evaluate its effectiveness as a proof-of-concept.

5.1 Existing Mitigations and a Security Hole

We study two representative mitigations, Anvil [1] and G-CATT [3], and explain how they are affected negatively by the faulty assumption using the aforementioned example of the vulnerable row (Fig. 3).

Anvil. Anvil defends rowhammer attacks by refreshing potential victim rows when the signs of rowhammer attacks are detected. The potential victim rows are the neighboring rows of the detected aggressor rows and thus Anvil refreshes the presumed neighboring rows.

However, according to the faulty assumption of Anvil, Anvil regards Row_b and Row_c as potential victim rows when Row_a is the aggressor row (Fig. 3b). Therefore, if attackers repeatedly access the aggressor row Row_a, bit flips may occur on Row_d, which was not refreshed by Anvil. As a result, Anvil can detect rowhammer attacks but cannot refresh all the victim rows.

G-CATT. G-CATT defends rowhammer attacks by putting a row between rows of different security domains (e.g., kernel and user) to physically separate the rows. Since rowhammer attacks only corrupt rows that are adjacent to aggressor rows, attackers cannot corrupt victim memory on G-CATT.

However, according to the faulty assumption of G-CATT, G-CATT expects that Row_a and Row_d are already separated (Fig. 3b). Therefore, if an attacker process is allocated in Row_d, Row_a is vulnerable to rowhammer attacks.

5.2   Method to Improve Existing Mitigations

To perfectly defend against rowhammer attacks, the existing mitigations must be improved with the proper physical row indexes. There are two methods to improve the existing mitigations with our discovered mapping algorithm.

The first method regards all possible neighboring rows of each and every case of the mapping algorithm schemes as the actual neighboring rows. This method takes additional runtime overhead to manage additional rows but our method to find the mapping algorithm is not required. The second method finds the mapping algorithm by using our proposed method before performing the existing mitigations. This method is only possible when the victim's DRAM modules are vulnerable enough to be able to be reverse engineered and initial time to find the mapping algorithm. However, this method does not need an additional runtime overhead compared to the first method.

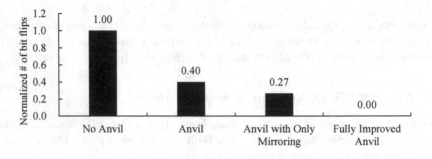

Fig. 5. Normalized number of bit flips with module A on Sandy Bridge.

5.3   Evaluation

We measured the bit flips by rowhammer on module A to evaluate the effectiveness of the improved mitigation that considers the exact mapping algorithm schemes. First, to show the security hole of existing mitigations, we performed single-sided rowhammer on Anvil with only the mapping algorithm for banks. Next, we improved Anvil into two cases: one is improved by considering only address mirroring, and the other is improved by considering both address mirroring and row twisting. We perform single-sided rowhammer again on those two improved Anvil methods (Fig. 5).

Anvil and Anvil with only mirroring might refresh actual victim rows because some refreshed rows are actual victim rows in spite of the faulty information about the neighboring rows. However, not all potential victim rows are actual victim rows, and thus Anvil and Anvil with only mirroring cannot refresh all of the actual victim rows. Fully improved Anvil, which is modified by using our mapping algorithm, shows no bit flips. This result shows that the fully improved mitigation can effectively defend against rowhammer attacks. In addition, we believe that G-CATT also properly prevents rowhammer attacks if the exact mapping algorithm is applied to G-CATT.

6   Conclusion

We introduced a method to reverse engineer the mapping algorithm for rows and revealed an exact mapping algorithm for rows. This method uses the feature that rowhammer induces bit flips only on the neighboring rows of aggressor rows. Using this method, we can infer the exact row arrangement. As a result, we demonstrate that previous work has faulty assumption that physically contiguous rows have also contiguous physical addresses.

Based on the exact physical row index, we can induce bit flips more efficiently than the conventional rowhammer method which does not consider the exact physical row index. Note that more bit flips make the rowhammer attack more successful because there are more candidates of exploitable bit flips. Also, we have shown that it is possible to make bit flips in the system with rowhammer mitigation methods if they were used with the faulty assumption. Finally, we have improved the existing mitigation and showed that the improved mitigation perfectly protects against rowhammer attacks.

Acknowledgement. This work was supported by the National Research Foundation of Korea (NRF) grant funded by the Korea government (MSIP) (No. 2017R1A2B4010914).

References

1. Aweke, Z.B., et al.: ANVIL: software-based protection against next-generation rowhammer attacks. ACM SIGPLAN Not. **51**(4), 743–755 (2016)
2. Baumann, R.: The impact of technology scaling on soft error rate performance and limits to the efficacy of error correction. In: International Electron Devices Meeting, IEDM 2002, pp. 329–332. IEEE (2002)
3. Brasser, F., Davi, L., Gens, D., Liebchen, C., Sadeghi, A.R.: Can't touch this: software-only mitigation against rowhammer attacks targeting kernel memory. In: Proceedings of the 26th USENIX Security Symposium (Security), Vancouver, BC, Canada (2017)
4. JEDEC: DDR3 SDRAM Unbuffered DIMM Design Specification, rev. 1.06 (2013)
5. Khan, S., Lee, D., Mutlu, O.: Parbor: an efficient system-level technique to detect data-dependent failures in dram. In: 2016 46th Annual IEEE/IFIP International Conference on Dependable Systems and Networks (DSN), pp. 239–250. IEEE (2016)
6. Kim, Y., et al.: Flipping bits in memory without accessing them: an experimental study of dram disturbance errors. In: 2014 ACM/IEEE 41st International Symposium on Computer Architecture (ISCA), pp. 361–372, June 2014
7. Kim, Y., Seshadri, V., Lee, D., Liu, J., Mutlu, O.: A case for exploiting subarray-level parallelism (SALP) in dram. ACM SIGARCH Comput. Arch. News **40**(3), 368–379 (2012)
8. Min, D.S., Langer, D.W.: Twisted line techniques for multi-gigabit dynamic random access memories, US Patent 6,034,879, 7 March 2000
9. Min, D.S., Seo, D.I., You, J., Cho, S., Chin, D., Park, Y.: Wordline coupling noise reduction techniques for scaled drams. In: 1990 Symposium on VLSI Circuits, Digest of Technical Papers, pp. 81–82. IEEE (1990)

10. Pessl, P., Gruss, D., Maurice, C., Schwarz, M., Mangard, S.: DRAMA: exploiting dram addressing for cross-CPU attacks. In: USENIX Security Symposium, pp. 565–581 (2016)
11. Razavi, K., Gras, B., Bosman, E., Preneel, B., Giuffrida, C., Bos, H.: Flip Feng Shui: hammering a needle in the software stack. In: USENIX Security Symposium, pp. 1–18 (2016)
12. Seaborn, M., Dullien, T.: Exploiting the DRAM rowhammer bug to gain kernel privileges (2015). https://googleprojectzero.blogspot.kr/2015/03/exploiting-dram-rowhammer-bug-to-gain.html
13. Van Der Veen, V., et al.: Drammer: deterministic rowhammer attacks on mobile platforms. In: Proceedings of the 2016 ACM SIGSAC Conference on Computer and Communications Security, pp. 1675–1689. ACM (2016)
14. Xiao, Y., Zhang, X., Zhang, Y., Teodorescu, R.: One bit flips, one cloud flops: cross-VM row hammer attacks and privilege escalation. In: USENIX Security Symposium, pp. 19–35 (2016)

A Study on Analyzing Risk Scenarios About Vulnerabilities of Security Monitoring System: Focused on Information Leakage by Insider

Kunwoo Kim(iD) and Jungduk Kim(✉)(iD)

Chung-Ang University, Seoul 06974, Republic of Korea
kunwoo.kim317@gmail.com, jdkimsac@cau.ac.kr

Abstract. Information leakage by insider results in financial losses and ethical issues, thus affects business sustainability as well as corporate reputation. In Korea, information leakage by insiders occupies about 80% of the security incidents. Most companies are establishing preventive and prohibited security policies. Nevertheless, security incidents are unceasing. Such restrictive security policies inhibit work efficiency or make employees recognize security negatively. Due to these problems, the rapid detection capability of leakage signs is required. To detect the signs of information leakage, security monitoring is an essential activity. This study is an exploratory case study that analyzed the current state of security monitoring operated by three companies in Korea and provides some risk scenarios about information leakage. For the case analysis, this study collected each company's security policy, systems linked with security monitoring system, and system log used. As a result, this study identified vulnerabilities that were difficult to be detected with the current security monitoring system, and drew 4 risk scenarios that were likely to occur in the future. The results of this study will be useful for the companies that are planning to establish effective security monitoring system.

Keywords: Insider threat · Information leakage · Security monitoring

1 Introductions

With the development of information technology and the improvement of personal capacity in computing ability, the business efficiency using information technology is improving, whereas the security incident like information leakage is increasing. According to statistics, information leakage affects both the companies and customers, and in case of companies, customer confidence declines and market share reduces and in case of customers, secondary damage is expected by personal information leakage [1]. This means that information leakage is highly relevant to the sustainability of the company. One interesting fact is that there is a difference in the subject who involves in information leakage between Korea and foreign countries. In case of foreign countries, information leakage by hackers occurs three times more than information leakage by insider, on the other hand, in case of Korea, about 80% of the subjects who leaked information appear as insider [2]. As can be seen in the result of study, the current

© Springer Nature Switzerland AG 2019
B. B. Kang and J. Jang (Eds.): WISA 2018, LNCS 11402, pp. 159–170, 2019.
https://doi.org/10.1007/978-3-030-17982-3_13

security system in Korean companies has limitations in preventing insiders from leaking information although it is appropriate for defending external threats.

Currently in Korea, most companies are establishing and operating various security systems to prevent security incidents. However, despite such efforts, it is impossible to prevent security incidents perfectly as can be seen in the cases of the past. In other words, Korea has a high level of dependence on prevention-centered security measures including access control, document encryption by DRM (Digital Right Management), storage device control and email control. Nevertheless, security incident like information leakage inevitably occurs. Also, prevention-centered security measures involve various problems including hindrance to business efficiency and increase in negative awareness of security [3]. Of course, preventing security incident like information leakage is important, but it is necessary to improve the ability to detect and respond to the signs of leakage as quickly as possible.

However, it is not easy to detect the information leakage by insider quickly at all. The amount of event (access log, usage log, etc.) that is occurred by employees are vast and false positive also occurs often [4]. Also, the focus was on detecting unusual behavior in the past, but analyzing the misuse cases of employees who have an authority and look normal is a difficult task particularly in Korea [5]. Therefore, to monitor the signs of information leakage by insider effectively, it is necessary to analyze the current state of monitoring by companies and draw the improvement direction. This study is a case study on security monitoring to detect the signs of information leakage, among insider threats as quickly as possible. For the case study, this study collected the information related to security monitoring system being operated by companies in fields of finance, manufacturing, and information communication technology in Korea where information leakage incident occurs relatively frequently. And this study draws some limitations and suggestions by analyzing to which system the security monitoring system is linked and which logs are collected and utilized.

2 Theoretical Background

2.1 Insider Threat and Information Leakage

This section describes the definition and types of insider threat and looks at why insider threat is important and especially through which routes the information is leaked. There are various definitions on insider and in general, insider is defined as a person who can access IT system legitimately [6]. Therefore, an insider can be defined as a person who has the legal right to access the information assets of an organization logically or physically and thus may have a negative influence on confidentiality, integrity, and availability of information assets. In addition, the term can be distinguished from external attacker like hacker, by the term 'legitimately'.

As can be seen in the definition above, insider means a person who knows the internal affairs of an organization. Therefore, an insider is more threatening than an outsider, as an insider knows the value of confidential information held by an organization, how to use a system and its vulnerabilities, and how to detour security control

[7]. In addition, an insider's misbehavior is an ethical issue and if known to the outside, may have a bad influence on corporate reputation [1]. Therefore, security measures should be prioritized by focusing on security threats like insider's leakage of confidential information, even though incidents by a hacking attack have recently been increasing.

In general, an insider threat means the abuse and misuse of the authority given oneself to access the assets of an organization and use them [8]. The term 'abuse and misuse' includes unintended behavior like making a mistake as well as inappropriate behavior stemming from malicious intent. Therefore, an insider's security threat is an act that accesses a system or treats information and data in violation of an organization's security policy, either intentionally or unintentionally [9]. For example, when an employee accessed a vulnerable website and got infected by malignant code by mistake including leakage of company secrets to the outside, the leakage of secrets by hacking also belongs to insider's security threat.

An insider's security threat can be classified into Intentional Destruction, Detrimental Misuse, Dangerous Tinkering, and Naive Mistakes, depending on the behavior intention that may cause damage [10]. Intentional Destruction includes the act to destroy an IT system maliciously or delete information and data and Detrimental Misuse means the use of the authority given for a purpose of making personal gains or damaging the company. Dangerous Tinkering and Naive Mistakes mean an act to set up a system without using a strong password or considering the security, although there is no malicious intent. The information leakage is a malicious violation of security policy for personal gains and thus belongs to detrimental misuse and is classified as high-risk group. In addition, a recent study suggests the relevance between attitude and security [11]. However, there was no explanation about how to detect the deliberate risk-inclined behaviors.

2.2 Security Monitoring

Most companies in Korea are establishing and operating various security systems to prevent information leakage. If a lot of security system is established, the risk level of information leakage will be lowered, but business efficiency will also decline and thus the current trends are that they establish proper number of security system and detect unusual signs quickly. To detect unusual signs, monitoring is essential, and in general, the term monitoring is defined as collecting the information related to an individual [12]. Therefore, security monitoring can be defined as collecting the information related to whether employees are complied with security policies. The security monitoring can be divided largely into the following two dimensions [13]. The first is collecting the logs of the security system that protects information assets from the external attack using Intrusion Detection System, firewall and anti-virus, and detecting whether there was an attack or not. The second is collecting the logs of the security system that protects information assets from mistakes or malicious intention of internal employees and detecting unusual signs against organization's security policy.

For security monitoring, it is essential to collect and analyze a large amount of system logs, and in general, security monitoring is performed in four steps: log collection, log analysis, correlation analysis, and risk calculation [13]. A single log is significant, but it is difficult to determine the signs of information leakage with single log only exactly and there might be a lot of false positive. Therefore, currently in Korea, most companies determine unusual signs by analyzing the correlation with single log and multiple log [14]. Logs for security monitoring can be collected at network level, system level, and application level [15]. In other words, logs can be collected from business system, electronic approval system, and personnel information system as well as security system, and the system linked with security monitoring may depend on the type and size of company.

As an analysis result of the past security incident cases in Korea, it appeared that information was leaked largely via internet, email and removal storage device [16]. Most companies block the use of commercial messenger services and restrict email sending via commercial email accounts or control the use of groupware email. Companies in Korea also detect the access and file upload to unauthorized web sites, and control the use of removal storage device such as USB and CD to prevent information leakage. The information leakage can be detected by setting threshold values based on employee's average file system access and use history [17]. In addition, symptoms of information leakage include use patterns of removal storage device, email sending patterns, document extension conversion, and unusual searches of data stored within the DB that happened in PC [18].

Meanwhile, a recent study suggested insider threat detection techniques such as anomaly based approach, role based access control, scenario based, using Decoys & Honeypots and risk analysis using psychological factors [19]. However, the study did not contain what kind of data use and how to detect the malicious behavior in detail. In addition, overseas studies related security monitoring did not consider some security systems like digital right management and removal storage device control and thus are different from the environment of Korea. Studies in Korea related security monitoring conduct research on single security system or are not specific on which logs are utilized and thus for conducting research from comprehensive perspective, it is necessary to analyze the actual monitoring cases by companies and draw improvement measures.

3   Research Methodology

There are three types in a case study. The exploratory case study is a way to look at the scale or extent of an unfamiliar problem or to suggest ideas for solving problems. The descriptive case study is a method of observing a specific phenomenon and systematically recording the result. The explanatory case study is a method of observing specific phenomena and explaining causal relationships. This study belongs to exploratory case study with a flexible design according to Yin's classification and includes semi-structured interviews with document analysis [20]. Since Yin's classification is the most cited representative case study, this study was referred to as a research methodology. For a case study, this study analyzed the current state of security monitoring operated by three companies in Korea. Three companies, targets of this study are in fields of finance, information communication technology and manufacturing, and the companies that could have a big ripple effect at the national and individual level in case of occurrence of information leakage were selected. For collecting companies' data, we pledged to ensure companies' anonymity and use the data for research purposes only.

3.1 Industrial Background

Company A is a bank that provides various banking services including deposit, loan, foreign exchange, and investment. It belongs to a large-sized bank that holds about 25 million customers and critical information includes customer information and credit information. As the company has experience with security incident in the past, it is enforcing considerably strict and limited security policy. Company B belongs to field of information communication technology industry that now provides internet portal service, mobile community service, and cloud service. Major information includes customer information and service development information. As the company thinks employees' creativity and speed of service development important, its organizational culture is relatively freewheeling. Company C is a company that manufactures belongs to large-sized company. The critical information is parts design drawing because the company involves in B2B business, and the number of individual customers is less than other companies. An organizational culture is hierarchical, but as the company requires employees to be creative, the intensity of security policy is between company A and B.

3.2 Data Collection and Analysis

For the case study, we visited three companies and collected data and information about security monitoring system. At the first, systems linked with security monitoring system were identified to check the coverage of security monitoring system against information leakage. Company A has 15, Company B has 11, and Company C has 8 systems linked with security monitoring system. Of these, 4 security systems, Storage device control, Digital right management(DRM), Email control and Website access control system are linked with security monitoring system operated by all three companies. Table 1 shows a list of systems linked with security monitoring system operated by three companies and its function.

The four security systems mentioned above have similar main functions, but can be different in their operation depending on the policy. In case of Company A, most security policies are based on blocking as default because its organizational culture is hierarchical and rigid. Thus, an approval for exception is necessary. Specially the internal network is separated from the external network, the company is blocking so that the external network cannot be accessed with the computer connected to the internal network.

Company B requires employees to be creative and relatively freewheeling organizational culture is formed and thus when it comes to security policy, its security policy is opposite to the Company A's. Use of storage device and DRM decryption are possible by entering reason only and the number of sending emails is not restricted. Also, when it comes to website access, it is permitted to access all sites that are even not registered in blacklist including harmful website.

Company C is applying security policy at intermediate level between Company A and B. For example, prior to use of storage device, pre-approval is necessary like company A. On the other hand, DRM decryption is possible as long as the document is created by the user, and in case of email sending, approval is required only if the data over 10 MB are attached. Also, it is possible to access all websites that are not registered in blacklist like Company B.

Table 1. A list of system linked with security monitoring system and its function

No.	Linked system	Function	Company		
			A	B	C
1	Information asset mgmt.	To manage hardware and software asset	O	O	O
2	Storage device control	To control unauthorized storage device use	O	O	O
3	Digital right mgmt.	To manage document encryption and decryption	O	O	O
4	Email control	To control groupware and commercial email sending	O	O	O
5	Website access control	To control unauthorized website access and file transfer	O	O	O
6	N/W access control	To control of unauthorized access to internal network	O	O	O
7	HR mgmt.	To manage information about employees	O	O	O
8	Physical access control	To control in and out of authorized and unauthorized people	O	O	–
9	Personal info. identification	To identify document that contains customer's information stored in PC	O	O	X
10	Server access control	To control unauthorized access to server of business application	O	O	–
11	DB access control	To control unauthorized access to DB of business application	O	O	–
12	Illegal software block	To control installation of illegal software	O	–	–
13	Printer control	To control document printout	O	–	–
14	Wireless intrusion prevention	To identify and block unauthorized wireless AP	O	–	–
15	Customer info. processing	To manage collection, use, storage and destruction of customer information	O	X	X
16	Design drawing mgmt.	To control read, screen capture, download of design drawing	X	X	O

* O: linked with security monitoring system/X: not established/–: not linked

Analysis of the policies of the three security monitoring systems and the security systems of the three companies shows that there is a difference in operation of the security monitoring system according to environmental factors such as the field of the company and the culture of the organization. This means that analyzing the logs collected and used by the security monitoring systems of the three companies makes it possible to generalize the monitoring status and to conduct in-depth analysis. In the other word, it is possible to identify vulnerabilities that are hard to detect using security monitoring system by analyzing logs collected for security monitoring.

4 Results

The logs collected by the linked system in the Table 2 were analyzed and the vulnerabilities difficult to detect in common by three companies and the weak points by each company were drawn. At the first, the three companies all appeared not having collected the file types from the removable device control system. In this case, employees can change file type that not supported to DRM encryption and the leakage is difficult to detect because it is hard to conduct the correlation analysis of the logs collected from removable device control, DRM, and email control system. In case of company A and B, both are not collecting the HDD (Hard Disk Drive) information from the information asset management system. Thus, employees can release information by connecting the detachable HDD to PC where security software is not installed with slave. In case of company B, attached files and related logs are collected from the email control system, however a log related to the body of the message is not collected. Thus, it still has vulnerability in that email can be sent by attaching the service development information including source code to the body. In case of Company C, as the company does not collect access log and output log, it is difficult to detect the behaviors to print out and export the document to the outside. Therefore, based on the above log analysis results, it is possible to derive scenarios related to information leakage.

Table 2. Linked system and collected log

No.	Linked system	Collected log	Company		
			A	B	C
1	Information asset mgmt.	Employee name, user ID, Dept., position, PC name, MAC, IP, OS info., on/off status, power on time, power off time	O	O	O
		HDD serial number, number of HDD, HDD detachment code	X	X	O
2	Storage device control	PC name, MAC, IP, employee number, employee name, user ID, Dept., position, media type, start time, end time, file name, file size, number of file, download time, upload time, fail time	O	O	O
		Exception type, use request time, approval time, approval code	O	X	O
		Reason of use	X	O	X

(*continued*)

Table 2. (*continued*)

No.	Linked system	Collected log	Company		
			A	B	C
3	Digital right mgmt.	Employee name, user ID, Dept., position, document name, document type, creation time, creation user name, edit time, encryption time, decryption time, number of decryption, number of decryption fail, number of print, online/offline login code	O	O	O
		Exception type, decryption request time, approval time, approval code	O	X	X
		Reason of decryption	X	O	X
4	Email control	Employee name, user ID, Dept., position, sender name, send time, send IP, title, attached file name, attached file size, number of attached file, receiver name, receive time, receive IP, CC	O	O	O
		E-mail message, approval time, approval code	O	X	O
5	Website access control	Host address, access URL, access time, client IP, server IP, user ID, attached file name, attached file size, number of attached file, block URL, access time of block URL, search history	O	O	O
		Exception type, access request time, approval time, approval code	X	X	O
6	N/W access control	User ID, MAC address, IP, OS info., start time, session time, end time, policy code, access approval code, access fail code, security S/W installation code	O	O	O
7	HR mgmt.	Employee name, Dept., position, e-mail address, phone number, mobile phone number, fax number, address, birth date, gender, employment date, resignation date, employment status	O	O	O
		Attendance time	X	O	X
8	Physical access control	Employee name, employee number, Dept., position, badge number, access time, gate number, access fail time	O	O	–
9	Personal info. identification	Employee number, Dept., PC name, MAC, IP, search time, number of identification, information grade, number of personal information, file path, file name, file size, file creation time, file edit time	O	O	–
10	Server access control	User ID, access time, end time, system name, sever IP, client IP	O	O	–
11	DB access control	DBMS IP, DBMS server port, service number, policy number, login time, logout time, query number, query execution time, query end time	O	O	–

(*continued*)

Table 2. (*continued*)

No.	Linked system	Collected log	Company		
			A	B	C
12	Illegal software block	S/W ID, S/W type, S/W name, manufacturer, license type, license duration, expire date, serial number, user ID, blocked S/W name, blocked S/W code, installation time, installation block time	O	–	–
13	Printer control	User ID, user name, Dept., document, title, number of page, print date, number of copy, printer ID, printer port, printer IP, personal information inclusion code, print request time, reason of print, approval time, approval code, approval after print, expected document discard date	O	–	–
14	Wireless intrusion prevention	Time, host name, host location, IP, SSID, event code, event block, AP category, access time, end time	O	–	–
15	Customer info. processing	Processing ID, Processing name, customer name, user ID, user IP, use time, use category (creation, edit, read, download, print)	O	–	–
16	Design drawing mgmt.	Employee name, user ID, Dept., position, IP, design drawing number, design drawing name, authority code, read time, print time, print screen time, download time, reason of download	–	–	O

* O: collected/X: not collected/–: not linked

As seen in the above section, three companies all are operating the security monitoring system, but have still some vulnerability difficult to detect information leakage. This section draws risk scenarios about information leakage by using such vulnerability and provides improvement directions. Risk scenarios and related companies are summarized in Table 3.

The first risk scenario belongs to information leakage using the vulnerability related to change of file type. If employees recognize that their behaviors are being monitored, they can export information to the outside using approved storage device by changing the file type to graphic file (JPG, GIF etc.) or text file (txt), i.e. by deceiving the file as personal data rather than work data in order to minimize the doubts of administrator or security staff. To detect such scenario, it is necessary to collect additional file type logs from removable device control, DRM, and email control system and track the history of document change of the same name, size, and type.

The second risk scenario belongs to information leakage using the vulnerability related to detachable HDD. In case of company A's security policy, approval is necessary for DRM decryption and company B should enter reason for decryption. Also, if the decryption pattern increases, this can be detected as unusual sign through security monitoring system. However, if DRM decryption is conducted in constant patterns, the security monitoring system has limitations in that it is difficult to detect by recognizing this as normal behavior. Moreover, the use of removable device is being controlled, however the security monitoring system does not collect the HDD related logs. Thus, there is a possibility to decrypt DRM in constant patterns and keep important document in storage and then export the detachable HDD to the outside. Lock can be installed to the frame of PC however employees might release the lock arbitrarily, and security staffs have to put a lot of time and effort to regular check of lock on PC used by all employees. Therefore, company A and B need to collect additional HDD information to detect whether HDD is detached or not as quickly as possible.

Table 3. Risk scenarios about information leakage

No.	Scenario	Company
1	Information leakage using approved removal device after changing file type	A, B and C
2	Information leakage detaching HDD after decryption of DRM in regular pattern	A and B
3	Information leakage via email after copying contents of document to the body of the email	B
4	Taking document out on weekends after printing the document on weekdays	C

The third risk scenario is related to information leakage via email. Company B is monitoring the email sent to the outside, but unlike company A and C, there are no restrictions on the email sending. Also, email sending monitoring focuses on attached file and does not collect the body of email and related logs. Therefore, company B's important information such as customer information and system development information can be sent to the outside through the body of email. Therefore, to detect such leakage, it is necessary to add rules to detect the type of important information like Social Security Number or if major scripts used for coding in case of system development are inserted into the body of email to detect information leakage.

The final risk scenario is related to information leakage through printout. In case of company C, the history of printout is left when printing the encoded document with DRM, however it is difficult to detect if storing the document that decrypted DRM in constant patterns and then going to work during holidays and printing out in quantity, because the security monitoring system does not collect separate logs from the printer. Moreover, as access logs are not collected from the physical access control system, it is difficult for the employees who do not go to work during holidays to go to work during the holidays and look for the abnormal signs. Of course, it is difficult to install individual access control devices residing in several companies within one building, but the attendance patterns during holidays can be identified if utilizing the other logs including document work history and website access history that occur during holidays. Also, if decrypted document ends, DRM is automatically encoded and thus if a lot of document are encoded with DRM suddenly, it is necessary to add the rules to detect this into the security monitoring system.

5   Conclusions

Information leakage by insider is recognized as the company's ethical issue and known to have bigger ripple effects than the information leakage by external attack like hacking. Especially in Korean companies, 80% of the subjects who involve in information leakage are insiders and so information leakage by insider emerges as a serious social problem. On one hand, most Korean companies are establishing preventive security policies but security incidents are occurring every year, and to overcome this, it is necessary to improve the ability to detect the signs of leakage as quickly as possible. The security monitoring is a necessary task for detecting the signs of information leakage. Overseas security monitoring related studies were conducted focusing on the methods to detect the attack from the outside and did not consider the security system operated by Korean companies. On the other hand, Korean security monitoring related studies conducted research on single security system or were not specific on which logs were utilized, and so to study from comprehensive perspective, it is necessary to analyze the actual monitoring cases of the companies.

This study analyzed the current state of security monitoring system operated by three companies in Korea. For a case study, company's security polices, systems linked with security monitoring system and logs were collected. Also, after identifying the vulnerability difficult to detect with the current security monitoring system, the risk scenarios that were likely to occur in the future were drawn and the methods to detect this were proposed. In this study we collected the security monitoring cases of the companies that held different industrial field, organizational culture, and security policy and generalized them to some extent. The result of this study will be useful for the companies that are planning to establish security monitoring system. Also, overseas companies that have similar security policies to Korean companies are expected to improve the detection performance of security monitoring system by referring to the risk scenarios.

Acknowledgments. This research was supported by the MSIT (Ministry of Science and ICT), Korea, under the ITRC (Information Technology Research Center) support program (IITP-2018-2014-1-00636) supervised by the IITP (Institute for Information & communications Technology Promotion).

References

1. Garrison, C.P., Ncube, M.: A longitudinal analysis of data breaches. Inf. Manag. Comput. Secur. **19**(4), 216–230 (2011). https://doi.org/10.1108/09685221111173049
2. Chang, H.B.: A study on the countermeasure by the types through case analysis of industrial secret leakage accident. J. Inf. Secur. **15**(7), 39–45 (2015)
3. Scholtz, T.: Consider a people-centric security strategy (2013). Gartner G00249357
4. Barnes, D.J., Hernandez-Castro, J.: On the limits of engine analysis for cheating detection in Chess. Comput. Secur. **48**, 58–73 (2015). https://doi.org/10.1016/j.cose.2014.10.002
5. Cho, S.K., Jun, M.S.: Privacy leakage monitoring system design for privacy protection. J. Korea Inst. Inf. Secur. Cryptol. **22**(1), 99–106 (2012)

6. Magklaras, G.B., Furnell, S.M.: A preliminary model of end user sophistication for insider threat prediction in IT systems. Comput. Secur. **24**(5), 371–380 (2005). https://doi.org/10.1016/j.cose.2004.10.003
7. Walton, R.: Balancing the insider and outsider threat. Comput. Fraud Secur. **11**, 8–11 (2006). https://doi.org/10.1016/S1361-3723(06)70440-7
8. Magklaras, G.B., Furnell, S.M.: Insider threat prediction tool: evaluating the probability of IT misuse. Comput. Secur. **21**(1), 62–73 (2001). https://doi.org/10.1016/S0167-4048(02)00109-8
9. Theoharidou, M., Kokolakis, S., Karyda, M., Kiountouzis, E.: The insider threat to information systems and the effectiveness of ISO17799. Comput. Secur. **24**(6), 472–484 (2005). https://doi.org/10.1016/j.cose.2005.05.002
10. Stanton, J.M., Stam, K.R., Mastrangelo, P., Jolton, J.: Analysis of end user security behaviors. Comput. Secur. **24**(2), 124–133 (2005). https://doi.org/10.1016/j.cose.2004.07.001
11. Pattinson, M., Parsons, K., Butavicius, M., McCormac, A., Calic, D.: Assessing information security attitudes: a comparison of two studies. Inf. Comput. Secur. **24**(2), 228–240 (2016). https://doi.org/10.1108/ICS-01-2016-0009
12. Stalla-Bourdillon, S.: Online monitoring, filtering, blocking…. What is the difference? Where to draw the line? Comput. Law Secur. Rev. **29**(6), 702–712 (2013). https://doi.org/10.1016/j.clsr.2013.09.006
13. Ambre, A., Shekokar, N.: Insider threat detection using log analysis and event correlation. Procedia Comput. Sci. **45**, 436–445 (2015). https://doi.org/10.1016/j.procs.2015.03.175
14. Park, S.J., Lim, J.I.: A study on the development of SRI (Security Risk Indicator)-based monitoring system to prevent the leakage of personally identifiable information. J. Korea Inst. Inf. Secur. Cryptol. **22**(3), 637–644 (2012)
15. Furnell, S.: Enemies within: the problem of insider attacks. Comput. Fraud Secur. **2004**(7), 6–11 (2004). https://doi.org/10.1016/S1361-3723(04)00087-9
16. Park, J.S., Lee, I.Y.: Log analysis method of separate security solution using single data leakage scenario. Trans. Comput. Commun. Syst. **4**(2), 65–72 (2015)
17. Thompson, H.H., Whittaker, J.A., Andrews, M.: Intrusion detection: perspectives on the insider threat. Comput. Fraud Secur. **2004**(1), 13–15 (2004). https://doi.org/10.1016/S1361-3723(04)00087-9
18. Liu, A., Martin, C., Hetherington, T., Matzner, S.: A comparison of system call feature representations for insider threat detection. In: Proceedings from the Sixth Annual IEEE SMC, pp. 340–347 (2005). https://doi.org/10.1109/IAW.2005.1495972
19. Sanzgiri, A., Dasgupta, D.: Classification of insider threat detection techniques. In: Proceedings of the 11th Annual Cyber and Information Security Research Conference. ACM (2016). https://doi.org/10.1145/2897795.2897799
20. Yin, R.K.: Case Study Research Design and Methods, 5th edn. Sage Publications, Thousand Oaks (2014)

Analysis and Visualization of Threats

AlertVision: Visualizing Security Alerts

Jina Hong[1], JinKi Lee[2], HyunKyu Lee[2], YoonHa Chang[2], KwangHo Choi[2],
and Sang Kil Cha[1(✉)]

[1] KAIST, Daejeon, Korea
{jina3453,sangkilc}@kaist.ac.kr
[2] AhnLab, Seongnam, Korea
{jinki.lee,hyunkyu.lee,yoonha.chang,kwangho.choi}@ahnlab.com

Abstract. Security is not just a technical problem, but it is a business problem. Companies are facing highly-sophisticated and targeted cyber attacks everyday, and losing a huge amount of money as well as private data. Threat intelligence helps in predicting and reacting to such problems, but extracting well-organized threat intelligence from enormous amount of information is significantly challenging. In this paper, we propose a novel technique for visualizing security alerts, and implement it in a system that we call AlertVision, which provides an analyst with a visual summary about the correlation between security alerts. The visualization helps in understanding various threats in wild in an intuitive manner, and eventually benefits the analyst to build TI. We applied our technique on real-world data obtained from the network of 85 organizations, which include 5,801,619 security events in total, and summarized lessons learned.

Keywords: Threat intelligence · Alert visualization · Alert correlation

1 Introduction

Security is a growing concern for enterprises and organizations with ever-evolving attack techniques. Today's security threats involve complex attack scenarios, and are designed to cause persistent damage against specific targets. They are often called an Advanced Persistent Threat, or APT in short [37]. APT actors typically leverage 'advanced' techniques such as code obfuscation and metamorphism [27] in order to thwart the detection.

Traditional defense approaches, e.g., Intrusion Detection System (IDS) [2], are *not* sufficient to handle APTs, because their focus is only on *attack instances*. That is, conventional defenses are mainly about understanding the behavior of malware instances, analyzing what kind of vulnerabilities are exploited, or figuring out what kind of techniques are used to bypass defenses. However, such information can vary depending on the victim as well as the attack campaign. Furthermore, responding to each and every threat by analyzing them is not feasible anyways in practice as they appear on a daily basis.

© Springer Nature Switzerland AG 2019
B. B. Kang and J. Jang (Eds.): WISA 2018, LNCS 11402, pp. 173–184, 2019.
https://doi.org/10.1007/978-3-030-17982-3_14

To deal with APTs, enterprises now try to utilize Threat Intelligence (TI), which is well-refined knowledge about threats with *outward* focus. That is, TI includes information beyond attack instances such as the behavioral patterns of the threat actors, their intent, and their characteristics. It is widely known that TI can help prevent security threats in a *proactive* manner [1].

Although TI-based defense is a promising direction, extracting TI from massive information obtained in wild is challenging because there are too many attack instances to consider. Companies employ Security Information and Event Management (SIEM) systems to detect threats and collect the corresponding events, which typically produce thousands of events per hour. It is not clear how to interpret and correlate those events to understand the attackers behind the scene. Furthermore, there can be false alerts from SIEM systems, which can easily confuse the TI generation process.

The current best practice in building TI is to correlate alerts generated from various IDS/IPS systems and identifies high-level patterns of current attacks. This process is often called *alert correlation* [23], and it can be used to identify unknown threats in the future. Most research in this field currently focuses on improving their accuracy [30,32,36], but an automated way of visualizing the correlation between security alerts is largely unexplored to date.

In this paper we present a simple and effective approach to visualize security alerts obtained from SIEM systems. We argue that such visual aids help analysts understand the characteristics of the attacks and the attackers behind, which often do not change regardless of the attack campaign: attackers tend to behave similarly even though the actual attack methodology may vary. To this end, we implement AlertVision, a visualization system for SIEM alerts, and evaluate it on real-world SIEM logs, which constitute 5,801,619 alerts in total.

To visualize security alerts, AlertVision first groups them based on their property, and produces a set of alert sequences. Each grouped sequence represents a feature of attack incidents, e.g., an attack source IP or a target service. Our system then computes similarity between the sequences, and visualizes their relationships in a graph. The key intuition here is that two or more features that are seemingly irrelevant can be similar to each other, and visualizing their relationship can often help understand the meaning of the incidents. To figure out the similarity between two distinct event sequences, it leverages a sequence alignment algorithm used in bioinformatics [34].

The primary challenge of AlertVision is to draw a graph where the coordinates of the nodes are not known, but only the distances, i.e., the similarity, between them are known. We leverage a force-directed graph drawing algorithm [7], which can draw a graph in a space based only on their relative distances. The resulting graph provides a useful insight to analysts because it can reveal that two *seemingly different* alert sequences are indeed similar to each other in the graph. Unlike traditional cluster analysis such as hierarchical clustering, the graph instantly presents visual evidence to analysts.

Our main contributions are as follows.

1. We propose a technique for visualizing relationship between attackers, which can help in understanding the meaning of security incidents.
2. We evaluated our technique on a large dataset obtained from real SIEM devices in wild.
3. We empirically show that security analysts can benefit from our visualization framework in terms of detecting previously unknown attacks.

2 Background

This section introduces the concept of local sequence alignment algorithm and force-directed graph layout algorithm, which serve as the basis of our alert visualization approach.

2.1 Local Sequence Alignment Algorithm

Sequence alignment is a way of arranging sequences. There are mainly two categories: local and global sequence alignment. Local sequence alignment algorithm finds similar subsequences between two sequences. Global alignment algorithm aims to obtain an end-to-end alignment between two sequences, whereas local alignment algorithm focuses on subsequences. Since we are dealing with SIEM event sequences that are different in their size and their look, we use local sequence alignment algorithm to obtain the similarity between the subsequences.

The most popular local sequence alignment algorithm is Smith-Waterman [34], which is a variation of Needleman-Wunsch algorithm [25]. Smith-Waterman algorithm is widely adopted in various areas in security such as malware analysis [15] and intrusion detection [3]. The algorithm takes in two sequences $s_1 = a_1, a_2, \ldots, a_m$ and $s_2 = b_1, b_2, \ldots, b_n$ of length m and n, respectively, and computes a scoring matrix H as follows. First, it constructs a $(m+1)$-by-$(n+1)$ scoring matrix H, where $H_{k0} = H_{0l} = 0$ for $0 \le k \le m$ and $0 \le l \le n$. It then fills in the scoring matrix with the following equation where $s(a, b)$ is a similarity score of the two elements a and b, and W_k is the penalty of having a gap of length k:

$$H_{ij} = \max \begin{cases} H_{i-1,j-1} + s(a_i, b_j), \\ \max_{k \ge 1}\{H_{i-k,j} - W_k\}, \\ \max_{l \ge 1}\{H_{i,j-l} - W_l\}, \\ 0. \end{cases} \quad (1 \le i \le m, \ 1 \le j \le n)$$

Finally, it traces back from a cell in H of the highest score to the one with a score 0, which constitutes the most similar subsequence of s_1 and s_2.

The time complexity of the classic Smith-Waterman algorithm is $O(m^2n)$, but Gotoh et al. [8] proposed an algorithm of $O(m + n)$ time complexity, and Myers et al. [24] showed an algorithm of $O(n)$ space complexity. There are also several linear-time and linear-space sub-optimal algorithms [11], which make local sequence alignment even more practical. Furthermore, there are several recent attempts to leverage GPU to accelerate the Smith-Waterman algorithm [26, 28].

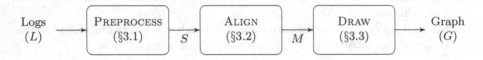

Fig. 1. Overview of AlertVision.

2.2 Force-Directed Graph

Force-directed graph drawing [7] is an algorithm used for graph layout and visualization. It takes advantage of the idea of Coulomb's law and Hooke's law to determine the position of nodes. In particular, there are attractive forces between nodes that are far apart, and are repulsive forces between nodes that are close to each other. The algorithm moves nodes based on these forces until it reaches an equilibrium state. We leverage this idea to visually represent security alerts. Although alert logs typically do not have the notion of coordinates, we can assign specific positions for each alert based on their relative similarities with force-directed graph drawing. As a result, we can apply a simple and cheap clustering algorithm such as k-means clustering to perform a cluster analysis on alert logs instead of using an expensive one such as hierarchical clustering [33].

3   AlertVision Design

At a high level, AlertVision takes in security logs generated from SIEM systems and returns a graph that visually correlating security alerts in the logs. Figure 1 shows the overall architecture of AlertVision. AlertVision consists of three major modules: PREPROCESS, ALIGN, and DRAW. First, PREPROCESS parses alert logs L and produces sequences of alerts S. Next, ALIGN finds similar subsequences from S using a local sequence alignment algorithm, and produces a matrix M that stores similarity between every pair of S. Finally, DRAW returns a graph where a sequence in S represents a node based on their similarity M.

3.1   Preprocess

AlertVision first preprocesses alert logs L to generate a set of alert sequences S by grouping alerts based on a specific attack feature. An attack feature includes a source IP address initiated the attack and a corresponding attack signature. By grouping alerts based on a feature, we can potentially realize relationship between feature values. For example, we may be able to realize the similarity between specific attacks if we visualize alert sequences grouped by their attack signatures.

In our current implementation, we focus on logs obtained from Network Intrusion Detection Systems (NIDS). In particular, we focus on source IP addresses of alert logs. By definition, every entry in NIDS logs contains its source IP address, i.e., an IP address that initiated the attack. By collecting a sequence of alerts for each IP address, we know what kind of attacks are introduced from an IP address in which order. Furthermore, assuming that attack payloads sent from the same IP address are from the same attacker, we can group the logs, and can potentially figure out similarities between attackers. From our experiments we found that an attacker tends to use the same set of IP addresses during an attack campaign even though actual payloads they use may differ. One notable example is APT, which typically includes multiple stages of independent attacks.

3.2 Align

ALIGN takes in a set of grouped sequences S, and produces a similarity matrix M, which contains similarity scores for every pair of grouped sequences in S. The similarity scores are used to visualize the relationship between the sequences in the next step. To compute M, we focus on local similarity between two sequences. Specifically, we first use Smith-Waterman algorithm to compute a local alignment with the gap penalty $W_k = 1$, and the similarity score 2 and -2 for matching and mismatching elements, respectively. In our implementation, we say two alerts match if they have the same IDS signature.

Since Smith-Waterman returns the most similar subsequence of given two sequences, we use the subsequence as the measure of similarity. In particular, we compute the sum of similarity score (in the scoring matrix H) for every element in the subsequence, and normalize the sum by dividing it by the minimum length of the two sequences, because the sum may differ significantly based on the length of the given sequences. Note that any resulting subsequence can only be as long as the minimum length of the given sequences. Thus, the normalized similarity should be always less than two, and greater than zero. To make the score be in the range from zero to one, we further divide the score by two, which is the maximum similarity score we gave.

For instance, given two sequences $s_1 = a_1, a_2, \ldots, a_m$ and $s_2 = b_1, b_2, \ldots, b_n$ where $m < n$, let us assume that we have obtained the most similar subsequence $s_3 = c_1, c_2, \ldots, c_l$, and the sum of the similarity score for s_3 was x. We then normalize the sum with: $\frac{x}{2m}$. Each element in the resulting matrix M represents a normalized similarity score.

3.3 Draw

The final step of AlertVision is to draw a graph based on the similarity matrix M we computed in the ALIGN phase. Each nodes in the resulting graph represents a sequence of alerts generated in the PREPROCESS step. The key challenge here is to decide where to place each node in a graph because there is no such notion as position for each of the sequences. To draw a graph based only on the relative distances between nodes, we leverage force-directed graph drawing [7] discussed in

Sect. 2.2. To represent the relationship between nodes, we draw edges only when two nodes are similar to each other based on our similarity measure. Specifically, we draw an edge between two nodes when their similarity score is higher than 0.9, i.e., 90%. The algorithm starts by placing every node in random positions in a two-dimensional coordinate plane, and terminates when all the nodes are in an equilibrium state.

4   Evaluation

We now evaluate AlertVision on real-world alert logs obtained from real SIEM devices. Specifically, we answer the following questions to evaluate our system.

1. Can we observe some meaningful correlation between alert sequences that are close to each other in a graph generated from AlertVision? (Sect. 4.2)
2. How do sequence clusters change over time? Can we see similar clusters over time? (Sect. 4.3)
3. Is there a specific attack incident that we can identify from the generated graphs? (Sect. 4.4)

4.1   Experimental Setup

We collected 6-months (from January to June in 2017) logs from real SIEM devices installed in 85 enterprises, which constitute 5,801,619 alerts for NIDS in total. There were 96,260 unique source IP addresses used in the alerts excluding private IP addresses; since one private IP address does not stand for one independent attacker, we disregarded private IP addresses. We ran PREPROCESS to make a mapping from a source IP to an alert message, which resulted in 96,260 mappings in total. We then removed mappings which have a sequence of only a single alert. Note that such a short sequence cannot affect the result of Smith-Waterman algorithm and removing them can help reduce overhead of ALIGN. As a result, we obtained 29,268 unique attack sequences in total. In the rest of this section, we discuss our research questions based on the results of PREPROCESS.

4.2   Alert Sequence Correlation

We ran ALIGN and DRAW on the sequences obtained in Sect. 4.1. Figure 2 presents six graphs we obtained by running AlertVision on monthly logs from Jan. 2017 to Jun. 2017. Each node (dot) in the graphs represents a sequence, i.e., a group of alerts. The graphs clearly show which sequences are similar to each other: we can easily recognize clusters of nodes from the graphs. We found that each cluster in the graphs contain similar attack sequences. For example, SQL injection attacks formed a large cluster in each of the graphs, and several web-based attacks such as XSS and XPATH injection formed multiple clusters that were close to each other. To further analyze the correlation between the alerts, we grouped the nodes based on their attack characteristics.

Particularly, there were 504 unique attack signatures in our dataset, and we manually categorized them into six categories based on their attack characteristics: (1) SQL injection, (2) vulnerability scanning, (3) XSS, (4) SSH password guessing, (5) web-based attacks, and (6) known CVE exploitation. We separated the XSS group with the web-based attack group because we found relatively

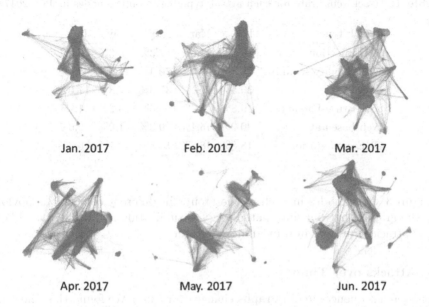

Fig. 2. Visualization of 6-month alert logs we collected from real-world SIEM devices.

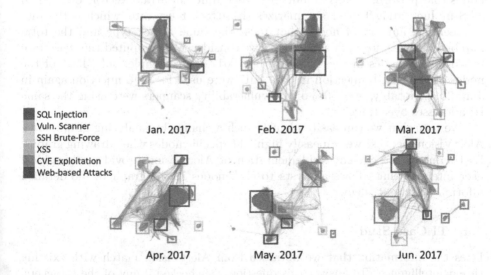

Fig. 3. Visualization of 6-month alert logs with categorization. (Color figure online)

many attack instances for XSS compared to other web-based attacks. The CVE exploitation group includes any attacks that are associated with known CVE. For example, we observed many exploits on Apache Struts in early 2017, which is associated with CVE-2017-5638.

Table 1. Attack reuse rate for each attack type based on the nodes in Jan. 2017.

Attack type	Feb.	Mar.	Apr.	May	Jun.
SQL injection	16.5%	11.6%	7.3%	5.6%	4.3%
Vulnerability scanning	63.8%	62.7%	70.4%	51.9%	54.4%
XSS	30.5%	27.2%	37.3%	27.8%	17.0%
SSH Brute-Forcing	19.8%	8.4%	5.5%	3.2%	1.9%
Web-based attacks	30.2%	15.1%	9.3%	11.2%	12.0%
CVE exploitation	18.8%	18.8%	18.8%	12.5%	6.3%

Figure 3 shows nodes in each of the groups in different colors. It is obvious from the graphs that our automated graph visualization algorithm was able to cluster attack sequences into meaningful clusters.

4.3   Attacks over Time

Do clustered sequences in our graphs change over time? We found that the same IP addresses tend to perform distinct attacks over time. For example, 83% of nodes that performed XSS in Jan. 2017 used different attack vectors other than XSS in Jun. 2017. Table 1 summarizes the attack reuse rate, which is the rate between the number of nodes that reuse the same attack type and the total number of nodes, for each attack type we consider. We computed the reuse rate based on the nodes in the graph of Jan. 2017. For example, only 4.3% of the nodes used for SQL injection in Jan. 2017 were used for SQL injection again in Jun. 2017. Notably, over 50% of the vulnerability scanners were using the same IP addresses over time.

We note that we can easily identify such a change by analyzing graphs with AlertVision, because we can easily highlight specific nodes when drawing graphs. Furthermore, the current implementation of AlertVision provides a graphical user interface that allows analysts to click nodes in the graph to see detailed information about them.

4.4   TI Case Study

Does the information that we obtained from AlertVision match with existing threat intelligence? To answer this question, we checked if any of the attackers' IP addresses in our dataset are listed in the IBM X-Force TI service [12]. We found that several known IP addresses for attackers in the TI were indeed in the same group in our graphs. Figures 4 and 5 show that known command-and-control (C&C) servers and botnet addresses from the TI were in the same group in the graphs, respectively. Both figures illustrate a case for Jan. 2017, but the same trend appears in other graphs.

This result signifies the value of AlertVision as a tool that helps analysts understand the meaning of the attacks. For example, the IBM TI shows some of the nodes in our graphs are identified as a bot, but other nodes in the graph that are close the identified bots may be other bots controlled by the same botnet master as their behaviors are the same as the identified bots.

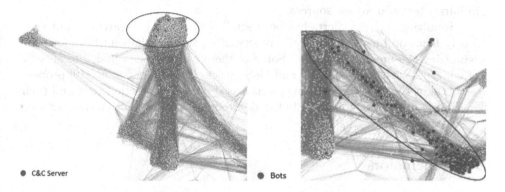

Fig. 4. Clustered C&C servers.   **Fig. 5.** Clustered botnet bots.

5   Related Work

Leveraging data mining and big data analytics for security has a long history. For instance, behavior-based anomaly detection [6,18] is a powerful defense mechanism that is still being used today. However, such techniques only focus on detecting attack instances, but not on identifying and analyzing the actors of the attacks.

Many researchers have recently turned their attention to refining security data obtained from various sources to build TI and to understand the meaning of threat instances due to recent advances in security threats. There are currently several attempts to classify threats [5,13,16,21,35,39] by leveraging ontology formally defined for describing security threats [5]. Although effective, those approaches are largely manual. Several attempts to defining data structures for TI have been made too. STIX [1] provides a unified way for expressing TI. Qamar *et al.* [29] recently extends STIX to represent semantics and contextual information of TI. Kapetanakis *et al.* [14] leverage traces on the victim machines left by attackers, e.g., modified/deleted files or registry entries, in order to generate attacker profiles. However, collecting such information is not feasible in practice as it requires installing host-based logging application for every machine, which may raise privacy concerns. On the other hand, our approach only uses the existing SIEM events in order to generate profiles. Furthermore, our system visualizes the relevance between security alerts, which can provide valuable insight for the TI analysts. Note that AlertVision presents a *unique design point* in mining useful knowledge from security alerts with visualization. Therefore, our technique is complementary to the existing works.

There have been a wide range of research on correlating similar SIEM events, which is often called, alert correlation [20,31,40]. Alert correlation techniques are used to detect botnets [9,17] as well as to discover attack patterns from alert logs [4,23,30,32,38]. Ours is in the same line of research, but our focus is not on correlating attack instances themselves, but on visually representing the similarity between attack sources.

Visualizing security alerts has been studied by several researchers, but they mostly focus on how to graphically representing the raw data itself, but not on visualizing the meaning of them. Some of them can only be applied to specific attack types such as Worm [10] and DoS attacks [22]. Livnat *et al.* [19] propose a general method for representing alerts based on their detection time and their location in a network topology, but it does not capture the correlation between those alerts.

6   Conclusion

In this paper, we presented a novel visualization technique for providing practical insights for security analysts. We applied our technique on a large-scale dataset obtained from real enterprise networks, and showed its effectiveness in terms of understanding attacks and extracting TI from alert logs. The proposed technique is indeed used internally now in AhnLab, Korea.

Acknowledgements. We thank anonymous reviewers for their helpful feedback. This research was supported by AhnLab.

References

1. Barnum, S.: Standardizing cyber threat intelligence information with the structured threat information expression (STIX^{TM}). Technical report, MITRE (2012)
2. Cha, S.K., Moraru, I., Jang, J., Truelove, J., Brumley, D., Andersen, D.G.: SplitScreen: enabling efficient, distributed malware detection, pp. 377–390 (2010)
3. Coull, S., Branch, J., Szymanski, B., Breimer, E.: Intrusion detection: a bioinformatics approach. In: Proceedings of the Annual Computer Security Applications Conference, pp. 24–33 (2003)
4. Cuppens, F., Ortalo, R.: LAMBDA: a language to model a database for detection of attacks. In: Proceedings of the International Workshop on the Recent Advances in Intrusion Detection, pp. 197–216 (2000)
5. Fenz, S., Ekelhart, A.: Formalizing information security knowledge. In: Proceedings of the International Symposium on Information, Computer, and Communications Security, pp. 183–194 (2009)

6. Forrest, S., Hofmeyr, S.A., Somayaji, A., Longstaff, T.A.: A sense of self for Unix processes. In: Proceedings of the IEEE Symposium on Security and Privacy, pp. 120–128 (1996)
7. Fruchterman, T.M.J., Reingold, E.M.: Graph drawing by force-directed placement. Softw.: Pract. Exp. **21**(11), 1129–1164 (1991)
8. Gotoh, O.: An improved algorithm for matching biological sequences. J. Mol. Biol. **162**(3), 705–708 (1982)
9. Gu, G., Perdisci, R., Zhang, J., Lee, W.: BotMiner: clustering analysis of network traffic for protocol- and structure-independent botnet detection. In: Proceedings of the USENIX Security Symposium, vol. 5, pp. 139–154 (2008)
10. Heoh, S.T., Ma, K.L., Wu, S.F., Zhao, X.: Case study: interactive visualization for internet security. In: Proceedings of the IEEE Conference on Visualization, pp. 505–508 (2002)
11. Huang, X., Miller, W.: A time-efficient, linear-space local similarity algorithm. Adv. Appl. Math. **12**(3), 337–357 (1991)
12. IBM: IBM X-Force threat intelligence. https://www.ibm.com/security/xforce
13. Jouini, M., Rabai, L.B.A., Aissa, A.B.: Classification of security threats in information systems. Procedia Comput. Sci. **32**, 489–496 (2014)
14. Kapetanakis, S., Filippoupolitis, A., Loukas, G., Murayziq, T.S.A.: Profiling cyber attackers using case-based reasoning. In: Proceedings of the UK Workshop on Case-Based Reasoning (2014)
15. Kirat, D., Vigna, G.: MalGene: automatic extraction of malware analysis evasion signature. In: Proceedings of the ACM Conference on Computer and Communications Security, pp. 769–780 (2015)
16. Kotenko, I., Polubelova, O., Saenko, I., Doynikova, E.: The ontology of metrics for security evaluation and decision support in SIEM systems. In: Proceedings of the International Conference on Availability, Reliability and Security, pp. 638–645 (2013)
17. Lee, K., Kim, J., Kwon, K.H., Han, Y., Kim, S.: DDoS attack detection method using cluster analysis. Expert Syst. Appl. **34**(3), 1659–1665 (2008)
18. Lee, W., Stolfo, S.J.: Data mining approaches for intrusion detection. In: Proceedings of the USENIX Security Symposium, pp. 79–93 (1998)
19. Livnat, Y., Agutter, J., Moon, S., Erbacher, R.F., Foresti, S.: A visualization paradigm for network intrusion detection. In: Proceedings of the Annual IEEE SMC Information Assurance Workshop, pp. 92–99 (2005)
20. Luh, R., Marschalek, S., Kaiser, M., Janicke, H., Schrittwieser, S.: Semantics-aware detection of targeted attacks: a survey. J. Comput. Virol. Hacking Tech. **13**(1), 47–85 (2017)
21. Luh, R., Schrittwieser, S., Marschalek, S.: TAON: an ontology-based approach to mitigating targeted attacks. In: Proceedings of the International Conference on Information Integration and Web-based Applications and Services, pp. 303–312 (2016)
22. McPherson, J., Ma, K.L., Krystosk, P., Bartoletti, T., Christensen, M.: PortVis: a tool for port-based detection of security events. In: Proceedings of the ACM Workshop on Visualization and Data Mining for Computer Security, pp. 73–81 (2004)
23. Mirheidari, S.A., Arshad, S., Jalili, R.: Alert correlation algorithms: a survey and taxonomy. In: Wang, G., Ray, I., Feng, D., Rajarajan, M. (eds.) CSS 2013. LNCS, vol. 8300, pp. 183–197. Springer, Cham (2013). https://doi.org/10.1007/978-3-319-03584-0_14

24. Myers, E.W., Miller, W.: Optimal alignments in linear space. Bioinformatics 4(1), 11–17 (1988)
25. Needleman, S.B., Wunsch, C.D.: A general method applicable to the search for similarities in the amino acid sequence of two proteins. J. Mol. Biol. 48(3), 443–453 (1970)
26. Okada, D., Ino, F., Hagihara, K.: Accelerating the Smith-Waterman algorithm with interpair pruning and band optimization for the all-pairs comparison of base sequences. BMC Bioinform. 16(1), 321 (2015)
27. O'Kane, P., Sezer, S., McLaughlin, K.: Obfuscation: the hidden malware. IEEE Secur. Priv. 9(5), 41–47 (2011)
28. de Oliveira Sandes, E.F., de Melo, A.C.M.A.: Retrieving Smith-Waterman alignments with optimizations for megabase biological sequences using GPU. IEEE Trans. Parallel Distrib. Syst. 24(5), 1009–1021 (2013)
29. Qamar, S., Anwar, Z., Rahman, M.A., Al-Shaer, E., Chu, B.T.: Data-driven analytics for cyber-threat intelligence and information sharing. Comput. Secur. 67, 35–58 (2017)
30. Ramaki, A.A., Amini, M., Atani, R.E.: RTECA: real time episode correlation algorithm for multi-step attack scenarios detection. Comput. Secur. 49, 206–219 (2015)
31. Salah, S., Maciá-Fernández, G., DíAz-Verdejo, J.E.: A model-based survey of alert correlation techniques. Comput. Netw. 57(5), 1289–1317 (2013)
32. Shittu, R., Healing, A., Ghanea-Hercock, R., Bloomfield, R., Rajarajan, M.: Intrusion alert prioritisation and attack detection using post-correlation analysis. Comput. Secur. 50, 1–15 (2015)
33. Sibson, R.: SLINK: an optimally efficient algorithm for the single-link cluster method. Comput. J. 16(1), 30–34 (1973)
34. Smith, T., Waterman, M.: Identification of common molecular subsequences. J. Mol. Biol. 147(1), 195–197 (1981)
35. Spring, J., Kern, S., Summers, A.: Global adversarial capability modeling. In: Proceedings of the IEEE eCrime Researchers Summit on Anti-phishing Working Group, pp. 1–21 (2015)
36. Strasburg, C., Basu, S., Wong, J.S.: S-MAIDS: a semantic model for automated tuning, correlation, and response selection in intrusion detection systems. In: Proceedings of the IEEE International Conference on Computer Software and Applications Conference, pp. 319–328 (2013)
37. Tankard, C.: Advanced persistent threats and how to monitor and deter them. Netw. Secur. 2011(8), 16–19 (2011)
38. Treinen, J.J., Thurimella, R.: A framework for the application of association rule mining in large intrusion detection infrastructures. In: Proceedings of the International Workshop on the Recent Advances in Intrusion Detection, pp. 1–18 (2006)
39. de Vergara, J.E.L., Vázquez, E., Martin, A., Dubus, S., Lepareux, M.N.: Use of ontologies for the definition of alerts and policies in a network security platform. J. Netw. 4(8), 720–733 (2009)
40. Zhou, C.V., Leckie, C., Karunasekera, S.: A survey of coordinated attacks and collaborative intrusion detection. Comput. Secur. 29(1), 124–140 (2010)

A New Bayesian Approach to Exploring Damaged Assets by Monitoring Mission Failures Caused by Undetected Attack

Shinwoo Shim[1,2] and Ji Won Yoon[1(✉)]

[1] Graduate School of Information Security, Korea University,
Seoul, Republic of Korea
{shimshinwoo, jiwon_yoon}@korea.ac.kr
[2] Cyber Warfare R&D Lab, LIG Nex1 Co., Seongnam, Republic of Korea

Abstract. Modern military systems operated with a complex of computers and software may have mission failure which is caused by undetected attacks. In such situations, it is important to find out which assets are damaged. After identifying damaged assets, we need to immediately examine the damaged assets to defend against the attacks. However, it is not straightforward to explore the damaged assets because there are the complicated relationships among assets, tasks and missions. In this paper, we propose an effective methodology to infer the damaged assets given observed mission impacts in a Bayesian framework. We used Bayesian networks to model assets, tasks, missions and to set the relationships among them. Our approach visually infers and identifies the damaged assets with the probability. We show that proposed Bayesian framework is practical and useful with the use case experiment.

Keywords: Mission Impact Assessment · Bayesian network · Cyber warfare

1 Introduction

As more information technology appliances are used, it is more difficult to build effective situation awareness system which detects significant but unpredictable operational risks. This situation makes the system operators struggle to find out how the asset damages can affect missions. Therefore, defining the relationships among assets, task, missions and assessing asset damage, impact propagation are essential for military systems. There have been several researches on Battle Damage Assessment (BDA) and Mission Impact Assessment (MIA) to find out the current ability to perform missions under the asset damages.

Previous researches focused on the damage propagations from assets to tasks and missions. In such situations, a monitoring systems or sensors should detect the damages on the assets first. However, there can be attacks that cannot be detected by the monitoring systems or sensors. For example, if an enemy exploits a zero-day vulnerability and succeeds in the attack, the mission can fail while the damage on an asset is still not detected [1]. Such attacks can lead to the failure of missions without observing any damage on assets. Even though the enemy does not use a zero-day vulnerability, it

B. B. Kang and J. Jang (Eds.): WISA 2018, LNCS 11402, pp. 185–196, 2019.
https://doi.org/10.1007/978-3-030-17982-3_15

is hard to apply security patches to all the assets in time if there are hundreds of assets to manage.

If mission failure is caused by undetected asset damages, we should find out which assets were damaged. If there are a few assets for a mission, we can check all the assets one by one. However, if there are hundreds of assets involving a mission, it is impossible to check all the assets in a limited time. In this point of view, it is valuable to find undetected damaged assets by observing a mission failure. In this paper, we infer the damaged assets from an observation of the mission impact using a Bayesian network.

The main contribution of this paper can be summarized as follows: We introduce a new way in analyzing the relationships among assets, tasks and missions. Previous researches tried to assess the mission impact when asset damages are detected. Instead of assessing asset damage propagation, we focused on making damaged assets inference from observing mission impacts when there is mission failure caused by undetected attacks. To infer the damaged assets, we propose a Bayesian framework which can be constructed practically using Logical AND and Noisy-OR relationships. We can therefore infer the damaged assets by getting the probabilities of damages for each asset. We show that this methodology is practical and useful with use case experiments.

The remainder of this paper is structured as follows. In Sect. 2, we will review the related researches that have been done on the Mission Impact Assessment and Bayesian networks. In Sect. 3, we define the terms used throughout this paper. In Sect. 4, we describe the method for building a Bayesian network, which consists of assets, tasks, mission and their relationships. We show how we make damaged assets inference from an observation of a mission impact by constructing a Bayesian network. In Sect. 5, we describe the implementation of the Bayesian network and result of the experiments.

2   Related Work

Jakobson [2] proposed a conceptual framework and a method for assessing impact that cyber attack might have to cyber assets, services, and missions. The framework builds the model of a mission, service and assets, and impact dependency graph. It presents an algorithmic base how to calculate impacts that cyber attack cause, how the direct impacts propagate through the service, and mission dependencies and affect the operational capacity of missions.

Sun et al. [3] introduced System Object Dependency Graph (SODG) to capture the intrusion propagation process at low operating system level. On the top of the SODG, a mission-task-asset (MTA) map can be established to associate the system objects with tasks and missions. A Bayesian network for MTA can be constructed and it can be used to find missions being tainted and to assess quantitative mission impact.

Motzek et al. [4] proposed a mathematical mission impact assessment, based on a probabilistic approach using mission dependency models and resource dependency model. In mission dependency models, a Bayesian network is used for building a probabilistic dependency models and for assessing mission impact.

Previous works have focused on studying on how the asset damages propagate to missions. Previous works assume that the attacks are detected and then the mission impacts are calculated according to the damages. However, in this paper we assume the situation that we are not able to detect the attacks when missions fail. The goal of our study is to find the damaged assets when we observe mission failures caused by undetected attacks.

3 Terminology

Before we state the methodology, we define the word used throughout the paper.

- Mission - A set of tasks that fulfills a purpose or duty
- Task - A piece of work done as part of a mission
- Asset - Hardware or software that supports one or more tasks
- Impact - An quantitative assessment of how much a mission is affected by a given activity or situation [5]
- Damage - A quantitative assessment corresponding to the state(s) a given asset is in with respect to its ability to perform a given role [5]
- Vulnerability - A specific weakness in the protections or defenses surrounding assets

For example, "surface to air defense" for an area can be a mission and "detecting air tracks", "intercepting enemy fighter" can be tasks which support the mission. Equipment which comprises radar system like "transmitter", "receiver" and "signal processor" can be assets that support the task "detecting air tracks". An asset can support one or more tasks and a task can support one or more missions.

"Impact" and "Damage" seem to be similar terms. However, they are not the same. Impact is generally the result of some damage [6]. In this paper, we use "damage" for negative influence on assets and "Impact" for negative influence on tasks and missions.

4 Damaged Assets Inference Using Bayesian Networks

Bayesian networks are probabilistic models based on directed acyclic graphs and have capability for bidirectional inferences which can model the top-down (semantic) and bottom-up (perceptual) combination of evidence [7]. A key feature of Bayesian networks is the ability to locally interpret individual parameters, i.e. to locally interpret individual probabilities of conditional probability distributions [4]. This feature provides a direct understandability to all conditional probabilities, i.e. we can make an inference for undetected damaged assets from observing impacted missions using Bayesian networks.

We need to construct a Bayesian network to find out the damaged assets which are undetected when a mission fails. Figure 1 shows a Bayesian network for assets, tasks, missions and their relationships. In this example, we constructed a small network that has four assets, three tasks, and two missions for easy explanation.

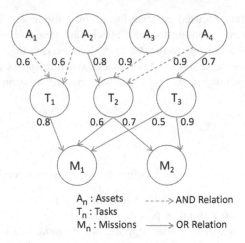

Fig. 1. A Bayesian network for assets, tasks, missions

When applying this methodology on the real military systems, experts who design or operate the military system are supposed to identify assets, tasks and missions and to construct the Bayesian network. The construction of a Bayesian network should be done by the experts who thoroughly understand the system to obtain the correct result.

Figure 1 is an example of a simple Bayesian network that describes assets, tasks, missions and the damage propagation. Figure 1 has is a little different from a typical Bayesian network. It has the probabilities on the edges instead of having conditional probability tables and it has the edges with AND or OR relations that a typical Bayesian network does not have. We will describe the notation of the Bayesian network and its application in the following sections.

4.1 Nodes and Edges

In Fig. 1, circles are nodes that denote assets, tasks and missions. For example, A_1 means the first asset, T_2 means the second task and M_1 means the first mission. We denoted assets, tasks and missions by number for simple notation. However, stating explanatory phrases like "surface to air defense" for nodes would be intuitive when building a Bayesian network.

Directed lines are edges that denote the probabilities that the child nodes are impacted when a parent node is damaged or impacted. For example, if A_2 is damaged, the damage can propagate to T_2 for the probability of 0.8. If T_3 is impacted, the impact can propagate to M_1 for the probability of 0.5 and to M_2 for the probability of 0.9.

Our purpose is not to figure out how much the assets are damaged with exact figures but to find out which assets are more probably damaged. Therefore, we define the state of the node to be binary, i.e. the states of assets can be damaged (True) or undamaged (False). The states of tasks and missions can be impacted (True) or not impacted (False).

4.2   Edge Relation

Military assets can be targets of enemies and tend to be attacked by them. Therefore, many military systems are constructed with redundancy. For example, a radar system can have two transmitters for high availability. In such a radar system, it can fulfill the task even though one transmitter is out of order and it can be impacted when both transmitters are out of order.

We depict redundancy relations with dashed edges in Bayesian networks. Parent nodes with dashed edges are in "AND Relation" which means that all the parent nodes should be damaged or impacted to impact the child node. For example, in Fig. 1, if A_3 is damaged and A_4, A_2 are not damaged, then T_2 is not impacted. Such concept of relations was also described in [2]. There can be two or more redundant assets in real situation, so two or more nodes can be in the same AND relation.

In addition to the concept in [2], we revised the AND relation to have the concept of groups. For example, in radar system stated above, a radar system can have two transmitters, and two receivers for high availability. In this situation, two transmitters can be two assets in a same AND group and two receivers can be two assets in another AND group. In such a radar system, it can fulfill the task even though one transmitter and one transmitter are out of order.

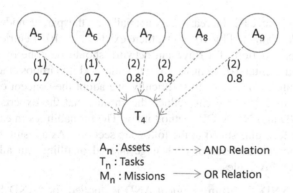

A_n : Assets $----\!\!\to$ AND Relation
T_n : Tasks
M_n : Missions $-\!\!\longrightarrow$ OR Relation

Fig. 2. Example of AND relation groups

An example for AND group is shown in Fig. 2 and it depicts a sub-graph of a Bayesian network. In Fig. 2, A_5, A_6 perform the same functions, and A_7, A_8, A_9 perform other same functions. Then $\{A_5, A_6\}$ becomes an AND group and $\{A_7, A_8, A_9\}$ becomes another AND group. Task T4 will not be impacted if at least one asset in each group is not damaged.

Relation other than "AND Relation" is "OR Relation", which means that only one damage or impact of parent nodes can affect the child node. We explain how the probabilities are calculated for AND relation and OR relation in Sect. 4.3.

4.3   Conditional Probability Tables (CPTs)

We should build conditional probability tables (CPTs) to make inference from a Bayesian network. CPTs state the probabilities of each node as the state of parent nodes changes. For example, Table 1 expresses the CPT for T_2 in Fig. 1. As we can see in Table 1, if a node has n parents, there are 2^n entries for the CPT of the node.

Table 1. Conditional probability table for T_2

A_2	A_3	A_4	T_2	
			T	F
F	F	F	0	1
F	F	T	0	1
F	T	F	0	1
F	T	T	0.81	0.19
T	F	F	0.8	0.2
T	F	T	0.8	0.2
T	T	F	0.8	0.2
T	T	T	0.962	0.038

The entries of the CPT increase exponentially as the parent nodes increase. For example, if a task is affected by 10 assets, there exists $2^{10} = 1024$ entries in a CPT. We stated that the construction of a Bayesian network should be done by experts. In this case, experts should enter 1024 entries for one node, and it is impossible for the human to enter all the entry. To resolve this difficulty, we adopt the concept of Noisy-OR [9, 10] and logical AND [8]. We can reduce the entities that the experts should fill out using logical AND and Noisy-OR methodology. The probabilities in each entry can be calculated by the formulas stated in the following sections. As a result, the experts only have to grade the probabilities of each edge instead of filling out all the entities in conditional probability tables.

Probability for AND Relation. Logical AND is applied for "AND Relation" and it means that damage can propagate only if all the parent nodes which have the "AND Relation" of same groups are damaged or impacted. The formula for logical AND can be expressed as:

$$p(X_i) = \begin{cases} 0, & \text{if at least one } X_j \text{ is False} \\ \prod_{j:X_j} p(e_i), & \text{otherwise} \end{cases} \quad (1)$$

$p(X_i)$ is the probability distribution of child node X_i. X_j is the parent node whose value is True. And e_j is the edge between child node X_i and parent node X_j and $p(e_j)$ is the probability of e_j.

Probability for OR Relation. Noisy-OR is applied for "OR Relation" and it means that damage or impact of only one parent node can affect the child node. The formula for Noisy-OR can be expressed as:

$$p(X_i) = \begin{cases} 0, & \text{if all } X_j \text{ is False} \\ 1 - \prod_{j:X_j} (1 - p(e_i)), & \text{otherwise} \end{cases} \tag{2}$$

The notation is same as logical AND.

Generalized Probability. In our Bayesian network, 'AND Relation' and 'OR Relation' can exist together and there can be several groups of 'AND Relation' edges for one child node. Therefore, the formula can be generalized as:

$$p(X_i) = \begin{cases} 0, & \text{if all } Y_k \text{ is False} \\ 1 - \prod_{k:Y_k} (1 - Y_k), & \text{otherwise} \end{cases} \tag{3}$$

where,

$$Y_k = \begin{cases} p(e_k), & \text{if } e_k \text{ is an OR relation edge} \\ \prod_{n:X_n} p(e_n), & \text{if } X_n \text{ is in AND group with n nodes} \end{cases}$$

Y_k is the parent node of X_i and other notation is same as Logical AND and Noisy-OR. The example of a CPT for logical AND and noisy-OR is depicted in Table 1. It shows the CPT for task T_2 in Fig. 1. A_3 and A_4 are in AND relation for T_2 and the edge probabilities are 0.9 each. One edge from A_2 to T_2 is in OR relation and has the probability of 0.8. When A_2, A_3, A_4 are all damaged (True), the possibility can be calculated using Eq. (3) and the result is $1 - (1 - 0.9 * 0.9) * (1 - 0.8) = 0.962$.

Risk of Assets. Risk of assets should be identified prior to the assessment. Risk of assets means how the assets are vulnerable or how the assets can be easily attacked by enemies. Risk of assets can be expressed as the probability of the assets to be damaged, i.e. $P(A_n)$.

The 'health' of the assets can be measured by security posture metric (SPM) [11]. SPM can be calculated by Common Vulnerability Scoring System (CVSS) [12] and SPM is a value between 0 and 1, where 1 represents a 'safe' asset. The formulation of SPM is shown in Eq. (4).

$$SPM(A_n) = \frac{1}{\sum_j \frac{1}{(1 - \frac{CVSS_{n,j}}{11})}} \tag{4}$$

$CVSS_{n,j}$ is the score of vulnerability A_n has. Scores range from 0 to 10, with 10 being the most severe. By using SPM we can calculate the probability of the asset risk as shown in Eq. (5).

$$P(A_n) = SPM(A_n) \tag{5}$$

This probability of an asset means how easily the enemy can damage or compromise the asset. In this paper, we used CVSS score for the quantitative measure and other methods can be used for calculating risk probabilities of assets.

4.4 Finding Damaged Assets

If we have the risk probabilities of each asset i.e. $P(A_n)$ and the CPTs for all tasks and missions, we can make an inference of damaged assets from observation of mission impacts. The probabilities of an asset damage given a mission failure can be calculated as shown in Eq. (6).

$$P_i(A_n) = P(A_n | M_i = T) \tag{6}$$

$P_i(A_n)$ is the conditional probability of asset A_n given the condition that mission M_i is impacted. For example in Fig. 1, if M_1 is impacted, the probability that A_2 can have damage is $P(A_2 \mid M_1 = T)$ and it can be calculated by summing out other nodes.

We can get the damage probabilities of all the assets and we can rank them. As a result, we can prioritize assets we should examine first when we observe a mission impact without asset damage detection.

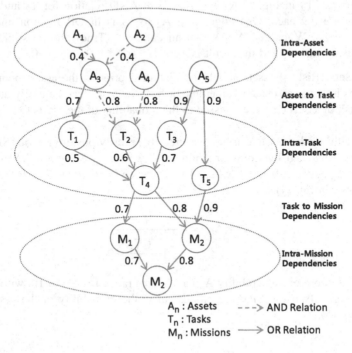

Fig. 3. An example of a Bayesian network that has intra-dependency relationships

4.5 Extension of Bayesian Networks

So far, we explained the Bayesian network which has inter-dependency, i.e. the dependency exists between asset nodes and task nodes, also between task nodes and mission nodes.

In our Bayesian framework, we can extend the network to have the concept of intra-dependency introduced in [2]. Intra-dependency means that there can be relationships among assets and also among tasks and missions.

The example of a Bayesian network that has intra-dependency is shown in Fig. 3. In this example, the graph is still directed acyclic, so our Bayesian framework can work by the methodology we described above. However, if there are nodes which have mutual dependency, then the graph becomes cyclic and the Bayesian framework would not work.

5 Experiments

In this section, we apply our methodology on a real world use case. The code implementation was made on MATLAB R2016b using Bayes Net Toolbox [13].

We present a simplified and abstract weapon system using a Bayesian Network described in Fig. 4. There are two missions, which are surface-to-air defense and the air-to-air defense and there exists two weapon systems, which are a surface-to-air defense system and an air-to-air defense system for each mission. Each mission comprises three tasks, which are detecting air targets, intercepting air targets and sharing information. Detecting air targets is a role of radar system and the assets can be signal processors and transmitters/receivers. To intercept air targets, missile launchers are needed for the assets. Sharing information is needed for exact situation awareness and communication equipment like tactical data link equipment is needed as assets. The explanation for each node is shown in Table 2.

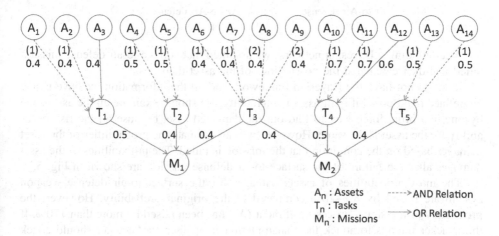

Fig. 4. A Bayesian network for air defense missions

As shown in Fig. 4, some assets have redundancy and the others do not have redundancy. For the simplification, we assume that the assets have the same risk probabilities for assets and impact propagation probabilities have similar values as shown in Fig. 4. We supposed that all the risk probability of asset is 0.3.

Table 2. Description for the nodes in the Bayesian network for air defense missions

Label	Description	Weapon system	Category
A_1	Transmitter/Receiver of radar	Surface-to-Air defense	Asset
A_2			
A_3	Signal processor of radar		
A_4	Missile launcher		
A_5			
A_6	Tactical data link equipment		
A_7			
A_8	Tactical data link equipment	Air-to-Air defense	
A_9			
A_{10}	Transmitter/Receiver of radar		
A_{11}			
A_{12}	Signal processor of radar		
A_{13}	Missile launcher		
A_{14}			
T_1	Detecting air targets	Surface-to-Air defense	Task
T_2	Intercepting air targets		
T_3	Sharing information	Surface-to-Air defense Air-to-Air defense	
T_4	Detecting air targets	Air-to-Air defense	
T_5	Intercepting air targets	Air-to-Air defense	
M_1	Surface-to-Air defense	Surface-to-Air defense	Mission
M_2	Air-to-Air defense	Air-to-Air defense	

After building a Bayesian network, we assumed that surface-to-air defense mission failed and then calculated the possibilities of the asset damages.

If we do not have the Bayesian framework and all the information we have is just predefined fixed possibility of asset vulnerability, we should examine all the assets one by one in a brute-force way to find out the damaged asset because all the risk probability for the asset is the same. However, we can estimate the probabilities of the asset damages based on the condition that the mission is failed. The probabilities of the asset damages after the failure of the surface-to-air defense mission are shown in Fig. 5.

The most probabilities of assets damages for the surface-to-air defense weapon system are raised by 8%–26% compared to the original probability. However, the probability of the signal processor of radar (A_3) has been raised by more than 170%. If the attacker intends to attack the transmitter/receiver, then the attacker should attack two transmitters/receivers at the same time because they have redundancy relationships.

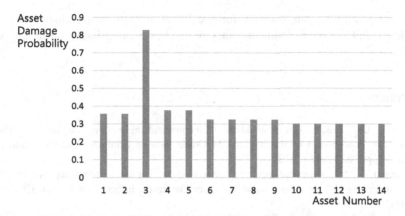

Fig. 5. Probabilities of assets damages based on the condition that the mission is failed

On the other hand, if the attacker intends to attack the signal processor, the attacker has to attack only one asset because the signal processor does not have a redundancy. Therefore, the Bayesian framework analyzes that it is easier for the attacker to attack the signal processor and raises its damage probability. Using the result of the analysis we can prioritize the assets to examine first.

In this use case, it can be intuitive to find out the most probable asset that an attacker would aim because the network is small and the relationships are not complicated. However, if the network becomes larger and the relationships get more complicated, it would be impossible to find out the most probable damaged asset by human intuition. In such cases, our Bayesian framework can prioritize the assets to be examined first.

6 Conclusion

In this paper, we have proposed a Bayesian network model for assets, tasks and missions and their relationships to infer damaged assets from observing an impacted mission. This methodology enables prioritizing the assets to be examined first when we fail to detect the asset damages.

We used an intuitive and mathematical method in modeling Bayesian networks and calculating the probabilities. Building Bayesian networks and setting conditional probability tables are intuitive and feasible for experts who are responsible for managing them. The experts define the assets, tasks, missions and set the relationships among them by AND relation or OR relation edges and then set probabilities of the edges that mean the impact probabilities of child nodes when the parent nodes are damaged or impacted. Instead of entering all the entities of conditional probability tables, the conditional probability tables are set automatically using the formula based on the edge values and the relationships among them. We showed that the inference is feasible and practical by the use case experiments.

We are continuing our research for the Bayesian framework which has mutual dependency and for other complementary researches relating issues on finding damaged assets.

References

1. Bilge, L., Dumitras, T.: Before we knew it: an empirical study of zero-day attacks in the real world. In: Proceedings of the 2012 ACM Conference on Computer and Communications Security, pp. 833–844 (2012)
2. Jakobson, G.: Mission cyber security situation assessment using impact dependency graphs. In: Proceedings of the 14th International Conference on Information Fusion, Chicago, IL (2011)
3. Sun, X., Singhal, A., Liu, P.: Who touched my mission: towards probabilistic mission impact assessment. In: Proceedings of the 2015 Workshop on Automated Decision Making for Active Cyber Defense, SafeConfig 2015, pp. 21–26, New York, NY, USA. ACM (2015)
4. Motzek, A., Möller, R.: Context- and bias-free probabilistic mission impact assessment. Comput. Secur. **65**(2017), 166–186 (2017)
5. Holspopple, J., Yang, S.J.: Handling temporal and functional changes for mission impact assessment. In: Proceedings International Multidisciplinary Conference on Cognitive Methods in Situational Awareness and Decision Support (CogSIMA), San Diego (2013)
6. Fortson, L.W.: Towards the development of a defensive cyber damage and mission impact methodology. AFIT Masters thesis, March 2007
7. Pearl, J., Russell, S.: Bayesian networks. In: The Handbook of Brain Theory and Neural Networks, 2nd edn, pp. 157–160. MIT Press (2003)
8. Munoz-Gonzalez, L., Sgandurra, D., Barrere, M., Lupu, E.C.: Exact inference techniques for the analysis of Bayesian attack graphs. IEEE Trans. Dependable Secur. Comput. **16**, 231–244 (2017)
9. Xie, P., Li, J.H., Ou, X., Liu, P., Levy, R.: Using Bayesian networks for cyber security analysis. In: 2010 IEEE/IFIP International Conference on Dependable Systems & Networks (DSN), Chicago, IL, pp. 211–220 (2010)
10. Henrion, M.: Practical issues in constructing a Bayes' belief network. In: Proceedings of Third Workshop on Uncertainty in AI, AAAI, Seattle, Washington, pp. 132–139, July 1987
11. Nakhla, N., Perrett, K., McKenzie, C.: Automated computer network defense using ARMOUR: mission-oriented decision support and vulnerability mitigation. In: 2017 International Conference on Cyber Situational Awareness, Data Analytics and Assessment (Cyber SA), London, pp. 1–8 (2017)
12. FIRST Org. Inc.: Common Vulnerability Scoring System v3.0. Specification Document. https://www.first.org/cvss/
13. Murphy, K.: Bayes Net Toolbox for Matlab. https://www.cs.utah.edu/~tch/notes/matlab/bnt/docs/bnt_pre_sf.html. https://github.com/bayesnet/bnt

Threat Modeling and Analysis of Voice Assistant Applications

Geumhwan Cho[1], Jusop Choi[1], Hyoungshick Kim[1(✉)], Sangwon Hyun[2],
and Jungwoo Ryoo[3]

[1] Sungkyunkwan University, Seoul, South Korea
{geumhwan,cjs1992,hyoung}@skku.edu
[2] Chosun University, Gwangju, South Korea
shyun@chosun.ac.kr
[3] Pennsylvania State University, Altoona, USA
jryoo@psu.edu

Abstract. Voice assistant is an application that helps users to interact with their devices using voice commands in a more intuitive and natural manner. Recently, many voice assistant applications have been popularly deployed on smartphones and voice-controlled smart speakers. However, the threat and security of those applications have been examined only in very few studies. In this paper, we identify potential threats to voice assistant applications and assess the risk of those threats using the STRIDE and DREAD models. Our threat modeling demonstrates that generic voice assistants can potentially have 16 security threats. To mitigate the identified threats, we also discuss several defense strategies.

Keywords: Voice assistant · Threat modeling · STRIDE · DREAD

1 Introduction

Voice assistant is a software program that helps users to interact with services (e.g., search engine) and applications (phone application) using voice commands with a more intuitive and convenient user interface mechanism. In general, voice assistant application runs as a background process and can be activated by using a reserved voice command (e.g., "Hey, Siri" and "Alexa"). Popular voice assistants including Siri (Apple), Alexa (Amazon) and Now (Google) help people shop online, send instant messages, and make phone calls, all through voice commands. However, to our knowledge there is no study analyzing security threats to voice assistants through a threat modeling process. Only a few studies experimentally demonstrated that commercial voice assistant applications are vulnerable to various forms of voice presentation attacks (e.g., [4,11]).

The goal of this paper is to identify potentially serious security threats to voice assistants and suggest several mitigation techniques to mitigate them. We first identify what threats exist and how risky the threats are by using the Security Development Lifecycle (SDL) threat modeling tool [10] that systemically

© Springer Nature Switzerland AG 2019
B. B. Kang and J. Jang (Eds.): WISA 2018, LNCS 11402, pp. 197–209, 2019.
https://doi.org/10.1007/978-3-030-17982-3_16

analyzes threats based on the data flow diagrams of a target system. The tool has been widely used for identifying security threats and analyzing corresponding security requirements. The key contributions of this paper are as follows:

- We provide a security analysis based on the SDL threat modeling methodology. We describe how a generic voice assistant application works with a data flow diagram. We then use the STRIDE approach [10] for categorizing 16 identified threats and the DREAD model [2] for assessing the risk of the threats (read Sect. 3).
- We discuss three possible attack scenarios that could lead to severe damages to systems using voice assistant applications (read Sect. 4) and suggest several defense mechanisms to mitigate those threats (read Sect. 5).

2   Background

2.1   Voice Assistant

Voice assistants have become more widely used for many purposes (e.g., playing music, setting timers and getting weather forecasts). Figure 1 shows an example architecture of voice assistant systems. A user initiates a voice assistant by issuing a voice command. For example, a user says, *"what time is it?"* and the voice assistant delivers the user's voice stream that the user requested to a voice assistant server. Next, the server interprets the voice stream and then requests the corresponding service to the cloud. The response to the user's voice command is delivered in the reverse order of the service request process. Consequently, the user can obtain the response of requested command.

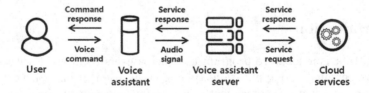

Fig. 1. A generic architecture of voice assistant systems.

2.2   Threat Modeling

Threat modeling is a process to identify potential threats to a system and evaluate the risk levels of identified threats. This process is helpful for reducing the risk from threats in the target system. In this paper, we use a threat modeling tool [10] to identify threats to voice assistant systems in a more systematic.

STRIDE is a threat classification model developed by Microsoft. STRIDE is an acronym containing the following concepts [10]. Our primary goal in this paper is to identify and categorize threats against voice assistant systems from the attacker's point of view, and the STRIDE model fits this goal.

- **S**poofing is an attempt to gain access to a system using a forged identity.
- **T**ampering is data corruption during network communication.
- **R**epudiation is a user's refusal to acknowledge participation in a transaction.
- **I**nformation disclosure is the unwanted exposure and loss of private data's confidentiality.
- **D**enial of Service (DoS) is an attack against system availability.
- **E**levation of privileges is an attempt to raise the privilege level of users by exploiting vulnerabilities.

DREAD is mainly used for quantifying the level of risks caused by threats [2]. In this paper, we used the DREAD model because it is especially useful to rank and prioritize threats according to their severity. Using the DREAD model, we can quantify the severity of each threat with numeric values (0, 5 and 10) assigned to each of the five categories described as follows [1], and consequently identify the threats that need to be dealt with higher priorities.

- **Damage Potential** measures the extent of the possible damage incurred by a threat. If the attacker could damage the entire system and data by exploiting a vulnerability, it would be the worst (10).
- **Reproducibility** measures how easy the attack or threat can be repeated.
- **Exploitability** is a metric that quantifies how much effort is required to launch an attack. If anyone can launch an attack, it would be the worst (10).
- **Affected Users** captures how many people would be affected if the attack was launched. It is usually a measure of what percentage of users are affected.
- **Discoverability** is a metric that indicates how easy a threat can be detected. If an attack is easily identifiable, it would be 10.

3 Security Analysis

3.1 Data Flow Diagram (DFD)

To identify security threats, we first draw a DFD (see Fig. 2) with the eight entities using the Microsoft's threat modeling tool [10]. `Human user` is an entity who uses the `Voice assistant application (app)` and controls `IoT devices` through the app. The voice assistant is working with a `Voice assistant server` to process a user's voice commands. The server typically converts the user's voice command to a service request message and sends it to an appropriate cloud server that can provide the service requested by the user. In addition, it is especially important to obtain a DFD that reflects the procedures of real-world voice assistant systems for practical modeling of threats. The DFD shown in

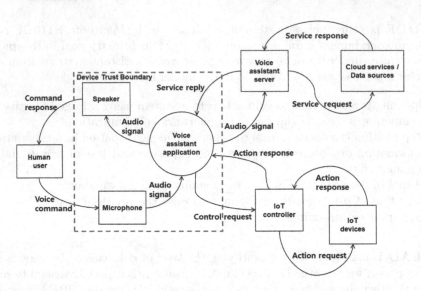

Fig. 2. DFD for generic voice assistant systems. The red rectangle indicates within voice assistant device. (Color figure online)

Fig. 2 has been constructed through our real development process, and has a strong similarity with popular voice assistant systems (e.g., Siri and Alexa).

The SDL threat modeling tool analyzed the DFD and automatically identified a list of 36 potential threats based on the STRIDE categories. We carefully examined the feasibility of attacks exploiting those vulnerabilities, identified that 20 of the identified threats are unrealistic in real-world settings, and finally selected 16 threats as valid ones by excluding the unrealistic threats. For example, in Fig. 2, the spoofing attack on voice command to `Microphone` has been proved as a feasible attack by some previous studies [4,11], thus we categorized it as a valid threat. As another example, on the other hand, the spoofing attack on command response to `Human user` is categorized as an invalid one, because it is unrealistic to assume that an attacker is able to put a fake speaker or physically compromise a victim's device without being detected by the victim.

3.2   Security Threat Analysis

To identify the security threats of the voice assistant system, we focus on analyzing threats associated with the following inbound/outbound data flows to/from the device (denoted as `Device trust boundary`) where `Speaker`, `Microphone` and `Voice assistant app` are placed; voice command, audio signal, service reply, control request, action response, and command response in Fig. 2. We do not consider the data flows inside the device trust boundary since we assume no physical attack against the voice assistant device. In addition, we ignore the data flows between `IoT controller` and `IoT devices` and between `Voice assistant server` and `Cloud services` in this analysis, which are not directly related with the voice assistant device. In the following, we will discuss 16 possible threats associated with the six data flows mentioned above.

Voice Command to Microphone. Human user issues a voice command to activate the Voice assistant app and the voice command first arrives at Microphone. We found four possible threats between Human user and Microphone.

– **Spoofing:** An attacker may attempt to spoof Microphone by impersonating a legitimate human user's voice. As a possible implementation, the attacker can simply record a victim's voices and replay them.
– **Tampering:** A voice command issued by Human user could be captured and modified by the attacker. Due to the broadcast nature of sound signals, anyone can hear and record the voice command. The attacker can then modify the recorded voice signals to generate the malformed voice command that causes unauthorized operations to be performed.
– **Denial of Service:** The role of Microphone is to receive the voice command from Human User and deliver it to Voice assistant app. The attacker can possibly launch a DoS attack by continuously injecting attack sounds to interfere with the normal voice command from the legitimate Human User. To secretly launch such attacks, the attacker might use hidden [4] and/or inaudible sounds [11] that a human cannot recognize and/or hear.

Audio Signal to Voice Assistant Server. Voice assistant app makes a request to analyze the audio signal (voice command) received from Microphone. Between Voice assistant app and Voice assistant server, spoofing attacks could be launched.

– **Spoofing:** The spoofing attack can be launched against Voice assistant server if there is no authentication mechanism. By impersonating a legitimate Voice assistant app, an attacker can transmit *unauthorized* audio signals to Voice assistant server. Consequently, the attacker can access the voice assistant service in an unauthorized manner.

Service Reply to Voice Assistant App. Voice assistant server sends a reply to Voice assistant app. From the reply, Voice assistant app decides what operation to perform. We identified four possible threats on this data flow as follows.

– **Tampering:** The service reply might be tampered by the attacker if there is no guarantee on the integrity of the service reply. That is, the attacker can capture a service reply and modify it to deceive Voice assistant app. Consequently, the attacker can deliver the malformed service reply to cause unauthorized operations on Voice assistant app or distribute unwanted information (e.g., advertisements) to Voice assistant app.

– **Information Disclosure:** The attacker might launch a sniffing attack of the service reply if there is no confidentiality protection of the service reply. For example, if the service reply is not encrypted, the attacker can extract some privacy sensitive information by eavesdropping the service reply.

– **Denial of Service:** The attacker could perform a DoS attack to disrupt the availability of Voice assistant app. The attacker has two options of DoS attacks. The attacker generates a service reply (with tampering attack) to contain malformed commands that might compromise the availability of Voice assistant app. The other option is to send a massive amount of service replies and consequently cause congestion on Voice assistant app.

– **Elevation of Privileges:** The attacker can generate malformed service replies containing malicious commands to exploit some vulnerabilities (e.g., vulnerable functions, insecure administrator password, etc.) on Voice assistant app. The execution of these malicious commands may allow the attacker to get a higher privilege than what is normally given by Voice assistant app.

Control Request to IoT Controller. Control requests are generated when Human user tries to control IoT devices with voice commands. We identified a threat that allows an attacker to spoof IoT controller with forged requests.

– **Spoofing:** A spoofing attack against IoT controller might be possible if there is no authentication mechanism between Voice assistant app and IoT controller. By impersonating Voice assistant app, the attacker can inject malicious control requests to IoT controller, and these forged control requests eventually allow the attacker to control security critical IoT devices (e.g., a digital door lock).

– **Tampering:** A tampering attack against IoT controller is possible if there is no integrity protection of control requests. Modifying control requests is to perform unauthorized operations on IoT devices (e.g., unlocking the door and forcibly turning on the fire alarm).

Action Response to Voice Assistant App. IoT controller responds Voice assistant app with an action response generated by IoT devices. The action response contains some information collected by IoT devices, such as the current temperature in the user's home, and also the status of IoT devices. We will explain six possible threats on the action response between IoT controller and Voice assistant app.

– **Spoofing:** Voice assistant app might be spoofed by an attacker if there is no authentication mechanism between Voice assistant app and IoT controller. The attacker can send an action response to Voice assistant app by impersonating IoT controller. As a result, the attacker can send any action response to Voice assistant app.

- **Tampering:** Without a proper integrity protection of an action response, an attacker can intentionally modify any captured action response and inject the forged action response to `Voice assistant app`.
- **Information Disclosure:** A sniffing attack against an action response is possible if there is no confidentiality protection of an action response. If an action response is transmitted without encryption, the attacker can easily obtain sensitive information from a captured action response.
- **Denial of Service:** The attacker can inject malformed action responses with some malicious commands whose execution causes intentional faults on `Voice assistant app`. In addition, the attacker can cause congestion on `Voice assistant app` by injecting an excessive amount of action responses. As a result, such DoS attacks can seriously disrupt normal operations of `Voice assistant app`.
- **Elevation of Privilege:** The action response could be misused by an attacker for illegal privilege escalation. For this attack, the attacker can generate an action response with malicious commands to exploit some vulnerabilities (e.g., vulnerable functions, insecure administrator password, etc.) and inject the action response to `Voice assistant app`. The execution of these malicious commands possibly allows the attacker to get a higher privilege than what is normally given by `Voice assistant app`.

Command Response to Human User. `Human user` obtains a service response via `Speaker`, which is the result of the voice command issued by `Human user`. We found that some sensitive information might be exposed to those who are physically close to `Speaker` because the command responses are usually broadcasted over air.

- **Information Disclosure:** `Speaker` simply broadcasts a service response over the air. Thus if the service response contains some sensitive information, anyone within the audible range can hear and/or record the service response. For this reason, `Human user` who wants to receive a command response from `Speaker` should carefully run `Voice assistant app`.

3.3   Risk Analysis

This section explains how we can evaluate the risk of each threat identified in Sect. 3.2 based on the DREAD assessment model [6, 10]. We focus on assessing how effective attacks are and how easy they are to launch. Each DREAD rating is the average of 5 categories and calculated using $(D + R + E + A + D)/5$.

We calculated the risk score (0, 5, and 10) of each of the 16 threats based on the DREAD model (see Table 1) and categorized the 16 threats into the following 3 orders of priority according to their risk scores: low (0 to 3), medium (4 to 7) and high (over 8). In summary, the 16 threats were categorized as follows: 2 threats in the low, 10 threats in the medium, and 4 threats in the high. In the following, we will describe the detailed procedure in which risk scores are calculated for several examples of threats (spoofing and DoS attack against `Microphone`, information disclosure of service reply).

Table 1. Risk assessment of voice assistant.

Data flow	Threat	D	R	E	A	D	Average
Voice command	Spoofing on `Microphone`	10	10	10	10	10	**10**
	Tampering with voice command	10	0	0	10	0	**4**
	DoS to `Microphone`	0	10	0	10	0	**4**
Audio signal	Spoofing on `Voice assistant server`	0	0	10	5	0	**3**
Service reply	Tampering with service reply	10	10	10	10	5	**9**
	Information disclosure of service reply	10	10	10	10	0	**8**
	DoS to `Voice assistant app`	0	10	5	10	10	**7**
	Elevation of privilege into `Voice assistant app`	10	10	0	10	0	**6**
Control request	Spoofing on `IoT controller`	10	10	5	10	0	**7**
	Tampering with control request	10	10	5	10	10	**9**
Action response	Spoofing on `IoT controller`	0	10	5	10	10	**7**
	Tampering with action response	0	10	0	10	10	**6**
	Information disclosure of action response	10	10	5	5	0	**6**
	DoS to `Voice assistant app`	0	10	10	10	10	**10**
	Elevation of privilege into `Voice assistant app`	10	0	0	0	0	**2**
Command response	Information disclosure of command response	0	10	10	10	0	**6**

Spoofing Attack Against Microphone. The open nature of the voice channels and the lack of authentication mechanisms make the voice assistants vulnerable to spoofing attacks such as voice replay attacks and voice impersonation attacks. As a result of spoofing attacks, an attacker can gain legitimate users' privileges (Damage Potential = 10). To launch such spoofing attack, the attacker generally require simple tools (e.g., recorders, speakers) without requiring sophisticated skills (Exploitability = 10), and this makes the attacks easy to launch and reproduce (Reproducibility = 10). Most voice assistants are focusing on text-to-speech translation and service provisioning without paying much attention to security (Discoverability = 10), thus the impacts of these types of attacks are significant (Affected Users = 10). Taking all these aspects into consideration, the DREAD rating is set to 10 and its priority is set to high.

DoS Attack Against Microphone. An attacker can launch DoS attacks against `Microphone` to disrupt the normal operations of voice assistants. Such DoS attacks interrupt legitimate users from using the voice assistant normally, but they do not directly damage the system and data (Damage Potential = 0). A simple form of DoS attack is playing audio files of attack sounds via a speaker, and this type of attack can not only be reproduced easily (Reproducibility = 10) but also affect most voice assistant users (Affected Users = 10). On the other hand, other types of DoS attack are not easy to launch because they require some specialized skills such as generating inaudible sounds (Exploitability = 0). In the case of using inaudible sounds, it is difficult for users to detect the attacks (Discoverability = 0). As a result, the DREAD rating is calculated as 4 and its priority is set to medium.

Information Disclosure of Service Reply. Service replies from `Voice assistant server` may be sniffed by an attacker. Depending on the types of data an attacker sniffs, it may be used to attack other parts of the system. Information disclosure can cause both direct and indirect damages to the system and data assets of users (Damage Potential = 10). With the assumption that service replies are not encrypted, sniffing service replies can be repeated whenever an attacker wants (Reproducibility = 10). In addition, sniffing attacks only require simple tools, and this makes these attacks easy to launch (Exploitability = 10). `Voice assistant server` is generally connected with a lot of users to provide them with services, and sniffing service replies from `Voice assistant server` can affect the privacy of all the users (Affected Users = 10). Due to the nature of information leakage, users do not know that their information has been leaked until the information is illegally used, and this makes it difficult to detect such sniffing attacks (Discoverability = 0).

4   Attack Scenarios

4.1   Spoofing Against Microphone Scenario

The open nature of voice channels and the lack of authentication mechanisms make voice assistants vulnerable to spoofing attacks such as voice replay attacks and voice impersonation attacks. Although audio microphones and speakers are enough to launch spoofing attacks, other sophisticated techniques such as signal processing can also be used to further improve the effectiveness of the attacks. For example, an attacker can use the so-called sound mosaic technique [8] to generate malicious voice commands from voice sound samples of victims, collected in advance. Specifically, the sound mosaic technique allows the attacker to generate malicious voice commands by dividing and concatenating victims' voice samples.

This technique is especially useful for impersonating famous people whose voice samples can be gathered easily.

Most of voice assistants do not provide voice authentication, that is, they do not care about who issues voice commands. This inherently makes them vulnerable to attacks injecting malicious voice commands. Although voice assistant devices are usually placed in the proximity of users, such attacks are still possible in this environment without raising the victim's attention, by injecting malicious voice commands that are only recognizable by machines but not by humans [4,11]. For example, an attacker can secretly embed inaudible malicious voice commands into a television broadcast or an announcement on elevators so that the malicious voice commands affect voice assistants in a stealthy manner.

4.2 DoS Against Microphone Scenario

Because the voice sounds are easily influenced by their surrounding environments, the voice assistant on a smartphone does not work well near a busy road or around a construction site. Therefore, it is possible to generate a sound which influences the voice assistant. DoS attack usually occurs in a network, and it is mitigated by blocking the packets or limiting the service requests. Unlike detecting traditional DoS attacks, the attack against the voice assistants is hard to recognize and prevent. Especially, if the attacker uses inaudible sounds for the DoS attacks, it is very hard for users to discover the attack occurring.

4.3 Information Disclosure of Service Reply Scenario

The service reply might contain a variety of information including the user's condition, what the user's interests are, some sensitive data and so on. The attacker can obtain much information by sniffing the communication channel. This leaked information can be used in social engineering attacks or phishing attacks. To mitigate this threat, packet encryption is the best strategy but the attacker may still infer some sensitive information from encrypted packets when encryption schemes are insecurely implemented. For example, traffic analysis (e.g., [7]) can be applied to obtain some sensitive information even when network packets are encrypted. Thus, the developer should carefully implement a secure encryption algorithm with a proper encryption mode and a padding scheme.

5   Recommendations

In this section, we offer some practical recommendations to mitigate potentially serious security scenarios described in Sect. 4.

To mitigate the spoofing attack in Sect. 4.1, destination authentication and liveness detection in data flows are required. That is, the voice assistant has to identify who the voice's owner is and whether the voice is generated in the present, not the past. One of the voice owner identification methods is the voiceprint analysis [5]. A voiceprint is the characteristics of a human voice,

Table 2. Suggested mitigation according to STRIDE category.

Data flow	Threat and mitigation
Voice command	**Spoofing on microphone:** Identify the authenticity of the voice command (e.g., voice recognition, voice liveness detection).
	Tampering with voice command: Provide a detection mechanism for distinguishing legitimate users' voice commands from forged ones.
	DoS to microphone: Deploy low-pass filter to cut off higher frequency than audio frequency.
Audio signal	**Spoofing on voice assistant server:** Identify the legitimate voice assistant app using authentication mechanism.
Service reply	**Tampering with service reply:** Protect the integrity of the service reply (e.g., HMAC), or use a secure channel.
	Information disclosure of service reply: Encrypt the service reply (e.g., TLS), or use a secure channel.
	DoS to voice assistant app: Limit the number of the service reply, or use a filter to distinguish malformed response or command.
	Elevation of privilege into voice assistant app: Check the validity of the input data (e.g., length of the input data).
Control request	**Spoofing on IoT controller:** Identify the legitimate voice assistant app using authentication mechanism.
	Tampering with control request: Protect the integrity of control requests (e.g., HMAC), or use a secure channel.
Action response	**Spoofing on IoT controller:** Identify the legitimate voice assistant app using authentication mechanism.
	Tampering with action response: Provide the integrity of action response (e.g., HMAC), or use secure channel.
	Information disclosure of action response: Encrypt the action response (e.g., TLS), or use a secure channel.
	DoS to voice assistant app: Limit the number of action response, or use a filter to distinguish malformed response.
	Elevation of privilege into voice assistant app: Check the validity of the input data (e.g., check the length of the input data) and use secure function within voice assistant app.
Command response	**Information disclosure of command response:** Avoid using command responses containing sensitive information about the user

and the characteristics are unique. In the cloud computing, the accuracy of the voiceprint authentication achieved 3.2% in FRR (False Reject Rate) [13].

The voiceprint method is vulnerable to recorded voice. Therefore, voice assistants have to use the liveness detection method. The liveness detection calculates phoneme localization with two microphones. Through the liveness detection method, the voice assistant can distinguish whether the input voice is from the user in real time or replayed. Zhang et al. [12] achieved over 99% accuracy and under 1% EER (Equal Error Rate).

To mitigate the denial of service attack of Sect. 4.2, limiting availability in data flows is required. That is, the voice assistant has to input the audible hertz sounds (e.g., 20–20,000 Hz) using signal processing for low pass filter. If the voice assistant only accepts the human audible sound ranging from 20 to 20,000 Hz, it is easier to detect anomalies. DoS attacks can be mitigated by limiting the number of the input data flows and filtering malformed data.

The simplest way to prevent the information disclosure in Sect. 4.3 is the encryption of data flows, such as SSL/TLS network protocols. However, imperfect encryption can still lead to information leakages. Many Android apps use SSL/TLS to protect their sensitive information. However, the sensitive data protected by SSL/TLS was vulnerable to Man-in-the-Middle attacks because some developers often used incorrect options or implementations [9]. In addition, the HTTPS protocol which is popularly used in protecting home banking, e-commerce, and e-procurement was vulnerable to Man-in-the-Middle attacks when the attacker had access to the victim's network [3] (Table 2).

The other threats can also be handled by a variety of mitigation methods. According to a given situation and capabilities, the mitigation methods should be properly chosen and implemented. Unsurprisingly, mitigation methods are not secure forever. Therefore, threat modeling analysts should periodically analyze possible threats and prepare proper strategies to mitigate those threats.

6   Conclusion

This paper analyzed potential security threats for voice assistant systems and suggested several mitigation strategies to reduces the risk of the identified threats through threat modeling analysis that has been widely used in the field of information security. Based on the threat analysis results, we also presented several attack scenarios. Finally, we proposed several practical defense strategies to mitigate the identified threats. In future work, we will implement the discovered attacks against real-world voice assistant systems to show their feasibility.

Acknowledgments. This work was supported in part by the ITRC (IITP-2018-2015-0-00403) and the NRF (No. 2017K1A3A1A17092614). The authors would like to thank all the anonymous reviewers for their valuable feedback.

References

1. Anand, P., Ryoo, J., Kim, H., Kim, E.: Threat assessment in the cloud environment: a quantitative approach for security pattern selection. In: Proceedings of the 10th ACM International Conference on Ubiquitous Information Management and Communication (2016)
2. Burns, S.F.: Threat modeling: a process to ensure application security. GIAC Security Essentials Certification (GSEC) Practical Assignment (2005)
3. Callegati, F., Cerroni, W., Ramilli, M.: Man-in-the-middle attack to the HTTPS protocol. IEEE Secur. Priv. **7**, 78–81 (2009)
4. Carlini, N., et al.: Hidden voice commands. In: Proceedings of the 25th USENIX Security Symposium (2016)
5. Garcia-Salicetti, S., et al.: BIOMET: a multimodal person authentication database including face, voice, fingerprint, hand and signature modalities. In: Proceedings of the 4th International Conference on Audio-and Video-based Biometric Person Authentication (2003)
6. Meier, J., Mackman, A., Dunner, M., Vasireddy, S., Escamilla, R., Murukan, A.: Improving Web Application Security: Threats and Countermeasures. Microsoft Corporation, Redmond (2003)
7. Park, K., Kim, H.: Encryption is not enough: inferring user activities on KakaoTalk with traffic analysis. In: Proceedings of the 16th International Workshop on Information Security Applications (2015)
8. Shih, T.K., Tang, N.C., Tsai, J.C., Hwang, J.N.: Video motion interpolation for special effect applications. IEEE Trans. Syst. Man Cybern. Part C (Appl. Rev.) **41**, 720–732 (2011)
9. Sounthiraraj, D., Sahs, J., Greenwood, G., Lin, Z., Khan, L.: SMV-HUNTER: large scale, automated detection of SSL/TLS man-in-the-middle vulnerabilities in android apps. In: Proceedings of the 21st Annual Network and Distributed System Security Symposium (2014)
10. Swiderski, F., Snyder, W.: Threat Modeling (Microsoft Professional), vol. 7. Microsoft Press (2004)
11. Zhang, G., Yan, C., Ji, X., Zhang, T., Zhang, T., Xu, W.: DolphinAttack: inaudible voice commands. In: Proceedings of the 24th ACM SIGSAC Conference on Computer and Communications Security (2017)
12. Zhang, L., Tan, S., Yang, J., Chen, Y.: VoiceLive: a phoneme localization based liveness detection for voice authentication on smartphones. In: Proceedings of the 23rd ACM SIGSAC Conference on Computer and Communications Security (2016)
13. Zhu, H.H., He, Q.H., Tang, H., Cao, W.H.: Voiceprint-biometric template design and authentication based on cloud computing security. In: Proceedings of 4th IEEE International Conference on Cloud and Service Computing (2011)

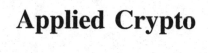

Applied Crypto

Secure Comparison Protocol with Encrypted Output and the Computation for Proceeding 2 Bits-by-2 Bits

Takumi Kobayashi[1] and Keisuke Hakuta[2(✉)]

[1] Interdisciplinary Graduate School of Science and Engineering, Shimane University,
1060 Nishikawatsu-cho, Matsue, Shimane 690-8504, Japan
s179506@matsu.shimane-u.ac.jp
[2] Institute of Science and Engineering, Academic Assembly, Shimane University,
1060 Nishikawatsu-cho, Matsue, Shimane 690-8504, Japan
hakuta@cis.shimane-u.ac.jp

Abstract. A secure comparison protocol computes a comparison result between private information from inputs without leakage of the information. It is a very important factor in many potential applications such as secure multi-party computation. These protocols under Yao's Millionaires' Problem output a plaintext of a comparison result. Because of this feature, however, these protocols are not suitable for some applications such as secure biometrics, secure statistics and so on. From this concern, we focus on a secure comparison protocol whose output is one bit encrypted comparison result. In recent works, the computation of such protocols proceeds bit-by-bit. For this reason, these protocols still have a problem about the efficiency. In this paper, as a first step of our study, we propose two secure comparison protocols with encrypted output. As an interesting feature, the computation of one of our protocols proceeds 2 bits-by-2 bits. We prove the correctness of our protocols and estimate the computational cost. Moreover we discuss the security of our protocols against semi-honest model.

Keywords: Homomorphic encryption · Privacy · Secure comparison ·
Secure multi-party computation · Semi-honest model ·
Yao's Millionaires' Problem

1 Introduction

A secure comparison protocol computes a comparison result between private information from inputs without leakage of any private information. It is a very important factor in many potential applications such as secure multi-party computation.

In 1982, Yao proposed a secure comparison protocol and suggested Yao's Millionaires' Problem [21]. Yao's Millionaires' Problem is as follows: "Alice and Bob

© Springer Nature Switzerland AG 2019
B. B. Kang and J. Jang (Eds.): WISA 2018, LNCS 11402, pp. 213–228, 2019.
https://doi.org/10.1007/978-3-030-17982-3_17

have non-negative integers a and b which are private information, respectively. Alice would like to know the comparison result $(a \leq b)$. How can Alice get a plaintext of the comparison result without leakage of any information about their private information?". Many researchers have tried developing an outperform protocol under Yao's Millionaires' Problem for a long term. Secure comparison protocols under Yao's Millionaires' Problem could be used to many potential applications. The examples of applications include: secure online-auction [5,14], secure biometrics [1], secure statistics, privacy preserving data mining [2,18] and so on [21]. However some applications in secure multi-party computation need a secure comparison protocol whose output is one bit encrypted comparison result as a subprotocol. Since a protocol under Yao's Millionaires' Problem outputs a plaintext of the comparison result, this protocol is not suitable for some applications such as secure biometrics [8,16] and secure statistics [9] and so on.

Motivated by the above concern, we focus on a secure comparison protocol whose output is one bit encrypted comparison result. The protocol outputs a ciphertext of a comparison result $(a \leq b)$ from Alice's input a and Bob's input b. There appears to be only a few publications in the literature which consider an encrypted output for integer comparison. We introduce some recent works in next subsection.

1.1 Recent Works

Several researchers proposed secure comparison protocols with an encrypted output and based on several building blocks. Note that a notion "$(a \leq b)$" stands for a truth value of a proposition "$a \leq b$" for non-negative integers a and b and other cases are defined similarly. For example, if $a \leq b$ is truth then a ciphertext of a comparison result $(a \leq b)$ is equal to that of "1". Damgård *et al.* proposed a comparison protocol with an encrypted output based on secret sharing [4–6]. Moreover Garay *et al.* proposed one with a ciphertext of a comparison result $(a > b)$ [12] using conditional gate [17]. More recently, some works using somewhat homomorphic encryption are proposed by Cheon *et al.* (cf. [3]). Their protocol outputs a ciphertext of a comparison result $(a < b)$. In addition, Veugen proposed a secure comparison protocol with a ciphertext of a comparison result $(a < b)$ using homomorphic encryption [19, Protocol 2]. Thus many comparison protocols have developed with several building blocks.

Secure comparison protocols are mainly classified as the following two protocols. Since the computation of some protocols proceeds bitwise in order to compute the comparison result, many comparison protocols still have a problem about the efficiency. In this paper, we call such a comparison protocol a BRC (Binary Representation Comparison) protocol, for short. On the other hand, the computation of some protocols proceeds an input size-by-an input size. We call such a comparison protocol an IRC (Integer Representation Comparison) protocol in this paper, for short. Each IRC protocol requires only a few rounds to compute the result [20, Protocol 4]. For this reason, an IRC protocol can be more efficient than a BRC protocol. However, compared to BRC protocols, a few IRC protocols with several building blocks have been proposed. Using several building blocks may makes secure comparison protocols more secure. Hence BRC protocols may outperform IRC protocols in terms of security.

Therefore we focus on a comparison protocol which the computation of the protocol proceeds w bits-by-w bits for a non-negative integer w. Namely, given l-bit non-negative integers a and b, the computation of the protocol proceeds w bits-by-w bits to compute the comparison result. We expect that computing w bits-by-w bits makes the comparison protocol more efficient. Moreover we expect that this protocol can be based on several building blocks such as BRC protocols. As a interesting feature, since this protocol proceeds w bits-by-w bits against l-bit input integers, we can treat large integers as the inputs of the protocol.

The goals of our study are follows: it is to develop a comparison protocol which the computation proceeds w bits-by-w bits for any non-negative w. Furthermore it is to discuss a suitable number of the bits in terms of both the efficiency and the security. This development means a generalization of a secure comparison protocols we propose in this paper.

As a first step for the generalization, we propose two comparison protocols whose output is one bit encrypted comparison result. Our first proposed protocol is a modification of Veugen's protocol [19, Protocol 2]. The computation of our first protocol and Veugen's one proceeds bit-by-bit. This modification makes an initialization of our first protocol simpler than Veugen's one. Moreover our second proposed protocol is based on our first protocol. The computation of this protocol proceeds 2 bits-by-2 bits.

1.2   Advantages of Our Protocols

Our first protocol is a first secure comparison protocol using only homomorphic encryption and outputting an encrypted bit of a comparison result $(a > b)$. Compared to a security of protocols using several building blocks, a security of the protocol using only one building block can be analyzed more easily. In addition a secure comparison protocol with an encrypted bit of a comparison result $(a > b)$ and using only homomorphic encryption still has been not proposed. This fact leads us to design our first proposed protocol. This protocol has potential for some application such as biometrics, statistics and so on. For example our first protocol can be applied for a secure division protocol [20, Protocol 1] and a secure comparison protocol [20, Protocol 4]. Moreover our first protocol has simpler algorithm than that of Veugen's one. This modification leads us to develop our proposed protocol 2.

Our second protocol proceeds 2 bits-by-2 bits to compute the comparison result. As a interesting feature, since this protocol proceeds 2 bits-by-2 bits against l-bit input integers, we can treat large integers as the inputs of the protocol. Moreover this second protocol is a first step for the generalization. We expect that the generalization leads us to develop more efficient secure comparison protocols.

1.3 Our Contribution

We consider a following scenario in this paper. "Alice and Bob have private integers a and b, respectively. They would like to compare their integers securely, but, they would not like to reveal the comparison result. Now Alice encrypts her messages using Bob's public key while Bob has the public key and its corresponding secret key. Then Alice only obtains an encrypted bit of the comparison result $(a > b)$." In other words, "Alice and Bob input private integers a and b. As a result, Alice outputs a ciphertext of the comparison result $(a > b)$ without leaking any information about private integers each other." We have two interesting contributions as follows.

1. We first propose a new comparison protocol whose output is one bit encrypted comparison result. Our first protocol is described as proposed protocol 1 in Sect. 3. Our first protocol and Veugen's one proceeds bit-by-bit to compute the comparison result. This protocol is a modification of Veugen's protocol [19, Protocol 2] and has simpler algorithm than that of Veugen's one. This modification leads us to develop our proposed protocol 2.
2. We secondly propose another comparison protocol whose output is one bit encrypted comparison result. Our second protocol is described as proposed protocol 2 in Sect. 4. Our second protocol is a modification of our first protocol. Our first protocol and some comparison protocols in recent works proceed bit-by-bit. On the other hand, our second protocol proceeds 2 bits-by-2 bits to compute the comparison result. In order to compute the comparison result, our second protocol needs a secure division protocol [20, Protocol 1] which needs a secure comparison protocol. Since an input size of the secure comparison protocol in the division protocol is enough small, the subprotocol in the division protocol is quite efficient. We describe the computational cost of our second protocol in Sect. 4.3. This second protocol is a first step for the generalization.

In Sect. 2 mathematical preliminaries are described, such as notation and Paillier encryption scheme [15] which is a common homomorphic encryption scheme. In Sect. 3 we propose a secure comparison protocol which is a modification of Veugen's protocol [19, Protocol 2]. Moreover we briefly discuss the correctness, computational cost and security. Here, the term "correctness" indicates that the protocol properly works to compute the outputs from the inputs. In Sect. 4 we propose a secure comparison protocol with the computation proceeds 2 bits-by-2 bits and prove the correctness of the protocol. Furthermore we estimate the computational cost and discuss the security. In Sect. 5 we conclude the paper by summary and future works.

2   Mathematical Preliminaries

We use the symbol $\mathbb{Z}$ to represent the rational integers. Let us denote by $\mathbb{Z}_{\geq 0}$ the set of non-negative integers, namely, $\mathbb{Z}_{\geq 0} := \{n \in \mathbb{Z} \mid n \geq 0\}$. For a positive integer $n \geq 2$, we denote the residue class ring modulo n by $\mathbb{Z}_n := \mathbb{Z}/n\mathbb{Z}$. Let p and q be $(k/2)$-bit primes which are chosen uniformly at random. We assume that $N = p \times q$ is a k-bit RSA modulus. As well with $\mathbb{Z}_n$, we denote the residue class ring modulo N and N^2 by $\mathbb{Z}_N = \mathbb{Z}/N\mathbb{Z}$ and $\mathbb{Z}_{N^2} = \mathbb{Z}/N^2\mathbb{Z}$, respectively. We represent the set $\{a \in \mathbb{Z}/N^2\mathbb{Z} \mid \gcd(a, N^2) = 1\}$ by $\mathbb{Z}_{N^2}^*$.

We refer the reader to [11, Definition 7.1] for the definition of a public key encryption scheme. We let κ be a security parameter of the scheme $\mathcal{E}$. A pair (pk, sk) which is an output of $\mathrm{Gen}(1^\kappa)$ constitutes a pair of corresponding public key pk and secret key sk. We represent the public key space, the secret key space, the plaintext space and the ciphertext space by $\mathcal{PK}$, $\mathcal{SK}$, $\mathcal{P}$ and $\mathcal{C}$, respectively.

$\mathrm{Enc}_{pk}(m)$ is the ciphertext of the plaintext $m \in \mathcal{P}$ using pk, whereas $\mathrm{Dec}_{sk}(c)$ is the decrypting result of the ciphertext $c \in \mathcal{C}$ using sk. In this paper, two maps Enc and Dec are defined as follows:

$$\mathrm{Enc} : \mathcal{P} \times \mathcal{PK} \to \mathcal{C} \qquad \mathrm{Dec} : \mathcal{C} \times \mathcal{SK} \to \mathcal{P}$$
$$(m, pk) \mapsto c, \qquad\qquad (c, sk) \mapsto m.$$

We refer the reader to [11, Definition 7.1] for the details.

2.1 Homomorphic Encryption

For our proposed protocols we need an additive and semantically secure homomorphic encryption scheme. A homomorphic encryption scheme and an additive homomorphic encryption scheme are defined as follows:

Definition 1 (Homomorphic Encryption [10, Definition 23.3.1]).
A public key encryption scheme with message space $\mathcal{P}$ and ciphertext space $\mathcal{C}$ is said to be homomorphic for the group $\mathcal{P}$ if there is some efficiently computable binary operation $\perp_1$ on $\mathcal{C}$ and $\perp_2$ on $\mathcal{P}$ such that, for all $m_1, m_2 \in \mathcal{P}$, if c_1 is a ciphertext of m_1 and c_2 is a ciphertext of m_2 (both with respect to the same public key) then $c_1 \perp_1 c_2$ is a ciphertext of $m_1 \perp_2 m_2$.

In Definition 1, if the binary operation $\perp_2$ is represented by the addition $+$, the public key encryption scheme is called an additive homomorphic encryption. One can apply any additive homomorphic encryption schemes to our protocols, such as Paillier encryption scheme [15], Damgård-Jurik encryption scheme [7] and DGK (Damgård, Geisler and Krøigård) encryption scheme [5,6]. In particular Paillier encryption scheme [15] is used for our proposed protocols in this paper. From homomorphic property, we have

$$\mathrm{Enc}_{pk}(m^{-1}) = \mathrm{Enc}_{pk}(-m) \text{ for } m \in \mathcal{P}.$$

Furthermore a multiplication operation between ciphertexts is denoted by ".".

2.2 Paillier Encryption Scheme

Paillier encryption scheme [15] is an additive homomorphic encryption scheme which is commonly used. We describe Paillier encryption scheme (Key Generation, Encryption and Decryption) as follows: note that $\lambda = \mathrm{lcm}(p-1, q-1)$, $a - 1 \equiv 0 \bmod N$ for any $a \in \mathbb{Z}_{N^2}$ [15, Theorem 9] and a map L is defined as

$$L : \mathbb{Z}_{N^2} \to \quad \mathbb{Z}_N$$
$$a \mapsto (a-1)/N.$$

1. <u>Key Generation</u>: Set a RSA modulus $N = p \times q$ where p and q are large prime numbers at random. Choose $g \in \mathbb{Z}_{N^2}^*$ at random. Check that g is a generator of $\mathbb{Z}_{N^2}^*$ by confirm whether $\gcd(\mathrm{L}(g^\lambda \bmod N^2), N) = 1$. If g is a generator of $\mathbb{Z}_{N^2}^*$, the public key is (N, g) and the secret key is (p, q).
2. <u>Encryption</u>: Given a message $m \in \mathbb{Z}_N$, select a random number $r \in \mathbb{Z}_N^*$. The ciphertext of the message m is $c = \mathrm{Enc}_{pk}(m, r) = g^m r^N \bmod N^2$.
3. <u>Decryption</u>: Given a ciphertext $c \in \mathbb{Z}_{N^2}^*$, compute the following equation:

$$m = (\mathrm{L}(c^\lambda \bmod N^2)/\mathrm{L}(g^\lambda \bmod N^2)) \bmod N.$$

Clearly, if $c = \mathrm{Enc}_{pk}(m, r)$, we obtain an original message m. We refer the reader to [15] for more details. We can see from below, Paillier encryption scheme is an additive homomorphic encryption scheme.

4. <u>Homomorphic property</u>: Given two messages m_1 and $m_2 \in \mathbb{Z}_N$, choose random numbers $r_1, r_2 \in \mathbb{Z}_N^*$. We represent two ciphertexts $c_1 = \mathrm{Enc}_{pk}(m_1, r_1) = g^{m_1} r_1^N \bmod N^2$, $c_2 = \mathrm{Enc}_{pk}(m_2, r_2) = g^{m_2} r_2^N \bmod N^2$. Then we have

$$\begin{aligned}
c_1 \cdot c_2 &= \mathrm{Enc}_{pk}(m_1, r_1) \cdot \mathrm{Enc}_{pk}(m_2, r_2) \\
&= (g^{m_1} r_1^N \bmod N^2) \times (g^{m_2} r_2^N \bmod N^2) \\
&= (g^{(m_1+m_2)}) \times (r_1 r_2)^N \bmod N^2 \\
&= \mathrm{Enc}_{pk}(m_1 + m_2, r_1 r_2).
\end{aligned} \tag{1}$$

3   Proposed Protocol 1

In this section we propose a comparison protocol whose output is one bit encrypted comparison result $(a > b)$. We use two maps $\mathcal{F}$ and $\hat{\mathcal{F}}$ throughout the paper. The two maps $\mathcal{F}$ and $\hat{\mathcal{F}}$ return a comparison result against input integers and are defined as follows. We define the map $\mathcal{F} : \mathbb{Z}_{\geq 0}^2 \to \{0, 1\}$ as

$$\mathcal{F}(a, b) = \begin{cases} 0, & (a > b), \\ 1, & (a \leq b), \end{cases} \tag{2}$$

and define the map $\hat{\mathcal{F}} : \mathbb{Z}_{\geq 0}^2 \to \{0, 1\}$ as $\hat{\mathcal{F}}(a, b) = \mathcal{F}(a, b) \oplus 1$, where "$\oplus$" is the exclusive-or operation.

Moreover we assume that Alice has a l-bit non-negative integer a and Bob has a l-bit non-negative integer b as follows:

$$a = \sum_{i=0}^{l-1} a_i 2^i = (a_{l-1}, \dots, a_0)_2 \in \mathbb{Z}_{\geq 0}, \quad a_i \in \{0, 1\},$$

$$b = \sum_{i=0}^{l-1} b_i 2^i = (b_{l-1}, \dots, b_0)_2 \in \mathbb{Z}_{\geq 0}, \quad b_i \in \{0, 1\}.$$

3.1   Description of Our Protocol 1 and Its Correctness

Our proposed protocol 1 is described as Algorithm 1. Our protocol 1 is a modification of Veugen's comparison protocol [19, Protocol 2]. Our protocol 1 and Veugen's one proceed bit-by-bit to compute the comparison result. Veugen's one outputs one bit encrypted comparison result $(a < b)$. On the other hand our protocol 1 outputs one bit encrypted comparison result $(a > b)$.

Set $a^{(i)} := (a_{i-1}, \ldots, a_0)_2 \in \mathbb{Z}_{\geq 0}$ and $b^{(i)} := (b_{i-1}, \ldots, b_0)_2 \in \mathbb{Z}_{\geq 0}$ for each i $(1 \leq i \leq l)$. Moreover we put t_i for $i = 0, \ldots, l$ as follows:

$$t_i := \begin{cases} 1, & (i = 0), \\ \mathcal{F}(a^{(i)}, b^{(i)}), & (1 \leq i \leq l). \end{cases}$$

Remark that

$$t_l = \mathcal{F}(a^{(l)}, b^{(l)}) = \mathcal{F}(a, b).$$

In our proposed protocol 1 the value t_{i+1} is computed for each i $(i = 0, 1, \ldots, l - 1)$. The goal of our proposed protocol 1 is that Alice outputs a ciphertext of $t_l = 1 - t_l = 1 - \mathcal{F}(a^{(l)}, b^{(l)}) = 1 - \mathcal{F}(a, b) = \hat{\mathcal{F}}(a, b)$ from their inputs a and b. This is achieved by computing $t_l = \mathcal{F}(a^{(l)}, b^{(l)}) = \mathcal{F}(a, b)$ and $\hat{\mathcal{F}}(a, b) = 1 - \mathcal{F}(a, b) = 1 - t_l$.

Our protocol 1 differs from Veugen's one in the following steps: (i) Initialization step, (ii) Randomization step, and (iii) Bit inverting step. In Initialization step, Alice encrypts a message "1", obtains $\mathrm{Enc}_{pk}(1)$, and substitutes $\mathrm{Enc}_{pk}(1)$ in $\mathrm{Enc}_{pk}(t_0)$. Furthermore Alice and Bob carry out iterations for i from 0 to $l - 1$ by $+1$. We alter steps 1–6 in Veugen's one to this step. In Randomization step, Bob chooses r' from random set at random and computes $(r')^N$. Moreover Bob randomizes $\mathrm{Enc}_{pk}(u_i)$ by computing $\mathrm{Enc}_{pk}(u_i) \times (r')^N$. We add this step between steps 22 and 23 in Veugen's one. In Bit inverting step, Alice computes $\mathrm{Enc}_{pk}(1) \cdot \mathrm{Enc}_{pk}(t_i)^{-1}$, substitutes $\mathrm{Enc}_{pk}(1 - t_i)$ in $\mathrm{Enc}_{pk}(t_i)$ and outputs $\mathrm{Enc}_{pk}(t_i)$. We add this step after step 38 of Veugen's one.

Furthermore we describe that how variables change in one iteration in proposed protocol 1 as Table 1. From Table 1, clearly, Alice obtains a ciphertext of $t_l = \mathcal{F}(a, b)$ in step 31. By bit inverse in steps 32–33, Alice finally obtains a ciphertext of $\hat{\mathcal{F}}(a, b)$. Thus we can see that our protocol 1 satisfies the correctness. Since the correctness of our protocol 1 is similar to that of Veugen's one we refer the reader to [19] for more details.

3.2   Computational Cost and Security of Our Protocol 1

Note that Enc, M, I, and Exp stand for the computational cost of one encryption, multiplication, inverse, and exponent, respectively. Our protocol 1 needs more 1 Enc, $0.5l + 3$ M, 2.5 I, and $0.5l$ Exp more than Veugen's protocol on average. While Veugen's protocol carries out $(l-1)$ iterations, our proposed protocol 1 carries out l iterations. Since we can guess that the input size l is enough large, our protocol 1 and Veugen's one have almost the same computation cost.

Algorithm 1. Our proposed protocol 1

Inputs: Alice : $a = (a_{l-1} \ldots a_0)_2$ and pk
Inputs: Bob : $b = (b_{l-1} \ldots b_0)_2$, pk and sk
Outputs: Alice : $\text{Enc}_{pk}(t_l)$ such that $t_l = \hat{\mathcal{F}}(a, b)$
Outputs: Bob : N/A

1: Alice encrypts a massage "1" and obtains $\text{Enc}_{pk}(1)$
2: Alice computes : $t_0 = 1, \text{Enc}_{pk}(t_0) \leftarrow \text{Enc}_{pk}(1)$
3: **for** i from 0 to $l - 1$ by $+1$ **do**
4:     Alice chooses c_i such that $c_i \in \{0, 1\}$ at random
5:     **if** $c_i = 0$ **then**
6:         Alice computes: $s_i = t_i, \text{Enc}_{pk}(s_i) \leftarrow \text{Enc}_{pk}(t_i)$
7:     **else**
8:         Alice computes:
9:             $s_i = 1 - t_i, \text{Enc}_{pk}(s_i) \leftarrow \text{Enc}_{pk}(1 - t_i) = \text{Enc}_{pk}(1) \cdot \text{Enc}_{pk}(t_i)^{-1}$
10:    **end if**
11:    Alice sends $\text{Enc}_{pk}(s_i)$ to Bob
12:    **if** $b_i = 0$ **then**
13:        Bob computes: $u_i = 0, \text{Enc}_{pk}(u_i) \leftarrow \text{Enc}_{pk}(0)$
14:    **else**
15:        Bob computes: $u_i = s_i, \text{Enc}_{pk}(u_i) \leftarrow \text{Enc}_{pk}(s_i)$
16:        Bob chooses r' from random set at random
17:        Bob computes $(r')^N$
18:        Bob randomizes $\text{Enc}_{pk}(u_i)$ by computing $\text{Enc}_{pk}(u_i) \times (r')^N$
19:    **end if**
20:    Bob encrypts b_i and obtains $\text{Enc}_{pk}(b_i)$
21:    Bob sends $\text{Enc}_{pk}(b_i)$ and $\text{Enc}_{pk}(u_i)$ to Alice
22:    **if** $c_i \neq 0$ **then**
23:        Alice computes: $\text{Enc}_{pk}(u_i) \leftarrow \text{Enc}_{pk}(b_i - u_i) = \text{Enc}_{pk}(b_i) \cdot \text{Enc}_{pk}(u_i)^{-1}$
24:    **end if**
25:    **if** $a_i = 0$ **then**
26:        Alice computes:
27:            $\text{Enc}_{pk}(t_{i+1}) \leftarrow \text{Enc}_{pk}(t_i + b_i - u_i) = \text{Enc}_{pk}(t_i) \cdot \text{Enc}_{pk}(b_i) \cdot \text{Enc}_{pk}(u_i)^{-1}$
28:    **else**
29:        Alice computes: $\text{Enc}_{pk}(t_{i+1}) \leftarrow \text{Enc}_{pk}(u_i)$
30:    **end if**
31: **end for**
32: Alice computes: $\text{Enc}_{pk}(t_l) \leftarrow \text{Enc}_{pk}(1 - t_l) = \text{Enc}_{pk}(1) \cdot \text{Enc}_{pk}(t_l)^{-1}$
33: Alice outputs $\text{Enc}_{pk}(t_l)$

Our protocol 1 has a following computational cost on average: Alice's Enc, M, I, and Exp are 1, $2l + 1$, $1.5l + 1$, and 0. Bob's Enc, M, I, and Exp are $1.5l$, $0.5l$, 0, and $0.5l$. Furthermore Total Enc, M, I, and Exp are $1.5l + 1$, $2.5l + 1$, $1.5l + 1$, and $0.5l$. We refer the reader to [19] for more details.

We briefly discuss the security of our proposed protocol 1. Our security analysis is similar to Veugen's one [19]. Differences of our protocol 1 from Veugen's one are Initialization step, Randomization step and Bit inverting step. In Initialization step, Alice and Bob do not communicate ciphertexts. In Randomization

Table 1. Variables in one iteration

c_i	a_i	b_i	s_i	u_i after step 19	u_i after step 24	t_{i+1}
0	0	0	$s_i \leftarrow t_i$	$u_i \leftarrow 0$	$u_i \leftarrow 0$	$t_{i+1} \leftarrow t_i + b_i - u_i = t_i$
0	0	1	$s_i \leftarrow t_i$	$u_i \leftarrow t_i$	$u_i \leftarrow t_i$	$t_{i+1} \leftarrow t_i + b_i - u_i = 1$
0	1	0	$s_i \leftarrow t_i$	$u_i \leftarrow 0$	$u_i \leftarrow 0$	$t_{i+1} \leftarrow u_i = 0$
0	1	1	$s_i \leftarrow t_i$	$u_i \leftarrow t_i$	$u_i \leftarrow t_i$	$t_{i+1} \leftarrow u_i = t_i$
1	0	0	$s_i \leftarrow 1 - t_i$	$u_i \leftarrow 0$	$u_i \leftarrow b_i - u_i = 0$	$t_{i+1} \leftarrow t_i + b_i - u_i = t_i$
1	0	1	$s_i \leftarrow 1 - t_i$	$u_i \leftarrow 1 - t_i$	$u_i \leftarrow b_i - u_i = t_i$	$t_{i+1} \leftarrow t_i + b_i - u_i = 1$
1	1	0	$s_i \leftarrow 1 - t_i$	$u_i \leftarrow 0$	$u_i \leftarrow b_i - u_i = 0$	$t_{i+1} \leftarrow u_i = 0$
1	1	1	$s_i \leftarrow 1 - t_i$	$u_i \leftarrow 1 - t_i$	$u_i \leftarrow b_i - u_i = t_i$	$t_{i+1} \leftarrow u_i = t_i$

step, Bob randomizes a ciphertext of s_i depending on b_i. Finally, in Bit inverting step, Alice just carry out bit inverse. Consequently our modification does not affect the security of Veugen's one. In addition, Veugen's one is secure against semi-honest model [19, Sect. 2.3]. We can see that our proposed protocol 1 is also secure against semi-honest model.

4 Proposed Protocol 2

In this section we propose a new comparison protocol whose output is one bit encrypted comparison result $(a > b)$.

4.1 Description of Our Protocol 2

Our proposed protocol 2 is described as Algorithm 2. The overview of Algorithm 2 is as follows. Our protocol 2 is a modification of our proposed protocol 1. Our protocol 1 and Veugen's one proceed bit-by-bit to compute the comparison result, while our protocol 2 proceeds 2 bits-by-2 bits to compute that.

We use two sets $\tilde{\Delta}$ and Δ, and an element σ in Δ as follows:

$$\tilde{\Delta} := \{0, 1, 2, 3\} \subsetneq \mathbb{Z}, \ \sigma \in \Delta := \{1, 2, 3\} = \tilde{\Delta} \setminus \{0\} \subsetneq \mathbb{Z}.$$

We represent the integer a as follows:

$$a = (a_{l-1}, \ldots, a_0)_2 = (A_{L-1}, \ldots, A_0) \in \mathbb{Z}_{\geq 0}, \ A_i := (a_{2i+1}, a_{2i})_2 \in \tilde{\Delta} \subsetneq \mathbb{Z}.$$

The non-negative integer b is represented as well. By padding zeros if necessary, we may assume that l is an even number in our proposed protocol 2. It is obvious that $L = l/2$.

Moreover we denote an integer representation of $(A_{i-1}, \ldots, A_0) \in \mathbb{Z}_{\geq 0}$ and $(B_{i-1}, \ldots, B_0) \in \mathbb{Z}_{\geq 0}$ by $A^{(i)}$ and $B^{(i)}$, respectively. Again we use a notation t_i and put t_i for $i = 0, \ldots, L$ as follows:

$$t_i := \begin{cases} 1, & (i = 0), \\ \mathcal{F}(A^{(i)}, B^{(i)}), & (1 \leq i \leq L). \end{cases}$$

Algorithm 2. Our proposed protocol 2

Inputs: Alice : $a = (a_{l-1}, \ldots, a_0)_2 = (A_{L-1}, \ldots, A_0)$, $d := 2^w = 2^2 = 4$ and pk
Inputs: Bob : $b = (b_{l-1}, \ldots, b_0)_2 = (B_{L-1}, \ldots, B_0)$, $d := 2^w = 2^2 = 4$, pk and sk
Outputs: Alice : $\text{Enc}_{pk}(t_L)$ such that $t_L = \hat{\mathcal{F}}(a, b)$, Bob : N/A
1: Alice encrypts and computes $\text{Enc}_{pk}(1), \text{Enc}_{pk}(d)$ and $\text{Enc}_{pk}(1)^{-1}$
2: Alice computes : $t_0 = 1, \text{Enc}_{pk}(t_0) \leftarrow \text{Enc}_{pk}(1)$
3: **for** i from 0 to $L - 1$ by +1 **do**
4:    Alice chooses c_i such that $c_i \in \{0, 1\}$ at random
5:    **if** $c_i = 0$ **then**
6:       Alice computes: $s_i = t_i, \text{Enc}_{pk}(s_i) \leftarrow \text{Enc}_{pk}(t_i)$
7:    **else**
8:       Alice computes: $s_i = 1 - t_i, \text{Enc}_{pk}(s_i) \leftarrow \text{Enc}_{pk}(1 - t_i)$
9:    **end if**
10:    Alice sends $\text{Enc}_{pk}(s_i)$ to Bob
11:    Bob encrypts B_i and obtains $\text{Enc}_{pk}(B_i)$
12:    **if** $B_i = 0$ **then**
13:       Bob computes: $u_i = 0, \text{Enc}_{pk}(u_i) \leftarrow \text{Enc}_{pk}(0)$
14:    **else**
15:       Bob computes: $u_i = s_i + B_i, \text{Enc}_{pk}(u_i) \leftarrow \text{Enc}_{pk}(s_i + B_i)$
16:    **end if**
17:    Bob sends $\text{Enc}_{pk}(B_i)$ and $\text{Enc}_{pk}(u_i)$ to Alice
18:    **if** $c_i \neq 0$ **then**
19:       Alice computes: $\text{Enc}_{pk}(u_i) \leftarrow \text{Enc}_{pk}(2B_i - u_i + 1)$
20:    **end if**
21:    **if** $A_i = 0$ **then**
22:       **if** $c_i = 0$ **then**
23:          Alice computes: $\text{Enc}_{pk}(B_i + d - 1)$
24:          Alice and Bob perform a division protocol: Alice inputs $\text{Enc}_{pk}(B_i + d - 1)$ and d, Bob inputs d and sk, Alice outputs $\text{Enc}_{pk}(\lfloor (B_i + d - 1)/d \rfloor)$
25:          Alice computes: $\text{Enc}_{pk}(t_{i+1}) \leftarrow \text{Enc}_{pk}(t_i + B_i - u_i + \lfloor (B_i + d - 1)/d \rfloor)$
26:       **else**
27:          Alice computes: $\text{Enc}_{pk}(B_i + d)$
28:          Alice and Bob perform a division protocol: Alice inputs $\text{Enc}_{pk}(B_i + d)$ and d, Bob inputs d and sk, Alice outputs $\text{Enc}_{pk}(\lfloor (B_i + d)/d \rfloor)$
29:          Alice computes: $\text{Enc}_{pk}(t_{i+1}) \leftarrow \text{Enc}_{pk}(t_i + B_i - u_i + \lfloor (B_i + d)/d \rfloor)$
30:       **end if**
31:    **else**
32:       Alice computes: $\text{Enc}_{pk}(u_i - A_i - 1 + d)$
33:       Alice and Bob perform a division protocol: Alice inputs $\text{Enc}_{pk}(u_i - A_i - 1 + d)$ and d, Bob inputs d and sk, Alice outputs $\text{Enc}_{pk}(\lfloor (u_i - A_i - 1 + d)/d \rfloor)$
34:       Alice computes: $\text{Enc}_{pk}(t_{i+1}) \leftarrow \text{Enc}_{pk}(\lfloor (u_i - A_i - 1 + d)/d \rfloor)$
35:    **end if**
36: **end for**
37: Alice computes: $\text{Enc}_{pk}(t_L) \leftarrow \text{Enc}_{pk}(1 - t_L)$
38: Alice outputs $\text{Enc}_{pk}(t_L)$

Remark that

$$t_L = \mathcal{F}(A^{(L)}, B^{(L)}) = \mathcal{F}(a, b).$$

In our proposed protocol 2 the value t_{i+1} is computed for each i ($i = 0, 1, \ldots, L-1$). The goal of our proposed protocol 2 is that Alice outputs a ciphertext of $t_L = 1 - t_L = 1 - \mathcal{F}(A^{(L)}, B^{(L)}) = 1 - \mathcal{F}(a, b) = \hat{\mathcal{F}}(a, b)$ from their inputs a and b. This is achieved by computing $t_L = \mathcal{F}(A^{(L)}, B^{(L)}) = \mathcal{F}(a, b)$ and $\hat{\mathcal{F}}(a, b) = 1 - \mathcal{F}(a, b) = 1 - t_L$.

In steps 1–2 of Algorithm 2, Alice carries out an initialization and denotes $t_0 = 1$. In step 3, Alice and Bob carry out iterations for i from 0 to $L - 1$ by $+1$. In steps 4–10, Alice blinds t_i ($= \mathcal{F}(A^{(i)}, B^{(i)})$) and sends it to Bob. Because of this blind, Bob cannot distinguish whether a massage s_i is t_i or $1 - t_i$ when Bob decrypts it. In steps 11–17, Bob computes $\text{Enc}_{pk}(B_i)$ and $\text{Enc}_{pk}(u_i)$ depending on B_i and sends them to Alice. In steps 18–20, Alice solves the blind. In steps 21–35, Alice computes $\text{Enc}_{pk}(t_{i+1})$ depending on A_i and c_i. In step 36, Alice obtains a ciphertext of $\mathcal{F}(a, b)$ through this iteration because we have

$$t_L = \mathcal{F}(a, b). \tag{3}$$

Finally, Alice obtains a ciphertext of $\hat{\mathcal{F}}(a, b)$ by bit inverse in steps 37–38. In steps 8, 15, 19, 23, 25, 27, 29, 32, and 37, each chipertext can be computed by the homomorphic property (1).

Moreover our protocol 2 needs a secure division protocol [20, Protocol 1] as a subprotocol. In this division protocol, Alice inputs a ciphertext of an integer x and a divisor d, and Bob inputs a divisor d and sk. At end of the protocol Alice obtains a ciphertext of the division result $\lfloor x/d \rfloor$ as the output. In step 24, 28, 33 of Algorithm 2, Alice and Bob need to perform the division protocol. On the other hand, since Alice can store a ciphertext of the division result, in steps 25, 29 and 34 of Algorithm 2, they do not need to do that. In addition, this division protocol needs a secure comparison protocol as a subprotocol. This comparison protocol requires to output a ciphertext of comparison result ($a > b$) for input integers a and b, with the size $\lfloor \log_2 d \rfloor$. We use our protocol 1 as the subprotocol.

4.2   Correctness

In this section we describe the correctness of our protocol 2. Now we recall that $\sigma \in \Delta = \{1, 2, 3\} = \tilde{\Delta} \backslash \{0\} \subsetneq \mathbb{Z}$. We depict Tables 2 and 3 which show that how does a value t_{i+1} depend on values c_i, A_i and B_i in our protocol 2. The value t_{i+1} is computed for each i ($i = 0, 1, \ldots, L-1$) using the following propositions:

Proposition 1. *For given integers $A^{(i+1)} = (A_i, \ldots, A_0) \in \mathbb{Z}_{\geq 0}$ and $B^{(i+1)} = (B_i, \ldots, B_0) \in \mathbb{Z}_{\geq 0}$ for $i = 0, \ldots, L-1$, if $A_i < B_i$ then we have $t_{i+1} = 1$.*

Proof. Here "$(i + 1)$-th iteration" stands for the iteration of steps 3–36 in Algorithm 2 for $i = 0, \ldots, L-1$. Since A_i and B_i are their most significant bits of the integers $A^{(i+1)}$ and $B^{(i+1)}$ in $(i + 1)$-th iteration, from Tables 2 and 3, we have $t_{i+1} = \mathcal{F}(A^{(i+1)}, B^{(i+1)}) = 1$. Thus Proposition 1 can be verified. $\square$

Table 2. Variables in one iteration (1/2)

c_i	A_i	B_i	Condition	s_i	u_i after step 16	u_i after step 20
0	0	0		t_i	$u_i \leftarrow 0$	$u_i \leftarrow 0$
0	0	σ		t_i	$u_i \leftarrow t_i + B_i$	$u_i \leftarrow t_i + B_i$
0	σ	0		t_i	$u_i \leftarrow 0$	$u_i \leftarrow 0$
0	σ	σ	$(A_i < B_i)$	t_i	$u_i \leftarrow t_i + B_i$	$u_i \leftarrow t_i + B_i$
0	σ	σ	$(A_i = B_i)$	t_i	$u_i \leftarrow t_i + B_i$	$u_i \leftarrow t_i + B_i$
0	σ	σ	$(A_i > B_i)$	t_i	$u_i \leftarrow t_i + B_i$	$u_i \leftarrow t_i + B_i$
1	0	0		$1 - t_i$	$u_i \leftarrow 0$	$u_i \leftarrow 2B_i - u_i + 1 = 0 - 0 + 1 = 1$
1	0	σ		$1 - t_i$	$u_i \leftarrow 1 - t_i + B_i$	$u_i \leftarrow 2B_i - u_i + 1 = 2B_i - (1 - t_i + B_i) + 1 = t_i + B_i$
1	σ	0		$1 - t_i$	$u_i \leftarrow 0$	$u_i \leftarrow 2B_i - u_i + 1 = 0 - 0 + 1 = 1$
1	σ	σ	$(A_i < B_i)$	$1 - t_i$	$u_i \leftarrow 1 - t_i + B_i$	$u_i \leftarrow 2B_i - u_i + 1 = 2B_i - (1 - t_i + B_i) + 1 = t_i + B_i$
1	σ	σ	$(A_i = B_i)$	$1 - t_i$	$u_i \leftarrow 1 - t_i + B_i$	$u_i \leftarrow 2B_i - u_i + 1 = 2B_i - (1 - t_i + B_i) + 1 = t_i + B_i$
1	σ	σ	$(A_i > B_i)$	$1 - t_i$	$u_i \leftarrow 1 - t_i + B_i$	$u_i \leftarrow 2B_i - u_i + 1 = 2B_i - (1 - t_i + B_i) + 1 = t_i + B_i$

Table 3. Variables in one iteration (2/2)

c_i	A_i	B_i	Condition	t_{i+1}
0	0	0		$t_{i+1} \leftarrow t_i + B_i - u_i + \lfloor (d + B_i - 1)/d \rfloor = t_i$
0	0	σ		$t_{i+1} \leftarrow t_i + B_i - u_i + \lfloor (d + B_i - 1)/d \rfloor = 1$
0	σ	0		$t_{i+1} \leftarrow \lfloor (u_i - A_i - 1 + d)/d \rfloor = \lfloor (d - (A_i + 1))/d \rfloor = 0$
0	σ	σ	$(A_i < B_i)$	$t_{i+1} \leftarrow \lfloor (u_i - A_i - 1 + d)/d \rfloor = \lfloor (d + t_i + (B_i - A_i - 1))/d \rfloor = 1$
0	σ	σ	$(A_i = B_i)$	$t_{i+1} \leftarrow \lfloor (u_i - A_i - 1 + d)/d \rfloor = \lfloor (d + t_i - 1)/d \rfloor = t_i$
0	σ	σ	$(A_i > B_i)$	$t_{i+1} \leftarrow \lfloor (u_i - A_i - 1 + d)/d \rfloor = \lfloor (d + t_i + (B_i - A_i - 1))/d \rfloor = 0$
1	0	0		$t_{i+1} \leftarrow t_i + B_i - u_i + \lfloor (d + B_i)/d \rfloor = t_i$
1	0	σ		$t_{i+1} \leftarrow t_i + B_i - u_i + \lfloor (d + B_i)/d \rfloor = 1$
1	σ	0		$t_{i+1} \leftarrow \lfloor (u_i - A_i - 1 + d)/d \rfloor = \lfloor (d - A_i)/d \rfloor = 0$
1	σ	σ	$(A_i < B_i)$	$t_{i+1} \leftarrow \lfloor (u_i - A_i - 1 + d)/d \rfloor = \lfloor (d + t_i + (B_i - A_i - 1))/d \rfloor = 1$
1	σ	σ	$(A_i = B_i)$	$t_{i+1} \leftarrow \lfloor (u_i - A_i - 1 + d)/d \rfloor = \lfloor (d + t_i - 1)/d \rfloor = t_i$
1	σ	σ	$(A_i > B_i)$	$t_{i+1} \leftarrow \lfloor (u_i - A_i - 1 + d)/d \rfloor = \lfloor (d + t_i + (B_i - A_i - 1))/d \rfloor = 0$

Proposition 2. *For given integers* $A^{(i+1)} = (A_i, \ldots, A_0) \in \mathbb{Z}_{\geq 0}$ *and* $B^{(i+1)} = (B_i, \ldots, B_0) \in \mathbb{Z}_{\geq 0}$ *and* t_i *for* $i = 0, \ldots, L - 1$, *if* $t_i = 1$ *and* $A_i = B_i$ *then we have* $t_{i+1} = 1$.

Proof. If A_i and B_i are equal in $(i+1)$-th iteration, from Tables 2 and 3, a value t_{i+1} depends on t_i. Now if $t_i = 1$, we have $t_{i+1} = t_i = 1$. Moreover we consider that A_i and B_i are equal for all i. Since we set t_0 to 1 in step 2 of Algorithm 2, we have $t_{i+1} = t_i = \cdots = t_0 = 1$. Thus Proposition 2 can be verified. $\square$

The correctness of our protocol 2 is that for Alice's input a and Bob's input b, if $a > b$ then Alice outputs $t_L = 1$ otherwise Alice outputs $t_L = 0$. A main idea of the proof is that Alice has Eq. (3) after L-th iteration. This is described as Theorem 1. From Theorem 1, Alice can obtain a ciphertext of $\hat{\mathcal{F}}(a, b)$ by computing $\mathrm{Enc}_{pk}(1) \cdot \mathrm{Enc}_{pk}(t_L)^{-1}$ in steps 37–38.

Theorem 1. *In Algorithm* 2, *after L-th iteration we have Eq.* (3).

Proof. From Propositions 1 and 2, Tables 2 and 3, it is not hard to prove that our protocol 2 is correct. □

Table 4. Computational cost of protocol 2 without subprotocols

c_i	A_i	B_i	Alice				Bob				Total			
			Enc	M	I	Exp	Enc	M	I	Exp	Enc	M	I	Exp
0	0	0	2	$5L+1$	$L+2$	0	$2L$	0	0	0	$2L+2$	$5L+1$	$L+2$	0
0	0	σ	2	$5L+1$	$L+2$	0	$2L$	0	0	0	$2L+2$	$5L+1$	$L+2$	0
0	σ	0	2	$3L+1$	$L+2$	0	$2L$	0	0	0	$2L+2$	$3L+1$	$L+2$	0
0	σ	σ	2	$3L+1$	$L+2$	0	$2L$	0	0	0	$2L+2$	$3L+1$	$L+2$	0
1	0	0	2	$8L+1$	$2L+2$	0	L	L	0	0	$L+2$	$9L+1$	$2L+2$	0
1	0	σ	2	$8L+1$	$2L+2$	0	L	L	0	0	$L+2$	$9L+1$	$2L+2$	0
1	σ	0	2	$7L+1$	$3L+2$	0	L	L	0	0	$L+2$	$8L+1$	$3L+2$	0
1	σ	σ	2	$7L+1$	$3L+2$	0	L	L	0	0	$L+2$	$8L+1$	$3L+2$	0
AVE			2	$5.375L+1$	$1.875L+2$	0	$1.5L$	$0.5L$	0	0	$1.5L+2$	$5.875L+1$	$1.875L+2$	0

4.3 Computational Cost

Now we recall notations Enc, M, I, and Exp. Note that Dec stands for the computational cost of one decryption. We first estimate the computational cost of subprotocols we need. As a subprotocol we use a secure division protocol [20, Protocol 1] which needs a secure comparison protocol. Veugen states that "Except for one execution of a secure comparison protocol, the remaining steps of this division protocol require 2 Enc, 3 M and 1 I by Alice, and 1 Enc and 1 Dec by Bob". Using precomputing techniques, in Paillier encryption scheme, we may assume that the computational cost of one decryption and one exponent are the almost same [15]. Furthermore we use our proposed protocol 1 as a secure comparison protocol in this division protocol. Since the input size of the comparison protocol is only $\lfloor \log_2 d \rfloor = \lfloor \log_2 2^w \rfloor = w = 2$, the comparison protocol is quite efficient. For one execution of the protocol, our proposed protocol 1 requires 1 Enc, 5 M, and 4 I by Alice, and 3 Enc, 1 M, and 1 Exp by Bob on average. Consequently, for L executions of the division protocol including the comparison protocol, an average of the computational cost are follows: Alice's Enc, M, I, and Exp are $3L$, $8L$, $5L$, and 0. Bob's Enc, M, I, and Exp are $4L$, L, 0, and $2L$. Furthermore Total Enc, M, I, and Exp are $7L$, $9L$, $5L$, and $2L$.

The computational cost in our protocol 2 without subprotocols is described in Table 4. We estimate the computational cost with assumption that Alice and Bob can store their ciphertexts which Alice or Bob has in their steps, respectively. Each line in Table 4 represents Alice's, Bob's or Total computational cost when c_i, A_i and B_i are respectively 0 or σ for all i. The bottom line in Table 4 represents the average of Alice's, Bob's or Total computational cost. As a result, an average of the computational cost in our protocol 2 including subprotocols is described as follows: Alice's Enc, M, I, and Exp are $3L+2$, $13.375L+1$, $6.875L+2$, and 0. Bob's Enc, M, I, and Exp are $5.5L$, $1.5L$, 0, and $2L$. Furthermore Total Enc, M, I, and Exp are $8.5L+2$, $14.875L+1$, $6.875L+2$, and $2L$.

Compared to the cost of our protocol 1, that of our protocol 2 is more expensive. Nevertheless, we propose our protocol 2 whose the computation proceeds 2 bits-by-2 bits for the generalization. We expect that the generalization leads us to develop more efficient secure comparison protocols.

4.4 Security

In this session we briefly discuss the security of our proposed protocol 2. Our security analysis is similar to Veugen's one [19]. We refer for more details to [19, Sect. 2.3]. We can see that our proposed protocol 2 is secure against semi-honest model [13, Definition 7.2.2].

Now we check that any information about the messages is not leaked in the protocol by looking their steps. In steps 4–10 of Algorithm 2, Alice blinds $\mathrm{Enc}_{pk}(t_i)$ by coin toss c_i and sends $\mathrm{Enc}_{pk}(s_i)$ to Bob. Due to the blind, Bob cannot distinguish whether a message s_i is t_i or $1-t_i$ when Bob decrypts $\mathrm{Enc}_{pk}(s_i)$. Next, in steps 11–17, Bob computes $\mathrm{Enc}_{pk}(u_i)$ depending on B_i. Moreover Bob sends $\mathrm{Enc}_{pk}(B_i)$ and $\mathrm{Enc}_{pk}(u_i)$ to Alice. Since the cryptosystem is semantically secure, Alice cannot get any information about the messages from these ciphertexts. Finally Alice and Bob cannot get any information about their messages each other.

5 Conclusion and Future Works

We proposed two secure comparison protocols whose output is one bit encrypted comparison result $(a > b)$. Our first protocol is a modification of Veugen's protocol [19, Protocol 2] and has simpler algorithm than that of Veugen's one. Our first protocol has potential for some applications such as biometrics, statistics and so on. Our second protocol is a modification of first one and proceeds 2 bits-by-2 bits. This protocol is a first step for a generalization of our secure comparison protocols. Our two protocols are secure against semi-honest model. Moreover we proved for the correctness and estimated the computational cost for our proposed protocols. Our work has interesting potential to many application such as secure biometrics, secure statistics and so on.

A goal of our study is developing a secure comparison protocol which the computation proceeds w-bits by w-bits for any non-negative integer w. As future works, we need to compare our protocols and other similar protocols. In addition we need to discuss the formal security of our protocols. Moreover we try developing a secure comparison protocol which the computation proceeds w-bits by w-bits by modifying our proposed protocol 2.

References

1. Blanton, M., Gasti, P.: Secure and efficient protocols for iris and fingerprint identification. In: Atluri, V., Diaz, C. (eds.) ESORICS 2011. LNCS, vol. 6879, pp. 190–209. Springer, Heidelberg (2011). https://doi.org/10.1007/978-3-642-23822-2_11

2. Bost, R., Popa, R.A., Tu, S., Goldwasser, S.: Machine learning classification over encrypted data. In: Network and Distributed System Security Symposium-NDSS 2015 (2015)

3. Cheon, J.H., Kim, M., Kim, M.: Optimized search-and-compute circuits and their application to query evaluation on encrypted data. IEEE Trans. Inf. Forensics Secur. 11(1), 188–199 (2016)

4. Damgård, I., Fitzi, M., Kiltz, E., Nielsen, J.B., Toft, T.: Unconditionally secure constant-rounds multi-party computation for equality, comparison, bits and exponentiation. In: Halevi, S., Rabin, T. (eds.) TCC 2006. LNCS, vol. 3876, pp. 285–304. Springer, Heidelberg (2006). https://doi.org/10.1007/11681878_15

5. Damgård, I., Geisler, M., Krøigård, M.: Homomorphic encryption and secure comparison. Int. J. Appl. Crypt. 1(1), 22–31 (2008)

6. Damgård, I., Geisler, M., Krøigård, M.: A correction to efficient and secure comparison for on-line auctions. Int. J. Appl. Crypt. 1(4), 323–324 (2009)

7. Damgård, I., Jurik, M.: A generalisation, a simplification and some applications of Paillier's probabilistic public-key system. In: Kim, K. (ed.) PKC 2001. LNCS, vol. 1992, pp. 119–136. Springer, Heidelberg (2001). https://doi.org/10.1007/3-540-44586-2_9

8. Erkin, Z., Franz, M., Guajardo, J., Katzenbeisser, S., Lagendijk, I., Toft, T.: Privacy-preserving face recognition. In: Goldberg, I., Atallah, M.J. (eds.) PETS 2009. LNCS, vol. 5672, pp. 235–253. Springer, Heidelberg (2009). https://doi.org/10.1007/978-3-642-03168-7_14

9. Erkin, Z., Veugen, T., Toft, T., Lagendijk, R.L.: Privacy-preserving user clustering in a social network. In: Workshop on Information Forensics and Security-WIFS 2009, pp. 96–100. IEEE (2009)

10. Galbraith, S.D.: Mathematics of Public Key Cryptography. Cambridge University Press, Cambridge (2012)

11. Goldwasser, S., Bellare, M.: Lecture notes on cryptography. Summer course on cryptography, pp. 119–120. Massachusetts Institute of Technology, 1996–2008 (2008). http://cseweb.ucsd.edu/~mihir/papers/gb.html

12. Garay, J., Schoenmakers, B., Villegas, J.: Practical and secure solutions for integer comparison. In: Okamoto, T., Wang, X. (eds.) PKC 2007. LNCS, vol. 4450, pp. 330–342. Springer, Heidelberg (2007). https://doi.org/10.1007/978-3-540-71677-8_22

13. Goldreich, O.: Foundations of Cryptography, vol. 2. Cambridge University Press, Cambridge (2001)

14. Kolesnikov, V., Sadeghi, A.-R., Schneider, T.: Improved garbled circuit building blocks and applications to auctions and computing minima. In: Garay, J.A., Miyaji, A., Otsuka, A. (eds.) CANS 2009. LNCS, vol. 5888, pp. 1–20. Springer, Heidelberg (2009). https://doi.org/10.1007/978-3-642-10433-6_1

15. Paillier, P.: Public-key cryptosystems based on composite degree residuosity classes. In: Stern, J. (ed.) EUROCRYPT 1999. LNCS, vol. 1592, pp. 223–238. Springer, Heidelberg (1999). https://doi.org/10.1007/3-540-48910-X_16

16. Sadeghi, A.-R., Schneider, T., Wehrenberg, I.: Efficient privacy-preserving face recognition. In: Lee, D., Hong, S. (eds.) ICISC 2009. LNCS, vol. 5984, pp. 229–244. Springer, Heidelberg (2010). https://doi.org/10.1007/978-3-642-14423-3_16
17. Schoenmakers, B., Tuyls, P.: Practical two-party computation based on the conditional gate. In: Lee, P.J. (ed.) ASIACRYPT 2004. LNCS, vol. 3329, pp. 119–136. Springer, Heidelberg (2004). https://doi.org/10.1007/978-3-540-30539-2_10
18. Vaidya, J., Clifton, C., Zhu, Y.: Privacy Preserving Data Mining. Springer, New York (2006). https://doi.org/10.1007/978-0-387-29489-6
19. Veugen, T.: Comparing encrypted data. Technical report, Multimedia Signal Processing Group, Delft University of Technology, The Netherlands, and TNO Information and Communication Technology, Delft, The Netherlands (2011)
20. Veugen, T.: Encrypted integer division and secure comparison. Int. J. Appl. Crypt. 3(2), 166–180 (2014)
21. Yao, A.C.C.: Protocols for secure computations. In: Proceedings of the 23rd Annual Symposium on Foundations of Computer Science-FOCS 1982, pp. 160–164 (1982)

Blockchain-Based Decentralized Key Management System with Quantum Resistance

Hyeongcheol An[1], Rakyong Choi[2], and Kwangjo Kim[1,2]([✉])

[1] Graduate of School of Information Security,
Korea Advanced Institute of Science and Technology (KAIST),
Daejeon, Republic of Korea
anh1026@kaist.ac.kr
[2] School of Computing, Korea Advanced Institute of Science
and Technology (KAIST), Daejeon, Republic of Korea
{thepride,kkj}@kaist.ac.kr

Abstract. The blockchain technique was first proposed called Bitcoin in 2008 and is a distributed database technology. Public Key Infrastructure (PKI) system, which is one of the key management systems, is a centralized system. There is a possibility of single point failure in currently used centralized PKI system. Classical digital signature algorithm; ECDSA has used the well-known cryptocurrencies such as Bitcoin and Ethereum. Using the Shor's algorithm, it is vulnerable to an attack by the quantum adversary. In this paper, we propose a blockchain-based key management system using quantum-resistant cryptography. Since it uses a GLP digital signature scheme, which is a secure lattice-based digital signature scheme. Therefore, our construction is based on quantum-resistant cryptography, it is secure against the attack of a quantum adversary and ensures long-term safety. In addition, we design a decentralized blockchain structure with extended X.509 certificate, and it is secure for the single point of failure.

Keywords: Blockchain · Quantum-resistant ·
Key management system

1 Introduction

IBM developed a quantum computer with 5-qubit in 2016 and a new quantum computer with 50-qubit in Nov. 2017. The research team of IBM has developed a quantum computer that allows the public to simulate a quantum computer through an IBM Q Experience [7]. Therefore, the emergence of the quantum computer is not theoretical but becomes practical. Public key cryptosystems,

This work was supported by Institute for Information & communications Technology Promotion (IITP) grant funded by the Korea government (MSIT) (No. 2017-0-00555, Towards Provable-secure Multi-party Authenticated Key Exchange Protocol based on Lattices in a Quantum World).

© Springer Nature Switzerland AG 2019
B. B. Kang and J. Jang (Eds.): WISA 2018, LNCS 11402, pp. 229–240, 2019.
https://doi.org/10.1007/978-3-030-17982-3_18

such as Diffie-Hellman (DH) key exchange protocol and RSA, are based on the difficulty of Discrete Logarithm Problem (DLP), Elliptic Curve DLP (EC-DLP), and Integer Factorization Problem (IFP). However, DLP and IFP can be solved within the polynomial time by Shor's algorithm [14] using the quantum computer. If universal quantum computers can be feasible, public key cryptosystems whose difficulties are based on the number theoretic problem will be broken in a polynomial time. Therefore, we need a secure public key cryptosystem against the quantum adversary. Post Quantum Cryptography (PQC) plays an important roles in building a secure cryptosystem against both classical and quantum adversaries.

A public-key cryptosystem needs Public Key Infrastructure (PKI), which guarantees the integrity of all user's public keys by binding them with its owner. The currently used PKI system is X.509 v3 [17] as recommended by the international standards. However, the X.509 PKI system has disadvantages such as centralization, single point failure, and fully trusted Certificate Authority (CA). CA is a trusted third party whose signature on the certificate guarantees the authenticity of the public key with each entity. Therefore, the currently used centralized PKI system has problems with availability, due to the centralized CA. The most famous cryptocurrency, Bitcoin [13] is the first decentralized virtual-currency. Bitcoin uses blockchain, which is a transaction database (or distributed ledger) shared by all peer nodes. With the transaction of the blockchain, anyone can find each block of information in the transaction history. Therefore, each peer node operates both client and server on their network at the same time, since the blockchain technique is decentralized.

In this paper, we propose QChain, a quantum-resistant decentralized PKI system with extended X.509 certificate. To construct QChain, we combine the blockchain and lattice-based cryptography which is one of PQC primitives. QChain is a practical method for managing public key cryptography in a decentralized manner.

2   Related Work

2.1   Blockchain-Based PKI

Emercoin (EMC) [8] is cryptocurrency, which is used for blockchain-based PKI system. EMCSSH integrates between the OpenSSH and EMC blockchain, providing decentralized PKI. EMC blockchain is based on both Proof-of-Work and Proof-of-Stake consensus protocol and forked from Peercoin. EMC uses the SHA-256 hash function, and it is not secure against the quantum adversaries by Grover's algorithm [5].

Matsumoto *et al.* suggest the Ethereum-based PKI system called IKP [12]. IKP's decentralized nature and smart contract system allow open participation offer incentives for vigilance over CAs, and enable financial resource against misbehavior. However, there are some security issues for Ethereum platform. In addition, IKP uses the quantum-resistant hash function called Ethash [15]. Ethereum is based on ECDSA signature algorithm, which is not secure against the quantum adversaries.

Yakubov *et al.* propose the blockchain-based PKI management framework [16] in 2018. They design a blockchain-based PKI, which modifies the X.509 certificates. X.509 v3 certificate standard consists of extension fields, which are reserved for extra information. They modify X.509 v3 certificate and design hybrid X.509 certificate, which consists of blockchain name, CA key and subject key identifier, and hashing algorithm in the extension field. This work is based on smart contract in Ethereum.

Certcoin [3] is the public and decentralized PKI system using blockchain technique and based on Namecoin. In revocation phase, they did not use Certificate Revocation List (CRL). They consider that Certcoin uses RSA accumulators, which is insecure against the quantum adversaries.

2.2 Lattice-Based Signature Scheme

Compared to the PQC primitives lattice-based primitives are faster and have smaller signatures size than others. In general since ring-LWE-based digital signatures can provide the smallest time-data complexity compared with others. Akleylek *et al.* proposed the ring-LWE based signature scheme called Ring-TESLA [1]. Secret key consist of a tuple of three polynomials $(s, e_1, e_2) \xleftarrow{\$} \mathcal{R}_q$, e_1 and e_2 with small coefficients. Polynomial $a_1, a_2 \xleftarrow{\$} \mathcal{R}_q$, and computes $b_1 = a_1 s + e_1 \mod q$ and $b_2 = a_2 s + e_2 \mod q$. To sign the message m, signing algorithm samples $y \xleftarrow{\$} \mathcal{R}_q$. Then, computes $c' = H(\lfloor v_1 \rceil_{d,q}, \lfloor v_2 \rceil_{d,q}, m)$ and polynomial $z = y + sc$. Signature value is a tuple of (z, c'). To verify signature (z, c') with message m, verification algorithm computes $H(\lfloor a_1 z - b_1 c \rceil_{d,q}, \lfloor a_2 z - b_2 c \rceil_{d,q}, m)$.

Güneysu *et al.* [6] published the GLP signature scheme based on ring-LWE problem. Polynomial ring defines $\mathcal{R}^{p^n} = \mathbb{Z}_q[\mathbf{X}]/(\mathbf{X}^n + 1)$ and $\mathcal{R}_k^{p^n}$ defines subset of the ring $\mathcal{R}^{p^n}$. $\mathcal{R}_k^{p^n}$ consists of all polynomials with coefficients in the range $[-k, k]$. To sign message μ, it needs cryptographic hash function H with range D_{32}^n. For $n \geq 512$ consists of all polynomials of degree $n - 1$ that have all zero coefficients except for at most 32 coefficient that is ± 1. First, we need to read 5-bit $(r_1 r_2 r_3 r_4 r_5)$ at a time. If r_1 is 0, put -1 in position $r_2 r_3 r_4 r_5$. Otherwise, put 1 in position $r_2 r_3 r_4 r_5$. In Sect. 3.1, we will describe modified GLP signature scheme.

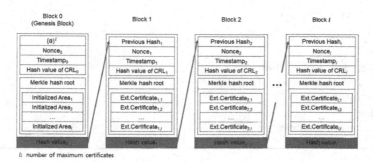

Fig. 1. Full structure of QChain

3 Our Approach

Our proposed quantum-resistant PKI scheme is based on the ring-LWE problem. In this section, we describe the full structure of QChain in detail. We construct QChain, which is quantum-resistant PKI using blockchain. In the following sections, we describe the structure of scheme and modified GLP signature scheme. We integrate the modified GLP signature scheme, that is first approach in blockchain. QChain uses the extension field of X.509 v3 certificate. Therefore, there is an advantage that it can be compatible with existing X.509 certificate standards.

3.1 Modified GLP Signature

GLP signature scheme is known to be faster than GPV [4] and LYU [10] scheme which belong to lattice-based signature scheme, and is believed to be secure against side-channel attacks till now. We has briefly described the GLP signature scheme in Sect. 2.2 In order to increase its performance, we modify the GLP signature scheme by integrating Number Theoretic Transformation (NTT) [7] like Algorithm 1. Let $\mathcal{R}_q^k$ be a subset of the ring $\mathcal{R}_q$, and that consists of all polynomials with coefficients in the range $[-k, k]$.

Algorithm 1. Modified GLP Signature

    Signing Key   : $r_1, r_2 \xleftarrow{\$} \chi_\sigma$

    Verification Key: $a \xleftarrow{\$} \mathcal{R}_q$, $\hat{a} \leftarrow \text{NTT}(a)$, $\hat{r_1} \leftarrow \text{NTT}(r_1)$, $\hat{r_2} \leftarrow \text{NTT}(r_2)$,

                $\hat{t} \leftarrow \hat{a}\hat{r_1} + \hat{r_2}$

    Hash Function   : $H : \{0,1\}^* \rightarrow D_{32}^n$

1 $\text{Sign}(\mu, a, r_1, r_2)$

2 **begin**

3      $y_1, y_2 \xleftarrow{\$} \mathcal{R}_q^k$;

4      $c \leftarrow H(ay_1 + y_2, \mu)$; $\hat{c} = \text{NTT}(c)$;

5      $\hat{z_1} \leftarrow \hat{r_1} * \hat{c} + \hat{y_1}$; $\hat{z_2} \leftarrow \hat{r_2} * \hat{c} + \hat{y_2}$;

6      $z_1 \leftarrow \text{NTT}^{-1}(\hat{z_1})$; $z_2 \leftarrow \text{NTT}^{-1}(\hat{z_2})$;

7   **if** $z_1 \notin \mathcal{R}_q^{k-32}$ *or* $z_2 \notin \mathcal{R}_q^{k-32}$ **then**

8 | go to line 3;

9   **else**

10 | return (z_1, z_2, c);

11 $\text{Verify}(\mu, z_1, z_2, c, a, t)$

12 **begin**

13   **if** $z_1, z_2 \in \mathcal{R}_q^{k-32}$ **then**

14 | $c \neq H(az_1 + z_2 - tc, \mu)$;

15 | return **reject**;

16   **else**

17 | return **success**;

3.2   Structure of QChain

Figure 1 shows the full structure of QChain. We use ring-LWE encryption scheme, which is quantum-resistant primitive in QChain. More precisely, the public key encryption scheme is based on ring-LWE by Lyubashevsky *et al.* [11] which is secure against the quantum adversaries.

Figure 2 shows extended certificate for QChain. In the structure of QChain, each block consists of the previous hash, nonce, timestamp, a centralized public key of the user, hash value of the block, and Merkle hash tree. Users can communicate with the application data using the public key cryptosystem based on ring-LWE scheme. QChain certificate contain the following fields:

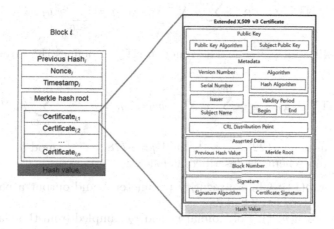

Fig. 2. Extended certificate for QChain

- **Version Number:** X.509 standards has three kinds of version. Version 1 is default format, and if the Initiator Unique Identifier or Subject Unique Identifier is present, that must use version 2. For more extension of certificates, the version must be used 3.
- **Signature:** This field includes signature algorithm and certificate signature. It covers all other field values and signs the certificate.
- **CRL Distribution Point:** This field includes a list of which establishes a CRL distribution points. Each distribution point contains a name and optionally reasons for revocation and the CRL issuer name, specifically, block leader.
- **Asserted Data:** This field consists of the previous hash value, Merkle root, block number. Previous hash value is based on the previous block.

If the leader is a malicious node, the certificate is abolished and a new leader is elected. Thus, it prevents malicious node of the leader. The leader has a CRL, and the user confirms revocation of the public key in the leader's CRL. The previous leader transfers the CRL and its hash value to the next leader when the leader changes.

3.3 QChain Scheme

The polynomial ring defines $\mathcal{R}_q = \mathbb{Z}_q[\mathbf{X}]/(\mathbf{X}^n+1)$. The error distribution χ_σ uses a discrete Gaussian distribution with standard deviation σ. For efficient encryption time, we use NTT operations. The NTT is commonly used in the implementation of lattice-based cryptography. NTT operation denotes $\hat{z} = \mathsf{NTT}(z)$. Cryptographic nonce and random number are randomly selected $nonce \xleftarrow{\$} \{0,1\}^n$ and $rand \xleftarrow{\$} \{0,1\}^n$. We denote the hash function and signature algorithm $H()$ and $Sign()$, respectively. The public and private key denote pk and $privK$, respectively. For a polynomial $\mathbf{g} = \Sigma_{i=0}^{1023} g_i X^i \in \mathcal{R}_q$, we define

$$\mathsf{NTT}(\mathbf{g}) = \hat{\mathbf{g}} = \sum_{i=0}^{1023} \hat{g}_i X^i \quad where, \hat{g}_i = \sum_{j=0}^{1023} \gamma^j g_j \omega^{ij}$$

where, $\omega = 49, \gamma = \sqrt{\omega} = 7$. The function NTT^{-1} defines the inverse of NTT function.

$$\mathsf{NTT}^{-1}(\hat{\mathbf{g}}) = \mathbf{g} = \sum_{i=0}^{1023} \hat{g}_i X^i \quad where, g_i = n^{-1}\gamma^{-i} \sum_{j=0}^{1023} \hat{g}_j \omega^{ij}$$

where, $n^{-1} \bmod q = 12277$, $\gamma^{-1} \bmod q = 8778$, $\omega^{-1} \bmod q = 1254$.

The QChain scheme is described as follows:

- QChain.Setup(1^λ): Choose security parameter λ and output a parameter n, q, and $\sigma = \sqrt{16/2} \approx 2.828$ [2].
- QChain.KeyGen(n, σ): Polynomial r_1 and r_2 sampled from the Gaussian distribution use NTT operation in polynomial multiplication and addition.

$$r_{1,i}, r_{2,i} \leftarrow \chi_\sigma; y_{1,i}, y_{2,i} \xleftarrow{\$} \mathcal{R}_q^k; a_i \xleftarrow{\$} \mathcal{R}_q; \quad \hat{a}_i \leftarrow \mathsf{NTT}(a_i);$$

$$\hat{r}_{1,i} \leftarrow \mathsf{NTT}(r_{1,i}); \quad \hat{r}_{2,i} \leftarrow \mathsf{NTT}(r_{2,i}); \hat{y}_{1,i} \leftarrow \mathsf{NTT}(y_{1,i}); \quad \hat{y}_{2,i} \leftarrow \mathsf{NTT}(y_{2,i});$$

$$\hat{p}_i \leftarrow \hat{r}_{1,i} - \hat{a}_i * \hat{r}_{2,i}; \hat{t}_i \leftarrow \hat{a}_i * \hat{r}_{1,i} + \hat{r}_{2,i};$$

The public key is $(\hat{a}_i, \hat{p}_i, \hat{t}_i) \in pk_i$ and the private key is $(\hat{r}_{1,i}, \hat{r}_{2,i}, \hat{y}_{1,i}, \hat{y}_{2,i}) \in privK_i$ for user i.

- QChain.GenesisBlock.Setup(): The genesis block is the first block of QChain. We also call it block 0, which is hardcoded into the software of our system. The genesis block does not have previous hash value. Therefore, we use $\{0\}^n$ for previous hash value in genesis block. We fix $i = 2^{10}$ in genesis block.

$$nonce \xleftarrow{\$} \{0,1\}^n; rand_i \xleftarrow{\$} \{0,1\}^n; where, 0 \leq i \leq 2^{10}$$

- QChain.GenesisBlock.Merkle(): We construct Merkle hash tree using random number $rand_i$, $timestamp$, hash function $H()$, and the signature algorithm $Sign()$. In genesis block, we fix $pk_i = rand_i$, $ID_i = i$, and $Username_i = i$. Then, we compute the top hash value H_{root} using each hash value of leaf nodes.

- QChain.GenesisBlock.Final(): We finally construct the genesis block in this final algorithm. To make a previous hash of block 1, QChain needs a hash value. Previous hash value computes as follows:

$$H_{Block0} = H(({\{0\}})^n || nonce || timestamp || H_{root})$$

- QChain.User.Setup(pk_i, H_{root}): In the user setup algorithm, it is similar to QChain.GenesisBlock.Setup() algorithm. The user setup algorithm operates as follows:

$$\text{Previous hash} \leftarrow H_{Block0};$$

$$nonce \xleftarrow{\$} \{0,1\}^n; pk_i \leftarrow \textbf{User public key} \in \{0,1\}^n; where, 0 \le i \le l \le 2^{10}$$

- QChain.User.Add($ID_i, Username_i, privK_i, Cert_i$): After the genesis block has been made by the QChain.User.Setup() algorithm, we add information about the user's public keys as follows:

$$H(ID_i); \quad H(Username_i); \quad (\hat{r}_{1,i}, \hat{r}_{2,i}, \hat{y}_{1,i}, \hat{y}_{2,i}) \leftarrow privK_i;$$

$$y_{1,i} \leftarrow \mathsf{NTT}^{-1}(\hat{y}_{1,i}); \quad y_{2,i} \leftarrow \mathsf{NTT}^{-1}(\hat{y}_{2,i});$$

$$(\hat{a}_i, \hat{p}_i) \leftarrow pk_i; \quad a_i \leftarrow \mathsf{NTT}^{-1}(\hat{a}_i);$$

$$c_i \leftarrow H(a_i y_{1,i} + y_{2,i}, ID_i); \quad \hat{c}_i \leftarrow \mathsf{NTT}(c)$$

$$r_{1,i} \leftarrow \mathsf{NTT}^{-1}(\hat{r}_{1,i}); \quad r_{2,i} \leftarrow \mathsf{NTT}^{-1}(\hat{r}_{2,i});$$

$$Sign(ID_i, a_i, r_{1,i}, r_{2,i});$$

Using ID_i and $Username_i$, we compute each hash and signature value. The output signature value is $(z_{1,i}, z_{2,i}, \hat{c}_i)$. Then, we construct Merkle hash tree same as genesis block process. The maximum users of each block are 2^{10}. Because we restrict the maximum depth of Merkle hash tree due to the memory complexity. The $Sign()$ algorithm is a modified GLP signature scheme.

- QChain.User.Verify($ID_i, pk_i, Sign(Cert_i)$): To verify the public key pk_i and $Sign(Cert_i)$ of the user, using the verify algorithm $Verify()$. The user verify algorithm runs as follows:

$$\hat{a}_i, \hat{t}_i \leftarrow pk_i; a_i \leftarrow \mathsf{NTT}^{-1}(\hat{a}_i); \quad t_i \leftarrow \mathsf{NTT}^{-1}(\hat{t}_i);$$

$$z_{1,i}, z_{2,i}, \hat{c}_i \leftarrow Sign(ID_i); c_i \leftarrow \mathsf{NTT}^{-1}(\hat{c}_i);$$

$$Verify(ID_i, z_{1,i}, z_{2,i}, c_i, a_i, t_i);$$

Using public parameters pk_i and $Sign(ID_i)$, we can easily verify the user.

- QChain.User.Enc(pk_i, m): To encrypt a message $m \in \mathcal{R}_2$, the encryption algorithm runs as follows:

$$(\hat{a}_i, \hat{p}_i, \hat{t}_i) \leftarrow pk_i; (a_i, p_i, t_i) \leftarrow (\mathsf{NTT}^{-1}(\hat{a}_i), \mathsf{NTT}^{-1}(\hat{p}_i), \mathsf{NTT}^{-1}(\hat{t}_i));$$

$$e_1, e_2, e_3 \leftarrow \chi_\sigma; \hat{e}_1 \leftarrow \mathsf{NTT}(e_1); \quad \hat{e}_2 \leftarrow \mathsf{NTT}(e_2); \hat{m} \leftarrow m \cdot \left\lfloor \frac{q}{2} \right\rfloor;$$

$$(\hat{c}_1, \hat{c}_2) \leftarrow (\hat{a}_i * \hat{e}_1 + \hat{e}_2, \quad \hat{p}_i * \hat{e}_1 + \mathsf{NTT}(e_3 + \hat{m}));$$

Then, we can generate $(\hat{c}_1, \hat{c}_2)$ and the ciphertext is $c = (\hat{c}_1, \hat{c}_2)$ using a user public key pk_i and message m.

- QChain.User.Dec($privK_i, c$): To decrypt message $c = (\hat{c}_1, \hat{c}_2)$, decryption algorithm as follows:

$$\hat{r}_{2,i} \leftarrow privK_i; (\hat{c}_1, \hat{c}_2) \leftarrow c; m' \leftarrow \mathsf{NTT}^{-1}(\hat{c}_1 * \hat{r}_2 + \hat{c}_2); m \leftarrow \mathsf{Decode}(m');$$

Decode() is an error reconciliation function. In QChain.Enc() function, we encode the message m. To decode the message m', we use Decode() function. The Decode() function defines as follows:

$$\mathsf{Decode}(m) := \left\lfloor \frac{2}{q} \cdot m \cdot \lfloor q/2 \rfloor \right\rceil \cdot \left\lfloor \frac{q}{2} \right\rfloor$$

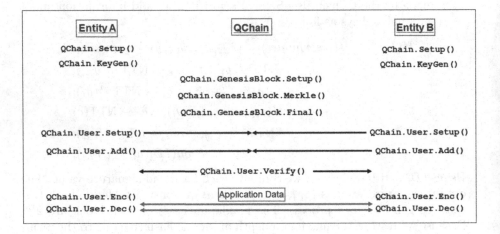

Fig. 3. A typical use case of QChain to setup secure communication

Figure 3 illustrates a typical use case of QChain to setup secure communication. The first QChain operator initiates genesis block (block 0). The operator has five-step algorithms. QChain.Setup() sets the parameter of QChain.KeyGen() makes a public and a private key of users. Then, QChain.Genesis Block.Setup(), QChain.GenesisBlock.Merkle(), and QChain.GenesisBlock.Final() algorithms operate to generate the genesis block. To register the public key, users set QChain.User. Setup() algorithm and they can register the public key with algorithm QChain.User. Add(). They can also verify the public key with algorithm QChain.User.Verify(). Using this algorithm, users can challenge to QChain for verifying the anonymous user. QChain will answer if it is an authenticated user or not. Finally, through algorithms QChain.User.Enc() and QChain.User.Dec(), users can communicate application data securely with each other.

4 Security Analysis

4.1 Generic Attack

Grover *et al.* suggest the database search algorithm called Grover's algorithm [5]. Our construction uses n_1-bit hash function. To break hash function, the complexity of brute-force attack is $O(\sqrt{2^{n_1}})$. Attacking a lattice-based cryptosystem, which has n_2-bit security key dimension with a finding shortest lattice vector using sphere-sieve also requires $2^{0.268n_2+O(n_2)}$-bit complexity [9]. Due to the ring-LWE problem is as hard as the worst case, so there is a decrease in attack amount as square root complexity despite the attack using the quantum computer. However, Shor's algorithm cannot attack our QChain construction. The encryption algorithm and digital signature of QChain are not based on IFP or DLP problems. Therefore, our construction is secure against Shor's algorithm. The attack complexity in a generic attack using a quantum computer is $min(O(2^{\frac{n_1}{2}}), 2^{0.268n_2+O(n_2)})$.

Using the classical computing attack, the hash function is secure if QChain uses the SHA3 hash function. Therefore, we can assume that the complexity of the hash function is $O(2^{n_1})$. The attack complexity of signature is $2^{0.298n_2+O(n_2)}$ [9]. Thus, total attack complexity in a generic attack using a classical computer is $min(O(2^{n_1}), 2^{0.298n_2+O(n_2)})$. However, the attack complexity of RSA and ECDSA is $O((\log n)^2(\log\log n)(\log\log\log n))$ using Shor's algorithm [14].

4.2 Feature Analysis

PKI system is required as register key or domain, update and look up, and revocation of the public key.

(i) Connection: QChain can keep offline states except initiating genesis block. On the other hand, X.509 v3 PKI system which is used for current international standard must keep online states in TTP-server side. If TTP of X.509 v3 PKI system is offline, the user cannot verify that the public key is authenticated or not.

(ii) Non-repudiation: QChain has the block which consists of user's public keys with their signatures. The user cannot deny their public information such as public key and user ID. X.509 v3 PKI system has a certificate which consists of a public key, username, and signature. Therefore, the user cannot deny their certificate.

(iii) Revocation: The complexity of revocation is $O(\log_2(n))$. QChain also uses a timestamp for each block and user's information. By using a timestamp for each block, the QChain operator can specify the time to expire on each block. Since the timestamp is used for each user, the QChain operator can determine the expiration time according to the characteristics of the user. Compared with QChain, X.509 v3 PKI system stores revocation in the user's certificate. The X.509 v3 PKI system also creates and uses CRL. Similarly, QChain can manage the revocation list by CRL.

(iv) Scalability: QChain increases linearly with scalability. Therefore, the complexity is $O(n)$. The advantage with QChain is that it does not need to increase the number of TTP servers even if the number of users and public information increases. However, the X.509 v3 PKI system must increase the computing power of the server in order to add the user's public information, because TTP of X.509 v3 PKI system stores and authenticates the user's public information.

(v) Trust Model: The main point of QChain is decentralized service for PKI system. Therefore, QChain does not need TTP where X.509 v3 PKI system must have TTP. Due to the existence of TTP, X.509 v3 PKI system has a problem of single point failure.

4.3   Comparision with Related Work

We compare the features between our construction and related work, such as Certcoin, IKP, and Emercoin. Table 1 shows the comparison of QChain and related work. In dependence on existing cryptocurrency system, Certcoin is based on Namecoin, which is forked from Bitcoin. Emercoin [8] is also based on Peercoin. Lastly, IKP [12] is based on Ethereum smart contract platform.

Table 1. Comparison of QChain and related work

System	QChain	Certcoin [3]	IKP [12]	Emercoin [8]
Dependence on existing cryptocurrency system	N	Namecoin (fork of Bitcoin)	Ethereum	Peercoin (fork of Bitcoin)
Extending X.509 certificates	Y	Y	N	N
Signature scheme	GLP	ECDSA	ECDSA	RSA
Complexity on signature using quantum computer	$2^{0.268n+O(n)}$	polynomial-time[a]	polynomial-time[a]	polynomial-time[a]
Hash function	Not specific	SHA256	Ethash	SHA256
Revocation method	CRL, Timestamp	Timestamp	Smart contract	Update by administrator

a: $O((\log n)^2 (\log \log n)(\log \log \log n))$

We extend the X.509 v3 certificate with extension fields. Certcoin also extends the same approach. However, IKP and Emercoin do not use X.509 certificate. Instead, they use smart contract and makes new blocks, respectively. Therefore, it cannot be applied currently used PKI standard. QChain only uses GLP digital signature scheme, which is one of the post-quantum primitives.

Other construction uses ECDSA and RSA digital signature. In other words, Certcoin, IKP, and Emercoin are not secure against quantum adversaries. In revocation method, our construction is based on CRL and timestamp. Utilizing CRL is the most efficient method of public key revocation. In addition, we use the timestamp to assist CRL. Unlike our construction, Certcoin uses only timestamps without CRL, which makes the disadvantage. Therefore, user needs to manually update a new certificate when the user needs to revoke the public key. IKP and Emercoin revoke by CA in the same way of current PKI standard as a smart contract.

5   Concluding Remarks

This paper proposes QChain, which is a decentralized PKI system that uses the blockchain technique based on the ring-LWE scheme. QChain provides a quantum resistant PKI system secure against the quantum adversaries who will appear in the near future by combining the blockchain technique and one of PQC primitives, lattice-based cryptography. Our construction uses extended X.509 certificate. Therefore, we can easily integrate current X.509 standards. For an efficient design of QChain, we use the NTT operations in polynomial multiplication and addition. We also modify the GLP signature scheme, which is based on the ring-LWE problem for the NTT operations. The generic attack on QChain is described for both quantum and classical adversaries. We consider the best-known generic attack algorithm, such as Grover's algorithm and sphere-sieve algorithm. Finally, we compare the currently used X.509 v3 PKI system with our QChain in feature analysis.

As future work, several directions should be explored from here. First, we will implement QChain as an open source project. Our implementation needs the consensus algorithm in the validating blocks. QChain is designed to release single-point of failure in the current X.509 v3-based key management system, that works like a kind of decentralized PKI. Thus, QChain can fit the consortium or private blockchain applications. In the practical implementation, SHA3 or other secure and efficient hash functions can be considered.

References

1. Akleylek, S., Bindel, N., Buchmann, J., Krämer, J., Marson, G.A.: An efficient lattice-based signature scheme with provably secure instantiation. In: Pointcheval, D., Nitaj, A., Rachidi, T. (eds.) AFRICACRYPT 2016. LNCS, vol. 9646, pp. 44–60. Springer, Cham (2016). https://doi.org/10.1007/978-3-319-31517-1_3
2. Brakerski, Z., Langlois, A., Peikert, C., Regev, O., Stehlé, D.: Classical hardness of learning with errors. In: Proceedings of the Forty-Fifth Annual ACM Symposium on Theory of Computing-STOC 2013, pp. 575–584. ACM (2013)
3. Fromknecht, C., Velicanu, D., Yakoubov, S.: A decentralized public key infrastructure with identity retention. Cryptology ePrint Archive, Report 2014/803 (2014). http://eprint.iacr.org/2014/803

4. Gentry, C., Peikert, C., Vaikuntanathan, V.: Trapdoors for hard lattices and new cryptographic constructions. In: Proceedings of the Fortieth Annual ACM Symposium on Theory of Computing, pp. 197–206. ACM (2008)

5. Grover, L.K.: A fast quantum mechanical algorithm for database search. In: Proceedings of the Twenty-Eighth Annual ACM Symposium on Theory of Computing-STOC 1996, pp. 212–219. ACM (1996). https://doi.org/10.1145/237814.237866

6. Güneysu, T., Lyubashevsky, V., Pöppelmann, T.: Practical lattice-based cryptography: a signature scheme for embedded systems. In: Prouff, E., Schaumont, P. (eds.) CHES 2012. LNCS, vol. 7428, pp. 530–547. Springer, Heidelberg (2012). https://doi.org/10.1007/978-3-642-33027-8_31

7. IBM Research: IBM Q experience (2018). https://www.research.ibm.com/ibm-q/. Accessed 20 Mar 2018

8. Khovayko, O.: Emercoin (2018). https://emercoin.com. Accessed 15 May 2018

9. Laarhoven, T., Mosca, M., Van De Pol, J.: Finding shortest lattice vectors faster using quantum search. Des. Codes Crypt. **77**(2–3), 375–400 (2015)

10. Lyubashevsky, V.: Lattice signatures without trapdoors. In: Pointcheval, D., Johansson, T. (eds.) EUROCRYPT 2012. LNCS, vol. 7237, pp. 738–755. Springer, Heidelberg (2012). https://doi.org/10.1007/978-3-642-29011-4_43

11. Lyubashevsky, V., Peikert, C., Regev, O.: On ideal lattices and learning with errors over rings. In: Gilbert, H. (ed.) EUROCRYPT 2010. LNCS, vol. 6110, pp. 1–23. Springer, Heidelberg (2010). https://doi.org/10.1007/978-3-642-13190-5_1

12. Matsumoto, S., Reischuk, R.M.: IKP: turning a PKI around with blockchains. Cryptology ePrint Archive, Report 2016/1018 (2016). http://eprint.iacr.org/2016/1018

13. Nakamoto, S.: Bitcoin: a peer-to-peer electronic cash system (2008)

14. Shor, P.W.: Algorithms for quantum computation: discrete logarithms and factoring. In: Proceedings, Annual Symposium on Foundations of Computer Science-FOCS 1994, pp. 124–134. IEEE (1994)

15. Wood, G.: Ethereum: a secure decentralised generalised transaction ledger. Ethereum Proj. Yellow Pap. **151** (2014)

16. Yakubov, A., Shbair, W., Wallbom, A., Sanda, D., et al.: A blockchain-based PKI management framework. In: The First IEEE/IFIP International Workshop on Managing and Managed by Blockchain (Man2Block) Colocated with IEEE/IFIP NOMS 2018, Tapei, Tawain, 23–27 April 2018 (2018)

17. Yee, P.: Updates to the Internet X. 509 public key infrastructure certificate and certificate revocation list (CRL) profile (2013)

A Construction of a Keyword Search to Allow Partial Matching with a Block Cipher

Yuta Kodera[✉][ID], Minoru Kuribayashi[ID], Takuya Kusaka[ID],
and Yasuyuki Nogami[ID]

Graduate School of Natural Science and Technology, Okayama University,
Okayama, Japan
yuta.kodera@s.okayama-u.ac.jp,
{kminoru,kusaka-t,yasuyuki.nogami}@okayama-u.ac.jp

Abstract. This paper considers a new construction of a keyword search including partial matching on an encrypted document. Typically, an index-based searchable symmetric encryption has been investigated. However, it makes a partial keyword matching difficult without a designated trapdoor. Thus, our objective is to propose a keyword search scheme which enables us to search a part of a keyword only by building trapdoors of each original keyword. The main idea is to insulate each character of a keyword into a bitstream of the sequence generated by a pseudorandom number generator. It achieves a partial search by giving a restriction on the length of a keyword.

Keywords: Searchable symmetric encryption ·
Partial keyword matching · Block cipher · NTU sequence

1 Introduction

On the behind of development of information and communication technology (ICT) society, recent cryptosystems are required to be high-functionality such as it can search a keyword or take the sum of a certain information on an encrypted data. The reasons for these requirements can be said that users have begun to store their secret information in a cloud storage and a system manager wanted to utilize the storage by a big-data analysis without any information leakage.

A searchable encryption (SE) is introduced as a solution to achieve keyword searching without decrypting documents on a server. There are mainly two types in the SE system; searchable symmetric encryption (SSE) [1–5] and public-key encryption with keyword search (PEKS) [6,7]. As the names stand, the former is based on a symmetric-key encryption such as AES [11], and the latter is based on a public-key encryption such as the pairing-based cryptography.

In this paper, we especially focus on SSE with a block cipher from the viewpoints of the efficiency of an encryption scheme even for a huge data. The SSE

© Springer Nature Switzerland AG 2019
B. B. Kang and J. Jang (Eds.): WISA 2018, LNCS 11402, pp. 241–252, 2019.
https://doi.org/10.1007/978-3-030-17982-3_19

is proposed by Song in [1] and recent research on an SSE is mainly constructed by using an index table, which associates a keyword with documents, because of its efficiency. For example, [2] is a well know SSE scheme as an index-based SSE scheme, and it firstly defined the security model for the SSE. As well as the above scheme, [4] proposed an index-based scheme and has additionally focused on the efficient updates and compact client storage. The schemes have been paid much attention from researchers and been widely used for the basic construction of SSEs. However, the index-based SSE has the difficulty of searching substring of a keyword with the same trapdoor of a usual search.

Thus, we purpose to construct an SSE scheme which allows a partial keyword search by using the same trapdoor of a usual keyword search by adopting the basic idea of [2]. In short, a trapdoor of a keyword is registered in an index table which is correlated with the identifier of documents. The keyword is actually concealed throughout the trapdoor function and a server evaluates whether a trapdoor is involved in the table or not. However, the table makes a flexible partial matching search difficult because the substring of a keyword is needed to be registered in advance.

This paper proposes a new keyword search scheme for a block cipher to achieve a partial keyword search on encrypted data. There are mainly two viewpoints which we focused on. First of all, a character is represented by a combination of 8-bit in common computational systems. Secondly, a pseudorandom number generator, called NTU sequence, is considered to have advantages as a trapdoor function to allow a partial matching.

Although the length of a trapdoor is always fixed with the length of a block cipher, by making the seed value flexible, a user can easily generate a distinct trapdoor from the same keyword. In addition, since every trapdoor is actually a binary random sequence of the certain length, an adversary will not easily guess which keyword is embedded in the trapdoor. The construction of a trapdoor also helps to find a substring of a keyword without a designated trapdoor for the substring with a restriction on the length of a keyword.

2 Preliminaries

2.1 Notations

Let a word $w = (w_0, w_1, \ldots, w_{n-1})$ of length n be a concatenation of 8-bit characters w_k ($0 \leq k < n$). For a set S, let $\#(S)$ denotes the number of elements in S. Let D and $KW(D_j)$ denote a collection of documents and a set of keywords in D_j, where D_j is a document in D and $0 \leq j < \#(D)$, respectively. The list of every distinct keyword is written by $L_{KW} = \{KW(D_0), \ldots, KW(D_{\#(D)-1})\}$. The bit size of a block cipher is written by N_b throughout this paper, e.g. $N_b = 128$ for AES cryptosystem.

2.2 Mathematical Fundamentals

Let $\mathbb{F}_p$ and $\mathbb{F}_{p^m}$ denote a prime field and its field extension, respectively. Let θ be a primitive element in $\mathbb{F}_{p^m}$, then every non-zero $\mathbb{F}_{p^m}$-element can be represented by the powers of θ as θ^i, where $0 \leq i \leq p^m - 2$.

For an element in $\mathbb{F}_{p^m}$, let us define trace function denoted by $\text{Tr}\,(\cdot)$. The trace function is defined as the sum of conjugates of an input as follows:

$$\text{Tr}\,(x) = \sum_{j=0}^{m-1} x^{p^j}, \tag{1}$$

where $x \in \mathbb{F}_{p^m}$. It is noted that the output of trace calculation always belongs to the prime field.

Let a be a prime field element and let us define Legendre Symbol as follows:

$$\left(a \big/ p\right) = a^{\frac{p-1}{2}} \pmod{p} = \begin{cases} 0 & \text{if } a = 0, \\ 1 & \text{else if } a \text{ has a square root in } \mathbb{F}_p, \\ -1 & \text{otherwise.} \end{cases} \tag{2}$$

For the output of the Legendre Symbol, a mapping function $M_2(\cdot)$ which maps $\{0, 1\}$ to 0 and -1 to 1.

2.3 Pseudorandom Number Generator

A pseudorandom number generator (PRNG) [12,13] has been widely adopted for security applications. In this paper, we consider using a PRNG to embed a keyword so that the secret-key holder can obtain encrypted documents even if the holder sent a partial keyword.

There are several famous PRNGs. For example, RC4 [14] was a practical PRNG which is in fact utilized to SSL and WEP. However, the security of RC4 has been suspected and some of the applications stop using due to its vulnerabilities [15]. Blum-Blum-Shub (B.B.S.) [16] is also a practical PRNG which can efficiently generate a binary sequence over a prime field. For a product of distinct primes p and q which satisfies $p, q \equiv 3 \pmod 4$ denoted by $N = pq$, B.B.S. outputs a pseudorandom sequence $b_0 b_1 b_2 \ldots$ where $b_i = parity(x_i)$ and $x_{i+1} = x_i^2 \pmod N$. It is found that the security of B.B.S. is supported by the difficulty of prime factorization of a large composite number N as well as RSA. However, the appearance of a quantum computer brings a threat to the RSA-security. In addition, the randomness properties of B.B.S. is mainly evaluated only by a statistical test suite such as NIST SP 800-22 [17].

On the other hand, Nogami et al. have proposed a pseudorandom number generator called NTU sequence which randomness properties are theoretically supported. Its advantage is the easiness to embed a keyword in a sequence. Therefore, the NTU sequence is focused on in this paper.

2.4   NTU Sequence

The NTU sequence defined below is a geometric sequence generated over an odd characteristic field which retains a provable randomness properties [9] such as the period, the correlation, the linear complexity [8]. These properties are the measurements of the difficulty of predicting the next bits.

Definition 1. *For a set of seed values* $\theta \in \mathbb{F}_{p^m}$ *and* $i \in [0, p^m - 2]$, *an NTU sequence generator* $PRNG_{NTU}(\theta, i)$ *generates a bitstream* $s_i s_{i+1} s_{i+2} \cdots$, *where* θ *denotes a primitive element in* $\mathbb{F}_{p^m}$, *and* s_i *is derived by Eq.* (3).

$$s_i = M_2 \left(\left(\mathrm{Tr}\left(\theta^i\right) \Big/ p \right) \right). \tag{3}$$

Although the $PRNG_{NTU}(\theta, i)$ can achieve the maximum linear complexity, the distribution of the output bits is not balanced due to the mapping function $M_2(\cdot)$. Thus, a technique for uniformization has been proposed in [18] to improve the distribution with negligibly small negative effects to the other properties.

Originally, the NTU sequence is generated by mapping $\{0, 1\}$ to 0 and -1 to 1. However, this mapping induces the difference on the number of appearance of 0 and 1. For a series of trace values in $\mathbb{F}_p$, the Legendre Symbol and the mapping function play the following roles. The Legendre Symbol firstly classifies a trace value to 0, quadratic residue (QR) and quadratic non-residue (QNR) according to the quadratic residuosity problem. Then the mapping function binarizes the its sequence consisted of $\{0, 1, -1\}$. It is noticed that the number of QR and QNR in a set of non-zero prime field element $\mathbb{F}_p \backslash \{0\}$ is the same, which is given by $\frac{p-1}{2}$, it is found that replacing the 0 by QR or QNR evenly when $\mathrm{Tr}(\cdot) = 0$ can induce a balanced sequence.

It replaces $\mathrm{Tr}(\cdot) = 0$ by a non-zero coefficient of the least degree of the input θ^i. Here, it is noted that an element in $\mathbb{F}_{p^m}$ is actually represented as an m-dimensional vector with a basis. The procedure is illustrated in Algorithm 1, where $\mathrm{Coeff}(\theta^i, j)$ denotes the coefficient of degree j of θ^i.

Algorithm 1. Uniformization technique for NTU sequence

$PRNG_{NTU}(\theta, i)$
  begin
    $a = \mathrm{Tr}\left(\theta^i\right)$
    $j = 0$
    while $a == 0$ and $j <= m$
      $a = \mathrm{Coeff}(\theta^i, j)$
      $j = j + 1$
    end while
    $s_i = M_2 \left(\left(a \Big/ p \right) \right)$
  end

In [9], a constant prime field element, denoted by $A \in \mathbb{F}_p$, is added to the output of $\mathrm{Tr}\left(\theta^i\right)$. In short, the generation procedure of NTU sequence has been revised as follows:

$$s_i = M_2 \left(\left(\left(\mathrm{Tr}\left(\theta^i \right) + A \right)\Big/_p \right) \right), \tag{4}$$

where s_i is an i-th coefficient of the sequence for $0 \le i \le p^m - 2$.

Then, it was found out that the period of this NTU sequence becomes longer than the original NTU sequence. In addition, the linear complexity is experimentally shown, and it has been partially proven theoretically in [10]. The result indicates that the difficulty of predicting the next bits remains reasonably high.

By combining the uniformization technique and the result described above including the experimental observation, a new keyword search scheme is considered with taking full advantage of NTU sequence.

2.5   Searchable Symmetric Encryption (SSE)

A searchable symmetric encryption [2–4] is the one of ideas for searching a keyword over encrypted data. It is realized by utilizing an index table which correlates a keyword to documents. For example, Curtmola et al. have proposed an index-based adaptively secure SSE scheme [2].

Figure 1 simply shows an image of adaptive keyword search with an index table. Firstly, a user scans a collection of documents to generate keywords and builds an index with utilizing trapdoors. After that, the user encrypts documents with a symmetric cryptosystem, and then uploads the index and encrypted documents to a server. Then, the user can search a keyword which has already registered in the index. However, the scheme does not allow a partial matching keyword search if a substring of a keyword is not registered in the index.

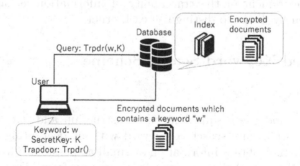

Fig. 1. Illustration of an adaptive SSE scheme

In the security of an SSE, a server which holds encrypted data is regarded as an adversary and an SSE scheme is desired keep the information leakage as small as possible with respect to keywords and documents. There are some unavoidable leakage such as history, access pattern and search pattern defined in [2]. For a document set D and a keyword w, they are defined as follows:

Definition 2 *(History). A q-query History over D denoted by $H = (D, w)$ is a tuple of documents D and keywords $w = (w_1, w_2, \ldots, w_q)$, which are obtained throughout q times communication between a client and a server.*

Definition 3 *(Access pattern). The access pattern $Access(H)$ induced by H is the result of each search via a trapdoor. It is the collection of documents that contains a keyword w_k $(1 \le k \le q)$.*

Definition 4 *(Search pattern). The search pattern $Search(H)$ induced by H is given by a symmetric binary matrix M which (j, k)-element is represented by*

$$M_{jk} = \begin{cases} 1 & if\ w_j = w_k, \\ 0 & otherwise. \end{cases} \tag{5}$$

For these information, Curtmola et al. defined Trace induced by a q-query history as follows:

Definition 5 *(Trace). The Trace denoted by $Trace(H)$ consisted of lengths of documents in D, the access pattern $Access(H)$, and the search pattern $Search(H)$.*

According to Curtmola et al. [2], it is said that the Trace is the minimal information leakage, and thus the Trace becomes one of the benchmarks to evaluate the security of an SSE scheme.

It is noted that the trace function used in the generating procedure of NTU sequence and the above Trace is completely different idea. In detail, the former is a mapping function for $\mathbb{F}_{p^m}$-element with respect to $\mathbb{F}_p$. However, the latter denotes a measurement of the traceability of information leakage. Thus, the latter is written by Trace to distinguish each other.

3   Proposed Keyword Search Scheme

3.1   Overview

A server-client model is assumed in our construction and our objective is to enable a user to partially search a keyword without decrypting documents so that a server cannot obtain information as small as possible. This is because of the possibility that a malicious server tries to guess information with respect to the stored secrets and keywords throughout queries from a user.

A keyword $w = (w_0, w_1, \ldots, w_{n-1})$ is a concatenation of characters w_k, where w_k is dealt as an 8-bit character in this paper, where $1 \le n \le N_b/8$ and N_b is the bit length of the block of a block cipher. In addition, the list of keywords is a finite set in lexicographical order which is generated from the target collection of documents and a user searches a keyword in the list including its substring.

Let w_k be an k-th character of a keyword w. The embedding function for w_k is defined by utilizing the NTU sequence $PRNG_{NTU}(\theta, i)$ over the fixed prime field $\mathbb{F}_{257}$ and modified trace function.

Definition 6 *(Embedding function). For w_k, the embedding function with NTU sequence denoted by $PRNG_{NTU_{w_k}}(\theta, i, w_k)$ is a deterministic function which yields a bit by using the following modified trace calculation instead of* $\mathrm{Tr}\left(\theta^i\right)$.

$$\mathrm{Tr}_{w_k}(\theta^i) = \mathrm{Tr}\left(\theta^i\right) + w_k \quad (\mathrm{mod}\ 257) \tag{6}$$

3.2   Definition

A keyword search scheme, which allows a partial matching, is consisted of six polynomial-time algorithms defined below.

Definition 7 *(Generate secrets). The function $Gen_{Sec}(m)$ returns a set of secrets including a secret-key for a block cipher. It takes a positive integer m as the input such that $\lambda = \frac{257^m - 1}{128}$ becomes sufficiently large (e.g. more than 2^{256}), where λ is the period of an NTU sequence. Then, $Gen_{Sec}(m)$ generates a primitive polynomial $f(x)$ of degree m over $\mathbb{F}_{257}$, a seed value pair (θ, i), a secret-key K_{trpdr} for the trapdoor function and a secret-key K_{SKE} for a block cipher, where $f(\theta) = 0$ and $0 \leq i \leq 257^m - 2$. It is noted that the size of the secret-key K_{trpdr} is the same as K_{SKE}.*

Definition 8 *(Trapdoor). The trapdoor function $Trpdr(\theta, i, \boldsymbol{w}, K_{trpdr})$ is a deterministic algorithm run by a client. It requires seed values θ and an integer i, a word $\boldsymbol{w} = (w_0, w_1, \ldots, w_{n-1})$ of length n and the secret-key K_{trpdr} as the input. $Trpdr(\theta, i, \boldsymbol{w}, K_{trpdr})$ returns the binary sequence $\boldsymbol{t}$ of the same size of a block of a block cipher, which involves the keyword $\boldsymbol{w}$ as the trapdoor of the keyword.*

Definition 9 *(Encryption). The function $Enc_{K_{SKE}}(\theta, i, \boldsymbol{D}, K_{SKE})$ is a deterministic algorithm run by the secret-key holder. It takes a seed values θ and i, a collection of documents $\boldsymbol{D}$, and the secret-key K_{SKE} as the input. Firstly, the function begins to scan every document to list up the distinct keywords $\boldsymbol{L}_{KW}$ contained in the documents. Then, a trapdoor of a keyword in $\boldsymbol{L}_{KW}$ is prepared by utilizing NTU sequence with θ^i. Finally, the documents are encrypted by a typical encryption scheme with K_{SKE} and the trapdoors are concatenated to each document which contains the keyword as the header. It is noted that the number of trapdoors is required to be memorized for the decryption. The simplest way is fixing the number of trapdoors to the maximum number of keywords in a document.*

Definition 10 *(Perfect matching search). The function $PerfectMatch(\boldsymbol{t})$ is carried out on the server with a trapdoor $\boldsymbol{t}$ as the input. It returns encrypted documents, which are believed to involve the keyword, based on the high reliability.*

Definition 11 *(Partial matching search). The function $PartialMatch(\boldsymbol{t})$ is carried out on the server with a trapdoor $\boldsymbol{t}$ as the input. It returns encrypted documents, which are considered to contain the substring of a keyword.*

Definition 12 *(Decryption). The function $Dec(\boldsymbol{D}_{enc}, K_{SKE})$ recovers documents with the typical decryption scheme after eliminating each header of an encrypted document. Since the secret-key holder knows how many trapdoors are concatenated to a document, the user can remove the header just ignoring them. The input are a collection of encrypted documents $\boldsymbol{D}_{enc}$ and the secret-key K_{SKE}.*

3.3   Trapdoor Function Based on NTU Sequence

For a keyword $\boldsymbol{w} = (w_0, w_1, \ldots, w_{n-1})$, a trapdoor of $\boldsymbol{w}$ is derived by the following steps.

Step 1. Set $j = 0$ and θ^i.

Step 2. Calculate a sequence of trace values $(tr_{j,0}, \ldots, tr_{j,7})$ by $\mathrm{Tr}_{w_k}(\theta^{i+8j+k})$, where $tr_{j,k}$ is an output of trace calculation and $0 \leq k < 8$.

Step 3. Generate a bitstream for every j and k by $s_{i+8j+k} = M_2\left(\left(^{tr_{j,k}}/257\right)\right)$ and concatenating the previous bitstream.

Step 4. If $j < n$, then return to Step. 2. Otherwise go to the next step.

Step 5. If the length of the bitstream is less than the bit size N_b of a block of a block cipher, then generate an NTU sequence until the bitstream reaches the length N_b by $PRNG_{NTU}(\theta, i+j)$ with utilizing the uniformization technique introduced in Sect. 2.4, where $8n \leq j < N_b$.

Step 6. Taking bit-wise XOR with $s_0 s_1 \ldots s_{N_b-1}$ and a secret-key K_{trpdr}. Finally, output a trapdoor $\boldsymbol{t}$.

The above procedure is also illustrated in Fig. 2, where k_j and t_j are j-th bit of K_{trpdr} and $\boldsymbol{t}$, respectively. In short, the NTU sequence in this procedure works as a mapping function from an 8-bit space to an another 8-bit space. In addition, this generation scheme gives a redundancy for a trapdoor of a keyword. The redundancy means that a trapdoor easily becomes a different one by changing θ^i.

3.4   Partial Matching

As shown in Fig. 3, $PerfectMatch(\boldsymbol{t})$ can find a trapdoor $\boldsymbol{t}$ from the header of an encrypted document by taking bit-wise XOR and evaluating whether $\boldsymbol{t}_j \oplus \boldsymbol{t} = \boldsymbol{0}$ or not, where $\boldsymbol{t}_j$ denotes a j-th trapdoor of a keyword.

Since a trapdoor is built as a binary sequence of length N_b, a user has to uniquely select the binary sequence from N_b dimensional binary vector space when the user searches a keyword.

Although the idea of the partial matching is similar to the perfect matching, $PartialMatch(\boldsymbol{t})$ does not evaluate the whole length of a trapdoor. The function checks the first $8l$-bit patterns of a trapdoor with the header of a document where l is the length of a substring of a keyword. Thus, it returns a collection of ciphers that may be contained the substring of a keyword or the keyword itself. The probability of matching is given by

$$\Pr[\boldsymbol{t} = \boldsymbol{t}_j] = \left(\frac{1}{2^8}\right)^l, \tag{7}$$

where t_j is a trapdoor in the header of a cipher. In this sense, it can be said that l is a control parameter for the function to enhance the correctness of matching.

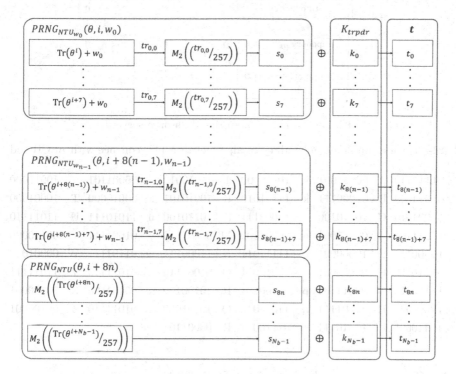

Fig. 2. Behavior of the trapdoor function for a keyword w.

3.5 Secure Update

Every header of documents is needed to be updated when a user wants to add a keyword. The secure update in our construction is recommended to remake the trapdoors with a different seed value set (θ, i). This is because of the flexibility of a trapdoor function, which means it can generate another trapdoor from the same keyword. Therefore, it is expected that the property is considered to prevent an adversary from stealing information about keywords and documents.

4 Considerations

4.1 An Example of Embedding

A numerical example of embedding a character to NTU sequence. Table 1 denotes an example of sequences of length 8 when embedding an alphabet to NTU sequence with ASCII code. Here, it is noted that the results in the table are just calculating $PRNG_{NTU_{w_k}}(\theta, i, w_k)$, where $i = 0, 1, \ldots, 7$ and w_k is each character represented by ASCII code. As the result shows, a character seems to be able to distinguish each other even after embedding in an NTU sequence.

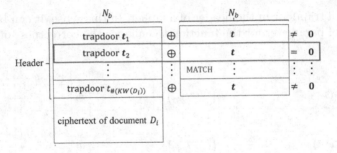

Fig. 3. An image of storing data on a server

Table 1. An example of embedding an alphabet to NTU sequence with ASCII code

a	01111110	A	00010001	j	10110000	J	11010010	s	00001101	S	10011000
b	01011010	B	01000111	k	11111010	K	10010101	t	00010000	T	10001000
c	11001010	C	10110100	l	11000111	L	10110100	u	11010111	U	11011110
d	10011100	D	00011001	m	00001000	M	01001110	v	01001111	V	00110000
e	11000111	E	10000001	n	11111011	N	11000111	w	01101111	W	00001000
f	01010110	F	00000001	o	01010011	O	01000110	y	01011110	Y	11011111
g	11110010	G	00011101	p	00100101	P	10100100	x	00101100	X	10100001
h	10000000	H	11101111	q	11011011	Q	10101000	z	01011110	Z	00100001
i	10110001	I	11110111	r	01110011	R	00001101				

4.2 Comparison of the Required Data Size

Figure 4 illustrates the total number of substrings for each length of keywords when adopting AES for a block cipher, where $1 \leq n \leq N_b/8$. It shows that the proposed method can carry out a partial search with maximumly one-eighth storage than the conventional index-based construction. This property enables us to implement the SSE scheme with low memory consumption.

4.3 Security

The proposed scheme has both positive and negative aspects comparing to [2]. The negative aspects are that the size of trapdoor becomes larger and the efficiency on searching is sacrificed. However, one of the most meaningful contributions of this work is the realization of partial keyword search by using the same trapdoor. Although a header size is increased from an original file size, fortunately, it conceal the original file size from a malicious server.

Let us consider the probability of a collision of trapdoors. As shown in Table 1, each character is mapped into an 8-bit binary via the NTU sequence independently. Thus, the probability for w and w' of length n is given by

$$Pr[Trpdr(\theta, i, w) = Trpdr(\theta, i, w')] = \left(\frac{1}{2^8}\right)^n. \tag{8}$$

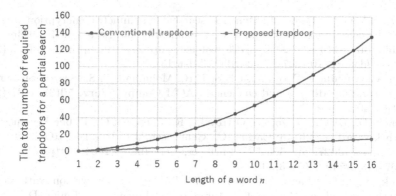

Fig. 4. The total number of substrings for each length of keywords

Thus, a failure at keyword search decreases in proportion to the increase of n.

Due to the page limitation, the more detailed security including about information leakage throughout our search scheme is omitted in this work.

5   Conclusion

We proposed a construction of a keyword search scheme which allows a partial matching search without registering a designated trapdoor of the substring of a keyword. It is realized by embedding each character of a keyword to an 8-bit binary sequence using a PRNG of NTU sequence. This is because of the ease of embedding an 8-bit character and the flexibility as trapdoor function. The sequences are concatenated to a ciphertext and are used for searching. Since a trapdoor is generated by taking the full advantage of the generation procedure of the PRNG, the randomness and the flexibility are quite high.

Although the security of the proposed method is discussed with the viewpoint of difficulty of collision of keywords, the formal description of security proof is still left for our future work.

Acknowledgement. This work was partly supported by JSPS KAKENHI Grant-in-Aid for Scientific Research (A) 16H01723.

References

1. Song, D., Wager, D., Perrig, A.: Practical techniques for searches on encrypted data. In: Proceeding 2000 IEEE Symposium on Security and Privacy, S & P 2000 (2000). https://doi.org/10.1109/SECPRI.2000.848445
2. Curtmola, R., Garay, J., Kamara, S., Ostrovsky, R.: Searchable symmetric encryption: improved definitions and efficient constructions. J. Comput. Secur. **19**(5), 895–934 (2011)
3. Wang, G., Liu, C., Dong, Y., Han, P., Pan, H., Fang, B.: IDCrypt: a multi-user searchable symmetric encryption scheme for cloud applications. IEEE Access **6**, 2908–2921 (2018). https://doi.org/10.1109/ACCESS.2017.2786026

4. Yavuz, A.A., Guajardo, J.: Dynamic searchable symmetric encryption with minimal leakage and efficient updates on commodity hardware. In: Dunkelman, O., Keliher, L. (eds.) SAC 2015. LNCS, vol. 9566, pp. 241–259. Springer, Cham (2016). https://doi.org/10.1007/978-3-319-31301-6_15

5. Poh, G.S., Chin, J., Yau, W., Choo, K.R., Mohamad, M.S.: Searchable symmetric encryption: designs and challenges. ACM Comput. Surv. **50**(3), 1–37 (2017). Article 40

6. Boneh, D., Di Crescenzo, G., Ostrovsky, R., Persiano, G.: Public key encryption with keyword search. In: Cachin, C., Camenisch, J.L. (eds.) EUROCRYPT 2004. LNCS, vol. 3027, pp. 506–522. Springer, Heidelberg (2004). https://doi.org/10.1007/978-3-540-24676-3_30

7. Baek, J., Safavi-Naini, R., Susilo, W.: Public key encryption with keyword search revisited. In: Gervasi, O., Murgante, B., Laganà, A., Taniar, D., Mun, Y., Gavrilova, M.L. (eds.) ICCSA 2008. LNCS, vol. 5072, pp. 1249–1259. Springer, Heidelberg (2008). https://doi.org/10.1007/978-3-540-69839-5_96

8. Massey, J.L., Serconek, S.: Linear complexity of periodic sequences: a general theory. In: Koblitz, N. (ed.) CRYPTO 1996. LNCS, vol. 1109, pp. 358–371. Springer, Heidelberg (1996). https://doi.org/10.1007/3-540-68697-5_27

9. Nogami, Y., Uehara, S., Tsuchiya, K., Begum, N., Ino, H., Morelos-Zaragoza, R.H.: A multi-value sequence generated by power residue symbol and trace function over odd characteristic field. IEICE Trans. **E99–A**(12), 2226–2237 (2016)

10. Tsuchiya, K., Ogawa, C., Nogami, Y., Uehara, S.: Linear compleixty of generalized NTU sequences. In: IWSDA 2017 (2017). https://doi.org/10.1109/IWSDA.2017.8095739

11. Daemen, J., Rijmen, V.: The Design of Rijndael. Springer, Heidelberg (2002). https://doi.org/10.1007/978-3-662-04722-4

12. Blum, M., Micali, S.: How to generate cryptographically strong sequences of pseudorandom Bits. SIAM J. Comput. **13**, 850–864 (1984)

13. Divyanjali, Ankur, Pareek, V.: An overview of cryptographically secure pseudorandom number generators and BBS. IJCA, 19–28 (2014). In: ICACEA

14. Poonam, J., Brahmjit, S.: A survey on RC4 stream cipher. IJCNIS **7**, 37–45 (2015)

15. AlFardan, N., Bernstein, D.J., Paterson, K.G., Poettering, B., Schuldt, J.C.N.: On the security of RC4 in TLS. In: USENIX Security 13, pp. 305–320 (2013). ISBN: 978-1-931971-03-4

16. Blum, L., Blum, M., Shub, M.: A simple unpredictable pseudorandom number generator. SIAM J. Comput. **15**, 364–383 (1986)

17. Rukhin, A.: A Statistical Test Suite for Random and Pseudorandom Number Generators for Cryptographic Applications NIST, SP 800–22, Revision 1a (2010)

18. Kodera, Y., Miyazaki, T., Kusaka, T., Arshad, A.M., Nogami, Y., Uehara, S.: Uniform binary sequence generated over odd characteristic field. IJIEE **8**(1), 5–9 (2018)

Compact LEA and HIGHT Implementations on 8-Bit AVR and 16-Bit MSP Processors

Hwajeong Seo[✉], Kyuhwang An, and Hyeokdong Kwon

Hansung University, Seoul, Republic of Korea
hwajeong84@gmail.com, tigerk9212@gmail.com, hdgwon@naver.com

Abstract. In this paper, we revisited the previous LEA and HIGHT implementations on the low-end embedded processors. First, the general purpose registers are fully utilized to cache the intermediate results of delta variable during key scheduling process of LEA. By caching the delta variables, the number of memory access is replaced to the relatively cheap register access. Similarly, the master key and plaintext are cached during key scheduling and encryption of HIGHT block cipher, respectively. Second, stack storage and pointer are fully utilized to store the intermediate results and access the round keys. This approach solves the limited storage problem and saves one general purpose register. Third, indirect addressing mode is more efficient than indexed addressing mode. In the decryption process of LEA, the round key pair is efficiently accessed through indirect addressing with minor address modification. Fourth, 8-bit word operations for HIGHT is efficiently handled by 16-bit wise instruction of 16-bit MSP processors. Finally, the proposed LEA implementations on the representative 8-bit AVR and 16-bit MSP processors are fully evaluated in terms of code size, RAM and execution timing. The proposed implementations over the target processors (8-bit AVR processor, 16-bit MSP processor) are faster than previous works by (13.6%, 9.3%), (0.6%, 8.5%), and (3.4%, 1.5%) for key scheduling, encryption, and decryption, respectively. Similarly, the proposed HIGHT implementations on the 16-bit MSP processors are faster than previous works by 38.6%, 33.7%, and 33.6% for key scheduling, encryption, and decryption, respectively.

Keywords: LEA · HIGHT · AVR · MSP · Software implementation

1 Introduction

In WISA'13, Lightweight Encryption Algorithm (LEA) was announced by the Attached Institute of ETRI [4]. Unlike previous Substitute Permutation Network (SPN) block ciphers, LEA algorithm follows simple Addition Rotation XOR (ARX) architecture which shows high speed computations in software and hardware implementations. Furthermore, the implementation is a regular fashion, which is secure against timing attack. In ICISC'13, LEA implementations on

© Springer Nature Switzerland AG 2019
B. B. Kang and J. Jang (Eds.): WISA 2018, LNCS 11402, pp. 253–265, 2019.
https://doi.org/10.1007/978-3-030-17982-3_20

high-end ARM-NEON and GPGPU platforms are introduced [11]. The works present efficient parallel implementations in Single Instruction Multiple Data (SIMD) and Single Instruction Multiple Thread (SIMT). In WISA'15, low-end 8-bit AVR processor is also evaluated [10]. The author presented speed and size optimized LEA implementation techniques for 8-bit AVR processors and compared the performance with representative ARX block ciphers, including SPECK and SIMON. The work proved that LEA is the most optimal block cipher for embedded environments. In WISA'16, both ARM and NEON instruction sets are fully utilized in interleaved way [12]. The work showed the interleaved approach efficiently hides the pipeline stalls between ARM and NEON instruction sets. Recently, block cipher competition is held by Luxembourg University (FELICS Triathlon). Many light-weight block ciphers are submitted and finally LEA and HIGHT implementations achieved the efficient block cipher implementations for Internet of Things (IoT) by considering three factors, including RAM, ROM, and execution timing [6]. The descriptions of compact LEA implementations are well described in [9]. In CHES'06, lightweight block cipher, HIGHT, was introduced [5]. The HIGHT block cipher consists of simple 8-bit wise ARX operations. The lightweight implementations were also reported in [9]. As listed above, many works have proved that LEA and HIGHT block ciphers are the promising block ciphers for both high-end computers and low-end microprocessors. However, still there are large room to improve the performance for 8-bit AVR and 16-bit MSP processors. In this paper, we re-visit previous results of LEA and HIGHT implementations on the 8-bit AVR and 16-bit MSP processors.

The remainder of this paper is organized as follows. In Sect. 2, we recap the basic specifications of LEA and HIGHT block ciphers, FELICS triathlon, and target 8-bit AVR and 16-bit MSP processors. In Sect. 3, we present the compact implementations of LEA and HIGHT block ciphers on 8-bit AVR and 16-bit MSP processors. In Sect. 4, we evaluate the performance of proposed methods in terms of code size, RAM, and execution timing. Finally, Sect. 5 concludes the paper.

2   Related Works

2.1   LEA Block Cipher

In WISA 2013, Lightweight Encryption Algorithm (LEA) was announced by the Attached Institute of ETRI [4]. The LEA block cipher only consists of simple Addition-Rotation-XOR (ARX) operations, which replaces the expensive S-box operations. These lightweight features are appropriate to achieve the high performance for both software and hardware platforms. Furthermore, ARX operations are secure against timing attack and simple power analysis.

2.2   HIGHT Block Cipher

In CHES'06, lightweight HIGHT block cipher was introduced [5]. HIGHT block cipher also consists of ARX operations and supports 64-bit block size and 128-bit key size. The basic operations are 8-bit wise addition, rotation, and XOR, and the number of round is 32. HIGHT block cipher is particularly efficient for low-end device and hardware implementations.

Table 1. First and second winners of FELICS triathlon (block size/key size)

Rank	First triathlon	Second triathlon
1	LEA (128/128)	HIGHT (64/128)
2	SPECK (64/96)	Chaskey (128/128)
3	Chaskey (128/128)	SPECK (64/128)

2.3 FELICS Triathlon

In 2015, the open-source software benchmarking framework named Fair Evaluation of Lightweight Cryptographic Systems (FELICS) was held by Luxembourg University. This is similar to SUPERCOP benchmark framework but the system is particularly targeting for low-end embedded processors, which are widely used in IoT and M2M services. Total three different platforms, including 8-bit AVR, 16-bit MSP, and 32-bit ARM, were selected and three different metrics, such as execution time, RAM, and code size were evaluated. The implementations are evaluated in three different scenarios including cipher operation, communication protocol, and challenge-handshake authentication protocol. In the FELICS Triathlon, more than one hundred different implementations of block and stream ciphers are submitted by world-wide researchers. In the competition, LEA won first triathlon and HIGHT won second triathlon (See Table 1). The other block ciphers, including SPECK and Chaskey, also show the competitive performance on low-end processors [1,6].

2.4 8-Bit Embedded Platform AVR

The 8-bit AVR embedded processor is equipped with an ATmega128 8-bit processor clocked at 7.3728 MHz. It has a 128 KB EEPROM chip and 4 KB RAM chip. The ATmega128 processor has RISC architecture with 32 registers. Among them, 6 registers ($r_{26} \sim r_{31}$) serve as the special pointers for indirect addressing. The remaining 26 registers are available for arithmetic operations. One arithmetic instruction incurs one clock cycle, and memory instructions or 8-bit multiplication incurs two processing cycles. The detailed instructions are given in Table 2. Previous 8-bit microprocessor results showed that LEA is estimated to run at around 3,040 cycles for encryption on AVR AT90USB82/162 where AES best record is 1,993 cycles [4,7]. The paper does not explore the specific LEA implementation techniques, but we assume that they used the separated mode to optimize performance in terms of speed by considering high performance. In case of AES encryption, they used the conventional lookup-based approach to reduce memory consumption [7]. The lookup tables are the forward and inverse

Table 2. Instruction set summary for AVR

asm	Operands	Description	Operation	#Clock
ADD	Rd, Rr	Add without Carry	Rd ← Rd+Rr	1
EOR	Rd, Rr	Exclusive OR	Rd ← Rd⊕Rr	1
LSL	Rd	Logical Shift Left	C|Rd ← Rd<<1	1
ROL	Rd	Rotate Left Through Carry	C|Rd ← Rd<<1 || C	1

S-boxes in total 512 bytes, because 32-bit look-up table access is not favorable for the low-end processors due to the limited storages. S-box pointer is always placed in Z register and the variable is stored into SRAM for fast access speed. For the efficient mix-column computation, a left shift with conditional branch to skip the bit-wise exclusive-or operation is established. Finally, the MixColumns step is implemented without the use of lookup tables as a series of register copies, XOR operations, taking a total of 26 cycles. The InvMixColumns step is implemented in a similar way, but it is more complicated routines, which takes a total of 42 cycles.

2.5 16-Bit Embedded Platform MSP

The MSP430 is a representative 16-bit embedded processor board with a clock frequency of 8–16 MHz, 32–48 KB of flash memory, 10 KB of RAM, and 12 general purpose registers from r4 to r15 available [3]. Since these registers share pointer and user defined registers, the number of registers are much constrained than 8-bit AVR processors. The device also provides various arithmetics supporting full functions of ARX operations (See Table 3).

Table 3. Instruction set summary for MSP

asm	Operands	Description	Operation	#Clock
ADD	Rr, Rd	Add without Carry	Rd ← Rd+Rr	1
XOR	Rr, Rd	Exclusive OR	Rd ← Rd⊕Rr	1
RLA	Rd	Logical Shift Left	C|Rd ← Rd<<1	1
RLC	Rd	Rotate Left Through Carry	C|Rd ← Rd<<1 || C	1

In [2], the implementation is based on the byte-oriented version, but the author has modified it to take advantage of the 16-bit platform. The first change was to improve the AddRoundKey function computing the bit-wise exclusive-or of 128-bit blocks in order to bit-wise exclusive-or 16-bit words at a time. The second change was to improve the use of 16-bit friendly lookup tables. The Subbytes, Shiftrows and Mixcolumns steps are combined in a single computation.

This is well known 32-bit optimization of using precomputed tables with 256 elements method. They exploited this for 16-bit version and it costs around 2 KB rather than 4 KB, conventional approach requires.

3 Proposed Method

3.1 Optimization of LEA for 8-Bit AVR Processors

For LEA implementation on 8-bit AVR, 32-bit ARX operations with the 8-bit instructions should be optimized. The 32-bit addition in 8-bit instruction can be implemented in four consecutive 8-bit addition instructions (add, adc). Similarly, the 32-bit exclusive-or operation is implemented with four 8-bit exclusive-or instructions (eor). For the 32-bit rotation operations, assembly-level optimizations are required to get a small code size and fast execution timing. The optimized rotations are described in Table 4 [9].

Table 4. 32-bit rotations on 8-bit AVR, where Z and T are zero and temporal registers [9]

⋘1	⋘8	⋘16 (⋙16)	⋙8	⋙1
LSL X1	MOV T, X4	MOV T, X1	MOV T, X1	BST X1, 0
ROL X2	MOV X4, X3	MOV X1, X3	MOV X1, X2	LSR X4
ROL X3	MOV X3, X2	MOV X3, T	MOV X2, X3	ROR X3
ROL X4	MOV X2, X1	MOV T, X2	MOV X3, X4	ROR X2
ADC X1, Z	MOV X1, T	MOV X2, X4	MOV X4, T	ROR X1
		MOV X4, T		BLD X4, 7
5 cycles	5 cycles	6 cycles	5 cycles	6 cycles

In addition, the special right rotation offset by 3-bit is optimized through the special routine by 1 clock cycle (See Table 5). Instead of bit selection (bst and bld), the rotation bits are cached in temporal registers and applied to the destination register at last. This approach even reduces the 1 line of code size in each round.

Key Scheduling. The key scheduling process generates the round key from master key and delta variables. For the high performance implementation, the number of memory access should be optimized. 128-bit master keys are reserved in the 16 general purpose registers. The part of delta variable (32-bit) are also reserved in the 4 general purpose registers, which are directly utilized when the delta variables are required. The remaining delta variables (96-bit) are loaded and stored again in the stack storages to avoid the overwriting of original delta variables in the memory.

Table 5. 32-bit rotations on 8-bit AVR by 3-bit offsets, where $X1 \sim X4$ are data registers and T is temporal register [9]

without bst/bld	with bst/bld
CLR T	Iteration #3{
	BST X1, 0
Iteration #3{	LSR X4
LSR X4	ROR X3
ROR X3	ROR X2
ROR X2	ROR X1
ROR X1	BLD X4, 7 }
ROR T }	
EOR X4, T	
17 cycles	18 cycles

Encryption and Decryption. The encryption process consists of 24 rounds. Since same process is iterated in every 4 rounds, the length of loop is set to 4. 16 and 8 general purpose registers are assigned to the plaintext and temporal storages, respectively. The callee-saved register pair (R28, R29) is not used, which saves 2 bytes and 8 clock cycles for PUSH and POP instructions. The rotation operations are implemented in techniques of Tables 4 and 5. The decryption process is reversed order of encryption. Main difference is round key access. The last index of round key is accessed and decremented to the first index. With this order of round key, the ciphertext is decrypted to the plaintext.

3.2   Optimization of LEA for 16-Bit MSP Processors

The 32-bit addition operation on 16-bit MSP is implemented with two 16-bit addition instructions (add, addc). The 32-bit exclusive-or operation is implemented with two 16-bit exclusive-or instructions (xor). The optimized rotation techniques on 16-bit MSP are covered in [8,9]. The optimized rotations are described in Table 6. For 8-bit left rotation, swpb and xor instructions are utilized. The swpb instruction performs byte-wise swap operation on the 16-bit variable, which exchanges the 8-bit values between lower and higher parts. Afterward, three xor instructions extract the swapped results. For 8-bit right rotation, the opposite routine of left rotation is required. For 1-bit right rotation, the bit instruction is used to check the least significant bit of the lower register (X2) and set the carry flag. Afterward the carry flag is updated to the most significant bit of the higher register (X1).

Table 6. 32-bit rotations on 16-bit MSP, where T is temporal register [9]

$\lll 1$	$\lll 8$	$\lll 16\ (\ggg 16)$	$\ggg 8$	$\ggg 1$
RLA X2	SWPB X1	MOV X1, T	MOV.B X1, T	BIT #1, X2
RLC X1	SWPB X2	MOV X2, X1	XOR.B X2, T	RRC X1
ADC X2	MOV.B X1, T	MOV T, X1	XOR T, X1	RRC X2
	XOR.B X2, T		XOR T, X2	
	XOR T, X1		SWPB X1	
	XOR T, X2		SWPB X2	
3 cycles	6 cycles	3 cycles	6 cycles	4 cycles

Key Scheduling. Unlike 8-bit AVR processor, 16-bit MSP processor only equips 12 general purpose registers. For this reason, the register utilization is more important than AVR processor. 8, 1, and 3 general purpose registers are assigned to master key, delta variable address pointer, and temporal storages, respectively. However, additional 9 general purpose registers for counter and delta variables are required. In order to resolve the limited number of registers, stack pointer (R1) is utilized. Particularly, 128-bit delta variables, counter, and address pointer for round key are stacked and restored whenever the values are required in the code.

Encryption and Decryption. The register utilization of encryption process is also important on 16-bit MSP processor. 8, 1, and 3 general purpose registers are assigned to plaintext, round key address pointer, and temporal storages. The counter variable is not stored in the register so the variable is stored in the stack. In LEA encryption, 6 32-bit round keys are required in each round. Among them, three round keys share same round key. This shows that only 4 round keys are required to perform the LEA encryption. However, MSP processor only provides very limited number of general purpose registers and four round keys cannot be reserved in the 3 16-bit registers. For this reason, part of 16-bit shared round key is reserved in the one register and the two registers are used to load the remaining round keys. In the straight-forward implementation, 8 16-bit indirect and 4 16-bit indexed memory access (28 clock cycles) are required[1]. By using cached round key, 8 16-bit indirect and 2 16-bit indexed memory access (22 clock cycles) are required. The rotation operations are performed by using Table 6. Four rounds are implemented and iterated by 6 times to complete the 24 rounds.

Decryption step is reversed order of encryption operation and the ARX operations of decryption step can be performed by following encryption step. The main difference is memory access pattern. The encryption routine accesses the

---

[1] Indirect memory access requires 2 clock cycles and indexed memory access requires 3 clock cycles.

round keys from the first to the last round keys. However, the decryption routine accesses the round keys from the last to the first round keys. Furthermore, MSP processor only supports incremental memory access and does not support decremental memory access. For the optimized memory access, the memory address offset is manually calculated. First, the offset is calculated. Second, the memory address is accessed by using indirect memory address mode in incremental order. In the straight-forward implementation, 12 16-bit indexed memory access (36 clock cycles) are required. By using manual offset correction, 10 16-bit indirect and 4 offset correction (24 clock cycles) are required.

3.3   Optimization of HIGHT for 16-Bit MSP Processors

The basic word size of HIGHT block cipher is 8-bit wise. For this reason, straight-forward implementation of HIGHT on 16-bit MSP is inefficient. In this section, we explore the efficient 8-bit wise operations for 16-bit instructions of MSP processors

Key Scheduling. In the key scheduling process, 12 general purpose registers are utilized. In particular, 8, 1, 1, 1, and 1 general purpose registers are assigned to master key variables, round key pointer, delta pointer, master key pointer, and loop counter, respectively. The master key pointer and loop counter are also used for temporal storages by pushing the data into the stack. The most expensive operation of key scheduling process is the update of delta variable. The detailed delta update is as follows.

$$\delta_{i+6} \leftarrow \delta_{i+2} \oplus \delta_{i-1}$$

The delta update requires bit-wise computations, which is inefficient for byte-wise platforms. For this reason, we used LUT-based approach to accelerate the performance. Another consideration is efficient 8-bit word handling for 16-bit MSP processors. The input/output length of LUT is 8-bit and memory access is expensive. In order to reduce the number of LUT accesses, 2 8-bit LUT results are loaded at once and used with post-processing. The detailed descriptions of round key generation are given in Algorithm 1. The round key generation requires addition of delta variable and master key. In Step 1, lower part of master key (M0) is moved to TMP1. In Step 2, 16-bit delta variable pair is loaded to TMP2. In Step 3 and 4, master key and delta variable is added and stored to the round key (RP). Similarly, from Step 5, higher part of master key (M0) and delta variable (TMP2) are prepared by using SWPB instruction. Finally, higher part is also stored to the round key (RP).

In each round key generation, the offset of master key is rotated by one. In the proposed implementation, two 8-bit master keys are stored in the 16-bit register and 8-bit wise rotation is inefficient for this alignment. For this reason, two rounds are directly performed and then the offset is updated by 2-word as follows.

Algorithm 1. Round key generation with 2 8-bit LUT access on MSP

Input: first and second master key pair (M0), delta variable pointer (DP),
temporal registers (TMP1, TMP2)
Output: round key pointer (RP)
1: MOV.B M0, TMP1
2: MOV @DP+, TMP2
3: ADD.B TMP2, TMP1
4: MOV.B TMP1, 0(RP)

5: MOV M0, TMP1
6: SWPB TMP1
7: SWPB TMP2
8: ADD.B TMP2, TMP1
9: MOV.B TMP1, 1(RP)

MOV M3, TMP1 → MOV M2, M3 → MOV M1, M2 → MOV M0, M1 → MOV TMP1, M0

MOV M7, TMP1 → MOV M6, M7 → MOV M5, M6 → MOV M4, M5 → MOV TMP1, M4

Encryption and Decryption. In the encryption operation, 12 general purpose registers are utilized. In particular, 8, 1, 1, 1, and 1 general purpose registers are assigned to plaintext, round key pointer, plaintext pointer, F0 function pointer, and F1 function pointer. The plaintext point is used for both temporal storage and loop counter by pushing the data into the stack. The expensive operations are F0 and F1 functions as follows.

$$F0 = X^{\lll 1} \oplus X^{\lll 2} \oplus X^{\lll 7}$$

$$F1 = X^{\lll 3} \oplus X^{\lll 4} \oplus X^{\lll 6}$$

The functions consists of XOR and rotation operations, which can be written in 2 256-byte pre-computed tables. In each round, four times of LUT accesses are required. The detailed descriptions of one round computation is given in Algorithm 2. In order to reduce the number of memory accesses, all plaintext variables are loaded to the 16-bit registers in 8-bit wise. The round key access is performed in byte wise since the number of temporal register is not enough to retain the round keys. The encryption round is performed with the F0/F1 LUT accesses and byte-wise XOR and addition operations. 8 rounds of encryption codes are written and iterated by 4 times to complete the 32 rounds. Similarly, the decryption round is performed in reversed order of encryption operation.

Algorithm 2. 1 round of HIGHT encryption using F0 and F1 LUTs

Input: plaintext registers (A0, A1, ..., A7), F0 pointer (F0P), F1 pointer (F1P), temporal register (TMP), round key pointer (RP)

Output: plaintext registers (A0, A1, ..., A7)

```
 1: MOV F1P, TMP
 2: ADD A0, TMP
 3: MOV.B @TMP, TMP
 4: XOR.B 0(RP),TMP
 5: ADD.B TMP, A1

 6: MOV F0P, TMP
 7: ADD A2, TMP
 8: MOV.B @TMP, TMP
 9: ADD.B 1(RP),TMP
10: XOR.B TMP, A3

11: MOV F1P, TMP
12: ADD A4, TMP
13: MOV.B @TMP, TMP
14: XOR.B 2(RP),TMP
15: ADD.B TMP, A5

16: MOV F0P, TMP
17: ADD A6, TMP
18: MOV.B @TMP, TMP
19: ADD.B 3(RP),TMP
20: XOR.B TMP, A7
```

4 Evaluation

We evaluated LEA and HIGHT implementations on representative processors that are commonly used in IoT devices, namely 8-bit AVR and 16-bit MSP processors. The performance on the low-end devices (AVR and MSP) was evaluated in terms of code size (byte), RAM (byte), and execution time (clock cycle). In Table 7, the performance evaluation of LEA and HIGHT block ciphers is presented. This evaluation was based on the scenario of FELICS framework. The FELICS framework considers three scenarios, namely cipher operation, communication protocol, and challenge-handshake authentication protocol. Among them, we selected the cipher operation (i.e. scenario 0) to measure the performance of encryption and decryption operations. Scenario 0 evaluates the performance of the round key generation, encryption, and decryption for a single block. The results include the implementation of speed optimized assembly. The detailed descriptions are given in Table 7.

In 8-bit AVR processor, the proposed implementation achieved the highest performance among previous LEA implementations. Particularly, key scheduling, encryption, and decryption requires 203, 167, and 170 clock cycles/byte and enhances the performance by 13.6%, 0.6%, and 3.4%, respectively. Interestingly, the proposed implementation requires smaller RAM size than previous works since it only utilized the 16 callee-saved registers. For the code size, encryption and decryption operations achieved the 8 and 14 bytes smaller than previous works. For the key scheduling routine, previous works by [9] implemented only single round of key scheduling. However, the proposed work utilized the cached delta value and four rounds are implemented. For this reason, the size of key scheduling is larger than previous works but this achieved the highest perfor-

Table 7. Comparison results of LEA and HIGHT block ciphers on 8-bit AVR and 16-bit MSP in terms of code size (byte), RAM (byte), and execution time (clock cycle/byte)

Impl.	Code size (bytes)				RAM (bytes)			Execution time (cycles per byte)		
	EKS	ENC	DEC	SUM	EKS	ENC	DEC	EKS	ENC	DEC
LEA–AVR										
[4]	-	-	-	-	-	-	-	-	190	-
[10]	-	924	-	-	-	592	-	-	169	-
[9]	520	862	890	2,272	467	433	433	235	168	176
This Work	1,068	854	876	2,798	444	416	416	203	167	170
LEA–MSP										
[9]	314	650	654	1,618	456	440	440	193	129	129
This Work	830	596	650	2,076	450	416	416	175	118	127
HIGHT–MSP										
[9]	402	1,134	1,138	2,162	290	676	676	119	222	223
This Work	448	520	526	1,494	296	674	674	73	147	148

mance and for the 128 KB processor, 0.5 KB is not high overheads. Similarly, in 16-bit MSP430 processor, the proposed LEA implementation achieved 175, 118, and 127 clock cycles for key scheduling, encryption, and decryption, respectively, which shows that the proposed implementations are faster than previous works by 9.3%, 8.5%, and 1.5%, respectively. Only code size of key scheduling achieved lower performance but other factors are better than previous works.

For the case of HIGHT block cipher, the proposed approach achieved the highest performance among them. The proposed implementation fully utilized the general purpose registers to cache the master key and plaintext/ciphertext for key scheduling and encryption/decryption operations. Particularly, 2 8-bit words delta variables are loaded and finely re-ordered to reduce the number of memory access for key scheduling. The proposed HIGHT implementation achieved 73, 147, and 148 clock cycles for key scheduling, encryption, and decryption, respectively, which shows that the proposed implementations are faster than previous works by 38.6%, 33.7%, and 33.6%, respectively.

5   Conclusion

One of the biggest challenges for Internet of Thing (IoT) is establishing the secure communications between resource constrained embedded processors. In order to ensure secure and robust transactions, we should conduct the encryption operation on sensitive and important information. In this paper, we explore the optimal implementations pursuing high speed and small memory footprint for the LEA and HIGHT block ciphers. This paper particularly concerned on the number of memory accesses by using cached approach. This enhances the performance over the 8-bit AVR processor by 13.6%, 0.6%, and 3.4% for key scheduling, encryption, and decryption, respectively. The performance gain is also observed on the 16-bit MSP processor by 9.3%, 8.5%, and 1.5% for key scheduling, encryption, and decryption, respectively. Similarly, the proposed HIGHT implementations on the 16-bit MSP processors are faster than previous works by 38.6%, 33.7%, and 33.6% for key scheduling, encryption, and decryption, respectively.

Acknowledgement. This work was supported as part of Military Crypto Research Center (UD170109ED) funded by Defense Acquisition Program Administration (DAPA) and Agency for Defense Development (ADD).

References

1. Beaulieu, R., Shors, D., Smith, J., Treatman-Clark, S., Weeks, B., Wingers, L.: The SIMON and SPECK lightweight block ciphers. In: Proceedings of the 52nd Annual Design Automation Conference, p. 175. ACM (2015)
2. Gouvêa, C.P.L., López, J.: High speed implementation of authenticated encryption for the MSP430X microcontroller. In: Hevia, A., Neven, G. (eds.) LATINCRYPT 2012. LNCS, vol. 7533, pp. 288–304. Springer, Heidelberg (2012). https://doi.org/10.1007/978-3-642-33481-8_16
3. Gouvêa, C.P., Oliveira, L.B., López, J.: Efficient software implementation of public-key cryptography on sensor networks using the MSP430X microcontroller. J. Cryptogr. Eng. **2**(1), 19–29 (2012)
4. Hong, D., Lee, J.-K., Kim, D.-C., Kwon, D., Ryu, K.H., Lee, D.-G.: LEA: a 128-bit block cipher for fast encryption on common processors. In: Kim, Y., Lee, H., Perrig, A. (eds.) WISA 2013. LNCS, vol. 8267, pp. 3–27. Springer, Cham (2014). https://doi.org/10.1007/978-3-319-05149-9_1
5. Hong, D., et al.: HIGHT: a new block cipher suitable for low-resource device. In: Goubin, L., Matsui, M. (eds.) CHES 2006. LNCS, vol. 4249, pp. 46–59. Springer, Heidelberg (2006). https://doi.org/10.1007/11894063_4
6. Mouha, N., Mennink, B., Van Herrewege, A., Watanabe, D., Preneel, B., Verbauwhede, I.: Chaskey: an efficient MAC algorithm for 32-bit microcontrollers. In: Joux, A., Youssef, A. (eds.) SAC 2014. LNCS, vol. 8781, pp. 306–323. Springer, Cham (2014). https://doi.org/10.1007/978-3-319-13051-4_19
7. Osvik, D.A., Bos, J.W., Stefan, D., Canright, D.: Fast software AES encryption. In: Hong, S., Iwata, T. (eds.) FSE 2010. LNCS, vol. 6147, pp. 75–93. Springer, Heidelberg (2010). https://doi.org/10.1007/978-3-642-13858-4_5
8. Park, T., Seo, H., Liu, Z., Choi, J., Kim, H.: Compact implementations of LSH. In: Kim, H., Choi, D. (eds.) WISA 2015. LNCS, vol. 9503, pp. 41–53. Springer, Cham (2016). https://doi.org/10.1007/978-3-319-31875-2_4
9. Seo, H., Jeong, I., Lee, J., Kim, W.-H.: Compact implementations of ARX-based block ciphers on IoT processors. ACM Trans. Embed. Comput. Syst. (TECS) **17**(3), 60 (2018)

10. Seo, H., Liu, Z., Choi, J., Park, T., Kim, H.: Compact implementations of LEA block cipher for low-end microprocessors. In: Kim, H., Choi, D. (eds.) WISA 2015. LNCS, vol. 9503, pp. 28–40. Springer, Cham (2016). https://doi.org/10.1007/978-3-319-31875-2_3
11. Seo, H., et al.: Parallel implementations of LEA. In: Lee, H.-S., Han, D.-G. (eds.) ICISC 2013. LNCS, vol. 8565, pp. 256–274. Springer, Cham (2014). https://doi.org/10.1007/978-3-319-12160-4_16
12. Seo, H., et al.: Parallel implementations of LEA, revisited. In: Choi, D., Guilley, S. (eds.) WISA 2016. LNCS, vol. 10144, pp. 318–330. Springer, Cham (2017). https://doi.org/10.1007/978-3-319-56549-1_27

Author Index

Printed in the United States
By Bookmasters